The Roman Self in Late Antiquity

The Roman Self in Late Antiquity

Prudentius and the Poetics of the Soul

Marc Mastrangelo

The Johns Hopkins University Press
Baltimore

© 2008 The Johns Hopkins University Press
All rights reserved. Published 2008
Printed in the United States of America on acid-free paper
9 8 7 6 5 4 3 2 1

The Johns Hopkins University Press
2715 North Charles Street
Baltimore, Maryland 21218-4363
www.press.jhu.edu

Library of Congress Cataloging-in-Publication Data
Mastrangelo, Marc.
The Roman self in late antiquity : Prudentius and the poetics of the soul /
Marc Mastrangelo.
p. cm.
Includes bibliographical references and index.
ISBN-13: 978-0-8018-8722-2 (hardcover : alk. paper)
ISBN-10: 0-8018-8722-4 (hardcover : alk. paper)
1. Prudentius, b. 348. 2. Virgil—Influence. 3. Literature, Comparative—
Latin, Classical and post-classical. I. Title.
PA6648.P7M37 2007
871′.01—dc22   2007023329

A catalog record for this book is available from the British Library.

*Special discounts are available for bulk purchases of this book. For more
information, please contact Special Sales at 410-516-6936 or
specialsales@press.jhu.edu.*

The Johns Hopkins University Press uses environmentally friendly book
materials, including recycled text paper that is composed of at least 30
percent post-consumer waste, whenever possible. All of our book papers
are acid-free, and our jackets and covers are printed on paper with
recycled content.

Contents

Acknowledgments

The love of literature and its history is behind the research and writing of this book. Such a sentiment is necessary these days—though by no means sufficient —in order to publish a book of literary criticism that focuses on a noncanonical, ancient author. I view the work of Prudentius as a dynamic, living presence within the long tradition of Roman literature reaching back to Lucretius and Vergil and looking ahead to Dante. Often given only a minor role in literary history, Prudentius' literary value and contribution remain underappreciated.

For all the risks that such a project entails, the intellectual adventure has been most rewarding. My interactions with friends and colleagues, who have guided, encouraged, and challenged me, are a great part of this reward. I am delighted to offer my thanks for their generosity and excellence. Peter K. Marshall and Michael Comber cultivated their pupil's confidence and sense of the literary. Freewheeling conversations with Jim McGowan on poetry and life have also made their mark. Christopher Pelling, Melinda Schlitt, Ted Pulcini, Andrew Rudalevige, Leon Fitts, Meghan Reedy, John Harris, and Lucile Duperron read sections of the manuscript and improved it substantially. Christopher Francese read, discussed, and commented on the manuscript, clarifying key arguments. He has been a constant source of knowledge and encouragement. From the beginning of this project, Angeliki Tzanetou selflessly gave her time and considerable talents to comment on successive drafts and clarify the argument and its presentation. Our discussions on literature and ideas remain central to my intellectual life. Joseph Pucci, who first introduced me to Prudentius, read multiple drafts, generously sharing his expertise in all things late antique with unflagging enthusiasm. Emily Hulme helped with the Latin translations and references. Michael Lonegro deserves special thanks for his willingness to entertain the publication of the manuscript, and for his editorial skill and patience.

The Dickinson College Research and Development Fund and the Roberts Fund of the Department of Classical Studies allowed me to work in far-flung libraries and reap the benefits of presenting work to audiences in Urbana–Champaign, State College, Cambridge, Oxford, London, Bryn Mawr, Providence, and Amherst. The support and friendship of a thriving department has been invaluable: Leon Fitts, Christopher Francese, Christofilis Maggidis, Barbara McDonald, and Joanne Miller personify collegiality. I am fortunate to teach at an institution that values Classical Studies and to have students who push me to think creatively about my subject. Finally, this brief expression of gratitude would be incomplete without acknowledging Lucile, Joseph, and Julien, who time and time again save me from the world's vicissitudes.

Meis Fratribus

The Roman Self in Late Antiquity

Introduction

haec dum scribo vel eloquor
vinclis o utinam corporis emicem
liber quo tulerit lingua sono mobilis ultimo!   (Prudentius, *Praefatio*, 43–45)
While I write or speak of these things,
how I wish to break free from the chains of my body
to the place where my nimble tongue's last sound carries me!

With these programmatic words the late antique poet Prudentius announces that his poetry will allow him to transcend his oppressed, earthly condition and achieve salvation. The passage perhaps would have reminded Prudentius' readers of the poet Horace, who, nearly four centuries earlier, had made a similar boast that his poetry would be an enduring monument to his talent and thus would free him from the limits of mortality (*Carm.* 3.30). Prudentius refashions the Roman convention of the immortality of the poet. For Prudentius, immortality is achieved in the poetic expression of his Christian faith. And although in these programmatic lines he communicates his overwhelming desire for personal salvation, there is also a clear sense of his connection to the canon of Roman poets.[1] Like them, Prudentius indicates his self-awareness of his craft by calling attention to the practice of poetry through the word *lingua*, a metonymic designation for poetry itself. In the work of Prudentius, *lingua* stands for poetry (*Cath.* 3.94) and the correct faith (*catholicam linguam*, *Apoth.* 2), which must be disseminated through writing, speaking, and singing. In reworking the Roman convention of poetic immortality—and by propagating his poetic self-awareness—Prudentius fuses the aspirations and accomplishments of the Roman poetic tradition with an explicit wish for salvation defined by Christian faith.

Prudentius' inventive and skillful fusion of Roman poetry and Christianity breaks new ground in two distinct but related ways. Poetry cannot only treat and promote a personal conversion along with its spiritual groundings, but can also articulate a vision of Roman Christian empire. This political function of poetry hearkens back to the achievement of Roman epic, especially Vergil's *Aeneid* and its meditation on Rome's imperial identity. In his collected works, Prudentius' treatment of imperial *Romanitas,* as well as his Christian concern for his own and others' salvation, inaugurates a new Christian literature. Prudentius' poetry gives voice to a vision of Rome as a divine empire, whose national identity is determined by both past imperial successes and the assertion of a Christian political ideology. Simultaneously, Christian spiritual ideas of free will and individual salvation shape Prudentius' representation of a Christian Rome. Prudentius' broad notion of poetry engages with and redefines *Romanitas* and *Christianitas* both individually and collectively.

In the Roman empire of the fourth century, Constantine had sealed paganism's doom and cemented Christianity as the dominant paradigm in political, social, and intellectual matters. Prudentius and other members of the Roman elite such as Augustine, Paulinus of Nola, and Ambrose experienced powerful conversions that led them to embrace Christianity completely. For Prudentius and other intellectuals, Christianity's divine "truths" and Rome's earthly, imperial success furnished subject matter for a new Christian literature. To write meant to express personal convictions about a spiritual life and create new genres in order to persuade other like-minded Romans to live up to orthodox Christian ideals and rules. Prudentius' personal wish for his own life in the preface develops into a highly wrought strategy in his work as a whole, through which he seeks to persuade complacent readers to commit to Christ and Rome.

Prudentius promotes this Christian mission while reasserting Roman poetry's past artistic and cultural authority. Strikingly, the poetry from his tongue will offer an ambitious literary manifesto in which, as I will argue, Roman poetry renews itself by integrating the new intellectual, theological and political realities of the post-Constantinian world. Not since the Epicurean Lucretius wrote in the middle of the first century BCE, had a Roman poet demonstrated the ultimate value of poetry as a source of knowledge and as a means to accomplish salvation. Furthermore, for Prudentius, poetry is just as much a political as religious vehicle. It expresses the imperial dimension of

Roman Christian identity. Not since Vergil had there been a Roman poet so effective at establishing a master narrative for his people.

For centuries scholars have not hesitated to credit Prudentius with an important legacy, and this comes in the form of assigning the poet a grand status. For instance, in the eighteenth century the great Latinist Bentley called Prudentius "the Christian Vergil and Horace," and thirty years ago Macklin Smith, whose monograph on Prudentius remains essential reading, pronounced Prudentius " the best Latin poet between the Augustan age and the twelfth century."[2] Several book-length studies and a bevy of articles over the past two decades certainly have contributed to a better understanding and appreciation of Prudentius' poems.[3] Recently, in addition to traditionally historical and philological studies, scholars have produced poststructuralist readings of poems that illuminate issues of gender, narrative stance, and hermeneutics.[4] Implicit in much of this scholarship is the desire for a more muscular, literary-historical profile for the poet.

Despite all this, Prudentius has never been given his due in literary history. From the *Church History* of the early fourth-century historian Eusebius to the recently published *Cambridge History of Early Christian Literature,* he and his fellow poets have been excluded from serious discussions of the late antique intellectual milieu, and, as a result, poetry remains marginalized as an index of the period's revolutionary contribution to the history of ideas.[5] Prudentius remains an outlier because scholars have failed to include him and his contemporary Christian poets within the literary, political, and intellectual setting of fourth-century Rome. Studying Prudentius either from an exclusively doctrinal perspective or in isolation from the fourth century's intellectual renaissance has done him a disservice. Even recent critical work on Prudentius' poetry, much of which is valuable and interesting, has not concerned itself with the poet's relationship and contribution to fourth-century intellectual history.[6] Thus, I seek a broader, deeper, and more long-range view of the poet's originality by considering his work as a successful artistic synthesis of literary, historical, philosophical, and theological ideas. Specifically, I claim that Prudentius' use of his intellectual inheritance, as manifested in the Roman epic tradition, the Bible, Christian theology and pagan philosophy, constitutes a vigorous contribution to the fourth-century reformulation of Greco-Roman literary and intellectual tradition. This reformulation is best understood as an effort to produce a "grand narrative" or "meta-narrative" of Roman Christian identity in all its cultural, ideological, and intellectual expression.[7]

A grand or master narrative is "central to the representation of identity, in personal memory and self representation or in the collective identity of groups."[8] An essential function of Roman epic was to restate national identity through a master narrative of larger than life figures.[9] The *Aeneid,* in Philip Hardie's words, made a powerful "claim to totality," fashioning a narrative that reached beyond cultural and literary categories into the realm of history itself.[10] By recasting his intellectual inheritance as a historical, philosophical, theological, and literary synthesis that makes use of the pagan, Hebrew, and Christian traditions, Prudentius' poetry, as a whole, achieves a master narrative. The resulting vision of Roman Christian identity not only accomplishes the goals of the epic master narrative—to shape historical memory and collective ideology—but also, by engaging with a wide range of intellectual and ethical ideas, reflects a renewed concept of self and its relation to the political community and the world.[11]

The foundations for Prudentius' literary accomplishment can be seen in the story of his life, which culminates in a radical conversion experienced by other prominent thinkers and writers of the day. He was born in 348 in Northern Spain[12] and, as befitted an aristocrat, attended the schools of rhetoric, which, he says, taught him the art of lying (*Praef.* 7–15).[13] He went on to have a distinguished civil career, which took him all the way to the imperial court of Milan under the administration of a fellow Spaniard, Theodosius I (*Praef.* 16–20).[14] He began writing poetry in his later years, after his civil career, which he viewed as part and parcel of a life of sin. Like other aristocratic contemporaries such as Paulinus of Nola, Marius Victorinus, and Augustine, Prudentius rejected his past life and underwent a conversion experience[15] in which an accomplished *vir Romanus* with an already Christian proclivity retires from his prestigious career and becomes a radically committed Christian. The voice of this new phase of his life was poetry, which he composed for God's glory and as a complete artistic expression of Roman Christian identity.

My study of Prudentius' poetry engages the *Aeneid,* contemporary poets, the Bible, Epicurean, Platonist, and patristic texts. Such a range of texts requires a variety of approaches to allusion in Prudentius's poetry ranging from direct, intentional references to a broad intertextual analysis that compares shared language and thought. Recent critics of golden and silver age Latin poetry have developed groundbreaking methods of allusion, resulting in stimulating literary criticism.[16] For the most part, however, such methods have eluded much of the literary criticism of late fourth-century poets.[17] I draw upon these methods of allusion with the goal of opening new directions for the interpretation of the Prudentian corpus. I approach Prudentius' texts as part of a system of language —poetic and otherwise—shared in varying degrees by Prudentius, Vergil, the Bible, Platonist texts, and patristic literature. Prudentius' poetic pose as persuader, converter, and cajoler circumscribes my approach to intertextuality and allusion in his work. I include the literary, historical, philosophical, and theological contexts of language shared between Prudentius and other writers in order to illuminate the meaning of passages and the poems as a whole.

This approach to allusion and intertextuality is partly determined by the relationship between the poet and the audience that is delineated in the Prudentian corpus. Prudentius himself defines the relationship between the author and audience in his work, arguing that the reader's *fides* ("faith") becomes the bulwark of the soul[18] because it represents a soul persuaded by an author (Moses, the author of the *Pentateuch*, John the author of *Revelation*, and Prudentius himself) to acknowledge its free will and make a correct moral choice. In the *Hamartigenia* ("The Origin of Sin"), a poem dedicated to exposing false doctrine and solving the problem of evil, Prudentius addresses the reader directly: *sanctum, lector, percense volumen; / quod loquor invenies dominum dixisse* (Reader, read through the holy book; you will discover that the Lord spoke as I say [he did]; *Ham.* 624).[19] The context of this address is a treatment of Christian free will in which Prudentius argues that each individual has a choice to do good or bad, and consequently, he concludes, the soul generates its own sin. But along with this emphasis on free will, he suggests a strong role for poetry—namely, that it speaks to the reader with the authority of scripture. For Prudentius, poetry is a speech act parallel to the way Christians imagined the world to be created by the Word.[20]

The first man and scriptural (and poetic) exemplar, Adam, parallels the experience of the reader. This scriptural character is the prototypical example of free will, for he is "the judge of his own mind (*Iudex mentis propriae, Ham.* 700)." Second, Adam was "persuaded" by the serpent, not coerced (*suadellis, suasisse, suaserat, Ham.* 714, 715, 718). Words persuaded Adam to choose badly but the words of the Bible as well as—so Prudentius implies—the words of his poetry can persuade a reader to make good choices. Prudentius' poetry is an act of persuasion toward a reader who exercises free will. The *Hamartigenia* and Prudentius' other works are designed to persuade, to engage a reader of faith who is amenable to persuasion. Both reader and author must participate fully in this process. The words of scripture or poetry *de scripturis* bind author and reader in the process of persuasion and choice (free will) in which *fides* tips the balance toward goodness. The *Psychomachia* best exhibits this reader/author partnership because Prudentius' allegorical presentation of the soul with its warring virtues and vices assumes that, like Adam, there is a persuadable reader of faith (or not) who, once presented with the facts and arguments *de scripturis,* will exercise his freedom of choice well (or badly). While having a clear effect at the ethical level, the *Psychomachia*'s concern with persuasion has political implications as well, for, as a former elite bureaucrat in Theodosius' administration, Prudentius exhorts his reader, through language and metaphors of war and civil war, to embrace a Roman Christian empire.

The example of Adam functions as a typological instrument of persuasion directed at the reader. For he represents a figure from the Old Testament whose fate as the "first man" is reversed by the new first man, Jesus. The reader must recognize this connection and apply it to himself: will the reader choose to live as an Adam or a Jesus? Typology is the method by which Prudentius presents the reader with choices from which he must choose. In addition, typology in Prudentius' works functions as an essential and flexible trope central to his poetic program. Biblical typology produces one-to-one correspondences between persons and events from Old and New Testament texts. Prudentius innovates by adding Roman figures such as Romulus, Numa, and others to this conventional typological framework. In general, Prudentius' poetry employs typology as a literary trope where connections between his source material (Old and New Testaments, Roman historical tradition), poetic stories and characters (personifications, martyrs), and an implied reader (a seeker of divine knowledge) express religious, ethical, and political concepts. The use of typology allows Prudentius to develop a sophisticated salvation history from Creation to Rome and beyond. This unified, historical continuum serves as the foundation of a new allegorical poetry, which expresses the political, intellectual, and literary ideals of his age.

The centrality of typology in this study presupposes the ability of the reader to recognize Prudentius' biblical figures and events, and interpret them. Typology demands that both the reader and the author be complicit in recognizing particular exegetical interpretations of the biblical material. Jean-Louis Charlet, whose work on fourth- and early fifth-century poetry is influential, sees the poetry of the fourth century as a combination of neoclassicism and neo-Alexandrianism rolled into a triumphalist expression of Constantino-Theodosian ideology.[21] Moreover, scholarly criticism of Prudentius often begins from a bias that used to infuse critics' views of "Silver" Latin poetry—namely, that early Christian poetry is a product of rhetorical excess. Whereas the triumph of Christianity plays an important role in my analysis of Prudentius' poetry and Prudentius' use of rhetoric is a worthwhile investigation, I focus on an under-developed critical approach, which is rooted in the notion that poetry in *la renaissance constantino-théodosienne* took an exegetical turn.[22] My view is that the rich and varied components of "exegetical poetry" have yet to be explicated. Exegetical poetry interprets texts, proclaims truths, and asserts doctrines. It is fundamentally a Christian poetry, and Christianity is a religion based on texts. Unlike pagan religion, the sacred texts acted as a common store, both of agreement and disagreement, for Christians to interpret and thus stabilize their religion's rules, rituals, and principles.

Prudentius' poetry joins patristic literature in this exegetical mission. The interpretation and assertion of an interpretation of the Old and New Testaments are the bulwarks upon which fourth-century Christians forged their faith and spiritual identity. Prudentius develops this stance into an aspect of his literary manifesto that poetry, unlike most patristic prose works, communicates to a wide audience the most deeply held principles concerning God and the soul. This Christian poetry is built on an exegetical stance toward specific aspects of Greco-Roman literary and intellectual traditions. Thus, Prudentius interprets biblical texts, Roman poetry and history, the history of pagan philosophy and Christian theology, with a view toward delineating the Roman-Christian self and state.[23]

The devaluation of poetry in the fourth century, at least for the intellectual class, has been an impetus for the arguments of this book. Certain barriers to the appreciation of Prudentius' impact originate in the longstanding conventional wisdom that any literary innovations of the time are to be found almost exclusively in patristic prose. Eusebius' *Church History* inaugurated this entrenched view by focusing on patristic prose writers alone.[24] This preference for prose is especially unfortunate because, for other ages of antiquity, the work of poets is usually understood as engaging and reflecting core artistic, intellectual, and cultural issues.[25] In both the Greek and Roman world, poets traditionally retained the status of wise interpreters of their cultures. The status accorded the poet in ancient Athens is evident from Plato's effort to debunk the myth of the poet's divine inspiration (*Ion*) and reject Homer's central position in Greek education (*Republic*, books 2, 3, and 10). On the Roman side, Vergil's recitations of the *Aeneid* to an expectant Augustus and his court, as well as the speedy inclusion of the poet's work in school curricula, confirm poetry's centrality in shaping and reflecting Roman ideas and identity. But in the fourth century, poetry, including Vergil's works, which Romans were still reading, had lost the cultural authority to shape directly Roman identity. There was an opportunity for poetry to reassert its cultural and intellectual centrality.

In Prudentius' day poetry was second to prose in terms of prestige and, one could argue, intellectual heft. This was so for two reasons. First, by celebrating the Bible as the pinnacle of literature, complete with divinely inspired poetry, the church encouraged the dominance of prose genres that functioned as critical defenses and explications of the Bible. Prose works became, for all intents and purposes, literary criticism of the Bible with the function of propagating and stabilizing scripture's theology and doctrine throughout the empire. Clergy who could write persuasive, philosophy-like treatises on the Trinity or on scripture became intellectual stars. The most preeminent church fathers of the fourth-century West, Ambrose, Jerome, and Augustine, whose writings helped to secure the priority of orthodox doctrine, earned sainthood. Moreover, because of their persuasive abilities, these figures were able to maintain and exploit close connections with the Roman political hierarchy and, as a result, came to represent the Roman state to their audience. Christian poets of the period did not garner such power and prestige.[26] Second, Roman poetry had reached an impasse. The mission of poets under the new world order of the Christian Roman Empire had yet to be clarified, especially against the rich aesthetic heritage of their pagan predecessors whose works contributed to Rome's idea of itself. In Prudentius' youth, poets responded to this challenge by assembling full and half lines of Vergil's verses to tell the story of the Creation and the Incarnation. These centones possess their own distinctive place in literary history and represent early steps on the way to a poetry that would encompass the contrary currents that make up Roman Christian identity.[27] The centones of Juvencus and Proba, in particular, define themselves against the pagan past by substituting Christian for pagan content.[28]

Prudentius takes up the challenge with far-reaching results for poetry. He is the first Christian poet to engage Roman literary tradition as Roman poets of the past had done—namely, through the complicated poetic strategies of imitation and emulation. The interplay between tradition and originality, which guided the epic successors of Vergil—including Ovid, Lucan, and Statius—guides Prudentius as well. Prudentius integrates his Christian message within an intertextual dialogue with his literary predecessors, a dialogue that is possible in the fourth century because of the compatibility between *Christianitas* and *Romanitas,* between Rome the city and the city of God, and finally, between the Roman Empire and Christian government.[29] To be sure, hostility toward paganism is part of the rhetorical pose of Christian writers, including Prudentius, but this must not handicap a modern reader's ability to understand the poetry's synthesis and interpretation of the pagan and Christian intellectual traditions.

In the fourth century, poetry, though less prestigious as a form of expression for the intellectual class, became more prevalent in everyday life, for example, in the form of hymns for the liturgy. The poetry of Prudentius succeeded in satisfying daily liturgical needs into the Middle Ages with his *Cathemerinon,* a set of hymns for the liturgical calendar. Prudentius, however, also makes a significant challenge in the name of poetry against the ascendancy of prose in the late fourth century. His dogmatic works, the *Hamartigenia* and *Apotheosis,* his attack on Roman paganism in the *Contra Symmachum* I and II, his genre-forming contribution to the history and cult of the martyrs (*Peristephanon*), and his groundbreaking, allegorical epic of the battle between the virtues and the vices (*Psychomachia*) all attempt an extraordinary integration of his historical, theological, and literary inheritance. With this in mind, each chapter in this volume lays out a series of arguments that aim to reposition Prudentius and his poetry at the center of late antique intellectual and artistic life.

1. *Epic Successor? Prudentius, Aeneid 6 and Roman Epic Tradition.* Mark Vessey has argued that the career and corpus of Jerome (c. 340–420 CE), a central intellectual figure of the fourth century, established him as the first "Christian *literatus.*"[30] Jerome was neither interested in prescribing a new Christian rhetoric nor in overturning the classical literary canon. Rather, he wished to define Christian literature in contrast to and emulative of pagan poetry, composed according to a set of rules associated with the Bible.[31] Jerome conceived of an "antiliterature" based on scripture. A Christian writer was therefore a writer *de scripturis,* not an imitator of biblical forms, but "an interpreter of the Bible text itself, one who cleaves to the letter and fastens on to its sense."[32] There is much to agree with in Vessey's insightful formulation of Christian literature. All Christian writers, both poetry and prose writers, saw the Bible as their template for literary production. The creation of the world and humans in *Genesis,* the incarnation of Christ in the Gospels, the end of times in *Revelation,* and the stories in between, provided the content and

structure of Christian literature, yet to apply mechanically Vessey's claims for Jerome to Prudentius would be inadequate because he was a Roman poet practicing in the wake of centuries of Roman poetic tradition that included Lucretius, Vergil, Horace, Ovid, Lucan, and Statius. Any literary historical evaluation of his poetry must include his work's engagement with Roman tradition to the same degree as its relationship to the Bible. Hence in chapter 1, I show a programmatic relationship between Prudentius and his epic predecessor Vergil that establishes the soul as the focal point of moral and political development. By such a bold and transformative engagement with Vergil's *Aeneid*, I argue, the *Psychomachia* stakes its claim as the national epic for Christian Rome because it reflects an ideal Christian self in a Roman context.

2. *Christian History and the Narrative of Rome.* Gerard O'Daly has commented that "[Prudentius'] poetry contains some of the most far reaching attempts in late antiquity to remodel the history and cultural traditions of Rome along Christian lines."[33] Prudentius lived and wrote in one of the most important times in the history of the West. In this age of upheaval, both pagans and Christians competed to possess the idea of Rome in its forms and traditions. In such times history itself is up for grabs, available to be claimed by whatever side wins the political, religious, and intellectual battles. In the fourth century, Christians were winning these battles and thus staking their claim to a particular view of history. This view is crystallized in the imperial theology of the era's most important historian, Eusebius, and in the commentaries of the church fathers. However, Prudentius as well puts forward a Christianizing view of history and an imperial theology, both of which lie behind many of the poetic choices he makes.

In chapter 2 I argue that Prudentius employs typologies, pairs, or triads of events or characters from biblical and Roman historical traditions that are connected and interpreted according to subsequent events. The *Psychomachia*'s narrative of the battle between the virtues and the vices contains fragments of historical narratives from *Genesis, Exodus,* and *Revelation* as well as the paradigmatic narrative of Roman civil war. The *Peristephanon*'s martyr stories are combined with allusions to biblical narratives and narratives of Roman kings. Prudentius typologically connects the biblical events of creation, the incarnation, and the last judgment to the whole of Roman history, from Romulus to Theodosius, to form unified narrative of salvation history. Hence, a Roman and Christian imperial history is born. The poet's historiographical strategy can be summed up as follows: future events, constructed as a set of ideologically fixed points in time (e.g., the Incarnation), cause the stories of the past (e.g., Melchisedec's entertaining of the triple-formed angel) to exist as history. That is, on a metaphorical level, because the poet (and thus the reader) knows the future for certain, he or she can affirm what events in the past are to be included in the construction of history. Prudentius offers this circular, literary argument within the metaphorical space of a closed text: typology proves the legitimacy of specific future events, which, in turn, furnish the criteria for the selection and interpretation of past events. So, for instance, the victory of Chastity (*Pudicitia*) over Lust (*Libido*) in the *Psychomachia* recalls the killing of Holofernes by Judith in the Old Testament, which, in turn, prefigures and helps to legitimize the Incarnation of Christ as an historical event.

3. *Christian Theology and the Making of Allegory.* Regarding the history of thought, John Rist observed nearly twenty-five years ago that "the role of philosophy in the background of Christian writers . . . is largely misunderstood" and what is needed is "no less than a rewriting of the intellectual history of the fourth century."[34] Rist's appeal, especially regarding Roman Christian poets, remains a challenge to contemporary scholarship. As part of a response, I investigate Prudentius' use of theological and philosophical ideas, which remains fertile ground for both an understanding of fourth-century intellectual history and Prudentian allegory, which, until recently, was the central topic for critics assessing the poet's legacy.[35] To this end, chapter 3 revisits Prudentius' use of typology and argues that his typological interpretations of biblical texts contribute to the construction of the *Psychomachia*'s personifications of virtues and vices, and that typological interpretations form the substance of the *Psychomachia*'s allegorical representations of indescribable phenomena, such as God and the soul. By positing in language "what God is not," Prudentius, like most of the church fathers, poses an apophatic challenge in which the reader (and poet) attempts to gain knowledge of God and the soul without the benefit of language, which is incapable of prescribing divine qualities. The poet's response to this linguistic impasse is to construct biblical typologies that produce nonlinguistic, allegorical effects that, in turn, convey a way of knowing the divine. It is impossible for descriptive and prescriptive language to make available to human beings this kind of knowledge.

4. *Pagan Philosophy and the Making of Allegory.* Prudentius also opera-

tionalizes a received tradition of pagan philosophy in order to further develop his indescribable allegorical creations. Chapter 4 argues that Prudentius attaches pagan Platonist and Epicurean ideas to the *Psychomachia*'s vices to show how a human soul ought not to behave. Thus, pagan philosophy informs the typological connection between vices, biblical villains, and an implied, non-radically converted Christian reader. Prudentius deploys pagan intellectual discourse in the portrayal of the personified vices while simultaneously exploiting Christian Platonist ideas in the description of the virtues such as metaphors of ascent in which the soul rises to commune with God. The poet is keenly aware of pagan philosophical ideas and integrates them into his poetry as part of his response to the apophatic dilemma.

5. *Self and Poetry.* My study envisions Prudentius' poetry as a product of a deeply ingrained typological view of the world where reality and history become illuminated through a series of prefigurings and correspondences. This worldview drives Prudentius' literary practice, view of history, interpretation of the Bible, free will, and finally, concept of self. In the epilogue, I suggest that in the work of Prudentius, typological thinking points to a concept of self that has both relational and individualist characteristics. The typological triad of the Father-Christ–human being provides a relational paradigm according to which a person's soul can become joined to God and other humans. The Roman Christian soul and citizen are one and the same: a metaphysical, political, and literary amalgam, whose communion with God drives his or her very identity. In the written record, this vision of the Roman self was temporary and lasted until Alaric's sack of Rome in 410 CE. Augustine would change the self's focus away from the city of Rome and refocus it toward the city of God. Prudentius' vision of the soul and its relation to God, however, remains a vital and vibrant example of a *mentalité* that saw no conflict between the "imperial Roman" and the "radical Christian."

On the other hand, the notion of free will in Prudentius' poetry—that is, the freedom to choose between "positive" and "negative" typologies and thus between faith in the Christian God and faithlessness—resides in the inner space of the soul and is independent from all other beings, including God. This individualist and separatist notion of the self results from, perhaps, the most important contribution of early Christian thought to Western intellectual history—namely, that the individual himself has the freedom and the will to act as he sees fit, for good or for ill and independently of a preordained fate. The self appears to gain an existence and autonomy unprecedented in Greco-Roman thought, a status that would periodically burst forth in subsequent intellectual history and counter Christianity's monarchic and imperial shepherding of peoples. Prudentius' poetry reflects both the coming of the autonomous self and the power of an authoritarian church. His corpus keeps faith with all the great poetry that preceded it by representing the central issues of its time in terms of a meditation on both the individual and the collective.

CHAPTER ONE

An Epic Successor?

Prudentius, *Aeneid* 6, and Roman Epic Tradition

The *Psychomachia*'s linguistic borrowing from the *Aeneid*[1] has led critics to rely on their interpretation of the *Aeneid* when approaching the *Psychomachia*. The implicit result of this working assumption is the proposition that the way in which one reads the *Aeneid* directly affects one's reading of the *Psychomachia*.[2] In light of this assumption and the documented literary dependence of the *Psychomachia* on the *Aeneid,* however, discussion has not fully exploited their rich intertextual relationship.[3] Generations of scholars uncovered linguistic parallels to demonstrate Prudentius' "parasitic" relationship with Vergil,[4] but more recent approaches construct this relationship differently: as either antagonistic, with the Christian poet painting his pagan rival as an inferior,[5] or ambivalent, representing an unresolved tension between pagan epic techniques and Christian content.[6] Yet these advances have not adequately revealed Prudentius' deep engagement with Roman epic tradition and its dominant author, Vergil—a state of affairs that has excluded the *Psychomachia* from its rightful place in the history of epic.[7] In three recent treatments of the subject, Prudentius is given no mention while Claudian, for instance, is given significant space.[8] Therefore, a reexamination of Prudentius' relationship with Vergil and of the Christian poet's role in the development of epic is in order.

To this end, I argue in this chapter that, from the first line of the *Psycho-machia* to its epilogue, Prudentius programmatically engages *Aeneid* 6 in an effort to transform the political, ethical, and metaphysical landscape of Vergil's master narrative.[9] *Katabasis,* the descent of the epic hero Aeneas to the under-world, an exercise in self-definition, and a harbinger of national and spiritual identity, provides a basis for the *Psychomachia*'s narrative, as well as for the rite of passage which its poet and reader must complete to reach their individual, and national, Christian identity.[10] This intertextual bond between the *Psycho-machia* and *Aeneid* 6 reveals a literary purpose.[11] From the first line of the *Psychomachia,* Prudentius places his poem squarely in the Roman epic tradi-tion, which Vergil spearheads. Specifically, Prudentius' manipulation of the notion of *katabasis* as a trial permits the Christian poet to appropriate several epic categories, such as the source of poetic inspiration, theology, the hero, and national identity. The invocation of the *Psychomachia,* the centrally placed battle between *Avaritia* and *Operatio,* and the epilogue, as well as other pas-sages, allude systematically to *Aeneid* 6, reinforcing the picture of the soul's journey from mortality and death to life and immortality. The journey turns on a moral and spiritual choice between virtue and vice. To choose virtue and Christianity represents a radical conversion that, if replicated in enough indi-viduals, engenders a Christian community—that is, a Christian Rome.[12]

The chapter falls into two sections. In the first part, which forms the bulk of the chapter, I shall demonstrate that the *Psychomachia* firmly implants the *Aeneid*'s *katabasis* within its structure and meaning through systematic allu-sion. This allusive program furnishes a way of reading the *Psychomachia* that exposes the poem's epic purpose and ambitions. In the briefer, final section of the chapter, I suggest several ways in which Prudentius' appropriation of Ver-gil's *katabasis* reworks fundamental categories of epic (e.g., the heroic trial, the nature of the hero, and the idea of Rome). I conclude that the Christian poet deserves the status of an epic successor to Vergil and the Roman epic tradition.

Prudentius Engages Vergil: Underworld, Soul, and *Katabasis*

In its first line, the *Psychomachia* so directly engages the *Aeneid* that it is difficult not to conclude that the Christian poet sees himself and this work as the epic successor to Vergil and the *Aeneid.*[13]

Christe, graves hominum semper miserate labores   (*Psych.* 1)
Christ, you always take pity on the heavy sufferings
of human beings

Phoebe, gravis Troiae semper miserate labores   (*Aeneid* 6.56)
Phoebus, you always take pity on the heavy sufferings
of Troy

Prudentius has adapted *Aeneid* 6.56, excepting the words *Phoebe* and *Troiae*. In one line the poet shows how everything has changed. No longer is Apollo the inspiration for poetry as the Augustans traditionally held;[14] no longer do pagan gods exercise divine authority; no longer do we live in a pagan past but, instead, dwell in a Christian present with a bright future; and finally, instead of a concern for Trojans becoming Romans it is now Romans who must become universal citizens in the new celestial order.[15] Prudentius' engagement with Vergil betrays a sense of literary history that ancient poets, as a group, furnish and is widespread throughout the history of epic. Vergil did to Homer what Prudentius does to him.[16] In the first line of the *Aeneid,* he replaces the *Odyssey*'s ἄνδρα with *arma* (echoing the sound of Homer), thus not only signaling his subject matter but also inviting the reader to compare the works of the authors.[17] As Gian Biagio Conte has reminded us, lines like these are where epic's defining characteristics are indicated "so that the new text enters the literary system as a literary work, as though by hereditary right."[18] Just as the text of the *Aeneid* through its engagement with Homer endeavors to transcend its genre and privilege itself in literary history, as it privileges Rome's *imperium* in history,[19] so *Psychomachia* 1, when it alludes to *Aeneid* 6.56, "announces" its own ambition to enter the epic "literary system" the *Aeneid* spearheads.[20]

If we examine further the contexts and words that the lines share, similarities and differences arise. Both Aeneas and Prudentius are praying. Aeneas is at his most priestlike in *Aeneid* 6, performing sacrifices, engaging in ritualistic activity, and acting as the conduit between his Trojan comrades, the oracular pronouncements of the Sibyl, and the seemingly oracular words of Anchises. The sacred words Aeneas hears hold the key to knowledge of his destiny and that of his men who desperately need a home. Analogously, the poet of the *Psychomachia* prays for himself and the human race, laying out in his poetry through the interpretation of sacred texts the knowledge of individual and collective salvation, which is allegorically portrayed in the *Praefatio* through the metaphor of home[21]—in fact, *domus* is the last word of the *Psychomachia*'s preface. Taken together with the *Psychomachia*'s entrance into the context of the Trojans' quest for home in *Aeneid* 6, the line overflows with surplus meaning. Aeneas and the Trojans seek an earthly city, enduring great difficulties and trusting in their destiny, whereas all human beings in the new dispensation (should) seek the heavenly city of the soul that is presented in the second half of the *Psychomachia* and is a construction that is well-ordered, peaceful, virtuous, and preserved by an abiding faith in the Christian god.

Like the Trojans' quest for home in the *Aeneid,* the search for home in the *Psychomachia* (that is, the search for salvation) requires the endurance of suffering, *labores.* The Trojans suffer at the hands of the Greeks, lose their city, and are forced to undertake a long and arduous journey. In the *Psychomachia,* human beings bring suffering upon themselves through original sin and their freely chosen, immoral behavior.[22] This suffering is overcome through a radical conversion of the soul, figured as a journey, in which a victorious struggle within each person between virtue and vice results in an ideal soul. In the *Psychomachia,* the exterior and worldly vicissitudes of Aeneas' and the Trojans' *labores* are rearticulated as taking place inside a person, in her soul, in the form of vice that causes suffering.[23] Moreover, rejection of vice by the Christian soul is an attempt to keep the world on the outside, where vice originates.[24] This movement from the exterior-oriented narrative of the *Aeneid* to the interior struggle of the person, hinted at in the first line of the *Psychomachia,* sets the stage for the poem's allusive appropriation of underworld landscape of *Aeneid* 6 to describe the soul's inner battle between the virtues and the vices. The soul's struggle becomes comparable to an epic descent into hell, a trial, so that the soul might become pure for meeting God.[25]

Miserate supports similar observations but from the perspective of the divine. When Aeneas states that Apollo "takes pity" on Trojan suffering, he is crediting the god with ending Trojan homelessness and further, as the reader of the *Aeneid* comprehends, granting civic glory to the proto-Romans. The idea of Rome casts a long shadow over the actions of Aeneas and the Trojans. Rome also plays an important role in the *Psychomachia*'s Christian worldview, if we take into account the poem's civic discourse (e.g., the civil war narrative during the *Avaritia* section), the civic themes and language of Prudentius' other works such as the *Contra Symmachum* and *Peristephanon* and, finally, the intertextual civic context of *Aeneid* 6. For Christ to "take pity" on human suffering is to forgive humans for their self-inflicted spiritual and ethical state, to watch over each person as she undergoes the trial with the vices, and to grant each individual's soul eternal life. As we see by the end of the poem, this can only happen if each person exercises her freedom to choose and construct her own temple/city of the soul as a faithful follower of the Christian God.

Through such conversions, the city of human beings, Rome, will prosper and live on.

A brief summary of the early section of *Aeneid* 6 will help set out certain themes and highlight diction that the *Psychomachia* purposefully exploits. *Aeneid* 6 opens with Aeneas arriving at the temple of Apollo and the cave of the Sibyl at Cumae, where he will receive guidance on how to reach the underworld (*Aeneid* 6.1–13). His mission is crucial because he will find out—in general terms at the very least—what the future holds for him and his men (*Aeneid* 6.11–13). While awaiting the arrival of the Sibyl, Aeneas and the men gaze at murals upon which the story of Daedalus is depicted (*Aeneid* 6.14–30). When the Sibyl arrives and startles them out of their bemusement over these images, Aeneas prays to Apollo—from whence the Prudentian invocation comes—to grant safe passage to Latium, in return for which he will build the god of prophecy a marble temple (*Aeneid* 6.56–76). After the Sibyl becomes divinely possessed, she predicts that the Trojans will experience "great dangers" (*magnis . . . periclis*) "grievous woes" (*graviora*), "wars" (*bella, horrida bella*), and "misfortunes" (*malis*) (*Aen.* 6.83–97). Aeneas replies that he has seen it all, *non ulla laborum, / o virgo, nova mi facies inopinave surgit* (*Aeneid* 6.103–104), and requests a meeting in the underworld with his father from whom he will receive a more detailed blueprint of the future.

Psychomachia 5–6 exhibits language familiar from *Aeneid* 6.55:

> dissere, rex noster, quo milite pellere culpas   (*Psych.* 5–6)
> mens armata queat nostri *de pectoris antro,*
> Say, our king, with what fighting force the soul
> is furnished and is able to expel the sins from
> the cavern of the breast,

> . . . funditque preces rex *pectore ab imo:*   (*Aeneid* 6. 55)
> . . . and the king [of the Teucrians] pours forth
> prayers from his inmost heart:

The context of Aeneas "praying" from his inmost being resonates with Prudentius' prayer and invocation to Christ. The association of the image of the cave with the soul or mind is explicit in Prudentius and implicit in *Aeneid* 6 where Aeneas' inner consternation is highlighted as he leaves the Sibyl's cave:

> . . . quibis altus Apollo
> praesidet, horrendaeque procul secreta Sibyllae,   (*Aeneid* 6.9–12)
> *antrum immane*, petit, magnam cui mentem animumque

Delius inspirat vates aperitque futura.
Where Apollo sits enthroned, and a vast cavern
hard by, hidden haunt of the dread Sibyl, into whom
the Delian seer breathes a mighty mind and soul
revealing the future.

ingreditur, linquens *antrum,* caecosque volutat   (*Aen.* 6.157–58)
eventus animo secum . . .
[Aeneas] wends his way, quitting the cavern, and
ponders in his mind the dark issues.

Both passages acknowledge the tension between receiving directions for future success and the ability to understand and carry out such prescriptions. Just as Aeneas must follow Apollo's directions via the Sibyl to found Rome, so must Prudentius, and the reader, follow Christ's doctrine in order to be part of the heavenly city.

The positions of Aeneas, the Sibyl and the *Psychomachia*'s poet and reader are analogous. Traditionally, the Roman *vates* is associated with the poet and a figure similar to the Sibyl, both of whom act as conduits for communication between humans and the divine. Vergil mentions the word three times within the first eighty lines of book 6 (*Aeneid* 6.12, 65, and 78), with the most vivid usage occurring at *Aeneid* 6.11–12, where the word describes the source of the Sibyl's power, and her function, which originates in Apollo, the Delian *vates*: *antrum immane, [Aeneas] petit, magnam cui mentem animumque / Delius inspirat vates aperitque futura.* The initial verses of book 6 emphasize divine prophecy and knowledge of the future.

The term *vates* does not occur in the *Psychomachia*.[26] Nor does the *Psychomachia* mention the Sibyl.[27] And as we have seen, Apollo's name is missing as well; however, by leaving out any mention of Apollo, *vates*, or Sibyl in the *Psychomachia*, yet by clearly recalling these names and their functions from *Aeneid* 6, Prudentius transforms the Vergilian context and highlights his own adaptation of the themes and ideas these figures represent. Christ, not Apollo, is the god we pray to for knowledge of our future; though the function of Apollo remains in the *Psychomachia*, it is transferred to Christ, who becomes the divine source of knowledge and literary inspiration. In the *Psychomachia*, Prudentius eliminates the *vates* as a mediator for gods and humans for divine knowledge. The roles of the Sibyl and Aeneas are therefore merged in the *Psychomachia* into that of Prudentius the poet. The poet is one less step removed from Christ, unlike Aeneas, who is separated from Apollo by the Sibyl and by the shade of his father, Anchises, both of whom provide knowledge.[28] Since Prudentius implicates the reader as the receiver of divine knowledge in the same direct manner as the poet, the flattening out of previous pagan hierarchies is accomplished. The implied reader and poet become equivalent— a quintessentially Christian maneuver.[29]

In addition, the positioning of the implied reader and poet in relation to the action of the poem (i.e., the actual battles) parallels the position of Aeneas regarding the pageant of Roman heroes in *Aeneid* 6, themselves a set of souls who will follow virtue or vice in their future life on earth. *Psychomachia* 5 and 6 contain two first-person plural forms, *noster* and *nostri*, which look back to the use of *hominum* at *Psychomachia* 1 and denote not only the poet (the so-called royal we) but also any other member of the human community who is presumably reading Prudentius' poem. The implied reader and the poet occupy equivalent places as subjects who will receive knowledge and therefore immortality. At the end of the invocation, *Psychomachia* 18–20, Prudentius articulates the way in which these subjects are to position themselves vis-à-vis the subsequent battles between the virtues and the vices:

> Vincendi praesens ratio est, si comminus ipsas
> virtutum facies et conluctantia contra
> viribus infestis liceat portenta *notare.*
> The way of victory is at hand, if it is permitted [for the poet/us]
> *to observe* at close quarters the very features of the Virtues
> and the monsters who struggle with dangerous force against them.

Prudentius' use of *notare* positions the poet and the implied reader as discerning observers who are so close to the conflict that they will be able to recognize the characteristics of both virtues and vices. This immediacy may be just what is necessary for the reader to make the right choice when he becomes the subject of this monumental struggle. The reader in the role of viewer, observer, and learner parallels Aeneas' position as he makes his way through the underworld with his father, who provides an intimate glimpse of Rome's future.

Vergil's underworld provides the terms of representation for the picture of the soul as embattled, which Prudentius immediately establishes.

> Ipse salutiferas obsesso in corpore turmas   (*Psych.* 14–15)
> *depugnare* iubes, . . .
> [Christ] You yourself command the relieving
> squadrons (i.e., the virtues) to fight it out in the

besieged body, ...

tu regere imperio populos, Romane ...   (*Aeneid* 6. 851–53)

... *debellare* superbos.
you, Roman, be sure to rule the world ...
... and crush the proud.

Psychomachia 14–15 portrays the soul under stress in a Christian epic where the text describes the virtues, the soldiers of Christ, who do battle within the soul. The verb *depugnare* occurs only here in the Prudentian corpus and appears to be a synonym for *debellare,* the verb from Anchises' famous dictum to Aeneas about the mission of Rome, *debellare superbos* (*Aeneid* 6. 853). Vergil never uses *depugnare* and uses forms of *debellare* in two other places for ultimate military conflict and for the mission of Rome to subdue the Italians and the proud.[30] The verb *depugnare* has the same meaning, "to fight it out," that is, to master one's enemy completely. And in the case of the *Psychomachia,* it is the virtues that will engage in such totalizing warfare. The shift to *depugnare* is appropriate because, whereas Vergil highlights war on a large scale (*bellum*), Prudentius includes a kind of fighting that is personal (*pugno*). The battle between the virtues and vices is a war, but it is also a personal struggle, a fight for survival.

Another Vergilian allusion in the invocation of the *Psychomachia* reinforces this picture of concern for the soul and its battles. *Psychomachia* 7–11 recalls *Aeneid* 1.148–53:[31]

exoritur quotiens turbatis sensibus intus   (*Psych.* 7–11)
seditio atque *animam* morborum rixa fatigat,
quod *tunc* praesidium pro libertate tuenda
quaeve acies furiis inter praecordia mixtis
obsistat meliore manu.
when there is disorder among our thoughts and
rebellion arises within us, when the strife of our evil
passions vexes the spirit, say what help there is then to
guard her liberty, what array with superior force
withstands the fiendish raging in our heart.

ac veluti magno in populo cum saepe *coorta est*   (*Aeneid* 1. 148–53)
seditio, saevitque *animis* ignobile vulgus,
iamque faces et saxa volant (furor arma ministrat),
tum pietate gravem ac meritis si forte virum quem

conspexere, silent arrectisque auribus astant;
ille regit dictis animos et pectore mulcet:
And as, when often in a great nation tumult has
risen, the base rabble rage angrily, and now brands
and stones fly, madness lending arms; then if by
chance they set eyes on a man honoured for noble
character and service, they are silent and stand by
with attentive ears; with speech he governs their
passion and soothes their breasts:

Prudentius adopts several key words from Vergil's simile (*exoritur* for Vergil's *coorta est, seditio,* and *anima*), as well as the main idea of the simile, which compares the calming of a storm to the soothing words of a leader to his people who have been rioting in a great tumult. These two passages capture nicely the concerns of both texts. Much has been written on the political and cosmic significance of the storm in *Aeneid* 1. Such a context is apt for the opening lines of the *Psychomachia,* which emphasizes the inner turmoil and eventual ordering and calming of the human soul. Further, Prudentius has introduced, however indirectly, a political tone to his poem in mentioning leaders and their people.

Beyond a concern for the soul and its conflicts, the *Psychomachia* takes from *Aeneid* 6 the themes of prophecy and knowledge of the future. In both works knowledge of the future is not merely knowing what is going to happen in detail, but knowing how to behave and what to do when trying circumstances obtain. The Sibyl warns Aeneas of the *labores* that await him and his men: namely, war, bloodshed, and suffering: *magnis . . . periclis* (*Aeneid* 6.83), *graviora* (*Aeneid* 6.84), *bella, horrida bella* (*Aeneid* 6.86), and *malis* (*Aeneid* 6.95). The early lines of the *Psychomachia* display similarly dark language: *graves . . . labores* (*Psych.* 1), *culpas* (*Psych.* 5), *turbatis sensibus* (*Psych.* 7), *seditio* (*Psych.* 8), *furiis inter praecordia mixtis* (*Psych.* 10), *ludibria cordis* (*Psych.* 16), *conluctantia* (*Psych.* 19), *viribus infestis* and *portenta* (*Psych.* 20). When Prudentius leaves the invocation's generalized, allegorical discourse of the soul for the first battle between *Fides* and *Veterum Cultura Deorum,* his language becomes more concrete and more Vergilian. So at *Psychomachia* 21–27, the prelude to the actual physical struggle, we encounter a flurry of allusions to Vergilian battle language.[32]

Two noteworthy cases are *Psychomachia* 21, *Prima petit campum dubia sub sorte duelli* ("[Faith], with an uncertain fortune, seeks the field of battle first"), and *Psychomachia* 27, *provocat insani fragenda pericula belli* ("[Faith] challenges the furious dangers of warfare about to break them down").[33] The first case places the reader into the situation of war where the outcome is always in doubt, especially apt since a Christian's salvation depends on a contested choice to follow good or evil. *Psychomachia* 21 is the first line after the invocation, and its concrete talk of war prepares the way for the allusion at *Psychomachia* 27 to the famous passages in *Aeneid* 7, where Allecto inflicts a lust for "insane war" on Turnus (*insania belli*, *Aeneid* 7.461). Further, just after Ascanius has killed the stag, Allecto describes the lust for "insane war" she causes in the minds of the Latins (*insani Martis*, *Aeneid* 7.550).[34]

Prudentius has appropriated these Vergilian contexts to underscore the intensity of the war about to take place between the virtues and the vices, and the inner, psychological discord that such a battle assumes. Moreover, the use of Vergil in these early lines of the *Psychomachia* builds tension by appropriating the atmosphere of the underworld from *Aeneid* 6. Near the end of the *Psychomachia*, Prudentius revisits *Aeneid* 6 and 7 when he writes that *bella horrida* (*Psych.* 902 and *Aeneid* 6.86 and 7.41) burn in humans' bones, because any victory over vice is temporary. The war must be fought continually. This instantly recognizable phrase, placed at such vital junctures in the *Aeneid*,[35] brings the *Psychomachia* full circle, and crystallizes the Christian message of this epic in the soul's allegorical description as an immortal and virtuous entity.

Additional thematic parallels serve to foreground the context of *Aeneid* 6 in the invocation of the *Psychomachia*. Prudentius exploits Vergilian material to highlight the theme of temple-building. At *Aeneid* 6.9–10, Aeneas lands at Cumae and makes his way immediately to the temple of Apollo (*at pius Aeneas arces, quibus altus Apollo / praesidet*). After another passing reference to the temple (*aurea tecta*), Vergil furnishes its aetiology (*Aeneid* 6. 14–33), in which we are told that Daedalus, after having landed safely in Cumae, built the temple for Apollo (*posuitque immania templa*). Finally, in Aeneas' prayer to Apollo, Aeneas himself promises, should he be victorious, to build Apollo a temple that looks forward to the Augustan structure built on the Palatine to commemorate the victory at the battle of Actium, the defining event of the Principate.[36] Parallel to the *Aeneid*'s focus after Book 6 on the victory of the Trojans over the native Italians, which itself suggests Augustus' total victory over his enemies, the central focus of the *Psychomachia* is the victory of the virtues over the vices—. Prudentius commemorates the virtues' victory by the detailed and monumental construction of the new Christian temple (*Psych.* 804–87), not only as a replacement for Solomon's temple but for Apollo's temple at *Cumae* as well.[37]

The language of initiation rites and mysteries, whose fundamental themes of death and rebirth saturate *Aeneid* 6, contributes in the *Psychomachia* to the figuring of the soul's journey as an epic descent.[38] Aeneas' trial confirms his divine and heroic status, putting him in the company of other epic figures: Odysseus, Hercules, Orpheus, Pollux, and Theseus. Aeneas' actions in Book 6 are a classic *katabasis,* a descent into death followed by a re-ascent into life.[39] This initiation story directly mirrors a movement from past and negative historical events to future and positive history. Aeneas' journey takes him from a past-oriented stance—from the shades of Palinurus, Dido, and Deiphobus— to the future-looking parade of Roman souls: *hac Troiana tenus fuerit fortuna secuta* (*Aen.* 6.62).[40] As William Fitzgerald has noted, the Daedalus story, the temple building, and the *ekphrasis* of *Aeneid* 6.14–36 imply "a historical transition from one culture to another," since both Aeneas and Daedalus are escapees from stories of disastrous love, figured on the diptych as a flight from east to west, from Crete to Athens.[41] Aeneas' prayer to Apollo makes explicit this temporal and thus historical and geographical shift, as Aeneas puts aside events of the past (e.g., the death of Palinurus and the Trojan tragedy) in preparation for the future.[42]

The *Psychomachia* reworks the religious and temporal strategies of *Aeneid* 6 through a careful allusive program. *Psychomachia* 30–31 describes the vice *Veterum Cultura Deorum* at the moment of her death: *Illa hostile caput falerataque tempora vittis / altior insurgens labefactat* ("But she (Faith), rising higher, smites her foe's head down, with its fillet-decked brows"). The vice is wearing the typically pagan religious *vittae*, which are worn by priests performing sacrifices or by the sacrificial object itself. This is also the headdress of poets in the Roman tradition who were thought to enjoy a divine status.[43] *Aeneid* 6.665 (*cinguntur tempora vitta*) contains an instance of this phrase in the same line position (though in the singular) as that of *Psychomachia* 30.[44] In the passage from the *Aeneid*, the archetypal poet Musaeus is leading Aeneas to Anchises. Just lines before, Vergil describes the inhabitants of this part of the underworld:

> quique sacerdotes casti, dum vita manebant,   (*Aeneid* 6. 661–62)
> quique pii vates et Phoebo digna locuti,

those who in their lifetime were priests and pure,
good bards, whose songs were suitable for Apollo,

Both poets and prophets wear the religious headdress; and in this passage the priests and poets are dead, associating the *vitta* not only with sacrificial activities, prophecy and poetry, but also with death. Two other occurrences of the phrase, in the same line position, at *Aeneid* 2.133 and 10.5 look forward and backward respectively, to the contexts of poetry, prophecy, and death in *Aeneid* 6. The headdress, mentioned at *Aeneid* 2.133, is worn by Sinon, the Greek who deceived the Trojans into accepting the Greek's gift-horse. In this passage, Sinon weaves a yarn in which he was to be a sacrifice, chosen by the Greeks in response to an oracle of Apollo mentioned several lines earlier. The headdress signifies his sacrificial status and his proximity to death. *Aeneid* 10.538, by contrast, portrays Aeneas about to kill a priest of Apollo, son of Haemon, who wears the headdress and acts as a sacrifice in revenge for the death of Pallas. Finally, when Laocoon is killed in *Aeneid* 2, he is described as *perfusus sanie vittas* (*Aeneid* 2.221). His headdress, which he wore as a priest making a sacrifice, ends up bloodied and worn by the dead.

These passages in the *Aeneid* are consistent regarding context and meaning. They argue for a parallelism between Christ and Apollo created through the categories of prophecy, poetic inspiration, and sacrificial death. They dovetail with the context of *Psychomachia* 30, which describes the death of all pagan gods, the personification of which wears the *vitta*. The passages, then, recall the tone and setting of Vergil's underworld which Prudentius painstakingly recreates at key junctures of his poem.

The next cluster of allusions to *Aeneid* 6 occur at *Psychomachia* 89–97, an excerpt from the speech of *Pudicitia* as she boasts over the dying *Libido:*

Tu princeps ad mortis iter, tu *ianua leti;*
corpora commaculans animas in *tartara mergis.*
Abde caput tristi iam frigida pestis abysso;
occide, prostibulum, manes pete, claudere Averno,
inque tenebrosum *noctis* detrudere *fundum!*
Te volvant subter vada flammea, te vada nigra
sulpureusque rotet per stagna *sonantia vertex.*
Nec iam christicolas, *furiarum maxima,* temptes,
ut purgata suo serventur corpora *regi.*
You are the leader to the path of death, you are the gate of death

staining our bodies you plunge our souls into Tartarus.
Hide your head in the grim pit, now you feeble pestilence;
die, harlot; seek the shades of the dead, be shut up in Avernus,
and be thrust down into the dark depths of night.
May the fiery rivers below roll you along, the black streams
and the whirlpool of sulfur swing you around through the resounding waters.
No longer, greatest of fiends, may you tempt the worshippers of Christ,
So that their cleansed bodies are preserved for their own king.

In this passage, we encounter a multitude of words and circumstances that recall the underworld setting of *Aeneid* 6.[45] Let us begin with the phrases *furiarum maxima* and *regi* (*Psych*. 96–97), which are paralleled at *Aeneid* 6.604–607:

. . . *epulae*que ante ora paratae
regificio luxu; *Furiarum maxima* iuxta
accubat et manibus prohibet contingere mensas,
exsurgitque facem attollens atque intonat ore.
. . . and before their eyes is spread a banquet
in royal splendor; the greatest of the Furies reclines
nearby and prevents their hands from touching the tables,
and she springs forth raising a torch and thunders with her voice.

Aeneas is in the midst of his tour of Tartarus, observing monsters, divine beings, and sinners who have committed an assortment of crimes having to do with the desire for power, money, and sex.[46] Prudentius mentions *Tartara* (*Psych*. 90), *manes* and *Averno* (*Psych*. 92),[47] all of which evoke a pagan atmosphere of the underworld and by extension help to describe Christian hell.[48] The phrase *ianua leti* at *Psychomachia* 89, a common epic formulation for the gates of the underworld,[49] reinforces the evocation of the pagan underworld. *Aeneid* 2.661 has *ianua leto* at the end of the line and forms part of Aeneas' appeal to Anchises to leave Troy with him before it is too late. The context of *Aeneid* 6 is preserved since both Aeneas and Anchises, the two main actors of *Aeneid* 6, are at the center of a life and death struggle in this passage.[50]

We can telescope this allusion further with the reference at *Psychomachia* 95 to *Aeneid* 6.652. The Prudentian phrase *sonantia vertex* picks up Vergil's *sonantia saxa*. Aeneas leaves Deiphobus, his last symbolic connection with the Trojan past, and comes to the fork in the underworld's road leading either to

Elysium or Tartarus. *Aeneid* 6.651–52 and *Psychomachia* 94–95 both describe the underworld river of Tartarus. In this place *Libido* will dwell for eternity. The context of these Vergilian passages suggests Aeneas leaving the past and death behind in preparation for the visit to the valley of Lethe later on in *Aeneid* 6. Such a journey (*iter*) parallels the experience of the poet/implied reader of the *Psychomachia*. Not only has Prudentius recalled Vergilian underworld language in a general way to connect the vice *Libido* to the pagan construction of hell, but he has also figured death and the options in the afterlife according to the architecture and narrative of *Aeneid* 6. *Pudicitia*'s words to *Libido* place the reader squarely in the context of *Aeneid* 6.604–607, in which the Sibyl describes the mythological inhabitants of Tartarus.

In the central battle of the *Psychomachia*, which pits *Avaritia* against *Operatio*, the reader once again encounters a series of allusions to *Aeneid* 6. Just after *Avaritia* enters, her personified attendants are listed (*Psych.* 464–66), three of which—*Metus, Fames*, and *Eumenides*—occur at *Aeneid* 6. 273–81.

Cura *Famis Metus* Anxietas Periuria Pallor   (*Psych.* 464–66)
Corruptela Dolus Commenta Insomnia Sordes,
Eumenides variae, monstri *comitatus aguntur.*
Care, Hunger, Fear, Anguish, Perjuries, Pallor
Corruption, Treachery, Falsehood, Sleeplessness,
Meanness, diverse fiends, go in attendance on
the monster.

vestibulum ante ipsum primisque in faucibus Orci   (*Aeneid* 6. 273–81)
Luctus et ultrices posuere cubilia *Curae,*
pallentesque habitant Morbi tristisque Senectus
et *Metus* et malesuada *Fames* ac turpis Egestas,
terribiles visu formae, Letumque Labosque:
tum consanguineus Leti Sopor et mala mentis
Gaudia, mortiferumque adverso in limine Bellum
ferreique *Eumenidum* thalami et Discordia demens,
vipereum crinem vittis innexa cruentis.
Just before the entrance, even within the very jaws
of Hell, Grief and avenging Cares have set their bed;
there pale Diseases dwell, sad Age, and Fear, and
Hunger, temptress to sin, and loathly Want, shapes
terrible to view; and Death and Distress; next, Death's

own brother Sleep, and the soul's guilty Joys, and,
on the threshold opposite, the death-dealing War,
and the Furies' iron cells, and maddening Strife,
her snaky locks entwined with bloody ribbons.

After *Avaritia* is killed, her attendants disperse (*Psych.* 629–31) and the light of the sun and heaven returns (*Psych.* 639). The dispersal of her attendants alludes to two more passages from *Aeneid* 6 (*Aeneid* 6.276–77, 6.381–83); and the return of light alludes to still another (*Aeneid* 6.640–41). These passages form the end frame of the *Avaritia* section.

> *His dictis curae emotae.* Metus et Labor et Vis   (*Psych.* 629–31)
> et Scelus et placitae fidei Fraus infitiatrix
> de*pulsae* vertere solum.
> At these words their cares departed. Fear and
> Suffering and Violence, Crime and Fraud that
> denies accepted faith, were driven away and fled
> from the land.

> aeternumque locus Palinuri nomen habebit.   (*Aeneid* 6.381–83)
> *his dictis curae emotae, pulsus*que parumper
> corde dolor triste;
> and forever the place shall bear the name of
> Pallinurus. By these words his cares departed,
> and for a little space grief is driven from his
> anguished heart;

> *purpuream* videas caeli clarescere *lucem.*   (*Psych.* 639)
> and light from heaven begins to shine
> resplendent to the view.

> largior his campos aether et *lumine* vestit   (*Aeneid* 6.640–41)
> *purpureo,* solemque suum, sua sidera norunt.
> Here an ampler ether clothes the meads with
> resplendent light, and they know their own sun,
> and their own stars.

Moreover, nearly in the middle of the *Avaritia* section, *Aeneid* 6 is made the focal point again. At *Psychomachia* 538–39, *Avaritia* describes the death of Achar, an Old Testament casualty of greed (*Joshua* 7). These lines contain Vergilian expressions from *Aeneid* 6:

Caedibus insignis murali et *strage* superbus   (*Psych.* 538–39)
subcubuit capto *victis* ex hostibus auro,
For though he won glory by the slaughter and
was exalted by the overthrowing of the walls, he
fell victim to the gold that was taken from the
beaten foe,

nocte tulit fessum vasta te *caede* Pelasgum   (*Aeneid* 6.503–504)
procubuisse super confusae *stragis* acervum.
on that last night, weary with endless slaughter
of the Pelasgians, you had fallen upon a heap
of mingled carnage.

Ille triumphata Capitolia ad alta Corintho   (*Aeneid* 6.836–37)
victor aget currum *caesis insignis* Achivis.
That one there (Lucius Mummius), triumphant
over Corinth, shall drive a victor's chariot to the
lofty Capitol, famed for Achaeans he has slain.

At *Aeneid* 6. 503–504, Aeneas speaks to the shade of Deiphobus, whose death he mentions (compare *Psych.* 94–95 which alludes to the Deiphobus scene as well). At *Aeneid* 6. 836–37, Anchises, during the pageant of Roman heroes, points out Lucius Mummius, who destroyed Corinth in 146 BCE. In this particular verse Anchises depicts Mummius in triumph after killing Greeks. The recollection of these Vergilian passages further contributes to the atmosphere of death and the underworld with which the center battle of the *Psychomachia* teems. The story of Achar, put into the mouth of a vice and evoking the language and environment of Vergil's underworld, produces a Roman epic version of a biblical story. Far from mock-epic or typical biblical epic, the passage performs an essential function of Roman epic: to restate national identity through a master narrative of larger-than-life figures.[51] Prudentius attempts to include Achar's story as part of the master narrative of salvation history that includes Rome.

If we analyze the sets of allusive passages which frame the central battle at the beginning and end, we see that the *Avaritia* section projects a vivid sense of psychology created through the personification of emotions. In addition, because these Vergilian recollections evoke the netherworld ephemera of *Aeneid* 6, the *Avaritia* scene becomes an essential part of the *Psychomachia*'s debt to Vergil, suggesting how the *Psychomachia* reworks the *Aeneid*.

In the first set of framing passages, *Psychomachia* 464–66 and *Aeneid* 6. 273–81, Prudentius emphasizes the personification of emotions as the constituents of a soul dominated by *Avaritia*. In the *Aeneid*, the poet has just invoked the gods of the underworld to grant that the truth be revealed.[52] Vergil describes the landscape as Aeneas and the Sibyl enter Pluto's realm. The Sibyl rushes into the cave, *antro se immisit aperto* (*Aeneid* 6.262), and Aeneas stands at the entrance, *vestibulum ante ipsum* (*Aeneid* 6.273).

In drawing on this scene, Prudentius envisions the landscape of the soul in the spatial terms delineated in *Aeneid* 6.[53] Vergil's underworld is a dark and forbidding region populated by disease, fear, hunger, and death. These monster-like beings translate well into the region of the soul in which *Avaritia* dwells. The spatial terms imply psychological concepts that Prudentius' poem imitates. The spatial-psychological connection materializes when the Sibyl exhorts Aeneas to take courage (*nunc animis opus, Aenea, nunc pectore firmo, Aeneid* 6.261) and rushes into the cave. This reading of Vergil in Prudentius is reinforced by the Vergilian phrase, *comitatus aguntur,* found at *Psychomachia* 466. The phrase refers to the personified followers of *Avaritia* and is taken from *Aeneid* 12.336, the context of which relates directly to the underworld scene of *Aeneid* 6 since Vergil deploys personifications, *Ira* and *Insidia,* to highlight Turnus' extreme psychological state during his Homeric *aristeia.* In essence, Prudentius has adapted Vergil's netherworld landscape and its attendant psychology to create a manifestly psychological space, bringing the epic struggle into the mental and emotional interior of the individual.

The set of allusive passages that form the end frame of the *Avaritia* section continue and solidify the psychological affinity between *Aeneid* 6 and the *Psychomachia. Avaritia*'s dreadful retinue disperses (*Psych.* 629–31) and is re-described as *curae emotae,* a phrase that Vergil uses at *Aeneid* 6. 382 of the nether-Palinurus who, upon being informed of his impending burial, experiences the dispersal of his cares. Rather than a subversive and hostile stance toward the *Aeneid,*[54] the *Psychomachia* has elaborated on ideas present in the Palinurus scene. Prudentius' allusion achieves a new epic vision by constructing on epic terms a psychological discourse in which inner, psychological qualities become narrative characters in order to describe the new epic battle within the soul.

Moreover, the journey of Palinurus and Aeneas toward their destinies takes them through the realm of death, an epic circumstance emulated in the *Psychomachia* by the poet/implied reader's journey within his own soul to eternal life. Prudentius' re-naming of the personifications (*Metus* et *Labor* etc.) as "dispersed cares" parallels Vergil's appositive of *dolor, curae emotae.*[55] These maneuvers evoke the underworld, which allegorically stands for the soul, as defined as mental states and emotions. Prudentius reads *Aeneid* 6 psychologically, constructing a world that does not exist in real space and time but is described through spatial and temporal discourse. The poet creates a place that is otherworldly, demonic, and full of surprises. Yet, in true Platonic style, the inhabitants of this world are real.[56] The way in which one negotiates the journey through this immaterial world determines one's destiny in the earthly world of change.

Prudentius uses Vergil in a similar way when the virtues, after the defeat of *Avaritia,* arrive at the double gate to their camp:

> *Ventum erat ad fauces* portae castrensis, ubi artum   (*Psych.* 665–66)
> liminis introitum bifori dant cardine claustra.
> They had reached the passage of the camp-gate, where
> a gate with double-door hinges furnishes a narrow entrance.

> *ventum erat ad limen,* cum virgo, "poscere fata   (*Aeneid* 6. 45–47)
> tempus" ait: "deus, ecce, deus!" cui talia fanti
> ante fores subito non vultus, non color unus,
> They had reached the threshold when the maiden said:
> "it is time to ask the oracles; the god, here is the god!"
> As she spoke such things in front of the doors, suddenly
> neither her demeanor nor her color was the same,

> inde ubi *venere ad fauces* grave olentis Averni   (*Aeneid* 6.201)
> Then, when they reached the jaws of stinking Avernus

The context of the *Psychomachia* passage is forbidding because, although the virtues believe that the battle against the vices is finished, the unwelcome surprise of *Discordia* awaits them within the walls of their camp.

The Vergilian passages have parallel contexts. The first takes place at Aeneas' initial contact with the Sibyl and the second occurs when Aeneas receives a clear sign indicating where to find the golden bough. The atmosphere of Misenus' death surrounds the giving of the sign, thus coloring Aeneas' success with a foreboding sense of sacrifice and of the difficulty of leaving the underworld. The *Psychomachia* exploits the tension and suspense of the *Aeneid* passages, which emphasize the uncertainty and unpredictability of these liminal moments in the underworld.[57]

Fauces (*Psych.* 665) participates in this emphasis, for it is a loaded word in the *Psychomachia,* standing for the throats of vices which at the moment of death are crushed by the virtues (e.g., the death of *Avaritia, faucibus artis / extorquent animam, Psych.* 592–93). *Fauces* recalls the contexts of *Aeneid* 6. 201 and *Psychomachia* 592–93 where, in the former, the word is used of the entrance into hell and, in the latter, of the corrupt throat passage of *Avaritia;* corrupt, because it spews forth heresy just as *Discordia*'s "breath-passage of her voice" does (*vocis . . . spiramina, Psych.* 717) following *Psychomachia* 665–66. Given these associations, with the use of *fauces* for the camp of the virtues, Prudentius suggests that the camp is still polluted with the concealed presence of *Discordia.*

The Vergilian context of the entrance into the pagan Sibyl's cave dovetails with the *Psychomachia*'s suggestion of a corrupt camp of the virtues. What is more, at *Aeneid* 6. 46–47 the description of the Sibyl's changed complexion and countenance parallels *Discordia*'s heretical ravings about the godhead: compare *deus est mihi discolor* (*Psych.* 710) with *non color unus* (*Aeneid* 6. 47). In this case, the allusion projects the pagan quality of the Sibyl and her oracular residence onto *Discordia,* a pagan character turned Christian heretic. The contexts of *Aeneid* 6. 45–47 and 201 influence the reading of the description of the virtues' camp and the characterization of the heretical interloper, *Discordia.*

The relationship between the two texts converges further if we compare *Psychomachia* 639 and *Aeneid* 6. 640–41. In the former, *Metus, Labor, Vis,* and *Scelus* have departed, causing the light of heaven and the sun to return. In the latter, Aeneas has just planted the golden bough at the threshold to the "Blissful Groves" where blessed souls of poets and prophets reside, bathed in light. The context of the *Aeneid* passage cannot be more appropriate to the purpose of the *Psychomachia.* The recollection of the groves from *Aeneid* 6 bestows epic stature on the departure of the minor vices in the *Psychomachia* while simultaneously exhibiting the change in the metaphysical positions from pagan hell to Christian tranquility. Prudentius does not engage in literary subversion, but exploits the *Aeneid* to delineate the terrain of the soul and its bifurcated nature (i.e., good/bad, light/dark, virtue/vice).

A final cluster of allusive passages occurs at the end of the poem, *Psychomachia* 889–90, thus creating a frame around the poem, the beginning of which, *Psychomachia* 1, mobilizes the allusive program:

grates, Christe, tibi meritosque sacramus honores   (*Psych.* 889–90)
ore pio; nam cor vitiorum stercore sordet.

[We give unending] thanks to you , Christ, and
offer to you honor that is deserved with loyal
lips; for our heart is foul with the filth of sin.

. . . di, talia Grais   (*Aeneid* 6. 529–30)
instaurate, *pio* si poenas *ore* reposco.
O Gods, with like penalties repay the Greeks
if with pious lips I pray for vengeance!

Immediately, one is struck by the fact that *Psychomachia* 889, with its appeal to
Christ, and in its rhythm and sound of the first and last pairs of words, recalls
Psychomachia 1, *Christe, graves hominum semper miserate labores.* Prudentius
returns to the beginning of his poem, signaling a transformative engagement
with the *Aeneid* and the Roman epic tradition. The "heavy suffering of human
beings" of the first line, itself a substitution for Trojan suffering, is replaced by
"thanks" to, and the "deserved honor" of, Christ. The metaphorical distance
traveled from Christ pitying humans to humans thanking Christ marks the
progress of the soul's journey in the *Psychomachia.* Although the soul continuously struggles against vice (as the last 23 lines of the poem assert), the allegory
of the ideal soul is offered as a model to be imitated by the poet/implied
reader.[58] *Psychomachia* 889 offers thanks to Christ for helping the poet/implied
reader through the trial of each one's soul. The focus shifts from the first line,
where all individuals (*hominum*) seek relief from suffering, to Christ (*tibi* is in
the same line position as *hominum*) who is the instrument of salvation. To
redeem themselves humans must look not to each other but to Christ—though
in order to look to Christ, humans must each exercise their own free will and
make a personal decision.

The phrase *ore pio* adds to this view by recalling Aeneas' words to Deiphobus in the underworld, a section of *Aeneid* 6 recalled in the battles between
Pudicitia and *Libido,* and *Avaritia* and *Operatio.* Although this expression is
found sparingly in Christian literature,[59] it is a fixture in Cicero and Livy, and
is used by Roman epic poets such as Vergil, Valerius Flaccus, and Silius Italicus.[60] This pagan epic diction is challenged in the next line by *stercore,* an un-
Vergilian word that describes the vice-laden part of the soul. The pull of these
two traditions within the phrases, *ore pio* and *vitiorum stercore,* in this one line
express each person's two-sided nature, a fundamental dualism that has its
roots in the epic hero himself, who is, like Aeneas, burdened by a choice
between action and inaction, glory and obscurity.

Both *Psychomachia* 889–90 and its Vergilian counterpart are prayers (*Aeneid* 6.529–30) to a god.[61] The *Psychomachia*'s return to Aeneas' meeting with Deiphobus situates Aeneas at the crossroad between the past and the future. His words represent the struggle of the Trojans to put to rest their tragic past and enter the "bright," Roman future. The parallel to the poet/implied reader is made palpable once again since Prudentius in these lines summarizes the struggle that each human soul must undergo to achieve immortality—that is, through the choice of virtue, to leave the past and move on to a perfect future.

Vergilian piety is paralleled by Christian virtue. Vergil's emphasis on piety in *Aeneid* 6 is well-known, expressed in Aeneas' unflinching commitment (after *Aeneid* 6 at any rate) to his journey and mission. Piety ultimately means he must act and endure according to rules he does not make, so that he may found the greatest earthly city. In the epilogue of the *Psychomachia*, the same quality of piety is invoked twice at *Psychomachia* 890 and 911, directing the reader/poet to take up the challenge of *horrida bella* within the soul (*Psych.* 902), so that virtues may expel vices (*Psych.* 911) and the soul may live forever in the heavenly city. In this way, Prudentius reads the *Aeneid* optimistically, though he seems to comprehend the *Aeneid*'s profoundly tragic situation.[62] That is, far from an ambiguous or ambivalent narrative of Aeneas' founding of Rome,[63] Prudentius' allusive program with *Aeneid* 6 helps to construct the *Psychomachia*'s salvational message.[64] Recollection of the journey of Aeneas adds epic weight and seriousness to the journey of the poet/implied reader.

Psychomachia 889 also contains the phrase *meritos . . . honores* which is found at *Aeneid* 3.118, 3.264, and 8.189. The contexts of the passages from *Aeneid* 3 evoke Apollo, Anchises, the idea of the journey, and knowledge of the future, elements which we have already seen in other allusions to the *Aeneid*. *Aeneid* 3 narrates the Odyssean journey Aeneas and his men take in the Mediterranean. *Aeneid* 3.118 narrates the sacrifices to Apollo and Neptune which Anchises performs in response to an oracle of Apollo on Delos. Aeneas reports the speech of Anchises (*Aeneid* 3.103–17), who begins by recounting the Trojan past and ends by exhorting Aeneas and the Trojans to move on, *sequamur* (*Aeneid* 3.114), as the past gives way to the future. The phrase *meritos honores* (*Aeneid* 3.264) also occurs within a speech of Anchises that takes place after the seer of Apollo, Celaeno, prophesies that the Trojans will not found their city until they "eat their tables." The founding of a new city translates into a new life for each and every Trojan. These passages embellish the end of the *Psychomachia*, which celebrates the metaphor of the soul as an ideal temple/city, perfected only after Christian doctrine is accepted, the vices have been expelled, and the virtues have attained complete control. Pagan epic contexts are exploited and reworked to serve Christian ideology.

In addition, Caelano's words warn of violence and wrongs to be endured before the Trojans reach their new home—a motif encountered earlier in the two works' intertextual relationship. Anchises prays to the gods to keep the Trojans safe during their impending sea voyage that will retrace the route taken by Odysseus. A brief Odyssean itinerary is given (*Aeneid* 3.270–75) as emblematic of the Trojans' long journey, made more unbearable by the fact that Odysseus, their most bitter enemy, followed the same path. The itinerary concludes at the shrine of Apollo at Leucas, which also recalls another shrine to Apollo at Actium.[65] The Trojans must retrace their past sufferings in order to reach their new home just as the poet/implied reader must face his vices within himself in order to construct the temple/city of the soul. The final resting place of the Trojans is mentioned by Celaeno:

> sed non ante datam *cingetis moenibus urbem,* (*Aeneid* 3. 255–57)
> quam vos dira fames nostraeque iniuria caedis
> ambesas subigat malis absumere mensas.
> but you shall not surround with walls your promised city before
> dread hunger and the wrong of violence toward us
> force you to gnaw with your teeth and devour your very tables.

The lines refer to the future and the unrealized city of the Trojans and contribute to the thematic and linguistic nexus of allusion, since the *Psychomachia*'s goal is to construct a purified soul in the form of the ideal city. The dark language of the first 20 lines of the *Psychomachia*, which evoked the foreboding language and atmosphere of the first section of *Aeneid* 6, is revisited in the pagan prophet's words (e.g., *malis,* 3. 257 and *iniuria caedis,* *Aeneid* 3.256—compare similar language of violence in *Psychomachia* 538–39 and *Aeneid* 6. 503–504, 836–37). Further, Anchises' plea invokes piety (*pios,* *Aeneid* 3. 266), the quality which *Psychomachia* 890 and 911 explicitly offer to Christ as a characteristic of the good Christian poet/implied reader. Both passages from *Aeneid* 3 contextually and thematically complement and reinforce the reference at *Psychomachia* 889–90 to *Aeneid* 6.529.

As for *Aeneid* 8.189, the context is the famous story of Hercules and Cacus which Evander narrates to Aeneas. In the passage, Evander states that the *meritos . . . honores* ("deserved offerings") are performed to keep his people safe from *saevis . . . periclis* (*Aeneid* 8.188). For Prudentius, violence matters less than the suggestion of sacrifice and ritual in these lines. Moreover, just as Hercules neutralizes the monster Cacus under a burning volcano, so do the virtues stamp out the vices. A reader of both the *Aeneid* and the *Psychomachia* may recall the violence of Hercules' story and perhaps even the ambivalent attitude toward Augustus and his regime that the story may suggest, but the "deserved offerings" which Prudentius directs at Christ lack ambivalence and appear to rework the pagan language of sacrifice into a Christian context. At the very least, the allusion reinforces a central theme of *Aeneid* 6, relief from the dangers and sufferings accumulated during the search for home. The *Psychomachia* capitalizes on this idea throughout its narrative.

Epic Ambitions: Readers, Heroes, and Identity

Acceptance of the claim that Prudentius' "reading" of *katabasis* in *Aeneid* 6 attempts to rival the *Aeneid* leads us to reflect on Roman epic tradition. To this end, I conclude by offering several suggestions regarding how the *Psychomachia* transforms the pagan epic tradition. First, the battle of the virtues and vices is figured in the *Psychomachia* as a *katabasis* of the soul, which Prudentius describes by appropriating the language and setting of Aeneas' descent into the underworld. The allusions to *Aeneid* 6, especially those that inform the battle between *Avaritia* and *Operatio*, establish an underworld atmosphere that evokes the Vergilian *katabasis*. Directly following this scene, Prudentius re-describes the Vergilian trial, but this time as the Old Testament story of the Exodus when the Jews, who allegorically stand for the virtues, escape the Egyptians, who stand for the vices, through the "psychological" depths of the Red Sea (*Psych.* 650–64). Note that these lines are the only formal, Vergilian simile in the *Psychomachia* (*non aliter, Psych.* 650 . . . *sic, Psych.* 663).[66] Yet this is not the end of the repetition. For once again Prudentius thrusts the reader into a *katabasis*-like milieu of the virtue/vice battles, when *Discordia* inaugurates another trial during which she unexpectedly threatens the virtues and is destroyed within the walls of the city of the soul. After her death, Prudentius describes the temple of the soul according to a New Testament source, Revelation. This description, which alludes to both Solomon's and Deadalus' temples, is built only after all of the vices have been vanquished. The third description of the trial of the soul is now complete, but this time ending on Christian terms after the cross-examination of *Discordia*, which is modeled on the questioning of Sinon in *Aeneid* 2 (and which contains language drawn from the second half of the *Aeneid*).[67]

There is a marked fall-off of Vergilian allusions in the temple section of the *Psychomachia*. The description of the temple of the soul represents the final step of a Christian trial in which the soul emerges from inner psychological battle against vice to a state of purity and readiness for communion with God. Hence, there is the Vergilian *katabasis* which underlies the *Avaritia/Operatio* scene, the *katabasis* of the Jewish Exodus through the Red Sea, and finally, the related trial beginning with the battle against the heretical *Discordia*. Prudentius describes the *Discordia* scene in a manner befitting the Vergilian underworld and ends the poem with the temple drawn from *Revelation*. This repetition represents a striking adaptation of the epic motifs of *katabasis* and the heroic trial. The sequence brings the reader from the pagan tradition and Jewish traditions to the Christian dispensation.

Secondly, the *Psychomachia*'s focus on the struggle within the soul results in the reconfiguration of Aeneas' dualistic nature,[68] which simultaneously projects "*Roma aeterna*" and also doubt, ambivalence, or even self-destruction. The epic hero, the *unus homo,* who stands for Rome, is wracked with conflict that is expressed, in the case of Aeneas, as a dialectic between *pietas* and *furor.* This dialectic reflects an uncertainty about Rome's moral and political authority. The killing of Turnus by Aeneas at the end of the epic signals this fundamental dualism. In Lucan, to cite one other example, we witness a series of oppositional character pairs, Caesar/Pompey, Caesar/Cato, which reflect the political duality of Principate/Republic.[69] In the *Psychomachia,* virtues and vices represent the residue of the moral and psychological dualism seen within Aeneas and his epic descendents. Confidence and an imperial swagger are delineated in the virtues and also, for example, in the *Peristephanon*'s martyr figures, who make the courageous and correct choice of following their faith; whereas doubt and self-destructive behavior are associated with the Vices.[70]

Aeneas as wanderer and seeker of future knowledge parallels the Christian poet who petitions Christ to aid him in finding his true future of immortality, thus ending his spiritual wandering. Through the Sibyl, Apollo speaks to Aeneas just as Christ speaks to Prudentius the poet. For Christ communicates to the implied reader *through* Prudentius, just as Apollo does to Aeneas *through* the Sibyl.[71] Thus parallel hierarchies appear in the schemes of Apollo-Sibyl-Aeneas in the *Aeneid* and Christ-Prudentius-implied reader in the *Psychomachia*. However, in the latter poem, the distance between the poet and the implied reader collapses, since the poem posits the reader and the poet to-gether as subjects seeking correct knowledge for the attainment of immor-tality. The collapse of the two terms, "Prudentius" and "implied reader," into one furnishes a more varied set of parallels with the hierarchy in the *Aeneid*. Therefore, comparisons are implied in the two texts between Prudentius the poet and Aeneas the founding father, the poet and implied reader as seekers/ wanderers, and the implied reader and Aeneas as seekers/wanderers. The *Psychomachia* fashions a close relationship between the implied reader and the text in complementary ways. For the poet and the implied reader become nearly equivalent while simultaneously the implied reader stands in a more intimate relationship with the divine.

Another aspect of Prudentius' restatement of epic dualism is that the poet/ implied reader takes on a psychological dualism summed up by the choice between virtue and vice. In choosing virtue, the poet/implied reader gains knowledge of, and acquires, an ideal soul. Prudentius' personifications are the allegorical parts that form a soul "on the page," but also the soul within the reader himself, who embodies a potential epic hero should he follow Christian doctrine. It is not the characters who are problematized in the *Psychomachia*, but rather the individual who reads and reflects on the characters as moral and religious examples. In keeping with the doctrine of Christian free will, the reader is compelled to make a choice between good and evil, faith and godless-ness, immortal life and death.[72] Thus, the epic dualism found in Vergil and Lucan becomes extratextual, projected onto the reader herself, and is figured as an internal conflict within the soul, resolved through choice. The choice of the reader is parallel to the choices that Aeneas and other epic heroes make, and even perhaps accompanied by the tragic overtones.[73] The reader is being called upon to become an epic hero, whose prize, like any other epic hero's, is immortality.

Finally, Prudentius' epic version of Rome, although not explicitly asserted, assumes Rome to be a Christian city that parallels the happy destiny of the Christian individual. Unlike in the *Aeneid*, Lucan's *Bellum Civile*, and the *Punica* of Silius Italicus, where Rome itself is problematized, the *Psychomachia* assumes a post-Constantinian golden age in which Rome is a stable and politi-cally homogenous state. Rome's political and military success is not prob-lematized.[74] Rather, Prudentius transfers his epic battles from the earthly and mythohistorical space of Troy, Latium, Pharsalia, and Zama, to the immaterial and divine realm of the individual soul. In the *Aeneid*, the assumption of an

Augustan golden age goes hand in hand with a reexamination of the past in the shadow of an uncertain future. Lucan juxtaposes the Principate's assumed benefits with a senseless civil war to devastating effect, and Silius ruminates on Rome's possible decline after the defeat of Hannibal.[75]

In the *Psychomachia,* the secure city where the virtues dwell at the end of their war against the vices is the celestial double of Rome, which, if we interpret the parallel, is now somewhat safe and secure because of each citizen's faith. The historical reality of martyrdom and the political/military victory of Constantine, both viewed unambiguously, combine to become the golden age successor to the Augustan return of the Republic in Vergil.[76] Therefore, the idea of Rome does not bring a dualistic meditation, alternating between confidence and melancholy expressed literarily but rather remains unabashedly pure, having reached an unassailable condition after Rome took up Christianity as the state religion.

Prudentius' version of Roman national identity, the representation of which is a basic function of epic, is tied to *Christianitas,* which becomes integrated into Roman society through each individual soul's radical conversion. The heroes of pagan Roman epic have a national and collective purpose, however fraught with contradiction it and they may be. Are there signs of this national hero who stands for the totality of Rome in Prudentius' poetry? In the *Psychomachia,* Prudentius deconstructs the Roman epic hero into each reader, who is part of a political purpose. Rather than founding the empire and unifying Rome through personal greatness, the reader is part of a reconstruction of Rome, one citizen at a time. The reader is not engaged in founding an empire through conquest and the imposition of political and cultural identity on a population but rather is a singular example of many, whose recognition of a Christian identity through a conversion of the soul is necessary for the construction of Rome as a Christian world nation. The conversion to Christianity represents a harmonious union between the religious and the political realms.[77] Each person must choose to know and to live by what is truly Christian in order to be truly Roman. Thus, collectivity through a private conversion experience is a goal of the new Christian epic.[78]

The idea of a Roman Christian collective guides Prudentius' use of history, which attempts to unify the Roman pagan, Christian, and Jewish traditions. The challenge of including these disparate traditions in a coherent story functions ideologically to create a new, dominant historical narrative—namely, salvation history. The use of Vergil hints at this project, revealing a change in the Roman epic categories of the nature of the divine, the heroic descent/trial, the nature of the hero, and the idea of Rome. Prudentius accomplishes this through a careful allusive program that simultaneously embraces and distances itself from his epic predecessor. In addition, a biblical allusive program, which takes the form of carefully chosen typologies, embraces Roman pagan history as it acknowledges the ultimate authority of Christian ideology in the construction of history.

CHAPTER TWO

Christian History and the Narrative of Rome

The *Psychomachia*'s deep engagement with the *Aeneid* exposes Prudentius' ambitious epic program and culminates in a redefinition of pagan Roman epic within the fourth-century Christian context. Rather than rejecting the Roman literary past, Prudentius' work follows Roman epic tradition and provides a new definition of national identity.[1] The construction of national identity is a cornerstone of the master narrative of epic from Homer and Vergil to Milton and Walcott. Poets contribute to a construction of national identity in epic narratives by exploiting history as narrative storytelling. For Greek and Roman epics, historical narratives furnished the content of fundamental cultural narratives that were propagated, promoted, and preserved. The writer who produces a culturally dominant historical narrative contributes to a people's idea of itself. Vergil and the epic writers who followed him participated in this high stakes literary game. The *Psychomachia* takes up where Vergil, Lucan, and others left off by reconfiguring the master historical narrative, but this time according to the conventions of Christian historiography.[2]

Scholars from Burckhardt to Momigliano, Barnes, and Cameron have seen Eusebius as the key figure in Christian historiography who links the sacred story of Christ and the Roman empire to create what has been called an "imperial theology."[3] Since Christianity was tolerated and even promoted by Constantine and subsequent emperors, Rome becomes part of historians' construction of universal sacred history. No longer is it the central purpose of writing history to prove the truth of Christianity. Rather, history for Prudentius and other Christian writers and readers after Eusebius is primarily a source of personal transformation in which the soul becomes the site for the definition of Christian identity. In fourth-century literature, history rarely functions as a discourse of political self-critique. In the *Aeneid*, however, the critique of Augustus generates a partisan or ambivalent version of *Romanitas*.[4] More than other literary works of the late fourth and early fifth centuries, the *Psychomachia* and the *Peristephanon* exhibit this fundamental shift in historical consciousness from history as an instrument of political self-critique to a more subjective use of history, which begins from Christian notions of soul and cosmos. This distinction between Prudentian and Vergilian epic notwithstanding, for Prudentius, the historical project does have a political purpose: the creation and consolidation of a Roman Christian self, originating in each reader's acceptance of Christian salvation history. In this chapter, I turn to Prudentius' use of Roman, Hebrew, and Christian history to illustrate the poet's transformative engagement with Roman historical narratives and the Roman self. My claim is that through the manipulation of salvation history, Prudentius transforms Roman historical narratives and notions of Roman identity inherited from epic tradition into a discourse of the Roman Christian self.

The practice of historiography is central to Prudentius' work. In the *Hamartigenia* (339–40), Prudentius refers to Moses as *historicus*, "a writer of history" who chronicles the world's birth as the traditional author of the Pentateuch. Furthermore, in a passage of the *Peristephanon*, the poet casts himself as a *historicus* who gathers information on a martyr in a cemetery.[5] In light of the *Psychomachia*'s universal span from *Genesis* to *Revelation*, it is not difficult to imagine Prudentius in the role of *historicus* in that poem, but the poet is no mere compiler of historical narratives. He is capable of a sustained and sophisticated historical critique. For instance, the *Contra Symmachum* demonstrates that Prudentius views the span of human history as teleological, functioning according to a process of development and evolution and culminating in a final event, the Last Judgment. He applies this approach to both Roman pagan and Old Testament history (*Symm.* 2.309–69). Prudentius also implies in the same work that the content of historical narratives can be subjected to a skeptical approach replete with analysis and judgment. In other words, Christians can explain the components of history according to the goal of history (i.e., the Last Judgment) and criticize a pagan view of history (e.g., Symmachus') by demonstrating its rational and factual shortcomings. In this manner, Prudentius from his advantageously Christian position in Post-Constantinian Rome shows Symmachus how pagans have misrepresented the facts.[6] The Christian historical tradition, which begins with the Old Testament, consists of, for the most part, ancient books (*antiquis . . . libris, Symm.* 2.337) that furnish reliable historical evidence for the beginnings of civilization. Prudentius's historiographical acumen is clear: he moves effortlessly from Judeo-Christian sources of history to Roman pagan sources, exposes inconsistencies of the typical Roman pagan view of religious history, and advocates the Old Testament historical text as a superior rival to pagan sources. Through such a program, the poet signals a transformation of the Roman pagan story of history.

Though recognizing the poet's tendency to combine Christian and pagan literary aspects, scholars and critics of Prudentius have said precious little concerning Prudentius' handling of Roman and Christian history.[7] My argument rests on the idea that the construction of salvation history informs Prudentius' poetic program in both the *Psychomachia* and the *Peristephanon*.[8] I show that underlying these two works is a synthesis of Roman pagan and biblical history that represents a version of Christian salvation history.[9] That is, Prudentius constructs salvation history from a fusion of Roman pagan history, Roman Christian history, which includes New Testament and martyr stories, and Old Testament history. He has incorporated into salvation history the whole of Roman history, from Romulus to Theodosius, as part and parcel of three fundamental events that define the orthodox version of Christian salvation history: Creation, the Incarnation, and the Last Judgment. The second part of my argument demonstrates that Prudentius' narrative of salvation history is intrinsic to the identity of the human soul—the soul of the reader mirrored in the battle within the soul (*Psychomachia*) and in the behavior of martyred souls (*Peristephanon*). The soul functions as a repository for both individual and political identity. In these poems, a Roman Christian's soul exists as a savable and immortal entity in virtue of salvation history's succession of events. Thus, Roman Christian identity is a function of Prudentius' version of salvation history. In essence, the soul is a product of a divinely directed history in which Rome plays a decisive role. This two-pronged argument has far-reaching literary implications. By setting his poetic stories within a unified backdrop of Roman and biblical historical narratives, Prudentius reinvigorates Latin epic and lyric in a period when Christian writers were redefining the forms, content, and purposes of Roman literature.

To construct salvation history, the poet employs typologies—namely, correspondences between actions and/or events from different time periods, which are systematized into a coherent representation of history insofar as the pairs are instrumental to a construction of historical narrative.[10] For Prudentius, history assumes the form of historical narrative, often built through the deployment of typologies, which determine the ordering and interpretation of events beginning with the Fall, extending through Roman civilization and the Incarnation, and ending in the Last Judgment.[11] Consequently, the individual narratives Prudentius finds in human history—i.e., persons and events in Roman and biblical history—are configured according to a typological framework that results in a version of Christian salvation history. So as we will see, Romulus becomes paired with Christ, or Judith with Mary and the immaculate birth of Christ. This modified version of traditional salvation history is an exercise in typology whereby mythohistorical events and persons of biblical and Roman historical traditions are connected and interpreted according to Christian doctrine.[12] The source of this synthesis, though, is biblical typology —i.e., figural interpretation—and functions as the principal strategy by which Prudentius achieves the unification of several national narratives (Roman pagan, Hebrew, Roman Christian) into salvation history. Each typology becomes meaningful through the assumption of a salvation history dominated by the significance of Christ's life.[13] Typology provides the literary structure for this unified historical narrative.

Thus, Prudentius defines a Christian soul/person[14] according to an effective and ubiquitous deployment of typologies. Typologies function to unify the pagan, Christian, and Hebrew historical traditions. Rome's monumental contribution to earthly history becomes embedded in the idea of Christian history. Prudentius' construction of historical narrative recontextualizes Roman history within a biblical historical framework and, consequently, asserts a Christian national identity. Christian identity takes shape as a story of the soul whose story is recounted in salvation history. "Historical" events such as Abraham's entertainment of the triple-formed angel, the Incarnation, the kingships of Romulus and Numa, and martyrdoms accumulate into a story of how the soul of a Roman Christian reader can obtain salvation. Even Roman pagan versions of civil strife, military success, and political dominance become part of salvation history and thus integral to the representation of the soul's salvation.[15] The ideal Roman Christian's soul not only acquires the qualities of Abraham and Christ through typological affinities with them and their stories but also reaffirms the power and the glory of the Roman empire because of the integration of Roman and divine histories. The Roman pagan past becomes palatable as part of salvation history, and, conversely, the Christian present and future resonate with Rome's political and military success.

Prudentius' typological unification of Roman pagan, Hebrew, and Christian historical traditions pervades both the *Psychomachia* and *Peristephanon* and emerges through a multifaceted narrative strategy that uniquely interweaves stories from different traditions into a complex whole. The inclusion of Roman pagan and Roman Christian history in salvation history sets the *Psychomachia* and the *Peristephanon* apart from other fourth-century works of poetry, including the poet's own. In the *Psychomachia*, Prudentius works with Old and New Testaments—though Roman pagan history is also invoked—to form a continuous narrative from *Genesis* to *Revelation,* from the stories associated with Abraham to the building of the new Christian temple.[16] The *Psychomachia*'s narrative of the battle between the virtues and the vices manipulates fragments of historical narratives from *Genesis, Exodus,* and *Revelation,* though he exploits the paradigmatic narrative of Roman civil war.

By distinction, Roman history in the *Peristephanon* is integral to the Christian narrative from Creation to resurrection, with two thrusts: one encompassing the pagan mythicohistorical past, from Romulus and Numa to the acquisition of a world empire, and the second drawing on the rich set of martyr stories that are central to Prudentius' vision of Rome's transition from paganism to Christianity. Martyr stories are combined not only with allusions to biblical narratives but also with allusions to narratives of Roman kings. From this bifurcated vision of Roman tradition, the *Peristephanon* emplots diachronically "real" events, which, in turn, fit neatly into the *Psychomachia*'s Old/New Testament narrative scope.[17] Romulus, the ancient Roman king, and Romanus, the Christian martyr, coexist on the time line of Creation—Incarnation—Last Judgment. What results is an historical master narrative—a reading of history as salvation history. Both poems taken together assume a version of salvation history that includes Rome as the earthly equivalent of Augustine's post-Alaric, divine city, the city of God. The two poems recontextualize Rome as a divine empire by integrating biblical history in the form of typologies with Roman politics and militarism.

Fabula, History, and Identity

My theoretical approach—developed in chapter 1, here, and further in the epilogue—is that Roman Christian identity itself becomes tied to the idea of narrative in general (*historia, fabula*) and to the recontextualization of Roman history in particular. For Prudentius in the late fourth-century, a Christian is a Roman who lives in and partakes of the grand biblical and salvic narrative, and because this narrative of salvation history is "internalized" as a story of the soul, Roman Christian identity is defined according to that narrative. Three passages from the *Apotheosis, Peristephanon,* and preface to the *Hamartigenia* directly reveal a relationship in Prudentius' literary strategy between narrative, typology, and Christian identity:

> omne quod est gestum notus auferat inritus, aurae   (*Apoth.* 1017–18)
> dispergant tenues. sit *fabula* quod sumus omnes!
> everything we do the frivolous South wind carries away,
> the feeble breezes disperse, what we all are is a story.

> Aedituus consultus ait: "Quod prospicis, hospes,   (*Pe.* 9. 17–20)
> non est inanis aut anilis *fabula.*
> *Historiam* pictura refert, quae tradita libris
> veram vetusti temporis monstrat fidem.
> The experienced caretaker said: "What you see, stranger,
> is not an empty and frivolous story. The picture expresses
> history, which has been recorded in the most ancient books
> and demonstrates the honest assurance of the ancient time.

> Ergo ex futuris prisca coepit *fabula*   (*Praef. Ham.* 25–26)
> factoque primo res notata est ultima,
> So the story of former times began from the stories
> that were to be and the last deed was indicated by the first,

Typically in fourth-century literature and elsewhere in Prudentius, *fabula* is a byword for a "false tale" and is associated with the lies that literature tells. The usages of the word in these three passages, especially the third passage, however, associate *fabula* with Prudentius' definition of history as a narrative of events constructed from typologies. The first passage connotes *fabula*'s sense of superficiality and falsity because it expresses the ephemeral quality of a human life as a story.[18] The passage nevertheless assumes that a story represents a human life in all its complexity and eventfulness, and the second passage shows that the story of certain individual lives—in this case, the life and murder of Saint Cassian—has historical import and meaning. The idea of "story"—namely, a causally related narration of events—is intrinsic to Prudentius' understanding of "history."[19] The *fabula* of a human life, especially of a martyr's life, can represent history and stand for true storytelling—namely, historical narrative.[20] The passage seems to juxtapose *fabula* and *historia* as opposites when it comes to truth, but in a cleverly Platonist way the passage argues for the right kind of *fabula,* one such as the story of Cassian, which in this passage begins from a painting (*pictura*) and in turn is written down as an important piece of history. The word *pictura,* though explicitly referring to a painting, connotes typological discourse and, as a result, can be understood to facilitate the passage's distinction between true and false *fabulae.* Indeed, the third passage, *Praef. Ham.* 25–26, affirms what is implied in the second passage, that the proper kind of *fabula* is the vehicle for the expression of history.[21] The idea is clear in the passage's assertion that true stories stand in a typological relationship with each other producing a historical narrative. One true story from the future can indicate another true story from the past—and vice versa.

A close analysis of these three passages shows how Prudentius has reworked the sense of *fabula* as the communication of true and significant events. Literature and history do have a close relationship. Rather than *fabula* as the "reality-lite" expression of ephemera that devalues literature as an untrustworthy earthly pursuit, I suggest that the human practice of literature can represent the historical reality of a life lived on earth. Because history comes directly from God and furnishes knowledge for eternal life, the categories of "history" and "a human life" remain in constant dialogue. Prudentius, unlike any fourth- and fifth-century Christian poets, comes as close as possible to establishing programmatically that literary storytelling (*fabula*) is the primary unit for the expression of salvation history. These units (i.e., stories, which culturally resonate with Roman Christians and are typologically associated throughout the expanse of time) ultimately feed into the construction of Roman Christian identity.[22]

Because *Apoth.* 1017–18 equates a human life with a story, it suggests the importance of human memory and human history.[23] *Pe.* 9. 17–20 suggests that a story contains other, "future" stories. *Praef. Ham.* 26 asserts that certain events that happened in the recent past, present, or the future are predicated on particular events in the more distant past. Most importantly, and counter-intuitively from a historiographical point of view, at *Praef. Ham.* 25, Pruden-tius states the typological relationship in reverse: a set of stories from the past such as those having to do with Abraham, Lot, and Sara, *originates* (*coepit*, literally "begins") in stories that follow them (*ex futuris*) such as the Incarna-tion or stories from the future—e.g., the Last Judgment. The future, con-structed as a set of ideologically fixed points in time (e.g., the Incarnation and Last Judgment), causes the stories of the past to exist as history. That is, historiographically speaking, this certain future determines what events in the past are to be included in the construction of history.[24] Prudentius offers this literary argument within the metaphorical space of a closed text where he employs typology to prove the historical legitimacy of specific future events, not merely that they happened or will happen but that carefully ordered events constitute metaphysical reality and salvational possibility. A person does not comprehend the structure and purpose of the universe nor his own possibility of immortality without understanding the meaning of ordered events (i.e., narrative). Prudentius' argument is circular: future events are contained in past events, which, therefore, legitimize future events. Because *fabula* and history are compatible, Prudentius implies that "history" is enacted through texts (like the *Psychomachia* and the *Peristephanon*) that represent a particular version and order of events rather than through the occurrence of events themselves.[25]

Taken together, these three texts suggest that the true stories of individual human beings are typological in nature. This constitutes the core of Pruden-tian history. A human life is a story that is typologically connected to the past.[26] *Apoth.* 309–11 shows that the concept of typology is at the core of Prudentius' thinking:

> Christus forma patris, nos Christi forma et imago.
> Condimur in faciem domini bonitate paterna
> venturo in nostram faciem post saecula Christo.
> Christ is the figure of the Father, and we the figure and image of Christ;
> we are made in the likeness of the Lord by the goodness of the Father,
> as Christ was to come into our likeness after ages of time.

Although these lines recount the hackneyed cliché of creation that humans were made in the form of God, the chiastic word order and typological vocabulary of *Apoth.* 309 connect human beings to the sweep of history from creation at the side of the Father through the Incarnation of Christ. The pronoun *nos* is at the center of the line framed by the Father and Christ who are further framed by the word *forma,* which, in turn is framed by Christ as the first word of the line and *imago,* another typological term, at the end of the line. Human beings complete the typological series that begins with the terms Father and Christ. The connection is ontological (Father—Christ—human) and, in a parallel manner, historical (Creation—Incarnation—Last Judgment). The self can be defined and interpreted according to its connections to past individuals and human events. This proposition is grounded on the idea that a significant action in the present or future is "predicted" by an act/event in the past.

However, because salvation history is conceived of by Prudentius and his readers as synchronic, encompassing a God's eye view of the past, present and future, the present or future act/event, with respect to the narrative whole, actually *determines* that past act or event.[27] How Prudentius interprets, or encourages the reader to interpret, a present or future event, determines which past events survive in a synchronically conceived salvation history. In his typological handling of Roman and biblical historical traditions, Prudentius compares and contrasts two acts/events—the human figures who perform them and the surrounding historical contexts—to create the ordered series of events of salvation history. This understanding of typology defines Prudentius' poetic construction of history. The story of history and the story of each person stand in a reciprocal relationship and exist because of each other. The identity of a person consists of his earthly (Roman) story, one that will hopefully connect him to the story of Christ and the Father. Hence, Prudentius has employed a literary trope, typology, as the connective means for identity and access to the divine.

Creating Historical Narrative: The Roles of Reader and Author

Lines 40–59 of the preface to the *Psychomachia* provide an archetypal example of Prudentius' definition and use of typology to emplot events and thus create a universal historical narrative. These lines show that the historical relationship between the Old and New Testaments is fashioned through typology, while simultaneously providing poetry a role in this negotiation: *Haec ad figuram praenotata est linea, / quam nostra recto vita resculpat pede* (This picture has been drawn beforehand to be a model for our life to trace out again with true measure; *Psych. Praef.* 51–52). The picture the poet means consists of Old Testament stories, here a series having to do with Abraham.[28] It is the recognition of the "mystic symbol" (*figura mystica; Psych. Praef.* 58), the number 318 (*Psych Praef.* 57), which stands for Christ crucified, that typologically binds the Old Testament to the New Testament. Melchisedec, a priest in the Old Testament who offers Abraham bread and wine, is the type who is fulfilled by Jesus in the New Testament, who is the antitype and the true priest. Prudentius gives Melchisedec credit for helping Sara conceive a baby in her old age and perhaps for prefiguring the Christian Eucharist. Christ makes the heart of an individual fertile and, of course, literally becomes the Eucharist. In this example, when biblical typology is plugged in, it evokes salvation history—that is, a span of human history whose central event is the Incarnation. An historical narrative, a connected set of historical events, is born. In addition, typology carries along with it the notion of fulfillment, which the reader realizes through correct understanding, correct interpretation, or correct application.[29] To realize that Jesus is the true priest that Melchisedec purported to be, the reader must understand and interpret both figures correctly and thus make the right application.[30] The author, Prudentius, must guide the reader, and the reader must be receptive to these promptings. In the *Psychomachia,* the Old Testament becomes the treasury of source material for the narrative of Christian salvation history. Hence, the construction of the Old Testament past according to New Testament events and doctrine becomes a vital part of Prudentius' work in the *Psychomachia.*

In the *Peristephanon,* Prudentius appropriates and, in effect, rewrites Roman history as a part of salvation history. Martyr stories serve this function and are the new entries into the historical narrative of Rome.[31] Martyrs as typological extensions of Christ function as ideal types for human beings, which include the poet and the reader. By calling special attention to martyr events, and juxtaposing them with pagan Roman reality, Prudentius succeeds in placing martyrs' stories in the Roman historical narrative. The implied typology of Christ/martyr/reader and the doctrinal material that underlies his telling of these stories (the doctrine of the soul) summon up the broader scope of salvation history; therefore, martyr stories as part of the content of Roman history serve to include it under the umbrella of an all-encompassing salvation history. The surface narrative of martyr stories (the near past) becomes part of the fabric of salvation history through the participation of the reader in the present. Prudentius influences the reader to see the martyrs not only as moral exemplars but also as crucial figures in a historical transition from a pagan Roman empire to a Christian Roman empire. To imitate martyrs is also to retell the history of Rome.

At *Pe.* 11.17–22, Prudentius describes his history project in terms of archival research accomplished through the study of inscriptions.[32]

Haec dum lustro oculis et sicubi forte latentes
rerum apices veterum per monumenta sequor,
invenio Hippolytum, qui quondam scisma Novati
presbyter attigerat nostra sequenda negans,
usque ad martyrii provectum insigne tulisse
lucida sanguinei praemia supplicii.

In surveying these memorials and hunting over them
for any letters telling of deeds of old, that might escape
the eye. I found that Hippolytus, who had at one time as
a presbyter attached himself to the schism of Novatus,
saying that our way was not to be followed, had been
advanced to the crown of martyrdom and won the
shining reward for suffering bloodshed.

The use of the two forms of *sequor* is instructive here. At lines 17–18, Prudentius says, "while I examine these things with my eyes and wherever throughout the tombs I follow (with my eyes) perhaps the hidden letters of ancient events. . . ." An implied meaning of *sequor* here is "to pursue," or "to go after a thing." The action of the verb bespeaks a process of looking at objects (that is, inscriptions at gravesites) in order to search for something (that is, historical information on martyrs). A further implied meaning of the verb at line 20 is "side with" or "adhere to (a doctrine)." Within the passage, Prudentius signals that for the reader to understand history and for the author to write history—and by extension poetry—both need to absorb and follow the right ideas. The story of Hippolytus is the story of person who started out "following" heretical ideas but later came around to Nicean orthodoxy. The verb *sequor* connects the poet as historical researcher with the martyr as the subject of historical research, and reader as a possible antitype for the martyr. The poet and reader do not have a hierarchical relationship because through their equally important activities of composition and reading both seek to become the ideal Roman Christian.

Other indications in the passage round out this picture. The language of historiography·is clear at line 18. Prudentius is examining "hidden letters," *apices,* on gravestones, which are evidence of past events (*rerum . . . veterum*). This archival research is, in effect, an exercise in Christian historiography, the purpose of which is, on the one hand, to recount the story of someone who adheres to proper Christian doctrine, despite a dubious beginning—perhaps a person like the reader—and, on the other hand, to construct a new history of Rome through the writing of martyr events, a historiographical choice that is partly determined by the Christian doctrine of the soul.[33] The doctrine is actualized in martyr events, which, in turn, become part of the narrative of salvation history. Moreover, the poet presents himself as a reader in this passage who is deciphering *latentes / rerum apices veterum.* These "hidden letters" paradoxically reveal hidden meanings to which a reader must be carefully attuned, whether the reader is a historical researcher like the poet or an insufficiently committed Christian like the implied reader. In this passage, the use of the adjective *latentes* in concert with *apices* suggests that Prudentius understands the act of reading not simply as a direct, one to one relationship between the reader and the words read but as a process of uncovering what words mean in a text. As other passages analyzed in this chapter will confirm, for Prudentius, figurative (allegorical) reading exists alongside figural reading. Words can mean "more" or "other" than what they literally stand for (more on this in chapter 3), but this process is not completely left up to the reader to navigate alone. The poet retains a role in this process as well. *Pe.* 11.17–22 establishes the poet as a historian who posits the martyr as a moral exemplar and includes him as a part of salvation history. Because the poet implicates the reader in this exemplar notion—that is, the poet encourages the reader to compare himself to the martyr—the reader becomes an actor in salvation history if he should adopt Christianity completely, thus triumphing at the Last Judgment. The same is true for the poet who constructs salvation history or whose texts are the means of expressing salvation history, for he occupies simultaneously the role of reader[34] immersed in the sources of salvation history and the prime mover behind a textual creation of salvation history.

Historical Memory in the Service of Christian Ideology

Another set of texts from the *Psychomachia* and *Peristephanon* reinforces the relationship between doctrine, typology, and the formation of historical narrative. Like the passages from the preceding section, they show how a typological correspondence, motivated by doctrinal assumptions, actually forms a historical narrative. Moreover, in each set of passages, the nuanced use of typology adds further to Prudentius' construction of history. In the *Peristephanon* passages (*Pe.* 10.401–25 and *Pe.* 10. 611–35), the apparent clash between pagan and Christian ideologies and histories does not eliminate the role of Roman pagan tradition in salvation history but, rather, carefully leaves room for the inclusion of the Roman past as a reference point for the construction of the martyr past. These two passages represent the first step in the process of converting the reader because they invite the reader to adopt this version of salvation history. The second step occurs in passages from the *Psychomachia* (*Psych.* 371–91 and 823–87), which show that typological correspondences only become productive through the faculty of human memory. Historical memory allows one to make the appropriate connections between events, individuals, and concepts that engender the recognition of a historical narrative and ultimately, Christian doctrine. To stimulate this historically oriented part of human memory, documents (certain Old Testament texts, Christian hymns, and poems) and monuments (the Christian temple) are essential. Prudentius' poetic program targets the memory of the reader, infusing it with the right content, furnishing it with an effective strategy (typology), and ultimately fashioning it according to a thoroughly Christian ideology. This program is aggressive, a species of *littérature engagée* and, though dependent on a receptive reader, nevertheless leaps forth from the purposefully composed words on the page. These words produce a version of scripturalism, which argues for the supreme historical, moral, and political authority of the Bible— and, by extension, Prudentius' sacred poetry. A particular version of salvation history becomes implanted in the reader's historical memory.

Taken together, *Pe.* 10.401–25 and *Pe.* 10. 611–35 reinforce the idea that Christian doctrine's application to source material contributes to the fashioning of Prudentius' universal historical narrative. The first passage is a prelude to the use of typology in the second passage. *Pe.* 10.401–25 is a fine instance of the lock-step relationship between the memory of historical events and Christian doctrine. The way in which these two categories function together has a direct effect on the health of the state (*pro saluta publica,* 402).

Hoc sanctum ab aevo est, hoc ab atavis traditum: (*Pe.* 10.416–20)
placanda nobis pro triumfis principis

delubra, faustus ut secundet gloriam
procinctus utque subiugatis hostibus
ductor quietum frenet orbem legibus.
This has been ordained from the beginning of time,
this has been handed down from our ancestors: that
we must make propitiation at the shrines to the emperor
for triumphs, so that his battle-array may be favorable, and
that when his enemies are subdued he as leader may govern
with his laws a peaceful world.

Asclepiades the prefect is arguing against the martyr Romanus, that Roman tradition—that is, the stories of how belief in the gods affects historical events —is founded upon the story of Jupiter's compelling the Romans to stay in the face of the Sabine threat (*Iovi Statori debet et dis ceteris,* 415). Line 416 makes it clear that the stories themselves form a tradition of ideas handed down from Roman ancestors, and these ideas, if honored through proper worship of the gods, actually influence historical events (*pro triumphis principis* and *sub-iugatis hostibus*) and are necessary conditions for good government (*quietum frenet orbem legibus*). Bad religious doctrine is an enemy of the state. Pruden-tius also points to the role of memory here in the form of generational and cultural memories that contain the proper ideological connections between events. These stories are passed on from generation to generation. Although they are the words of a pagan, the tales represent the basic set of assumptions that Prudentius and his opponents both accepted when they debated the supe-riority of Christianity versus paganism. The argument Asclepiades puts to Romanus at lines 406–10, in which he asserts that the Christian god and historical figures had no part in the founding of Rome, provides the rhetorical basis for Romanus' response regarding the interaction between history and Christian doctrine.

To this end, the second passage of the pair, *Pe.* 10. 611–35, connects Christian doctrine to historical writing through the typological symbol of the cross. This maneuver will produce a syncretism between Roman pagan and Roman Chris-tian history in the *Peristephanon,* thereby bringing the resultant narrative history under the aegis of Old and New Testament history. Prudentius is, in effect, arguing for a new story that will define Rome's cultural inheritance and produce a new kind of historical memory in Rome's people as they read works such as the *Peristephanon.*

Romanus' answer to Asclepiades' reading of history and government flows from the representation of pagan doctrine in the previous passage (*Pe.* 10.401–25). The differences are dramatic, but the result is not a gutting of the Roman historical tradition. In fact, what separates Prudentius from Paulinus of Nola, for instance, is that his use of typology—here the typology of the cross—cuts across and unites the whole of history. Paulinus' *Natalicia*, a series of poems dedicated to Saint Felix of Nola whose memory and importance Paulinus almost single-handedly managed to popularize, tends to emphasize typology as moral exemplar; Saint Felix's moral and spiritual qualities are akin to Old Testament heroes.[35] Paulinus' poetry shows little interest in the interface between imperial Rome and Christian Rome. By contrast, Prudentius attempts a unification of all three traditions, the Jewish, Christian, and pagan. In *Pe.* 10.611–35, the poet confronts the problem head on. Romanus expresses a scope of history more universal than Asclepiades does when he says at line 620 that Jupiter and Mars are gone and the things that presently exist will be gone as well. The cross is the only constant in this sweep of history (*nascente mundo,* 622) and is represented in signs and in writing, *expressa signis, expedita est litteris* (623). We can take these signs to be the other half of the cross typology; for instance, the number 318, the numerical equivalent of the Greek letters TIH, corresponds to Christ and the cross.[36] Thus, events are partly defined as such through Christian doctrine as represented in the cross and the writing of those events is guided by Christian doctrine. As *Pe.* 11.17–22 suggests, the close tie between typology and writing has become a fundamental means of proliferating and maintaining Christian ideology.[37] One need only witness the scene at *Apoth.* 598, where Prudentius portrays himself kissing, adoring, and even crying over the letters (*apices*) of the text of Isaiah. The letters on the page do not merely explain reality; they are reality. Such textualism, presumed in Prudentius' poetry, remains unfettered by geographical boundaries because its target is human memory. In fact textualism may furnish a significant part of the explanation of Christianity's establishment as a universal religion.[38]

Prudentius asserts the relationship between events, ideology, and writing at lines *Pe.* 10.626–30:

Reges, profetae, iudicesque et principes
virtute bellis cultibus sacris stilo
non destiterunt pingere formam crucis.
Crux praenotata, crux adumbrata est prius,

crucem vetusta conbiberunt saecula.
Kings, prophets, judges, and rulers by
their excellence, wars, rites, offerings, and the pen
did not cease to depict the form of the cross.
The cross was predicted, the cross was prefigured,
ancient ages absorbed the cross.

Line 626 presents a list of the authority figures that reflect in history the doctrine symbolized by the cross. The list shows interest in creating a historical narrative through the doctrinal power of the cross. Prudentius may have eliminated pagan gods, but the list leaves plenty of room for figures such as Romulus, Numa and Quirinus (i.e., *reges* and *profetae*) whom he will include in *Pe.* 2. Line 626's categories of kings, prophets, and the like are not only the makers of history but are also—more importantly, for the purposes of Prudentius—the historical means by which doctrine represented in the figure of the cross becomes ideology.

For Prudentius, history as the representation of reality is a function of doctrine. There is no correct interpretation of past events and ages unless the present and the future are understood from the point of view of Christian doctrine. Since the future posits the Second Coming, Last Judgment, and the immortality of the soul, both the present and the past demand a reading according to the future. The future, paradoxically, is absolutely set in a fundamental way. In other words, the future has already been interpreted and so remains fixed, but the "memory" of this future depends on the memory of the past, the Old Testament. In the *Peristephanon,* it is the present in the form of heresies, and the past in the form of Roman history, which require a Christian interpretation. Doctrinal assumptions fuel this interpretation, which in turn determines Christian political ideology. In both the *Psychomachia* and the *Peristephanon,* Christian doctrine simultaneously shapes and expresses itself through history. Doctrine functions ideologically because it influences events for the benefit of Rome and her citizens. These events become the purple passages of Roman history, the prism through which the notion of the state and its imperial and divine purpose pass into the minds and memories of Roman Christian citizens.

For Prudentius in particular, a narrative emphasis has brought with it epic and historical perspectives that, in turn, furnish an ideological mission. The asyndeton of nouns at *Pe.* 10.626–30 represents a dense compression of the concepts of morality, history, religious doctrine, and writing. Bravery, wars, acts of worship, offerings, and the pen are the constituents of historical production that the *Peristephanon* employs to construct salvation history, and a martyr's place in that history. Martyrs have become the new epic heroes whose narratives penetrate all genres of poetry: epic, lyric, epigram, and so forth. As I have suggested in chapter 1, this Christian hero becomes an individual and collective role model for the implied reader. Even though, technically, the *Peristephanon* is not epic, it is infused with the definitive aspect of epic poetry, heroes, the literary purpose of which is the reader's individual and national self-identity. Identity is conferred one reader at a time. A true Christian conversion through the reading of the *Psychomachia* and/or the *Peristephanon* forms a true Roman citizen. This citizen will understand Rome as part and parcel of salvation history and, in essence, as God's city on earth. The epic battle of the virtues and vices within the soul and the heroic example of Christian martyrs function as the blueprint of a Christian individual and her political identity. The Christian self carries the notion of moral choice with a view to immortality. Politically speaking, the legacy of Rome's military and political power for a Roman Christian becomes a right to inherit and administer empire.

Pe. 10. 401–25 and 611–35 assume that within Roman culture citizens possess a memory of events and interpretations of those events that determine the actual health and power of Rome. *Psych.* 371–91 and 823–87 advance this idea through the exhortation to know and remember important Old Testament texts and through the construction of a new monument built upon such knowledge and memory. At *Psych.* 371–91 typology once again is the agent through which certain historical narratives of the Old Testament work, but this time in reverse, as they trigger correct Christian doctrine. In her long speech to the army of virtues who falter at the sight of *Luxuria*, *Sobrietas* reminds them of a series of Old Testament stories that should trigger Christian doctrinal ideas. She recalls the story of the Jews thirsting in the desert and finding water from a miraculous rock and acquiring food (*Exodus* 16:14–15 and 17:3–6), a story that has its analogue in the Eucharist, which provides such a miracle at every liturgical service. From a historiographic perspective, Prudentius' typology has a double trajectory. For, on the one hand, the Eucharist helps to determine Prudentius' choice of Old Testament stories to foreground in his work, but, on the other hand, the Old Testament stories in themselves are significant because of the future events they indicate. Prudentius invokes the theme of memory as an exhortation to the reader who must remember, through the typological exemplars, the virtues, whom *Sobrietas* exhorts. These exemplars are immersed in a historical context resulting in a historical narrative that connects great expanses of ages, cultures, and modes of thinking.

Two more allusions to King David and Jonathan (*I Samuel* 14.24 and 15) illustrate the foolhardiness of tolerating vice and the necessity of repenting one's sins to gain forgiveness. The remembering of such history initiates the recognition of these doctrines. This is the reason behind the notable frequency of *Sobrietas'* exhortations to the virtues to remember Old Testament history: *Excidit . . . excidit* (*Psych.* 371), *State, precor, vestri memores, memores . . .* (*Psych.* 381), *meminisse decet* (*Psych.* 383), and *excitet egregias mentes* (*Psych.* 386). Certain historical events, if read and remembered, exhibit and cause the recognition of the Christian type,[39] because these events confirm Christian doctrine. Thus, the only passages of the Old Testament that are useful to Prudentius are the ones that can be interpreted according to Christian doctrine, and this approach encourages the creation of a historical memory in each Roman reader—an achievement fundamental to Christian historiography.

After the vices have been vanquished in the *Psychomachia*, Prudentius describes the building of a monument (i.e., a temple; *Psych.* 823–87) to celebrate the events and the doctrine that form an inseparable pair. The poet calls upon the Old Testament once again through allusions to Solomon and the erection of the Jewish temple (*Chronicles* 28: 2–3 and *I Kings* 5: 2–5) to create a typology between both temple stories.[40] Peace is the precondition for temple building (*Psych.* 809), and, just as the Jews were at peace when Solomon undertook the project, so the virtues are in a state of peace as they build the new temple, a structure that binds together the Old and New Testaments. The reader is spared no detail in the narrative of erecting the temple. Prudentius mentions the names of the twelve apostles inscribed over each doorway (*Psych.* 838–39), thereby placing the New Testament figures in the topmost parts of the temple. One New Testament and two Old Testament allusions establish the central place of *Sapientia* (Wisdom) in this new temple according to typological correspondences. *Psych.* 868 describes seven pillars of an inner chamber, clearly recalling *Proverbs* 9:1, where Wisdom's dwelling has seven pillars. *Matthew* 13: 45–46 is alluded to at *Psych.* 872–74, which assert the incalculable spiritual value of the white capstone of the pillars, purchased by all the material possessions of *Fides*. And finally at *Psych.* 875ff., Wisdom's scepter is discussed in terms originating from *Numbers* 17: 6–8. *Sapientia's* house and her accoutrements originate from the Old Testament, but they are appropriated by the new Christian history, which comes from the New Testament and beyond. This building acts as a historical document in itself, a *monumentum,* a concrete representation of the salvic historical narrative, which has been reformulated according to a clear hierarchy between Old Testament and New Testament stories and images.[41] The hierarchy expressed in Prudentius' version of the temple typology implies a supersessionist view in which Hebrew scripture is at the service of the new Christian dispensation and, further, Christians have superceded Jews as God's chosen people. In Prudentius, Christian historiography is supersessionist on two fronts: the Christian New Testament over the Hebrew Old Testament and the Roman Christian over the Roman pagan. We have arrived at another fundamental purpose of the Christian construction of history, a vigorous and muscular supersession of Judaism.[42]

In the *Psychomachia,* the narrative itself is expressed in several ways, from singing hymns that recall Old Testament events, as when the virtues sing the story of the parting of the Red Sea (*Psych.* 650–66), to building concrete structures that are adorned with Old Testament inscriptions and architectural imagery, to, finally, the *Psychomachia* itself, which encapsulates all three forms of historical memory— hymns, monuments, and epic poetry. It is clear that typology's natural effect of furnishing and fashioning events has allowed Prudentius to create a historical narrative recognizable from the individual monuments in the poem and from the poem itself as a monument. From the poem's point of view, such monuments would retain a vital political function and be the teachers of memory, present to each generation as institutionalized reminders of the central stories of salvation history, and, in this particular case, the reader's memory is formed according to a supersessionist ideology that is both hermeneutical and sociopolitical.

Conventional wisdom has held that early Christian historiography is deficient in political analysis because there is no discernible critique of the Christian government after Constantine. Thus, scholars such as Arnaldo Momigliano have asserted that Christian historical writers do not engage in political reflection as a Tacitus or a Thucydides does.[43] In other words, for Tacitus and Thucydides, the religious and the political are separate in their analyses of historical events.[44] Simply put, these authors did not underpin their historical writing with a panegyric and/or apologetic purpose directly related to a perceived, dominant religion. Eusebius, however, does follow this approach[45] and certainly did not engage in a political critique of Constantine, but the Christian use of history as seen in Prudentius (and in Eusebius as well) is political and ideological. The poet universalizes the moral component in historical writing, the un-universalized version of which the pagan authors certainly exploited. But Prudentius goes further. He infuses a divine morality into not only the product of Christian historiography (i.e., salvation history) but also the means of production, Christian historiography—that is, the writing of salvation history, which becomes infused with a divine and universal morality that pagan historiography, for the most part, understates in its representation of political and military events. Instead of an evaluative analysis, one encounters a sophisticated political exhortation in passages such as *Pe.* 10.626–30 in the form of a plea to the reader to convert to proper Christianity and thus become a proper Roman. To accomplish this, the reader must commit to the poet's offering of the syncretism of biblical and Roman historical narratives. This fashioning of historical memory is ideological in that Prudentius affirms both in his reading of history and in the reader a Christian Roman state. This is the essence of fourth-century Christian historiography boiled down from Prudentius' poetry.

Typological Terminology, Texts, and Memory

I have been arguing that Prudentius uses typology to form a narrative of salvation history, which includes Roman history. This historical narrative is meant to shape the memory of his reader. The ideological purpose is to assist in affirming the identity of a Christian, Roman individual, and of Christianity itself, the "oldest" and "truest" religion. For example, regarding the identity of Christianity, Prudentius constructs a supersessionist history that subordinates Jewish history by prioritizing the "New" Testament over the "Old" Testament. The same goes for Roman pagan *res gestae,* which are shoehorned into the scheme of Creation, Incarnation, and Last Judgment. How Prudentius exploits typology to help form the implied reader's memory becomes apparent in his innovative use of typological terminology, which was established by his patristic predecessors. In this section I want to show that Prudentius exhibits an impressive control over typological discourse, whose application to the construction of historical narrative in poetry is unique in the later Latin poetic tradition. Unlike his poetic descendents and contemporaries—for instance, Paulinus of Nola—Prudentius combines clear markers of history (i.e., historical names and events) with technical, typological terminology. This combination of historical content with the methodological language of constructing historical narrative redraws the relationship between poetry and history. Christian salvation history traditionally found its full expression in prose writing, scripture, and patristic commentary. With the work of Prudentius, such textualism is transferred to poetry. Poetry with its use of typology becomes the vehicle for the transmission of salvation history and thus the Christian collective and individual identity. Such ambition for poetry recalls the historical and political goals of Latin poetry seen primarily in Roman epic tradition.

The typological and historical terms of *Pe.* 10. 626–30 that I will focus on are *conbibere, forma crucis, praenotare, adumbrare,* and *saeculum.*[46] Quoting the Latin passage again will help contextualize these terms.

Reges, profetae, iudicesque et principes
virtute, bellis, cultibus, sacris, stilo
non destiterunt pingere *formam crucis.*
Crux *praenotata,* crux *adumbrata* est prius,
crucem vetusta *conbiberunt saecula.*

The combination of typological discourse with historical markers indicates Prudentius' concern to use typology in order to construct historical narrative. A striking expression at line 630 seems to crystallize Prudentius' thinking on this particular topic: *crucem vetusta conbiberunt saecula.* The word *saecula* denotes an idea of chronological expanse, not merely historical events *per se,* but a period of time containing individual events and in which an ethos or a dominant *mentalitè* persists. Prudentius knows well that the interpretation of events in previous periods of Roman history have been dominated by paganism; hence the vivid *conbiberunt* that gives a picture of previous periods as being completely reconstituted through the lens of Christian doctrine as represented by *crucem.* The cross has even absorbed the periods of Rome's past. This is not merely the Christian commonplace that the cross and its doctrine have been present throughout history—although Prudentius implies this as well—but, more originally, Prudentius in poetry packages Rome's past for the ideal Roman Christian's memory according to Christian doctrine, a future-oriented set of ideas, for the choosing and interpreting of past events (i.e., emplotting events to form a narrative). From a literary historical point of view, this is a revision of Vergilian and other Roman epic versions of history and *Romanitas.* Rome shall become the heavenly city on earth with citizens who practice the "true" religion.

Prudentius, more than any other fourth-century author, uses the verb *con-bibere*. The Prudentian corpus contains five uses that split into two groups. The first is a poetic usage, seen in Ovid,[47] which means a literal "drinking up" or "absorbing" of liquid, flames, and rivers. The second use is rare, more figurative, found in Cicero's philosophical works,[48] and means the absorption of customs and habits. Prudentius extends this particular meaning to the absorbing of doctrines (*Pe.* 10.50). At *Cath.* 4.16 we see a similar usage of the verb when the soul "drinks deep of God." Prudentius implies the "drinking of doctrine" again at *Psych.* 359, where *Sobrietas* exhorts the virtues not to become like a vice by "drinking up" bad doctrine.[49]

In other uses of the verb through the fourth century, the idea of "drinking" is applied to inanimate objects.[50] Paulinus of Nola uses a form of *conbibere* once (*Carm.* 24.111). And again we find inanimate objects as the focus of the usage:

> bibit unda navem, navis undam conbibit,   (*Carm.* 24.111–14)
> sorbentur et sorbent aquae.
> inebriati navitae potu salis
> tristi necantur crapula.
> The wave sucked in the ship, the ship drank in the wave,
> the waters were both swallower and swallowed.
> The sailors, drunk with the draught of salt water,
> died from this grim intoxication.[51]

In this first part of a lengthy verse epistle, Paulinus tells of the harrowing sea adventure of Martinianus, a messenger, whose boat sinks but whose life is preserved through his Christian belief. Nonbelievers do not survive, and this serves as an allegory of sorts for judgment day when the good (i.e., Christian) and the bad (i.e., non-Christian) will be sifted out. Regarding the use of *conbibit,* Paulinus places the verb in a context of drinking alcohol. As boat and sailors alike drink up the salt water, their state is described as a "grim intoxication."[52] Although a reader could associate the activity of this verb with the nonbelievers who might perhaps "drink up" bad doctrine, it is a stretch, for the passage appears to use the metaphorical language of inebriation for a primarily descriptive effect only. It is safe to conclude that Prudentius has indeed extended the meaning of *conbibere* in a Christian poetic context, especially at *Pe.* 10.630. Prudentius uses the verb in association with typology and history. The absorption of (Christian) doctrine is a figurative meaning of the

word used to evoke a figural method of history, and appears unique to Prudentius.[53] This meaning implies a reader who herself absorbs doctrine and reads
figurally in order to interpret the sweep and events of history.

Thus, the poet has enlisted nontypological words such as *conbibere* in service to his typological construction of narrative. As for the typological terminology at *Pe.* 10.626–30, *formam, praenotata,* and *adumbrata,* I have been
guided by the question of whether the poet's use of these words represents an
expansion of the conventional usage. To put the question in another way, since
the passage contains biblical and Roman markers of history (*Pe.* 10.626–27),
do the meanings of these typological terms become more sophisticated because they are juxtaposed with markers of history? I give a two-part answer to
this question. First, Prudentius appears to be the only poet of his age to employ
these words frequently in their technical, typological sense like the Church
Fathers. Juvencus (c. 330), Proba (c. 360), Ambrose (c. 339–97), Damasus
(c. 304–84), Sedulius (fifth century), Arator Victorius (d. 425/30), and Avitus
(d. c. 518) do not use these words at all in their poetry; and though Paulinus of
Nola uses such language, the typological sense of the terms is lacking. Thus, for
the first time in Latin poetry, we witness the technical use of typological terms
such as *praenotata, adumbrata,* and *forma,* in conjunction with biblical and
Roman historical names and events as part of the construction of a historical
narrative, epic in its scope and universal in its applicability to the past. All of
this in order to implant in the implied reader's memory an ideologically
specific historical narrative. Again, on a literary level, the effect of this poetic
project lies in its direct engagement with pagan epic, especially the *Aeneid,*
constituting a challenge to both pagan and Christian Latin poetry. Furthermore this combination of biblical typology and pagan poetic tradition produces a new kind of poetry.

If we analyze the use of *praenotata,* we see that Prudentius follows the
Patristic usage present in Tertullian, for instance,[54] that means "predicted" or
"designated beforehand." Events in the past, as seen in the Old Testament,
function as predictors of Christ's life and of sacraments. Both times Prudentius
uses the term, it is in precisely this way. Both occurrences come from the
Peristephanon and the *Psychomachia.* At *Pe.* 10. 629, the cross has been "predicted beforehand" by the Old Testament and at *Psych. Praef.* 50, the Old
Testament stories of Melchisedec, the triad of angels, and Sara's miracle birth
anticipate the birth of Christ. Prudentius has used *praenotata* to show a typological correspondence between the Old and New Testament texts, his deci-

sive step in a typical form of early Christian supersessionism, marked by the selective mining of the Old Testament's stories in service to the New Testament's signature story and doctrine. The poem invites the reader to adopt this supersessionist perspective through its persuasive (and implied) analysis of scriptural texts via typology. Thus, the method of typology applied to texts leads to the creation of a Christian memory of historical narratives in an implied reader.

None of his fellow Christian poets approximate this patristic and innovative use of typological term *praenotare*. Paulinus of Nola at *Carm.* 24.141, the same poem that contains his only usage of *conbibo*, uses the past participle, *praenotatos*, not in the sense of prediction but in the sense of "marked out," where the faces of the faithful will be marked with the sign of the cross (*cum praenotatos ora vexillo cruces*) on judgment day. Paulinus does not have a typological usage in mind. Perhaps we can go as far as to say that the word certainly is charged with doctrinal associations because, like Prudentius, Paulinus uses the participle with *crux*, a sign that means one has followed the right doctrine.[55] The only other usage of this word by Paulinus occurs not in his poetry, but in his letters (*Ep.* 32.12), and it is not typological. The verb in the passage means "to mark in front,"[56] As far as the forms of *praenoto* are concerned, Prudentius appears to have pioneered a poetic usage in which typology is part of a supersessionist historical construction fueled by a Christian doctrinal perspective.

In the very same line as *praenotata,* the participle *adumbrata* (*Pe.* 10.629) again furnishes a clear typological meaning, only, in this case, the word does not evoke so much the idea of prediction but the notion of an "outline," or "sketch," something that could be missed if one is not paying close enough attention. Prudentius uses the participle two more times (*Ham.* 335 and *Psych.* 556) and a subjunctive form of the finite verb at *Symm.* 2.56. *Symm.* 2.56 comes close to the *Peristephanon* usage because it has the sense of "to give a picture" or "depict" and stops short of "prefigure" though this meaning lurks under the surface.

> Cur etiam templo Triviae lucisque sacratis   (*Symm.* 2.53–56)
> cornipedes arcentur equi, cum Musa pudicum
> raptarit iuvenem volucri per litora curru,
> idque etiam paries tibi versicolorus adumbret?
> Why also are horny-hoofed horses excluded from the precinct
> of the goddess of the cross-ways and her consecrated groves,

after the Muse has carried away a chaste youth along the shore
in a flying chariot, and a wall too gives you a picture of the scene
delineated in many colors?

But the connection is perhaps even more subtle since the context of the passage
is a discussion of art. In a Platonist rant, painting and poetry (*Symm.* 2.45–50),
described as *socii* (*Symm.* 2.43), are associated with idolatry. Notwithstanding
the negative sense of the context, the poet has connected art and typology.
Even literary composition shares typological origins with narrative history.
Both are the direct products of the typological method. To represent something in art is to "depict" or "give a picture" of it, just as a future event "gives a
picture" of a past event, or vice versa. However faint the connection may seem,
Symm. 2.43–56 nevertheless employs typological language (note also *faciem,*
Symm. 2.43) in the context of the discussion of art. Prudentius appears to
conceive of poetry's function as primarily historical: poetry becomes the vehicle for history through typology for the purpose of influencing the memory of
the reader. If successful, the new poetry will correct the idolatry of the old
poetry.

Both *Ham.* 335 and *Psych.* 556 have the sense of *adumbrare* as "to feign" or
"counterfeit." Both senses of the participle and the finite verb are used by
Ambrose, Jerome, and Augustine, though the meaning of "obscured" or "coun-
terfeited" is far more frequent.[57] The third-century father Commodian wrote a
series of poems in which there is one occurrence of a form of *adumbrare.*[58] This
is the only passage I am aware of in Latin patristic literature and poetry that, like
the passage of Prudentius' *Peristephanon,* pairs up forms of *adumbrare* and
crux. Commodian employs the combination typologically to connect the cross
and the tree of knowledge. Paulinus uses the participle at *Carm.* 31. 366,[59] but
only in the sense of "shadowy" or "deceptive" when talking about how Christ
has gotten rid of shadowy ideas and images. Prudentius in two passages (*Pe.*
10.626–30 is the best example) has employed *adumbrare* in the context of the
capacity of an event in the past to sketch out or dimly indicate a future state of
affairs. Once again, unlike almost all his poetic contemporaries and descendents, he appropriates typological language to highlight the idea that narrative
history is central to the understanding of Christian doctrine. Typology plays a
main role in forming such a narrative and thus Prudentius is at pains to gather
together the language of typology to announce and complete this project.

The expression *formam crucis,* which Prudentius packs into the same passage along with *praenotata* and *adumbrata*, possesses a clear typological sense. There are not as many occurrences of the expression as one might think,[60] but a doubtful epigram of Ambrose and two examples in *Carm.* 19 of Paulinus offer a representative comparison group to Prudentius.[61] In the epigrammatic passage spuriously attributed to Ambrose, the usage of the phrase is not typological in the historical sense. The form of the cross is symbolic of the temple: *forma crucis templum est, templum victoria Christi, / sacra triumphalis signat imago locum* ("The form of the cross is the temple, the temple is Christ's victory, the triumphant, sacred image indicates the place"). The passage does clearly state a one-to-one correspondence between the cross and the temple, but it is clear that historical content is secondary—if present at all—to the symbolic value. That is, the meaning is figurative. A similar explanation works for the two passages from the corpus of Paulinus.[62] In both Paulinian passages the use of *forma* is literal, referring to the actual appearance and shape of the cross as a symbol of the church.[63] Paulinus is at pains to explain the symbolic value of the combination of six letters in terms of the life and death of Christ and its meaning for him. Thus, the expression *forma crucis* does not carry the typological associations, which connect the histories of the Old Testament, the New Testament, and Roman pagan tradition as in *Pe.* 10.626–30. Unlike Paulinus, Prudentius includes in the sense of the phrase *forma crucis* a pronounced figural meaning. The presence of the verb *signo* in the passages of Paulinus—as well as in the epigram attributed to Ambrose—emphasizes the symbolic and the figurative or doctrinal meaning of the cross. Nevertheless, Prudentius appears to be capturing a figural meaning in which the cross literally refers to historical events. As Dawson, who discusses Auerbach's idea that such an approach is antagonistically supported by an appeal to symbolic meaning, has recently put it, "Christian figural readers establish a relation between [what they believe to be] two historically real entities apart from the category of [symbolic] meaning" yet they adopt the "basic tension . . . between structural figural similarities among persons and events and semiotic figurative relations of meaning."[64] Prudentius' use of the phrase *forma crucis* and the other three uses under analysis here appear to fall on the figural and the figurative sides, respectively, though Prudentius does indeed appeal to doctrine, a nonliteral mode, to formulate his figural (i.e., typological) relationships in the first place.

The language of typology, while replete with symbolic associations for Prudentius, functions as the means to carry out an ambitious historical project seen in the *Peristephanon* and the *Psychomachia*. The language of history—i.e., names for persons and events that I have referred to as historical markers— works together with technical, typological terminology to suggest a unification of Roman pagan and Roman Christian history.[65] In his adaptation of this typological terminology from the church fathers and from his own innovations, Prudentius reaffirms history's authority over the reader, thus fashioning a poetics, which reintroduces poetry's historical and political function. Such a poetic program rivals the historical dialectic between mythic and Augustan Rome in Vergil's *Aeneid*. A political and ideological orientation manifests itself at the point of reception at which the individual reader accepts Prudentius repackaging of universal history. The history of the world comes to rest within the reader, the self, which chooses whether or not to accept the poet's version of history. The affirmative choice simultaneously permits the self to become a participant in salvation history and salvation history to include the self. This process is triggered by the power of words—i.e., a text, like the *Psychomachia* or the *Peristephanon*. Prudentius defines a poetics of history in which poetry prescribes by means of history to persuade the reader of Christian doctrine and ideology. Moreover, this poetry, which reinforces a strict textualism, is itself a new and authoritative version of biblical scripture.

The word *saeculum* is a historical,[66] rather than a typological, term and, as I have written regarding *Pe.* 10, sums up all previous ages as well as the present one. It appears with great frequency in fourth-century authors. It is revealing to examine the use of *saeculum* in the works of Prudentius and Paulinus of Nola. We will see that Prudentius, while engaging in conventional usages, expands and systematizes the use of *saeculum*. In several key passages, Prudentius creates a context in which *saeculum*, "an age," stands for both profane/ historical ages and sacred/eternal ones, all of which are to be united and integrated according to Christian doctrine. In his poetry,[67] Paulinus does not undertake such a project and appears satisfied to posit, on an abstract and general level, a historical age followed by an age of immortality. Unification on any level is not an issue, or, perhaps, is assumed. The word is ubiquitous in the work of both poets, but Prudentius is unique in creating the idea of a typologically gluttonous cross, as he does in *Pe.* 10, which not only appears in all historical ages but also absorbs them through the doctrine it represents.

In Paulinus' poetry, of the thirty-eight passages that contain the term, fourteen conventionally refer to "this age" or "this world" in which we humans live. Often this meaning carries with it the notion of Paulinus' rejection of his materialist age. The contemporary age is viewed as corrupt, difficult, and in need of cleansing (i.e., destruction).[68] There are several other uses as well.[69] I will focus on three passages where Paulinus uses *saeculum* in a typological context that has historical associations. The first passage is *Carm.* 6.305–10:

> non haec prima dedit domini sententiae, qua te
> admonuit claram mittens per nubila vocem,
> saecula multa prius sancti deus ore locutus
> Isaiae vatis, veteris qui maximus aevi:
> mittam, ait, ante tuos oculos, o nate, ministrum,
> qui sentosarum purget concreta viarum.
>
> It was not the first utterance of the Lord when he
> advised you by speaking aloud through the clouds;
> many generations earlier God spoke through the mouth
> of his holy prophet Isaias, the greatest of that ancient era.
> "My son," he said, "I shall send a servant before your face,
> who will cleanse the paved and thorny ways."

Carmen 6 is for all intents and purposes a biblical paraphrase of the life of John the Baptist. In this passage, Paulinus employs typology in a broad sense by invoking a prophecy from the book of *Isaiah* (40:3) that predicts the Baptist's existence and purpose. The term *saecula* here indicates "past ages," but more specifically "past generations," which denote the period of time between Old and New Testament history. Thus, Paulinus provides a correspondence between the old and the new in terms of the Old Testament's prediction of New Testament's events and characters. This is not a specific or focused typology but has the effect of unifying Jewish and Christian historical traditions. A similar method is used in the second passage under consideration, *Carm.* 31.403–406:

> iamque propinquantem supremo tempore finem
> inmutanda novis saecula parturiunt.
> omnes vera monent sacris oracula libris
> credere praedictis seque parare deo.
>
> The ages of the world, which must be transformed anew, is already
> pregnant with the end in its final moment. The oracles of
> truth warn everyone to believe in the books mentioned,
> and to prepare themselves for God.

Paulinus has given a contrite and gnomic assertion of the idea that the apocalypse and second coming can be found in the present through the aid of scripture. The "ages of the world," taken together, "must be transformed" and are "pregnant with" or "bring forth" "the end" of the world. He goes further by asserting that "oracles of truth" in the Roman world itself have warned of final judgment.[70]As with the previous passage, Paulinus furnishes the general principle from which typological methods originate. All past ages contain signs that predict and prefigure present and future events. The striking metaphor in the verb *parturio* exhibits how future events are embedded in present or past events. Moreover, the additions of scripture (*sacris . . . libris*) and Greco-Roman oracles (*vera . . . oracula*) provide the hard evidence for his argument and a plea for a scripturalist (and textualist) approach to the understanding of reality. Prudentius assumes these features present in the Paulinus passage in his approach to history and typology. Paulinus does have an interest in unifying all ages in this passage, defined as the Old and New Testaments, and even the Roman age is implied from the Roman "oracles of truth." Paulinus' version of this vision, however, is concentrated, indirect, and without a systematic application to historical narrative. It is not a central part of his poetic project as with Prudentius.

The final passage of Paulinus that merits mention connects the word *saeculum* to an exemplar typology, which posits positive or negative qualities in a person of a past age, which resurface again in a descendent. *Carm.* 21.220–38 is a rich example of a typological technique in which Paulinus indulges throughout his *Natalicia*.[71] The passage is noteworthy because Paulinus furnishes a framework of historical narrative by comparing Roman pagan and Christian consuls. The subject is the family Valerii, whose famous ancestor, along with Brutus, expelled the Roman kings long ago. A revealing excerpt from this section combines a historical sense with typological terminology:

sed nos fideli contuentes lumine   (*Carm.* 21.228–33)
retroacta vel praesentia humani status
miramur opera conditoris ardui
et praeparatos a vetustis saeculis
successionum mysticarum lineis
pios stupemus inpiorum filios
Yet as we gaze with the eyes of faith on the past
and present of the human condition, we marvel
at the achievements of that lofty founder, and we
are in awe of the holy sons of such unholy ones,
who have been prepared from the ancient epochs
by a line of mystical succession.

At first glance, Paulinus constructs an exemplar typology in which the legendary Valerius—here referred to as a "lofty founder' (*conditoris ardui*), is the type for the antitype Christian consul of the same name. Like a typical Roman, Paulinus respects the talents of the ancestor, but only to the extent they are applicable to problems and challenges of the human world. After all, the ancestor was a pagan and will burn in hell (*Carm.* 21.227). The historical language comes at line 229, *retroacta vel praesentia humani status.* Paulinus focuses on the history of the human condition, the human state before and after the birth of Christ, a crucial point on the timeline of salvation history. At lines 231–32 ("we are in awe of the holy sons of unholy ones who have been prepared from ancient epochs by a line of mystical succession") we encounter typological language (e.g., *mysticarum lineis*[72]) that clearly functions toward the purpose of providing moral exemplars.[73]

But what are we to make of the historical component, which is juxtaposed with this typological terminology? Is Paulinus, like Prudentius, constructing a narrative history that combines Judaic, Christian, and Roman pagan historical traditions into a vision of salvation history? Once again, bits and pieces of Prudentius' approach can be found in Paulinus, but, on the whole, the poetry of Paulinus does not support such a project. Paulinus' approach is to recognize the seeds of light (*lucis . . . semina, Carm.* 21.235) in these ancient pagan types and to distinguish between human talent, which can be passed on (*mens et voluntas lege naturae fuit, Carm.* 21. 238) and spiritual truth, which is only possible after the Incarnation and according to individual choice.[74] Thus, his primary concern is not historical, but moral and spiritual. The historical language in this passage does not refer to events, or traditions, but to the state of the individual regarding salvation. This colors the typological language as more exemplar-oriented; and the typological correspondence, a strict person to person model, specifies further the notion of *humani status.*[75] Paulinus, unlike Prudentius, appears to have little interest in redefining poetry in terms of its figural techniques that highlight the historical and political position of the reader. The Paulinian passage portrays a continuity between pagan and Christian generations of aristocrats who constitute the government of the empire. Rather than a political and ideological message designed to shake a Roman Christian reader from his complacency or restate the function of poetry in historical terms, Paulinus' discussion of a Roman senator exemplar is contained and limited. The reader is invited to compare himself morally and spiritually to an ideal Roman, but the memory of the reader is not targeted as a repository of history. In the *Peristephanon* and the *Psychomachia* the reader is asked to compare himself to historical martyrs or to a person undergoing a radical spiritual struggle in the context of biblical and Roman history. The influencing and creating of memory as a way toward the achievement of Roman Christian identity stands out as the purpose of Prudentius' work.

At *Pe.* 10.626–30, Prudentius employs *saecula* in an arresting typological and historical context. The subject of *conbiberunt* is *vetusta saecula,* a common expression referring to past ages of human history[76] that "drink up the cross." The cross unifies all periods of history not simply by its presence in these periods through various signs allegorically interpreted, but, more importantly, through its doctrinal power. Prudentius projects the power of the Christian God expressed in Christ's life, death, and resurrection onto human history itself. The historical meaning of the cross, foregrounded by typological vernacular like *praenotata* and *adumbrata,* is intensified and focalized by its direct application to *vetusta saecula.* The language of history has collided with the language of typology resulting in the bolstering and clarification of typological meaning. Prudentius has made a truly sophisticated theological statement. As I have already noted, poets such as Juvencus, Proba, Ambrose, and Damasus do not approach this concentration of historical and typological language, which Prudentius applies in the *Peristephanon* and *Psychomachia* to the details and events of Judeo-Christian and Roman history.[77]

Prudentius' use of *saeculum* is far richer than that of Paulinus and other poets of the age. For example, Prudentius refers to concrete and discrete periods of history. Where Paulinus uses the term to refer to "this age"—the generalized contemporary age (as Prudentius does as well[78]), Prudentius sometimes has a particular time period in mind, as, for example, in *Pe.* 2.277–80, where "the powerful men of this age" are paradoxically persons from the age of martyrs.[79] At *Cath.* 5.109–12 the term refers to the time and place of *Exodus* in the Old Testament.[80] At *Symm.* 1.72–78 *saecla* seems to conjure up a past golden age. Elsewhere, Prudentius envisions human history as a series of *saecula* that are defined by universal principles such as greed and the immortal soul.[81] Several passages that contain the word portray an age of Rome itself that learns and progresses toward the true knowledge and faith of the Christian age. A large range of historical and moral reference characterizes Prudentius' usages of *saeculum.*

Prudentius' interest in unifying the various historical periods under the umbrella of Christian doctrine can be seen elsewhere in his use of the term

saeculum. Cath. 5.161–64 furnishes an extraordinary example of what Prudentius strongly implied at *Pe.* 10.626–30.[82]

> per quem splendor honor laus sapientia
> maiestas bonitas et pietas tua
> regnum continuat numine triplici
> texens perpetuis saecula saeculis.
>
> through whom glory, honor, praise, and wisdom,
> as well as majesty, goodness, and love extend your
> kingdom with its triple godhead, uniting age
> to age forever.

The word *saeculum* nearly comes to stand for "history" itself. Line 164 makes
the point that Christ's glory and wisdom (among other things) "weaves together" both profane and eternal ages, *texens perpetuis saecula saeculis.*[83] This
act of weaving together represents the intersection of the vectors of literature
or poetry and history. The figure of Christ may manipulate the ages of history,
but the scriptures and other texts, including poems, do the work of constructing salvation history for the benefit of each individual Roman.

If we return to *Pe.* 10 and read lines 608–30, we discover two more usages of
saeculum (*Pe.* 10.608, 610) in which the term refers to those "of this world"
who, ignorant of the Christian god, still might be able to become wise regarding Christianity (*prudens dei*). The poet, by using a cognate of his own name,
may be reinforcing his own role in textualizing salvation history. There are
other signs of the poet injecting into his poetry the idea of composing life-
guiding texts. For instance, at *Psych.* 78–79, *Pudicitia*'s speech exploits the
connection from *John* 1 between the word (*verbum*) and flesh (*carnis*). The
phrase is noteworthy: *dum carnis glutinat usum,* "It (the word) sticks to the
experience of the flesh." The verb *glutino* is used of gluing, but also of "closing"
a wound (*OLD glutino,* 1b), which fits with the postlapsarian view of human
flesh as damaged or wounded. But, more important, as we saw with the
connection between *fabula* and *vita* in the introduction to this chapter, line 79
indicates that speech or words are part of the human experience. Although as
pure knowledge the Word may be divine, it takes the form of flesh (i.e., Christ)
and thus, as a result, interprets and transforms the flesh. The word is indeed
"attached to the experience of the flesh." *Verbum* can be seen as a chronicle and
interpretation of human experience, the process of history itself, and in the
end the method of extending and celebrating Christian doctrine.

As already mentioned, Prudentius recalls pagan Rome's founding stories *Pe.* 10.626–30. The notion of unification is explicit in this inclusion of historical narrative.[84] These three uses of *saeculum* in Prudentius (*Pe.* 10.608, 610, 629) show that sacred and profane history come together under the auspices of doctrine. Far from the profane ages being set against the eternal one, Prudentius is at pains to make profane history part of sacred history. I hope to have shown that Paulinus of Nola is representative of other poets of the day who, if they even use the term *saeculum,* conceive of *saecula* as either sacred or profane ages. Prudentius not only indicates a unification of sacred and profane ages, but his concerns are also literary: to elevate poetry to the status of texts that inform and convert.[85]

The synchronic effect of the marriage between typology and history is but one result of Prudentius' use of *saeculum* at *Pe.* 10.626–30. In addition, passages such as *Symm.* 1.511–40 make it clear that though the concept of *imperium sine fine* was taught to Rome by the likes of Vergil and Cicero, it is now part of Christian Rome. Again we witness the tendency of the poetry to appropriate Rome's imperial and literary past. In this case, the poet all but declares his notion of imperial theology whose human representation is Rome itself.[86] We are reminded of the basic task of Vergilian epic, which is to show the symbiotic relationship between divine history and Roman history. The literary task of combining sacred and profane ages is put in service to the promotion of divine empire. Second, textualism is the main mode of promoting this ideological view. In the *Peristephanon,* Prudentius presents the Christian martyr side of Roman history because it is imperative that "succeeding generations" of Romans be taught martyr stories (*Pe.* 1.73–78). The transmission of history is crucial to the purpose of Prudentius' poetry, which is to define Christian identity. Third, Prudentius use of *saeculum* promotes a vision of Christian identity, descending from God, but heavily laden with the ages of history. *Pe.* 1.58–59 contains the idea of a human being as a "likeness of God" (*dei formam*), that is, the antitype of the type God.[87] Prudentius asks whether such a creature will dedicate itself to the corrupt concerns of "this age." *Apoth.* 305–11 constructs a similar typological progression from God to Christ to humans. We are the antitype whose form comes to full fruition with the Incarnation, which happens only after ages of time. The wedding of typological associations with human and divine history creates the conditions for individual identity accomplished by means of reading texts. Prudentius propels texts, and thus his own poetry, as the *sine qua non* for his grand vision of Christian national and individual identity. So much for the traditional critical notion of Prudentian poetry and Christian poetry as a whole, often advanced on the surface by the poets themselves, that the new poetry's primary quality is humility, which relegates both poet and poetry to a silent and inferior role in the hierarchy of written discourse.[88]

In concluding this excursus on the use of the historical and typological terms of *Pe.* 10.626–30, it is clear that Prudentius uses a rich, varied, and metaphoric panoply of meanings. These meanings emerge from the context of the passages, contexts in which both typology and historical narrative are present. Through this juxtaposition and, ultimately, integration, Prudentius creates a poetry with a clear sense of theology where God works outside of historical time, an imperial theology that lionizes Rome's inclusion in salvation history, and, finally, a general focus on history as a defining criterion of self and state. This is another way that Prudentius reinvigorates Latin poetry at a moment in literary history when poetry's political and epic functions were waning. The "empire without end" is no longer a Vergilian construction. By means of a sophisticated and systematic deployment of typology's capability to unite and create historical narrative, Prudentius definitively claims Rome for Christian poetry and as a part of Christian identity.

Christ, Romulus, Numa, and Christian Poetry's Mission

Pe. 2.413–44 and *Psych.* 470–629 brilliantly crystallize the multifaceted relationship between typological practice, Roman markers of history, and the construction of salvation history. In each example, Prudentius repositions Roman pagan history within Christian history and ideology. In keeping with the project of textualizing a consumptive salvation history that respects Roman pagan history, Prudentius constructs audacious and tension-filled juxtapositions between Roman pagan markers of history and what he takes to be their Christian typological counterparts. Both examples from the *Peristephanon* and the *Psychomachia* employ typology to forge unexpected correspondences between Old Testament, Roman pagan, and Christian histories; the result is a consumptive construction of history, a unification of these historical narratives under the aegis of salvation history. The sacred and the profane exist side by side, alternating between Roman earthly and Christian heavenly realms. This nearly systematic juxtaposition implies, for example, the appropriation of the earthly symbolic meanings of Roman mythical figures of *Pe.* 2.

413, Romulus and Numa, thereby supporting the cause of Christian divine empire. Christ takes over Romulus' and Numa's imperial functions as founder, conqueror, spiritual leader, and protector of the people. *Psych.* 470–629 tells the story of Judas Iscariot's betrayal of Christ within the easily recognizable backdrop of Roman civil war. The picture of Roman civil strife as background to the New Testament story of greed foregrounds the reader (a Roman citizen) as a locus of moral choice either to act like Judas or pursue a life like the one of Christ. A life of greed is associated with personal and civil strife, whereas a life without greed, it is implied, is not. The reader encounters a biblical scene set within a quintessentially Roman context. The parallel yet integrated combination of biblical and Roman material both reflects and affirms the identity of the reader.

Pe. 2. 413–44 displays an unorthodox use of typology wherein the Roman figures of Romulus and Numa become types for the imperial, theological identity of Christ. The mythohistorical figures of Quirinus, Romulus, Remus, and Numa are "absorbed" by the figure of Christ.[89] Christ becomes the authority through which Rome was founded (*auctor horum moenium,* 416) and rules the world (*unis legibus,* 424; and *omne sub regnum Remi / mortale,* 425–26). The formulation of Christ as founder of Rome is unprecedented in fourth-century poetry. The passage is a prayer to Christ consisting of descriptive language directly connecting Christ to the Roman historical figures of Quirinus, (419) Remus (425), Romulus (443), and Numa (444) and couched in prescriptive language requesting Christ to grant that Rome come under a unified Christian worship (433–36 and 441–44).

It is helpful to examine more closely the ways in which these figures appear in Prudentius and other poets of the era. First the figure of Numa. We should note that Juvencus, Proba, Ambrose, Damasus, and Paulinus rarely—if ever—mention Numa. I take this as a clear sign of their lack of interest in or hostility to Roman mythohistory. Prudentius often mentions the name to indicate the negative, pagan side of history and religion.[90] In two places he mentions the founder of Roman pagan religion in a value neutral sense to denote a line of historical development on the pagan side. At *Symm.* 2.543, Numa is a historical figure, juxtaposed with the "descendants of Aeneas" and emblematic of the pagan side of history, the teleology of which leads to the historical dominance of the Christian god. At *Pe.* 2.513 Prudentius uses Numa as the foremost symbol of pagan Roman religion that occupies a certain point of history on the evolutionary line to Christianity.

This idea is replicated and then transformed into an extraordinary, if somewhat ambiguous, meaning at *Pe.* 2.444: *et ipse iam credat Numa.* Without making too much of this passage, it nonetheless strikes the reader that Numa, by the fourth century a hackneyed emblem of pagan religion, is invoked as a possible Christian. Prudentius does the same to Romulus in the line above, *fiat fidelis Romulus* (*Pe.* 2.443). This kind of sentiment is unparalleled elsewhere in the Prudentian corpus and in fourth-century poetry.[91] In this prayer to Christ, the founder and lawgiver of Rome, why is it desirable that Romulus and Numa be believers? Is Prudentius cutting Roman pagan historical names down to size? Have these names ceased to be historical figures for Prudentius and for fourth-century educated Christians in general? In response, it is clear that in *Pe.* 2, "Lawrence's fate is defined in civic terms."[92] At the end of *Pe.* 2, there is a prophecy of Theodosius' rule (lines 473–76); senators are converted and carry away the body of Lawrence (lines 489ff.). Thus, Lawrence' martyrdom takes place against the backdrop of Rome's political and civic institutions.[93] Second, Rome is a city founded by Christ but still associated with the contributions of the first, archetypal Romans, Romulus and Numa: that is, military and religious infrastructure. The military achievement of Rome is crucial to Prudentius' appropriation of the idea of Rome for the new Christian dispensation. As Rome's first religious leader who established the fundamentals of Roman religion, Numa's central role as religious founder is akin to Christ's after the Incarnation, and Romulus as the archetypal military and political organizer suggests Christ's role as imperial steersman of the empire. In fact, the attraction of Romulus and Numa to Christ and Christianity indicates a typological relationship between them and Jesus.

In the *Psychomachia,* Prudentius' typological constructions focus primarily on the Old and New Testaments with the Roman context of civil war in the background. We saw in the work of Paulinus of Nola that typology can be applied to oneself and one's ancestors; however, in *Pe.* 2. 413–44, given the vivid context of Lawrence as representative of the new Roman religion and assimilated into Roman civic and political institutions, Prudentius has taken this political and religious miscegenation further: he has constructed a typology between Christ and Romulus/Numa, in whom military, religious, and political power reside. The effect is both reciprocal and monumental. Romulus and Numa become endowed with Christian qualities that result in their inclusion in Prudentius' historical continuum—or at the very least they become part of the new Christian Roman family—and Jesus is amplified as an earthly, Roman ruler and ruler in heaven. The Roman past is assimilated into the Christian present and future. Once again, Prudentius has employed typological thinking to construct a unified historical narrative that functions allegorically. The allegory is the interpretation that Rome—the city, the empire, its characters and history—is part of salvation history.

What the *Peristephanon* passage attempts through simple yet audacious typological correspondences, *Psych.* 470–629 accomplishes by means of an organic literary scenario. Prudentius creates a hypothetical historical scenario of civil war, a condition that pervades pagan Roman history, to show that destructive historical events are caused by the pagan moral and theological doctrines that Romans adopted. In this section of the poem, both exemplar typology and historical typology overlap. The doctrine in question is represented by the vice *Avaritia*, and its personified representation gives a speech at 511–50 in which she uses a perverse historical typology to point out that the concept of greed is common to all versions of history, whether pagan, Old Testament, or New Testament history. *Avaritia* recalls the behavior of Judas Iscariot, the exemplar of greed, and Achar, a famous Old Testament exemplar of greed. She says that Achar was descended from an Old Testament patriarch who was a relative of Christ! Unlike our previous examples in which Old Testament antitypes are positively construed, in this case, the type fails to fulfill the antitype. The type Achar is offered up as someone who did not understand the real meaning of this ancestral/historical connection according to Christian doctrinal assumptions, and thus Achar (and Judas) suffers the worst of fates. In other words, salvation is denied.[94] Moreover, rather than a mocking, contradictory, or confusing use of typology, the implied typological correspondence between Judas/Achar, Avaritia, and Christ/humans serves to highlight the Christian doctrine of free will—that is, the choice individuals exercise between good and bad actions.

Immediately following this provocative historical reference, *Avaritia* summarizes Prudentius' view of the relationship between history and doctrine: *Quis placet exemplum generis, placeat quoque forma / exitii: sit poena eadem; quibus et genus unum est.* ("Those who choose to take his race as their pattern, let them choose also the form of his destruction; let those who own the same race suffer the same punishments," *Psych.* 544–45). The whole passage, lines 542–46, comprehensively states Prudentius' approach. It is not merely the stories themselves that one must know, but how to make meaning out of them. Typology by itself is no guarantor of understanding, but a preliminary step that creates a historical narrative containing the full and correct meaning. The key to making meaning is having a notion of doctrine itself. Moreover, *Avaritia*'s words point to the notion of typology as correct recognition and understanding of correspondences. Again we see the integration in Prudentius of figural and figurative meaning. Readers must go one further step into the realm of allegory understood as the interpretive function of history, a readerly activity vital to Prudentius' overall poetic program. This idea returns when *Discordia* blurts out her reprehensible doctrines, her heresies, inside the walls of the city (*Psych.* 709–14) that goad her to overthrow the city of the virtues. Of course, she fails and is dismembered by the virtues. We can conclude that the vice's words and actions represent a foiled attempt to create history. Her doctrines cannot be allowed to stand if the correct version of the Christ story is to be preserved. In addition, the Old Testament events, which are to form an inseparable unit with the Christ story would not stand either. Therefore, what is being contested in this example is the correct historical narrative. And this can only exist through the agency of correct doctrine, just as we saw in the debate between Asclepiades and Saint Romanus earlier. Prudentius, the reader of history, composes for a reader who reads history as he does. A human story taken from history, made meaningful through the manipulation of typologies, not only implies the reader himself in the typological continuum of salvation history, but also furnishes the fundamental scheme for the reader to understand Prudentius' reading of history.

Later in the civil war narrative, Prudentius emphasizes again the relationship between history and Christian doctrine, but this time from the perspective of the virtues. After just eliminating *Avaritia*, *Operatio* says, *Quaerite luciferum caelesti dogmate pastum* (Seek the food that brings light from heavenly teaching; *Psych.* 625) As in *Matth.* 6:26–34 and 10:9–10, Christian teaching is equated to food. The Roman civil war scenario has ended with a peaceful community, courtesy of New Testament doctrine. The powerful conclusion to this section of the poem reminds the reader that Rome with all of its tempestuous history has come to a political and ethical equilibrium thanks to the new Christian dispensation. The *Peristephanon* passage hinted at such an integration of the civic and political identity of Rome with a biblical reading of universal history, in which Romulus and Numa, as imperial divine figures, are absorbed by Christ. On a more personal level, though, the reader has also been reminded that she is part of salvation history. She must decide what kind of typological series of which she will be the final term. Both levels of reference, the divine-imperial and the personal-ethical, have the purpose of forming Prudentius' implied reader. This renewal of the ethical and political function of Roman poetry has become the mission of Christian poetry.

Conclusion

In the *Psychomachia,* Prudentius primarily combines Jewish and Christian history through typology to form salvation history. Typology is a flexible trope that can either be characterized as historical in nature or limited to moral exemplars. In the *Peristephanon,* by comparison, Roman pagan history is placed under the umbrella of Christian salvation history—we see this phenomenon in the *Psychomachia* as well. Both works illustrate the Christian appropriation of Roman and Old Testament historical events into a historical narrative that allegorically comes to mean salvation history. Methodologically, doctrine provides Prudentius with the set of assumptions that controls his choice and content of typologies and leads to the creation of a historical narrative. Historical narrative, formed through the method of typology, is unparadoxically a figural and figurative allegoresis, an interpretation that both is a version of salvation history and adds new meaning to the terms of the typology.

A good example of Prudentius' method occurs at *Psych.* 650–62, where he includes the events of the Jewish Exodus (e.g., *Ex.* 1–15) in salvation history because they are an allegory for Christ's coming and the liberation of the soul from its postlapsarian bondage. This meaning is realized through a series of typological connections between the Exodus and the Incarnation and Resurrection of Christ. Both the Old and New Testament events form a narrative, which acquires a meaning, different from the literal, ordered sequence of events. It is ultimately a meaning expressed to the reader as a judgment or a pattern—and in the *Exodus* example, the pattern is underwritten by the doctrine associated with Christ's existence and its implications for the human soul.[95] Conversely, individual events and persons acquire meaning and are included in the larger historical narrative through the application of the larger story to them, or when they are typologically associated to another specific event or person; for example, in the *Peristephanon,* Romulus, Numa, and the events in which they partake acquire new meaning when placed in the context of salvation history. The Roman kings become part of salvation history because Prudentius connects them with the figure of Christ. Such a process results in an allegory, a version of "truth," characterized by meaning-producing connections between present and past—pagan and biblical—formed according to a fixed future.[96] This syncretism of the Roman, Christian, and Jewish traditions bespeaks a view of Rome as a divine empire, and this picture of Rome is intrinsic to each of Prudentius' Christian readers. Thus, Prudentius reflects a post-Constantinian but pre-Alaric view that the Roman Empire and the new Christian dispensation are a linked pair.

In the *Aeneid*, Vergil had combined and reinterpreted Roman myth and history to produce a multilayered historical narrative. The *Psychomachia* and the *Peristephanon* constitute a restatement of biblical myth and history, which also includes and depends on the tradition of Roman historical writing that Vergil exploited in the *Aeneid* to define Roman national identity. As readers, we can discern the biblical and Roman historical threads in Prudentius' poems because they combine biblical and Roman traditions of historical writing through typology in order to redefine the idea of *Romanitas*. In the process of embracing specific examples of Roman history, Prudentius challenges the expression of Roman tradition as *res gestae*, in which events themselves, not a canonized text about events, primarily inform the idea of history.[97] This Roman historiographical approach becomes subsumed under a well-defined Christian approach in which Prudentius understands history as a codified and authoritative set of texts (i.e., the Bible). For Christianity, unlike pagan religion, sacred texts acted as a common store of agreement and disagreement, by which believers attempted to stabilize their religion in all its aspects, from ritual to history. This dependence on scripturalism—i.e., the authorization of one's experience of, and inquiry into, the world by direct reference to the Old and New Testaments—becomes the dominant approach to Christian historiography.[98] Prudentius christianizes Roman history by textualizing it as a narrative of salvation history. The *Psychomachia* and the *Peristephanon* together assert a literary argument for their own status as textual authorities of salvation history.

Prudentius' use of typology is historical and metaphysical in reach, rather than concerned only with exemplars, as we see in the Christian poetry of praise, for instance, the *Natalicia* of Paulinus of Nola. Prudentius critically embraces Roman historical narratives in his version of salvation history, a literary move unparalleled in fourth- and early fifth-century poetry. This synthesis is of such a scale, that it serves to reinvent Roman poetry. Prudentius constructs pagan/Christian typological correspondences, as well as merges pagan and Christian historical characters and scenes, resulting in a new definition of *Romanitas,* a central concern in pagan Latin epic. The absorption of *Romanitas* by *Christianitas* functions as a poetic argument for individual and national identity and divine empire. This literary achievement rivals the political and historical sophistication of the *Aeneid,* which helped shape Roman identity for centuries.

The Christian poet has chosen, ordered, and interpreted each set of stories and characters through the transformative power of Christian doctrine. The reader must interpret as well. I say "must" because, ultimately, Prudentius sees each reader as having a choice, just like Judas, and to make the right choice he or she must be "properly" informed. Prudentius informs us by means of a typological historical approach in which Christian doctrine is used to interpret the archives of Roman and biblical traditions and results in a unified sacred historical narrative that expresses a Christian ideology. This use of history is the foundation of Prudentius' poetic program. Crucially, this program requires a well-defined notion of reader reciprocity. Both Prudentius the guide, and the reader as the follower, must meet each other halfway. He assumes the implied reader be biased in favor of Christian doctrine and biblical stories and have a share in the political and civic life of fourth-century Rome. This reader understands the consequences of his choice profoundly because being a Roman Christian requires a complete spiritual and political commitment, one that makes politics and religion indistinguishable.

In the following chapter, I look at the allegory of the *Psychomachia* not so much as a political and religious exercise, but as an intellectual product of the desire to know God. In this chapter I have laid the groundwork for this investigation by linking the construction of salvation history with the method of typology. This relationship facilitates a picture of the Roman Christian reader whom Prudentius addresses in order to secure an authentic spiritual and political commitment. Salvation history, rather than being understood as a fluid linear string of events designed to position the reader and his hope for immortality, becomes a body of knowledge and proves the case for the omnipotence of the Father and the immortality of the soul. This allegorization of salvation history is designed to provide knowledge. Hence, the impetus to produce allegory relates to a quest for knowledge of the divine, whether of god or the soul. Prudentius' poetry grounds this quest in history, in "real" events that acquire the capability to project nonliteral (i.e., allegorical) meanings.

CHAPTER THREE

Christian Theology and the Making of Allegory

Most critics agree that the narrative use of allegory is Prudentius' main contribution to literary history.[1] The *Psychomachia* illustrates Northrope Frye's observation that allegory occurs "when the events of a narrative obviously and continuously refer to another simultaneous structure of events or ideas, whether historical events, moral or philosophical ideas, or natural phenomena."[2] The surface elements of the *Psychomachia* (the warring personifications, the Roman historical and literary landscape, the temple, and plot of the struggle between opposing moral and religious forces) refer to a "simultaneous structure of events or ideas." The characters in the poem are not merely epic warriors but are also abstract virtues and vices that demonstrate a Christian soul's content and structure. The temple is both a described object and a perfected human soul ruled by wisdom and ready for Christian salvation. The plot is not just a series of set piece battles between good and evil but, rather, the story of individual and collective spiritual struggle of Roman Christians.

The *Psychomachia* is the first text of Western literary history that modern critics analyze according to the tension between a literary work's fictional autonomy and its reference to other events, circumstances, and principles.[3]

Critics routinely assume that the *Psychomachia* subordinates narrative content to its additional meanings, whether they are disparaging the poem or praising it.[4] Rather than separating the two levels of meaning in this way, my approach views both the surface narrative's political and historical symbols and the deeper tropological meanings on an equal footing. Both are there to persuade a Roman Christian reader to be committed to the future of Christian Rome and his own salvation. The *Psychomachia* accomplished this ideological purpose by using allegory to translate the narratives of the Bible and Roman civilization into an inspiring spiritual message for a fourth-century Roman Christian. This use of allegory proved to be a highly influential strategy, and one whose effects can be traced throughout the Middle Ages.[5]

In his study of the intellectual background of the Cappadocian Fathers, Jaroslav Pelikan observes that in patristic texts, allegory is understood as a response to language of negation. Prudentius, too, displays a clear interest in apophatic or negative theology, the idea that human reason in the form of language can neither describe nor capture adequately the divine godhead and, by extension, the divine part of the soul.[6] Several prominent passages in the *Psychomachia* (*Praef. Psych.* 40–44, 59–60) and the first 175 lines of the *Apotheosis* make it clear that negative theological thinking and speaking are the starting point in Prudentius' work for the achievement of knowledge of God.[7]

Pelikan's observation points the way to a theory of Prudentian narrative allegory. The *Psychomachia* posits the linguistic puzzle of how to describe God and the soul and responds with a series of typologies that express interpretations of biblical texts and Christian dogma. These typological exegeses describe the soul's qualities and its inner struggle.[8] Abraham's life and actions, interpreted as the quality of faith, establish faith as a quality of the soul, an allegorical concept, which is then personified and placed in a narrative of the poem proper. Prudentius connects *Spes* typologically to David, whose hope overcame Goliath, and in turn to the reader, whose hope in Christ brings great rewards. Virtues and vices become allegorical personifications, but each of their literary identities begins as a typological interpretation of biblical stories and characters. Allegory formed from typological interpretation of the Bible makes it possible for the poet to communicate ideas that are incommunicable through normal object or referent language.

Whereas scholars have acknowledged that the *Psychomachia* is exegetical poetry,[9] little attention has been paid to the relationship of biblical exegesis to the poem's narrative allegory, and no scholar has proposed that the allegory of the poem be viewed as a response to the apophatic dilemma. Critics have underappreciated the importance of biblical exegeses to the poem's allegory-producing typologies. Biblical interpretations are crucial to the poem's typologies and therefore to the signifiers of the *Psychomachia*'s allegorical universe: the personifications, the battle narrative, and the temple.[10]

The Argument of the *Praefatio* to the *Psychomachia*

The *Praefatio* to the *Psychomachia* establishes the concepts and narrative that will be carried on through the end of the poem. The narrative describes the figure of Abraham and specific stories in *Genesis*. Prudentius' general aim is to prefigure in the life and narrative of the patriarch virtue's victory over vice at several levels: in the soul, in the city, and in the daily life of an individual person.[11] My purpose is to show that typology not only is the structuring principle of the *Praefatio* but also forms an allegorical response to the apophatic dilemma set out in the *Praefatio*.[12] Through the deployment of apophatic language—which denies that words, the instruments of reason, can represent the reality of God—the ability of human reason to understand divinity is portrayed as limited. Instead, the language of negation thrusts the reader into a world inexplicable through the literal meanings of words. Words either mean something other than what they normally mean or produce enigmatic and undecidable meaning. To guide the reader, Prudentius often furnishes typologies as alternative meanings to these apophatic words, typologies that express specific exegetical meanings of biblical passages.

In my treatment of the *Praefatio* I shift between two levels of explanation concerning the nature of Prudentius' allegorical technique. The first is more general and charts the relationship between text, reader, and author. The divine text of the Bible presents apophatic language. Prudentius interprets this language in the form of typologies intended to express specific meanings, and the reader can only understand the poet's intent by having a proper degree of doctrinal faith. Allegorical meaning occurs at the intersection of the reader's faith and the author's typological intent. The second scheme explains the production of allegory in the poem itself. The poet poses the apophatic problem of knowing God and the soul. The response is a series of typologies from biblical texts that produce allegorical meanings. In the *Praefatio*, the achieved allegorical meaning is that Christ is a mediator between God and the human soul. Prudentius further supports this idea by use of imagery of the soul as home to

Christ. The allegorical meaning of the typology of Christ and Melchisedec constitutes real knowledge, which is available to a reader of sufficient faith.

The Apophatic Text

Prudentius' use of apophatic language in the *Praefatio* to the *Psychomachia* vividly evokes the mystery of the priestly line from Melchisedec to Christ and the Father. Two passages provide a burst of negative language about the divine origins of Melchisedec and Christ:

dei sacerdos rex et idem praepotens   (*Praef. Psych.* 40–44)
origo cuius *fonte inenarrabili*
secreta nullum prodit *auctorem* sui
Melchisedec, qua stirpe quis maioribus
ignotus uni cognitus tantum deo.
The priest of God, himself a powerful king
Whose *mysterious birth* from a *source that*
cannot be named has *no ostensible author,* Melchisedec,
whose line and ancestors *no person knows,* for
they are known to God alone.

si quid trecenti bis novenis additis   (*Praef. Psych.* 57–60)
possint *figura noverimus mystica.*
mox ipse Christus, qui sacerdos verus est,
parente natus alto et *ineffabili*
if *we know through the mystic symbol* what
is the power of three hundred eighteen more.
Then Christ himself, who is the true priest,
Born of a father lofty and *unutterable.*

In the same manner as Gregory of Nyssa, Gregory of Nazianzus, or Ambrose, Prudentius has fore-grounded the apophatic idea that humans cannot know the essence of God nor even understand God's existence.[13] As a result, concerning the story of the visitation in the *Praefatio,* the existence of Christ as Son of God on earth brings a human being as close to God as she will ever come. The two Gregorys tend to speak in apophatic language (i.e., negative theological terms) concerning their descriptions of God and in their exegesis of *Gen.* 14:18 and *Heb.* 7:3. *Praef.* 40–44 employs the apophatic language as well, some directly from *Heb.* 7:3. At *Praef.* 41 and 42 Melchisedec's origin is described as *inenarrabili* and *secreta.* He has no *auctorem sui.* Further, at *Praef.* 44 his origin is *ignotus, uni cognitus tantum Deo.* Poetically, the language is suitable because Prudentius, like Paul in *Heb.* 7:1–3, is drawing a typological comparison between Melchisedec and Christ[14] (note especially *trinitas* [*Praef.* 45] and *trinitatis* [*Praef.* 63], as well as *Praef.* 41–42 and 60[15]).

We should understand these lines with the early verses of the *Apotheosis,* which climax with the same story of the visitation to the house of Abraham. At *Apoth.* 6 Prudentius asks, "Can God suffer? (*Passibilisne Deus?*), to which he begins his answer apophatically:

> . . . cuius species et imago   (*Apoth.* 6–8)
> nulli visa umquam; nec enim conprendier illa
> maiestas facilis sensuve oculisve manuve.
> His shape and form no one has ever seen;
> for that majesty is not easily grasped by thought, eye, or hand.[16]

The discussion that follows in the *Apotheosis* focuses on the unknowability of God, whose son Jesus gives humans a partial glimpse of the Father's essence.[17]

The poet mentions what he considers ridiculous notions of conceiving of God inside a human body (*Apoth.* 4), subject to death (*Apoth.* 5), and capable of suffering (*Apoth.* 6). Normal human capabilities cannot grasp God. God cannot be seen (*Apoth.* 9–12), nor can God's infinity be understood so as to limit it: . . .*et dietatis / inmensum adsumpto non temperat ore modove* ("nor does [the Father] qualify the infinity of his godhead by assuming countenance or mode," *Apoth.* 13–14). The Father cannot be seen directly (*Apoth.* 15–17), although his *specimen* in the form of the Son was seen by those who lived at that time (*Apoth.* 18–25). Prudentius uses *gnatum* at *Apoth.* 23 and *natus* at *Psych.* 60 of the Son, a participle formation with the same root as γεννήτος, which in the patristic tradition is a basic example of apophatic language. When used with regard to Christ and the Father, the Word shed its literal, human meaning and adopted an abstract, symbolic sense.[18] Just before the reference to Abraham, Prudentius restates his basic negative theological point: *Nam mera maiestas est infinita nec intrat / obtutus, aliquo ni se moderamine formet* ("The pure majesty is infinite, and does not come within our vision unless it takes *some tempering shape,*" *Apoth.* 26–27). Abraham's sighting of a triple-formed angel counts as *aliquo moderamine.*[19]

From an exclusively rational point of view, Prudentius holds what appears to be two mutually exclusive propositions that the Father who cannot mingle with mortal flesh (*non admiscenda caducis, Apoth.* 17) and that the Son who can be seen is the progeny of the Father (*ab ipso / infusum vidit gnatum, Apoth.* 22–23). *Apotheosis* 28–30 explicitly refer only to Christ as the visitor.[20]

> Hoc vidit princeps generosi seminis Abram,
> iam tunc dignati terras invisere Christi
> hospes homo, in triplicem numen radiasse figuram.
> Abraham, the leader of a noble race,
> a human being, the host of Christ who considered it
> worthy to visit the earth, saw the divinity, radiated
> into three figures.

Scholars have seen Prudentius' interpretation of *trinitas* as a "triple image of Christ," not as representing the Father, Son and the Holy Spirit.[21] Although this conclusion is valid, it does not express precisely what Prudentius accomplishes with the use of this story. The context of *Apotheosis* 28–30 is helpful in this matter. As already indicated, the text of the poem before the reference is full of apophatic language concerning the Father.[22] After *Apoth.* 28–30, the figure of Christ is understood as the only means for humans, who recognize him through faith, to gain access to the Father—i.e. the Word, which is not seen as it is, but issuing from the Father, and seen in the form of a human (compare *Psych. Praef.* 45–46). Therefore the typological reference to *Genesis* 18 evokes the role of Christ as the vehicle through which humans gain knowledge of the Father (*Patris est specimen, Apoth.* 18). Christ is the facilitator, the messenger, or the medium through which the rest of the Trinity can be known. This is clear from *Psych. Praef.* 62–63, which tell of Christ entering the "hut" of the soul to show it how to entertain the Trinity, *monstrans honorem trinitatis hospitae.* The apophatic language of the *Praefatio* to the *Psychomachia* sets the stage for a narrative vignette with the allegorical message that the figure of Christ is the one phenomenon that allows the soul of a human being to know God. This typological allegory, supported by *Apoth.* 28–30 and expressed as the relationship between Christ and knowledge of God in the human soul, is the positive meaning produced in response to the epistemological problem that apophatic language raises.

The Faithful Reader

The typological relationship between Abraham's trials and the victory of virtue over vice elicits the basic principle of faith, defined as belief in and commitment to Nicean Christian doctrine.[23] Prudentius telescopes the events from the *Genesis* narrative, which suit his typological purpose, summed up as an argument for the priority of faith in one's life and one's reading of Christian texts. For the reader, without faith, there is no understanding of the author's typological allegory that Christ is the mediator between humans and God. Faith begins in the *Praefatio* as a typological quality to be gleaned from narrative events of Abraham's life. The typology that Prudentius implies is Abraham-faith-reader, while at the end of the poem the personification of faith inhabits the temple of the soul along with another quality of the soul *Sapientia. Sapientia*'s characteristic of proper judgment shown in an ability to distinguish good from evil and divine from mortal is also portrayed narratively in the *Praefatio* to the *Psychomachia* with the visitation of the triple-formed angel and is stated at the end of the poem when a gift of *Fides* crowns *Sapientia*'s temple—both instances requiring a reader of faith to interpret these moments. Therefore, a clear association between faith and reason exists throughout the poem as qualities of the soul, which demonstrates the state of preparedness of an ideal soul to receive Christ, the mediator between the soul and the godhead (and perhaps between the very qualities of Faith and Reason themselves). Reason and faith are necessary conditions to understand the poem's interpretation of biblical events.

Prudentius strongly implies and the reader infers that the life and experiences of Abraham (described as *fidelis* in the first line of the *Praefatio*) are emblematic of faith (the near sacrifice of his son, the rescue of Lot, his wife Sarra's miracle birth, and the vision of the triple-formed angel). This allegory exists only because Prudentius the author has constructed his text in such a way that the Roman Christian reader recognizes (comes to know) the allegorical sense of the words. By delineating the limits of rationality through negative theology, Prudentius provides a "rationale" for the concept of faith as a necessary condition for knowledge of or communion with the divine. It is no coincidence that the psychological trait of faith and a psychologized notion of allegory (i.e., occurring in the minds of author and reader) share an epistemological function. Faith triggers the reader's allegorical response to the text.

The Faithful Reader's Recognition and the Poet's Typological Intent

It is illuminating to look more closely at the transition in the *Praefatio* from the language of negation to typological allegory, made possible through the reader's response, guided by faith, and through the author's organization of the text's words and ideas, also guided by faith. The *Praefatio* is driven by the assumptions of negative theology, leading to the abstract concept of faith (to be personified at *Psych.* 18), indicated typologically in the concrete events of the life of Abraham (i.e., faith indirectly "personified"). Abraham's connection to faith prefigures the construction of the ideal soul (the temple) in the *Psychomachia* and, further, the reader's faithful soul. Moreover, for the reader, Abraham's life story as a symbol of faith prefigures Christ's life and story as a means to the ideal soul. The thought of the *Praefatio* moves from the inability of humans to understand divinity, to the endorsement of faith as a vehicle for understanding, to, finally, (typological) allegorical assertions about the relationship between God and the soul.

The typologies in the *Praefatio* become recognizable only through faith, which is represented in the stories associated with Abraham: *senex fidelis prima credendi via / Abram* (The faithful old man is the first model of believing, Abraham; *Praef. Psych.* 1–2); just seven lines below, *deo . . . credito* (*Praef. Psych.* 8)[24]; and finally, much later, *vigilandum in armis pectorum fidelium* ("there must be armed vigilance in the hearts of the faithful," *Praef. Psych.* 52).[25] These passages form a sequence of thought that climax in the last instance. Abraham is indeed the archetypical faithful person who follows God's commands based on his faith. The adjective in *Praef. Psych.* 1, *fidelis,* is an apt description of what one ought to be, but by *Psych.* 8 we encounter faith as a necessary ingredient for the performance of actions (sacrifices[26])—what one with faith ought to do. The proper reader *performs* his faith by understanding the typological allegory. The reader's performance seamlessly achieves both understanding and acceptance.

By *Praef. Psych.* 52, Prudentius has developed some aspects of the virtue-vice allegory—the heart as faithful, armed, and needing a person's vigilance. Faith becomes the crucial ingredient that permits a person, in this case Abraham, to recognize Melchisedec's sacred significance and welcome the triad of angels into his house. These faithful actions bear fruit in the elderly Sara's birth of Isaac and, most important, as the type for the role and function of Christ within the human soul. Christ's unknowable and unsayable origins must be taken on faith though his existence in the flesh, parallel to Isaac's existence, is a concrete, earthly reality. In the typological correspondences of the *Praefatio*, Melchisedec and Isaac prefigure Christ as a miraculous mediator between human flesh and the pure divinity of God.[27] Faith is the necessary ingredient that facilitates these "logical" and "reasonable" inferences on the part of the reader. Therefore, the apophatic dilemma of God as pure divinity, untouched by mortal flesh, though God's son becomes flesh, is reoriented toward the practice of faith, which propels the reader to an allegorical and transcendent realm by means of the recognition of typological correspondences. In this way the *Praefatio* presents faith as a necessary condition for "knowing" (*noverimus, Psych.* 58) and participating in the mysteries of the godhead and its benefits to the soul.[28]

In the *Praefatio* to the *Psychomachia,* faith is necessary for understanding and knowledge. The *Praefatio* progresses from the story of Abraham's triumph in liberating Lot (*Praef. Psych.* 15–37 and *Gen.* 14), to the mention of Melchisedec (*Praef. Psych.* 38–44, *Gen.* 14:18,[29] and *Hebr.* 7:3[30]), to Sara's miracle pregnancy (*Praef. Psych.* 45–49, *Gen.* 18:1,[31] and 21:2–6[32]), to the climax of the mention of Christ (*Praef. Psych.* 59ff). *Praef. Psych.* 51–58 acts as a bridge from the Old Testament stories, which prefigure the life of Christ to the New Testament and the battle that will take place afterward within the soul. These lines provide the transition from the concrete battles and victory of Abraham to the more abstract battles, which will take place in the interior of a person against the immaterial forces of desire.

Similar to the use of Melchisedec, Abraham's story acquires meaning when one begins from the apophatic idea that the soul is best described not through linguistic predication, but through the typological correspondence between Abraham's concrete battles and the soul's interior struggles with vice. As he goes into battle, Abraham is described as *plenus deo* (*Praef. Psych.* 26). The parallel to *patris inplebit domum* (*Praef. Psych.* 68), in which the house of the Father is filled with a worthy heir (allegorically speaking, a healthy soul), is unmistakable. The transition to the allegorical realm of the soul is indicated by three further occurrences of the language of home. At *Praef. Psych.* 23 Abraham arms his servants who are from his own home (*vernulas*). At *Praef. Psych.* 46 he entertains the triformed trinity of angels in his modest hut (*mapalia*). At *Praef. Psych.* 55–58 the poet makes this language abstract with the notions of marshalling one's forces at home for the interior battle (*domi coactis . . . viribus*) and recognizing one's own home-grown servants that will be indispensable for victory (*vernularum divites*). The only way for a person to "recognize" such circumstances is for him to obtain this self-knowledge through the mystic symbols (*figura noverimus mystica*).

Prudentius comes to the apophatic idea that embracing unknowable phenomena (*figura mystica*) is necessary to win the battle between the virtues and vices. At this point, where rational explanation becomes useless, Prudentius introduces the figure of Christ by name (*Praef. Psych.* 59), whereas the reference of *Praef. Psych.*45 to the Savior is indirect and implied. At *Praef. Psych.*59 Christ is the concrete figure through whom we can win the immaterial battle within ourselves, but at *Praef. Psych.*45 he is only an abstraction that, paradoxically, occurs in the part of the poem that is concerned with concrete, exterior events (Abraham's battle to liberate Lot). The typology of Melchisedec and Christ permits the transition from the literal to the allegorical. Thus, through the redefinition of the term *domus* (from the literal "home" to the abstract "home of the soul") and from the stated example of Melchisedec to the implied coming of Christ, Prudentius allegorically makes a theological statement about the role of Christ as facilitator of knowledge of God that is consistent with the function of faith and reason.

The two most important aspects of Prudentius' treatment of Melchisedec are the apophatic language (*inenarrabili, secreta, nullum . . . auctorem sui, ignotus, uni cognitus . . . deo, Praef. Psych.,* 41–44) and his description of him as *sacerdos* and *rex* (*Gen.* 14:18). These descriptions activate the typology between Melchisedec and Christ, but, rather than emphasize the pair's similarities, the description of Christ as *sacerdos verus* (*Praef. Psych.*59) provides the reader an opportunity to recognize a contrast between the two figures—that is, Christ's superiority to Melchisedec. In fact, for Prudentius, Christ is the only "high" priest—the perfect priest who, through his death on the cross, has assumed the functions and office of all previous, imperfect priests back to Aaron, Moses' brother.[33] Moreover, similar to Christ's sacred and mysterious origin, Melchisedec's origin is unknown, yet another crucial typological contrast is that he does not entertain the triformed visitor, the typological representation of the Holy Trinity. This function is left for the faithful Abraham and his typological double, the reader of the *Psychomachia* who requires Christ's guidance for the task. At this point in the poem, Prudentius has juxtaposed the two typologies of "faithful Abraham—reader" and "Melchisedec—Christ," resulting in a coherent statement of the relationship between the human soul and the godhead. Christ in the flesh as the priest and mediator demonstrates to Abraham and us how to be hospitable to the Trinity and to Christ himself as part of the unknowable godhead within the soul (*Praef. Psych.*62–63); and, through him as mediator, we gain knowledge of his origin and the qualities necessary for an eternal communion with the God.

Human limitations receive their clearest expression in the apophatic language used of the Father, *parente . . . ineffabili.* With this apophatic premise and the response of the typological correspondences (Abraham/reader and Melchisedec/Christ), Prudentius allegorizes the process of uniting the human soul to God through Christ. Christ's role as the true priest allows him to officiate at the wedding between the Holy Spirit in the role of the groom and the soul in the role of bride (*Praef. Psych.*64–65). The end of the poem shall reunite these entities. Prudentius makes the parallel complete by mentioning how the soul, *expertem diu,* can give birth to a worthy heir for the house of the Father (*Praef. Psych.*68). The ending directly and typologically parallels the reference to Sara's late pregnancy, which occurs right after Abraham entertains the triformed visitor (*Praef. Psych.*47–49; note especially *fertilis* and *herede*). Typologically speaking, then, from the earthly yet miraculous birth of Isaac to the indefinable, abstract birth of the ideal soul produced from the union between the Holy Spirit and the human soul, Prudentius has once again demonstrated a sophisticated theological view, expressed in a typologically driven allegory; in this instance, a wonderfully rich conception of the relationship between the Trinity and the soul with Christ as facilitator between the two parties.[34] This progression of themes, a pattern repeated often in the poem, furnishes a literary unity to the *Psychomachia.*

For Prudentius, Christ is the *credendi via* or *vincendi ratio* regarding human knowledge of God. The Son's life and teachings represent a way for humans to obtain knowledge about God. Prudentian theology envisions Christ as a messenger coming to earth to bring the news of the Trinity, which would otherwise be incomprehensible to humans. Thus, Prudentius is certainly aware of the trinitarian associations of *Gen.* 14:18 (compare *Gen.* 18:2) but is endeavoring to clarify the limits of reason and the role of faith which "knows" and "sees" by means of the figure of Christ. The poetry expresses this theological position by beginning from apophatic language that poses the problem of knowing the godhead and the soul. Then, ingeniously and with great flexibility, Prudentius employs typology to create associations that uniquely distinguish Christ and his relationship to the Christian soul. These associations are only possible through the recognition on the reader's part of the faith that Abraham represents which, when personified, will fight the first battle of the *Psychomachia* proper. As a response to the apophatic dilemma, faith becomes the reader's contribution to knowing Christ and his own soul, defined as a predisposition toward Christian doctrine, and plays a vital role in recognizing the author's typological correspondences that produce the allegory of Christ as the mediator between the Father and the soul. For Prudentius, to understand and profit from the *Psychomachia,* the reader must be predisposed to the kind of faith that Christianity promotes.

Judith and the Typological Allegory of Purity and Union

At *Psych.* 56–69 Prudentius groups allusions to *Matth.* 25:7 (though, in general, he is recalling verses 1–13) and *Judith* 13ff.[35] The Gospel passage develops the metaphor of bridesmaids waiting for the bridegroom, a theme already raised in the *Praefatio.* In this case, however, humans are the bridesmaids and Christ is the bridegroom. Half of the bridesmaids are ready to receive the groom; readiness is defined as having their lamps (*lampades*) full of oil and thus being allowed to enter the place of the wedding (heaven).[36] The rest of the bridesmaids are left out of the wedding because they are not sensible, prudent, or prepared enough to receive Christ the groom. Common sense and reason are essential to the understanding of a successful union with God, which is constructed in terms of a marriage.

To this picture from the *Matthew* passage Prudentius adds the story of Judith (*Judith* 13ff.), which he says, "prefigures our times" (*tempora nostra figurat*) by prefiguring the birth of Christ by Mary through chastity. Judith, a symbol of the unbending (*aspera, Psych.* 62) principle of chastity, beheads Holofernes, the Assyrian king, in his own bedroom when he attempts to seduce her.[37] Prudentius' focus is on virginity and chastity because the virgin birth of Christ leads to reflection on the nature of Christ and his relationship to the Father.

Numquid et intactae post partum virginis ullum   (*Psych.* 70–88)
fas tibi iam superest? Post partum virginis, ex quo
corporis humani naturam pristina origo
deservit carnemque novam vis ardua sevit
atque innupta deum concepit femina Christum,
mortali de matre hominem sed cum patre numen.
Inde omnis iam diva caro est, quae concipit illum
naturamque dei consortis foedere sumit.
Verbum quippe caro factum non destitit esse
quod fuerat, verbum, dum carnis glutinat usum
maiestate quidem non degenerante per usum
carnis sed miseros ad nobiliora trahente.

Ille manet quod semper erat, quod non erat esse
incipiens; nos quod fuimus iam non sumus, aucti
nascendo in melius. Mihi contulit et sibi mansit.
Nec deus ex nostris minuit sua, sed sua nostris
dum tribuit nosmet dona ad caelestia vexit.
Dona haec sunt quod victa iaces, lutulenta Libido,
nec mea post Mariam potis es perfringere iura.

Well, since an immaculate virgin has borne a child, do you have
any claim remaining—since the day when a man's body lost
its primeval nature, and power from on high created a new flesh,
and a woman unwedded conceived the God Christ, who is man
in virtue of his mortal mother but God along with the Father?
From that day all flesh is divine, since it conceives him and takes on
the nature of God by a covenant of partnership. For the Word
made flesh has not ceased what it was before, that is, the Word,
by attaching to itself the experience of flesh; its majesty is not
lowered by the experience of flesh, but raises wretched men to
nobler things. He remains what he always was, though begins to be
what he was not; but we are no longer what we were, now that we
are raised at our birth into a better condition. He has given to me,
yet still remained for himself; neither has God diminished what is
his by taking on what is ours, but by giving his nature to ours he has
lifted us to the height of his heavenly gifts. It is his gift that you lie
down conquered, filthy Lust, and cannot, since Mary, violate my authority.

Thus, through the ingenious combination of Old and New Testament texts Prudentius forms a series of typological pairs. Two of the pairs arise from the Judith passage itself: with regard to chastity and virginity, Judith/Mary and Judith/*Pudicitia*. In relation to the health of his soul, the reader faces an ethical choice between two typological pairs when the Judith passage is combined with *Matth.* 25:7: Judith/reader, who are ready to receive the bridegroom, and Holofernes/reader, who are unprepared morally and spiritually to receive the bridegroom. The way to prepare oneself for the "marriage" with Christ is to have a chaste soul, pure of vice, and to understand who Christ is and what he offers a chaste soul. The discussion of Christ and his father at *Psych.* 70–88 constitutes a direct reflection on this typological nexus. The typologies and the reflection on them serve one purpose: a clear understanding of Christ's origins and the proper condition of the soul to receive him.

At *Psych.* 70, 71, and 88, Prudentius deploys the phrases *intactae post partum virginis, post partum virginis,* and *post Mariam,* respectively. These formulations express the idea that a new age has dawned in the history of humankind. The story of Judith typologically prefigures the events of Mary's virgin pregnancy and eventual birth of Christ, and also heralds the new post-Incarnation age (*tempora nostra figurat*)—and, by implication, the triumph of *Pudicitia.* Virginity and celebacy resulted in the greatest of all births and a clear opportunity for human salvation. The typological use of Judith ultimately suggests this allegorical version of the pure Christian soul, forming the climax of the poetry through *Psych.* 108.

This new epoch in the history of humankind means a new flesh (*carnem novam, Psych.* 73) that has acquired a divine nature (*diva caro, Psych.* 76). The Word, which undergoes the experience of flesh (*carnis . . . usum, Psych.* 79; and *usum / carnis, Psych.* 80–81), is in no way made inferior nor degenerate. The flesh, by contrast, has been improved—given the opportunity of immortality—by being joined with the Word (*ad nobiliora, Psych.* 81). The poet recalls *Luke* 1:34[38] and *John* 1:14[39] (*et verbum caro factum est*) in this section of the poem. The theological positioning is concisely expressed in an apophatic flourish at *Psych.* 82–84:

> Ille manet quod semper erat, quod non erat esse
> incipiens; nos quod fuimus iam non sumus, aucti
> nascendo in melius. Mihi contulit et sibi mansit.
> He remains what he always was, though begins to be what he was
> not; but we are no longer what we were, now that we are raised at
> our birth into a better condition. He has given to me, yet still
> remained for himself.

Thus, the Word—i.e., Christ—always remains what it was, though commencing to be what it was not, and humans were not what they are now. This language constitutes an apophatic challenge in which the godhead and human beings are defined in paradoxical and enigmatic terms.[40] The important, positive meaning that Prudentius gleans from this apophatic formulation, which is common in patristic discourse, is that human flesh and souls have fundamentally changed because of God taking on human form—while the godhead remains the same. This change in humans is explained not in ordinary thinking and speaking, but in historical terms through the typology of Judith/Mary and, in conceptual terms, through the typology of Judith/*Pudicitia*. The defeat of *Libido* by *Pudicitia* and the Judith story, a complex typological allegory, helps define the change in human flesh by portraying the purity acquired from chastity. In this section of the poem, this typlogical nexus does not explain the nature of the divine as much as it clarifies the manner in which a soul acquires the purity necessary for communion with the godhead through Christ as intermediary. The quality of the soul, chastity, is the necessary ingredient for the acquisition of purity in both body and soul. Therefore, knowledge of the soul, a particular aspect of the apophatic challenge in the *Praefatio* and *Psych.* 82–84, is taken up in *Psych.* 56–108.

Judith and *Pudicitia*

If we examine more closely Prudentius' representation of the failed seduction and decapitation story as well as Judith's character, we expose significant features of the typologies associated with chastity and Judith. Although Prudentius usually does not hesitate to sensationalize his material with graphic descriptions of death and violence, in this adaptation of the *Judith* passage, he is restrained. The only grisly parallel to the Old Testament passage is the severing of the head of Holofernes. Prudentius excludes the description of Holofernes' headless trunk rolling off his bed and the part of the narrative in which Judith places the head in a bag of food to bring to the Assyrian leaders. He keeps the focus on the characteristics of the soul, which are necessary for one to preserve one's chastity and therefore make one ready to receive Christ. Second, in the *Psychomachia* Judith does not hesitate to carry out the deed, whereas in the biblical version, she constantly seeks strength from God, without which she does not seem able to accomplish the action. At *Judith* 14:1–5, the matriarch is portrayed as a leader who gives orders and even predicts the outcome of the battle between the Jews and the Assyrians. She gains a personal power and authority *after* she kills Holofernes, whereas Prudentius characterizes her as a confident leader before and during the slaying of the Assyrian. These differences expose the characteristics emphasized in the typology between Judith and *Pudicitia*. Perhaps in deference to the epic genre the poet portrays the sure, confident, and heroic Judith. Prudentius typologically projects this part of Judith's biblical identity on to *Pudicitia* herself, who commands, leads, and gains total victory.

Pudicita's Sword and the Purity of the Soul

Judith's connection with Mary logically leads to the topics of the ontological nature of Christ, his relationship to the Father, and the status of human flesh (*Psych.* 76–86). *Pudicitia,* as she addresses the dying *Libido,* accuses her of corrupting human souls (*furiarum maxima, Psych.* 96). After the immaculate birth of Christ, there appears to be no role left for lust in human affairs (. . . *ullum / fas tibi iam superest?, Psych.* 70–71). In typical apologetic fashion, Prudentius explains the status of Christ whose birth and relationship to humans and the father flows from lustless origins. When *Pudicitia* finishes her speech, she cleans her bloody sword in the Jordan River and places it by a divine spring in a Christian temple, as it is inappropriate to keep it sheathed (*Psych.* 98–108). In addition to the allegorical reference to Christian baptism and purification, these ten lines allegorically refer to the chaste (body) and pure soul, which has become a reality with the birth of Christ. With the death of lust indicated typologically in the story of Judith, and in the death of lust's personification, Christians can become cleansed and preserved for the communion with their divine creator "so that cleansed bodies may be saved by their king" (*ut purgata suo serventur corpora regi, Psych.* 97).[41]

The sword, described in *Psych.* 98–108, is a metaphor for the journey of the body and soul. It has been cleansed through baptism (*abolens baptismate labem, Psych.* 103), spared the corrupting practice of sex (*nec iam contenta piatum / condere vaginae gladium, Psych.* 104–105), dedicated to the Christian church (*catholico in templo divini fontis ad aram / consecrate, Psych.* 107–108), and given eternal life (*aeterna splendens ubi luce coruscet, Psych.* 108). These elements of an individual soul's journey are allegorically indicated by the sword and are expressed throughout *Pudicitia*'s speech to *Libido.* In addition, the soul's journey is implicit in the exegesis of Judith's story, expressed as two typologies between her and contemporary human beings and her and Mary (*Psych.* 67–68, 71–73, 85–86, 89–90, and 97). In these passages, the reader understands that the point of biblical typologies and exegeses is knowledge concerning the nature and fate of the human body and soul. Thus, the story of Judith triggers a series of exegeses concerning the soul and, necessarily, concerning the nature of the godhead; for instance, the journey of the body and soul, and the fleshlessness of the Son. The allegory of the sword is the climax of this sequence, repeating symbolically what has already been stated in the explicit exegetical and typological passages littered throughout *Pudicitia*'s speech. Furthermore, at the level of personification allegory, the figures of *Pudicitia* and *Libido* instantiate the message that the presence of the quality of chastity in the soul excludes its opposite quality, lust. Only through the chastity of one's soul is one ready to receive the gift of immortality from God through Christ. The interpretation of the sword passage rests on the recognition that the typological discourse associated with Judith assumes a series of exegeses of biblical texts. Having understood this, the reader acquires knowledge.[42]

The progression of thought in the section of the *Psychomachia* beginning with the story of Judith and ending with the allegory of *Pudicitia*'s sword follows the path laid out in the introduction of this chapter. The Judith typology and the subsequent allegory of the Christian body and soul represent a response to an apophatic conundrum posed at *Psych.* 78–84 that attempts to explicate the ontological nature of Christ. That discussion is an exegesis of several New Testament texts and constitutes a response to the "unknowability" of God's relationship to the soul. The Judith/Mary typology represents the thrust of the response and leads to the allegory of the sword, which itself is a distilled exegesis of the concepts of chastity and purity found in the Judith story. In this way, the text of the *Psychomachia* poses the epistemological problem of the godhead and the soul and solves it by directly interpreting biblical texts and furnishing biblical typologies whose exegetical meaning is a quality of the soul, chastity. And, to reiterate, the reader must have the ability to discern the typologies and their allegorical meaning, an accomplishment requiring faith that Christ is who the New Testament says he is, and requiring the reasoning capacity to see the significance of the typological pairs Judith/Mary and Judith/*Pudicitia*. Allegory's burden of communication is both on the author and the reader.

The exegesis assumed in the pairing of Judith and Mary constitutes the power of typologies to "make" history. This analysis emphasizes the idea that the conceptual content of the typological relationships forms the exegeses of scriptural events. The preconceived relationship between the two juxtaposed events produces an interpretation of the events themselves. Exegesis in its very definition contains an ideological presumption, here summed up by a Christian doctrinal idea. Prudentius regularly engages in typological exegesis of New and Old Testament stories. The story of Judith (*Psych.* 58–75), who preserved her virginity by killing King Holofernes, prefigures Mary's chastity and consequently the Incarnation of Christ. Chastity is the concept that connects these two events, and Christ as the messiah and savior furnishes the ideological presumption. Both the connecting concept and the ideological component are necessary for the relationship between Judith and Mary to be historically and exegetically significant. The exegetical quality of the *Psychomachia* is comprehensive and contributes to a consumptive biblical history. An exegesis is the inspiration for a given typology and simultaneously the final message of a given typology.

The Reader as Old Testament Hero

Following the battle of *Pudicitia* and *Libido*, we encounter a series of battles that make use of three Old Testament figures: Job, Adam, and David. Job is mentioned in the *Patientia* (*Long Sufering*)—*Ira* (*Anger*) battle (*Psych.* 163), Adam and David in the *Mens Humilis* (*Lowliness*)—*Superbia* (*Pride*) battle (*Psych.* 226 and 290–91), and David when *Spes* (*Pride*) takes over from *Mens Humilis*. In each case, the biblical figures exhibit Prudentius' flexible and varied use of typology; in particular, a common thread that connects the three Old Testament heroes is that each figure and the elements of their stories that the *Psychomachia* recalls represent qualities of the soul that are central to the struggle within the soul. As with the character of Abraham in the *Praefatio*, these qualities are typologically projected on to the personifications in the text and on to the reader at a tropological level. The allegorical effect is an expression of the inner ethical state of the individual in perpetual conflict. Because there is an association between the Old Testament figures and the personified qualities that battle within the soul, the reader becomes typologically linked to the Old Testament heroes because, like Adam, Job, and David, he is faced with choices between virtuous qualities of the soul and vice-like ones. This typological connection underscores the poem's epic ambitions by recasting the epic hero not as a figure better than the reader but as the reader himself whose potential is actualized through the free choice of virtuous qualities. Prudentius' use of Adam, Job, and David puts him in the camp of the Alexandrine-influenced Christian fathers, Clement, the Cappadocians, and Ambrose, all of whom directed their exegesis of such stories and passages toward the explication of the inner life.[43]

At *Psych.* 162–71 Prudentius grants a significant number of verses to the figure of Job, who is portrayed as having accompanied *Patientia* throughout her battle with *Ira*.

> Haec effata secat medias inpune cohortes
> egregio comitata viro; nam proximus Iob
> haeserat invictae dura inter bella magistrae

fronte severus adhuc et multo funere anhelus,
sed iam clausa truci subridens ulcera vultu
perque cicatricum numerum sudata recensens
milia pugnarum, sua praemia, dedecus hostis.

So saying, she makes her way unharmed through the middle of the
battalions, escorted by a noble man; for Job had clung close to the
side of his invincible mistress throughout the hard battle, up to this
point serious in demeanor and panting from much slaughter, but now
with a smile on his stern face as he thought of his healed sores and by
the number of his scars, recounted his thousands of hard-won fights,
his own glory and his enemy's dishonor.

Prudentius focuses on *Job* 42, which recounts the protagonist's restoration.
The poet dartingly refers to *Job* 2:7–8, where Job becomes a leper (*ulcera*,
Psych. 166) and appears to be working from *Job* 42:12ff. when he says that Job's
winnings are permanent (*Psych.* 169–71). The poet has added Job's physical
participation in the battle against *Ira*'s squadrons, many of whom he kills
(*Psych.* 164–65), further emphasized by language not present in the biblical
text but referring to its stories (the notions of *millia pugnarum* and *dedecus
hostis, Psych.* 167–68). In this passage, Job serves to introduce the reader to an
important function of typology in the *Psychomachia*—namely, the biblical
character typologically corresponds to the personification[44] and to living human beings in the form of the reader.[45] As an Old Testament figure, Job
contributes to the historical importance of the soul's inner struggle and he is
the human symbol of suffering which Christ will come to be. Although not
explicitly mentioned, an association between Job and Christ surely is implied,
especially because the next two Old Testament figures, whom Prudentius includes, have clear connections with the New Testament savior.[46]

Prudentius exploits the figure of Adam to show the dark side of human
character. *Psych.* 226, "the venerable Adam clothed himself with skins" (*pel-
litosque habitus sumpsit venerabilis Adam*), is a clear reference to *Gen.* 3:21.[47]
The action of *Gen.* 3:21 takes place after God discovers that Adam and Eve have
eaten the apple of knowledge and sentences them to a life of hardship. So that
the man and the woman do not eat the fruit of immortal life, God expels them
from Eden to the east and guards the tree with a flaming, whirling sword. In
her retelling of this part of the Fall, *Superbia* leaves out the wife and mentions
only Adam putting on the skins. At *Psych.* 227 *Superbia* describes Adam as

nudus adhuc, which is a reference to *Gen.* 2:25, where both Adam and Eve are described as nude (*ambo nudi*) just prior to the appearence of the serpent. The difference between a nude and a clothed Adam exegetically translates to before and after the Fall, paradise and the world of suffering, immortality and mortality.[48]

In addition, unlike *Gen.* 3:21, Prudentius plays on an ambiguity present in *habitus,* which can either mean "dress" or "nature" (the nature of human beings).[49] Adam has "put on" the trappings of mortality and the world, thereby crucially altering his inner nature. The poet has taken the *Genesis* passage and given it both a literal—putting on skins as clothes—and an allegorical—putting on a (different) nature after the Fall—level. From the point of view of the poet-narrator, *Superbia* is the source of these events in Old Testament history—it invaded the two people, forever changing them. The pagan imagery that surrounds the character of *Superbia,* and the particular prominence of the concept in Roman historiography and literature, points to a nonbiblical set of sources for the idea of *Superbia.*

Prudentius' deployment of *habitus,* including the specific diction placed in *Superbia*'s mouth, produces an allegorical meaning from the biblical text. The exegetical tradition of the Fall typified by Irenaeus emphasizes the birth of disobedience,[50] which perhaps can be viewed as a form of pride. Yet it is clear that Prudentius adds a layer to the exegesis by imposing *Superbia* on the story. Prudentius cleverly shows us precisely at what point in the biblical historical narrative *Superbia* herself entered (*adhuc*). The poet puts into the mouth of a vice an exegesis of a central biblical story, a version of the story that focuses on Adam, thus implying the typology of Adam and Christ.[51] The Adam/Christ typology, which was well trodden in the patristic tradition, is frought with similarities and differences between the two figures.[52] Prudentius here concentrates on the difference of pride, which is exhibited in the actions of Adam (and Eve) but certainly not in the figure of Christ—and, we hope, not in us as we live our lives. At the level of human beings, the typology's meaning suggests the choice humans must make between virtue and vice. Thus, it is significant that such a difference between the two figures of Adam and Christ would be expressed by the personification of that difference, *Superbia.* Through a precise control over the deployment of his typologies, Prudentius projects onto the reader the tropological meaning of the typology in order to foreground to the reader his moral choice.

The use of the figure David and certain aspects of his defeat of Goliath put in relief the typological relationship between this Old Testament figure, *Spes*, and the reader and assert Prudentius' main exegetical strategy of interpreting biblical stories and passages, and employing typologies, according to an allegory of the soul's inner, ethical nature.[53]

> Vidimus horrendum membris animisque Golian   (*Psych*. 291–304)
> invalida cecidisse manu; puerilis in illum
> dextera funali torsit stridore lapillum
> traiectamque cavo penetravit vulnere frontem.
> Ille minax rigidus iactans truculentus amarus,
> dum tumet indomitum, dum formidabile fervet,
> dum sese ostentat, clipeo dum territat auras,
> expertus pueri quid possent ludicra parvi
> subcubuit teneris bellator turbidus annis.
> Me tunc ille puer virtutis pube secutus
> florentes animos sursum in mea regna tetendit,
> servatur quia certa mihi domus omnipotentis
> sub pedibus domini meque ad sublime vocantem
> victores caesa culparum labe capessunt.
> We have seen that Goliath, terrible as he was in body and valor,
> fell by a weak hand; a boy's right hand shot at him a little stone
> whizzing from his sling, and pierced a hole deep in his forehead.
> He, for all his stark menace, his boasting and his bitter speech,
> in the midst of his ungoverned pride and fearful raging, as he
> vaunted himself, terrorizing the winds with his shield, found what
> a little boy's toy can do, and wild man of war as he was, fell
> to a boy of tender years. That day the boy, in the bloom of valor,
> followed me; as his spirit bloomed he lifted it up towards my kingdom;
> because for me a safe home is kept at the feet of the all powerful
> Lord and men reach after me when I call them on high the victors
> who have cut down the sins that stain them.

The three terms of the typology (David/*Spes*/humans) are explicitly mentioned in sequence in *Spes*' speech at *Psych*. 285–304.[54] The virtue makes the claim that, like *Superbia*, who was present at and caused the Fall (*Psych*. 222–23), she was by David's side as he strode into the single combat (*Me tunc ille puer virtutis pube secutus, Psych*. 300).[55] Binary opposites of qualities of the soul are present to humans at all times and must be chosen by them. Moreover, personified inner qualities of the soul such as *Spes* and *Superbia* function as prime movers in individuals and as the source and associative feature of Prudentian typology. The reason the reader connects himself and David is precisely because of the quality of hope that the reader infers that he and David share. In this case, in the *Psychomachia*, *Spes*' words stimulate the reader to draw a correspondence between the reader and David when she calls human beings victors (like David) who eliminate sin (*Psych.* 303–304). Note as well the word order of *Psych.* 300, *Me tunc ille puer virtutis* . . . , in which *Spes* clearly marks the correspondence and hierarchy between her and David ("me-then-that-boy") and effects the transition from David to her in the subsequent lines.

The speech of *Spes* contains further typological correspondences that reflect an allegorical and complex picture of the soul. For instance, a dark and negative typology is implied with the mention of Goliath (*Psych.* 291) along with all of his menacing, non-Christian qualities (*Psych.* 295–96). The implied typology between Goliath/vice/human beings (the reader) presents the alternative we humans have as we navigate this world of good and evil. We must make a choice to complete either the typology of David/*Spes* or Goliath/vice. Prudentius furnishes two possible typological triplets, the actuality of which depends on the reader's choice. The sequence of David/*Spes*/reader also is preceded by two more terms, "God" and "Christ," that contribute to an overall typological scheme in *Spes*' speech. The first line of her speech presents God as the ultimate conqueror of vice (*frangit deus omne superbum, Psych.* 285). At *Psych.* 289 Christ is introduced via reference to *Matth.* 23:12 as saying that the proud shall fall and the lowly shall ascend. Immediately thereafter Prudentius launches into the David and Goliath story. Thus, the passage expresses a clear typological hierarchy from God to Christ, to *Spes* (or vice), to David (or Goliath), and, finally, to the reader.

In the exegetical tradition, Christ is closely associated with David, but not in the same way as with Adam. In this case, as well as in other passages of his corpus, Prudentius makes the point that David is part of a regal, generational succession that leads to Christ.[56] More important, this typological progression in the speech of *Spes* leads to a picture of the human soul that contains a life and death struggle between virtue and vice for the survival of the soul itself. The final term in the typological sequence is human beings (the reader), and each reader has a choice of which typological triplet she will complete. When David kills Goliath, his soul blooms and is lifted up (*florentes animos sursum in mea regna tetendit, Psych.* 301). For Prudentius, the best allegorical meaning of typology is the healthy condition of the soul, which in following virtue makes correct choices and acquires immortal life. Prudentius' treatment of Adam, Job, and David explicitly invites the reader to associate himself to these heroes and the virtues they struggle to achieve. The participation of the reader works on two levels: she must have the ability to recognize the typological connections between the biblical characters, abstract qualities, and her own soul; having made this recognition, she must choose between virtue and vice.

The association between the Old Testament figures and personified qualities of the soul recalls the epic motif of gods as foils to epic heroes. Prudentius has capitalized on the motif to assert a significant exegetical point about the presence of vice and virtue in the history of human beings. Also, because the reader becomes linked to the Old Testament figures, the pagan epic motif undergoes another mutation in which a common human being can identify with larger than life figures, such as the heroes of the Old Testament. A reader would never associate his life and destiny with Vergil's Aeneas or Lucan's Caesar. The treatment of Job, Adam, and David suggests the idea of reader as hero.

In the central section of the *Psychomachia,* Prudentius continues to interpret biblical texts in terms of typologies in order to connect biblical history to the inner life of the human soul. As I have mentioned in chapter 2, *Avaritia*'s speech (*Psych.* 530–50) typologically connects Judas Iscariot and Achar with greed, and with the reader. Prudentius gathers together an eclectic combination of biblical allusions at *Psych.* 530–50. The poet is able to reveal *Avaritia*'s sinister role, not only in New and Old Testament history but also in the soul of the human being. It is at this point of the *Psychomachia* that the reader understands that, although she has been neutralized for the moment, *Avaritia* is in some way immortal. Her eternal existence guarantees that human beings will have to make ethical choices.

Having mentioned the main details of Achar's story, *Avaritia,* a vice, asserts a fundamental rule of Christian typology: *Quis placet exemplum generis, placeat quoque forma / exitii; sit poena eadem. quibus et genus unum est* (*Psych.* 545–46).[57] There is a clear choice implied in the verb *placere;* humans (the reader) have the capability to choose the figures and stories on which to model their own lives. And it is also clear that whatever story one adopts, one necessarily takes on its ending, for better or worse. The existence of choice is indirectly shown in the mention of Christ who is a descendent of Achar (*Psych.* 543–44). The possibility of Achar as Christ's *exemplum* is implied and of course, to be rejected. By taking on the foibles of humanity, as his association with Achar implies, however, Christ himself becomes a member of a group that has the capability to choose greed with the worst results, or choose a different way. Once again, through an explicit and an implied typology—Greed/Judas or Achar/reader and Greed/Achar or Christ/reader, Prudentius portrays a vital capacity of the soul, the ethical will to choose. The *Psychomachia* creates a tension within human reality by first imposing greed on the whole of human history and then furnishing the opposing notion that Christ overcame *Avaritia* to redeem all humanity. The typological implication is that we must follow his difficult example through our sense of free will.

The Exodus as Typological Allegory: *Psychomachia*

Psych. 606–64 forms a discrete interpretive unit because of its use of a set of biblical texts, *Matth.* 6:26–34,[58] *Rev.* 3:21,[59] and *Ex.* 15:1–21.[60] The poet has crafted these passages and his narrative battle between the virtues and the vices into an effective allegorical response to the apophatic challenge. The dominant story is the exodus from Egypt in which the Jews escape through the parted Red Sea and undertake a journey through the desert where miracles furnish food and water. The basic elements of Prudentius' treatment are as follows. The Israelites sing as they look back at the sea (*cecinit . . . victor . . . / . . . Istrahel, Psych.* 650–51). When they complete the crossing, a mountain of water devours the dark-skinned Egyptians (*Psych.* 653–55). Fish return, the sand is covered with water, and the sea is normal once again. Prudentius portrays the Israelites beating timbrels (*Pulsavit . . . modulantia tympana, Psych.* 658) and exclaims that this event must be told to future generations—it is worthy of epic (*dei celebrans mirum ac memorabile saeclis / omnipotentis opus, Psych.* 659–60). We again encounter the image of the banks of water, rising up, parted, and suspended on either side (*Psych.* 661–62). Finally, Prudentius again mentions the virtues singing (*resultant / mystica dulcimodis virtutum carmina psalmis, Psych.* 663–64), and thus brings the story full circle and achieves connection between the Old Testament story and the virtues' triumph.

Both the *Matthew* and *Revelation* passages function as supporting texts that embellish the themes established by the *Exodus* episode. In the *Revelation* passage, Christ is beckoning the listener to "conquer" death and sin as Christ did and, looking forward to the building of the temple at the end of the poem, to occupy the throne of his father with him. *Psych.* 615–20 used the *Matthew* texts from the Sermon on the Mount, as well as discussions with his apostles, to imply the common typology between Moses and Christ. The *Psycho-machia*'s use of these biblical passages results in a sophisticated set of typological correspondences that are bound together by the moment and immediate aftermath of the victory of virtue over vice. Four events covering the past, present, and future are typologically related: the triumph of the Jews over the Egyptians, the triumph of Christ over death and a sinful human world, the victory of virtue's army over vice's army, and, finally, an individual soul's victory over vice and death. The final event in this series represents a preferred possibility in the present/future for the reader of the *Psychomachia*. Thus, the typological sequence ends in an allegory of the healthy soul which, lacking any distraction of vice, is prepared to live forever with its creator.

The *Psychomachia* develops the typological connections between these passages into an exegesis firmly grounded in the allegorical patristic tradition of Philo and Gregory of Nyssa. According to this tradition, the journey in the desert and the escape through the Red Sea is an allegorical type for the soul's own journey to knowledge. The soul's progress is defined according to the passions it casts off along the way. The swallowing up of the Egyptians by the Red Sea is the casting off of passions, in which the Egyptians symbolically occupy this role.[61] The *Psychomachia* adopts and refreshes this allegory by substituting the personified vices for the passions, which are eliminated from the world of the virtuous soul. The manna in the desert, as well as the water at Marah and at the rock of Horeb (*Ex.* 16, 15:23–25, 17:1–6), are interpreted by this particular branch of patristic tradition as nourishment for the soul— Prudentius' *luciferum caelesti dogmate pastum* (*Psych.* 625)—which requires the knowledge of God to survive rather than literal food and drink.[62]

For Prudentius, the fundamental purpose of the soul is the acquiring of divine knowledge through the adoption of steadfast faith in the Christian godhead. In this section of the poem, the acquisition of knowledge is constructed as a descent into hell, as figured in the *Exodus* story, a heroic trial that, once completed, guarantees the soul's immortality. The use of biblical typologies and the Vergilian underworld imagery at *Psych.* 606–64 is a response to the apophatic dilemma concerning the soul and the godhead. As I have argued in chapter 1, through his use of *Aeneid* 6 in the *Psychomachia*, Prudentius exploits Vergil's diction in order to depict the soul's characteristics and relationship to the godhead.

The Exodus as Typological Allegory:
Cathemerinon 5 and the *Psychomachia*

If we compare the two other passages in Prudentius' works which allude to the Red Sea part of the *Exodus* story (*Cath.* 5.31–137, and *TH* 12), we can conclude that the carefully wrought typological relationship between Moses, Christ, the reader and the resulting allegorical effect of the journey of the soul are supported by aspects of the Vergilian vision of the soul's fate. The typology associated with the exodus, and with a Vergilian model of the underworld catalyze an allegorical interpretation of the Exodus tale that expresses clearly and concretely an indescribable and immaterial entity, the soul.

Prudentius treats aspects of the *Exodus* story and the life of Moses in a multitude of places.[63] *Psych.* 606–64 and *Cath.* 5.31–137, however, allude to the pursuit of the Egyptians and Red Sea miracle. Prudentius would have known from New Testament, patristic, and catechetical sources regarding the exodus episode the typological and allegorical interpretations concerning the soul and godhead.[64] *Cath.* 5.31–137 exhibits the range of typological reference that Prudentius assumes in the *Psychomachia*. The first fifty lines of the passage read like a biblical paraphrase of *Ex.* 15–17. It becomes clear, however, that the main interest of this hymn for the lighting of the lamp is to elaborate an explicit typology between Moses and Christ.[65] Moses is mentioned at *Cath.* 5.31, after which a series of narrative details from *Exodus* commences, and Christ is invoked at *Cath.* 5.81–82, after which the poet credits Christ with the defeat of Egypt, the parting and closing of the Red Sea, the miraculous appearance of the waters of Marah and from the rock at Horeb, and the manna that suddenly descends upon the Jews in the desert. From mentioning the miracles of food and water in the story, Prudentius transitions to the soul itself: *cuius subsidio nos quoque vescimur / pascentes dapibus pectora mysticis* ("by his support we are also fed, nurturing our hearts with mystic feasts"; *Cath.* 5.107–108). The poet is attempting to use his assertion of Christ's nonphysical omnipresence throughout the Old Testament story as a bridge to the world of the immaterial. As seen in the *Praefatio* to the *Psychomachia*, Christ is the agent of the immaterial God and the mediator for the immaterial human soul. Thus, the literal food and water of Exodus is transformed into spiritual food through the typology of Moses/Christ and perhaps implies the Eucharist.

The Alexandrian patristic allegorical exegesis of the journey of the soul is paralleled here, though Prudentius' activation of the interpretation, the typology of Moses/Christ, appears abruptly without a securely established background context, such as the *Psychomachia*'s fabulistic world of the virtues and vices. Rather, *Cath.* 5.113–36 provides this world as a kind of appendix to the typology (*illic, Cath.* 5.113). After the details of the typology are asserted, the desert suddenly becomes a paradise of beautiful streams, meadows, and flowers where blessed souls (*felices animae, Cath.* 5.121) sing like the Jews who escaped the Egyptians through the Red Sea. Prudentius mentions hell, where, in a Christian variation on the pagan underworld, sinful souls on the day of Christ's birth receive relief from their suffering. Finally, at *Cath.* 5.137, Prudentius leaves this "heaven" and effects a transition to a scene at a Christian church on any given Sunday where this hymn will be performed—*nos . . . trahimus.*

Cath. 5.113–36, reads like a Vergilian description of the underworld in which the land of the blessed and accursed occupy equal poetic space. Literary criticism has often accounted for such Vergilian eruptions as instances of the clash between the pagan and developing Christian poetic tradition; however, this Latin epic scene is no mere pastiche. Rather, as I have argued in chapter 1 regarding the *Psychomachia*'s extensive use of *Aeneid* 6, Prudentius' poetry visually conceives of the afterlife in Vergilian imagistic terms. Prudentius has responded to the apophatic dilemma of the afterlife—we just do not know how to conceive of it—by integrating the Vergilian sensual version into Christian tradition. The presence of such vivid epic material juxtaposed to the *Exodus* story, however, may run even deeper. The *Cathemerinon* 5 passage and the *Psychomachia* understand the escape through the parting of the Red Sea as a descent into Hell, which the Jews—and, by a typological connection, Christian souls—must pass through in order to defeat death.

On the Christian side there is a clear precedent for such a reading of *Exodus* 15. Syriac literary tradition reads the episode in just this way,[66] but it would seem that the impetus for such a reading in this passage of *Cathemerinon* 5 would come from Greco-Roman epic tradition whose heroes often underwent the trial of descending to and emerging from hell. The *Avaritia* section of the *Psychomachia* is constructed along the lines of the Vergilian underworld and is followed by the descent of the Jews into the Red Sea, where they cast off the Eyptians (their vices). The extended passage in *Cath.* 5 puts the two scenes together once again. The Vergilian description of heaven in *Cath.* 5 and the *Psychomachia*'s dependence on Aeneas' descent of *Aeneid* 6 point to an underlying exegesis of *Ex.* 14:21–17:13 as a descent to hell, a supreme trial, to defeat death as Christ did when he rose from the dead.[67] The Vergilian coloring of the

Exodus story enables Prudentius to imply another typology related directly to the death and rebirth of Christ. The descent into and emergence from the Red Sea prefigures Christ (and the reader's soul) resurrected.

A series of transitions in this section of the *Cathemerinon* (*Cath.* 5.31–137) implies a typological scheme that becomes more integrated in the *Psychomachia*. Prudentius first focuses on the figure of Moses, whose escape from the Egyptians the poet elaborates in detail. He then concentrates on Christ as the prime mover behind the events that Moses performed to the visible eye. At *Cath.* 5. 105–107, the poet interjects a reference to human beings (*patribus* and *nos quoque vescimur*) whose understanding of the *Exodus* story and Christ's role in it provide the occasion to discuss literal and spiritual food. Next the poet moves from human beings to human souls and then to the place souls spend eternity, heaven. Finally, the poet signals that the sequence, which has the Exodus as its unifying thematic principle, has ended by returning to parishioners who sing the hymn. Thus, the sequence of subjects moves from Moses to Christ, to humans in general, to human souls, to paradise, and comes to rest with a human congregation in a church of the late fourth century.

With this sequence we can see the signs of Prudentius' flexible typology, which is fully deployed in the *Psychomachia*. The typological pairs of Moses/Christ, Christ/human, Christ/virtue, Jews in *Exodus*/Christian souls, and desert/heaven receive different emphases; for example, Moses/Christ is most explicit and desert/heaven is implied. The most important observation to be made from this analysis is that Prudentius understands the *Exodus* story as a rich source of typologies, which directly and indirectly lead to Christ and his role in saving the human soul.

This direct progression from a series of typologies to the allegorical effect of a Christian soul's journey places the treatment of *Matth.* 6:29–34, *Rev.* 3:21, and *Ex.* 15–17 at *Psych.* 606–64 in the allegorical tradition of Philo and Gregory of Nyssa. Ambrose, Jerome, and Tertullian prefer to use these scriptural passages in the context of marriage, divorce, and widowhood, whereas Prudentius, Gregory of Nazienzus, and Gregory of Nyssa see these passages as part of a project that illuminates the very structure and nature of the soul. They accomplish this by isolating particular qualities of the soul from the biblical texts. In the *Psychomachia*, the personifications and their actions stand for qualities of the soul. Therefore, when Prudentius compares personifications to characters in *Ex.* 15:21, he is interpreting this biblical passage as an allegory of the soul. The characters and events of the *Exodus* story represent the qualities and behavior of the human soul, and this is exactly how the Cappadocian Fathers read the Exodus episode and *Matth.* 6:29–34.

Regarding the uses of *Matth.* 6:29–34 and 10:10 by Prudentius and the Fathers, we can draw similar conclusions. In *Operatio*'s speech to the virtues after the death of *Avaritia* (*Psych.* 606–28), Prudentius implies a pair of typologies and asserts exegeses of passages from *Matthew* 6 and 10 to focus the reader's attention on the nature of the soul. The *Matthew* passages are taken from the Sermon on the Mount, in which Jesus is preaching to the people. Prudentius typologically suggests a parallel between *Operatio* addressing the virtues (and all human beings/the reader) and Christ delivering his sermon to the people—and in addition, Moses bringing the Law to the Israelites. Moreover, *Operatio* alludes to Christ's exhortations to his disciples (*Matth.* 10:10), the future priests of his religion, which in turn recalls the typological reference at *Psych.* 498 to priests as parts of the soul's army.[68] These typological correspondences between the apostles and the soul's priests (also implied are preachers of the Gospel) and between Christ, Moses, and the personification *Operatio* are integral to the allegorical effect of the soul's journey from human to immortal through divine connection.

Prudentius' exegeses of the *Matthew* and *Revelation* passages support this dynamic exegesis of the Exodus episode. The former reinforces the Moses/Christ typology because of Christ's Sermon on the Mount as the Christian antitype of Moses' receiving and dissemination of the Ten Commandments. What is more, the qualities of the soul isolated in the *Matthew* texts fit well with those of the narrative in *Psych.* 606–64. The focus of *Rev.* 3:21 on "conquering" colors the exegesis of *Exodus* 15–17 as a story of a people, an individual, and a soul conquering sin and death. It is this interpretation of *Exodus* 15–17 that Prudentius highlights as the triumph of the Jews after the collapse of the Red Sea onto the Egyptians.

The Vergilian picture of the underworld and a hero's successful emergence from it also color Prudentius' exegesis of the *Exodus* story. *Cath.* 5 and the general scheme of the *Psychomachia* allude to *Aeneid* 6's vivid picture of hell in order to aid in the description of the soul's condition. The soul must undergo a trial before it can emerge with the proper qualities for the necessary knowledge, which furnishes eternal life. This poetic maneuvering serves to create a clear and concrete explanation of the soul's ideal fate and its relation to God. The allegorical journey of the soul figured from the *Exodus* story, supported by *Matth.* 6:29–34 and *Rev.* 3:21, and the details of a Vergilian underworld landscape form an answer to the apophatic dilemma. *Psych.* 606–64 is an integrated response to this challenge first set out in the *Psychomachia*'s *Praefatio* and revisited in the second half of the poem.

The Temple and the Architecture of Typological Allegory

After the Virtues have won the battle and repelled the surprise ambush by *Discordia Heresis, Concordia* and *Fides* give speeches that sum up the ideal soul's condition. The speeches function as a preamble to the building of the temple, the final task of the poem (*Unum opus restat, Psych.* 804). *Fides* and *Concordia* build or, more accurately, "envision" the temple. These two virtues have ended up center stage because, on the one hand, faith marks the true way of knowledge—as the *Praefatio* and first battle between *Fides* and *Veterum Cultura Deorum* indicated, and, on the other hand, harmony as the banishment and destruction of vices represents the first and primary task of a soul. The temple, the symbol of the New Jerusalem, is understood as the antitype of Solomon's temple.[69] In essence, the final 110 lines of the *Psychomachia* engages in a literal typology of the two temples. The allegorical representation of the soul and its relation to God is at its most manifest.[70] To this end Prudentius constructs a set of biblical allusions at *Psych.* 799–822 to set the scene for the building of the Christian temple. He deploys references from 1 *Kings* 5:3–5 / 1 *Chron.* 28:2–6 (*Psych.* 805),[71] 1 *Kings* 6:22 (*Psych.*810),[72] and 1 *Kings* 8:6 (*Psych.* 813).[73]

From this material and its surrounding contexts the poet includes four successive stages of the Old Testament story of Solomon building the temple for the ark of the covenant: (1) David receives a message from God to have Solomon build the temple (1 *Chron.* 28:2–6), (2) Solomon announces that he will build the temple by the authority of his father David and God (1 *Kings* 5:3–5)—these first two stages furnish the situation that is replicated in *Fides*' speech of the announcement and divine sanction of a new temple; (3) the actual details of the building of the temple (1 *Kings* 6:22)—this connects directly with *Psych.* 826ff.'s allusion to *Rev.* 21's detailed description of the new temple; and (4) the ritualistic dedication of the temple by priests (1 *Kings* 8:6 and *Psych.* 813–14), which climaxes in a sacrifice of oxen and sheep (1 *Kings* 8:62–63). Moreover, at 1 *Kings* 8:16–17 Solomon recalls and connects the post-Exodus period of the Jews to David's idea of building a temple. Continuity of the poet's typological vision is evidence by the fact that 1 *Kings* 8 contains the Old

Testament material used to construct the typologies analyzed in the central part of the *Psychomachia:* David/Christ and the Jewish exodus/virtues' victory over the vices.

The allegory of the temple as the soul begins from the typology of the temples of Solomon and *Revelation.*[74] This specific typological relationship between the Old and New Testaments is the reference point from which the poet develops his climactic picture of the soul. The outer chamber of the temple displays the twelve names of the apostles over as many gates (*Psych.* 838–39). These written names represent the Holy Spirit which encircles the *arcana recondita mentis* (*Psych.* 840–41). That is, the apostles and the Holy Spirit see the apophatically unseeable, the inner chamber of the soul occupied by *Sapientia.* The Holy Spirit, itself an apophatic phenomenon,[75] provides access to the qualities of the apophatic soul but can only do so through faith, which, as seen from the story of Abraham, must have its origin in the human side of the soul.

The Old and New Testaments provide the typological framework for the very structure of the new Christian temple, and allegorically, of the soul itself. A decoration contributed by *Fides,* via an allusion to *Matth.* 13:45–46 (*Psych.* 873),[76] crowns this inner chamber, signifying that *Fides* and *Sapientia* occupy the same space in the soul—a very important point for Prudentius. *Sapientia* of the *Psychomachia* is represented through the Old Testament text *Prov.* 9:1 (*Psych.* 868 and 875)[77] and is portrayed as a lawmaker and governing entity. Prudentius relates these biblical passages in an ingenious way. Unlike in *Prov.* 9:1, the poet does not have *Sapientia* actually build the house, but rather the house is built for her. *Fides* is instrumental in this project because, similar to the merchant in the *Matthew* passage, she sells all of her material possessions (*Psych.* 872–74) so that she may buy the pearl that will be the roof (*Psych.* 870) of *Sapientia*'s temple. Having established *Sapientia*'s sway over both city and soul with the aid of *Prov.* 9:1, faith's complementary and equal role in the temple of the soul is fixed through the use of *Matth.* 13:45–46. This virtue's contribution crowns the inner part of the temple, where Wisdom and the Holy Spirit reside. Faith and Wisdom, both emanations of Christ from the scepter, become partners in the management of the soul as implied in the *Praefatio.* Thus, the poet masterfully relates and deploys *Prov.* 9:1 and *Matth.* 13:45–46. Faith and Wisdom, necessary for the communion with and knowledge of God through the mediation of Christ, are the most crucial characteristics of the human soul, occupying the central space of the temple.

Christ installs the virtues as a jeweler places gems in a setting. This concretization envisions Christ as the primary cause of the temple itself (*Psych.* 912). Once he has performed this task, he remains as an overseer, the divine being who looks down on the functioning temple. Christ and the Father occupy the top of a metaphysical hierarchy, remaining separate from the soul, with *Sapientia* understood as typologically related to Christ. In the human soul, wisdom reigns and Christ oversees. This fits well with a theological point (chapter 2, note 85), which posits Christ as intervening from outside of human history and God completely separate from history. In addition, Christ's role as installer of virtues in the soul indicates his mediating role as an aid to the soul's development and the link in the typological chain of the poem from virtues to biblical characters to the reader's soul. The verb *texat* (*Psych.* 913) suggests that typology is an activity of Christ on behalf of the soul because Prudentius elsewhere uses the verb to capture typology's function of binding together the New and Old Testaments (e.g., *Cath.* 5.164).

This rich representation of the temple typology of Solomon's Temple and the temple of the Christian dispensation is developed by means of two typological lines of thought: first, the thematic connection between Christ as a sacrificial offering and peace as a sacrificial offering; and second, the connection between Aaron's and *Sapientia*'s scepters. My analysis of these typological connections demonstrate Prudentius' flexible use of typology that constructs an allegorical representation of the soul, first laid out in the *Praefatio* and achieved in full at the end of the poem. The soul must be in a state of peace to be ready for receiving Christ, whose presence emanates through *Sapientia*'s scepter. Remaining true to the logic of the *Psychomachia*, these typological ideas follow from the presence of the apophatic point of view in the latter third of the poem. The typologies create effects that function as an allegorical response to the apophatic challenge, which I have earlier summarized as the acquisition and expression of knowledge of the relationship between God and the soul.

The Apophatic Challenge Revisited

In the second half of the poem, the apophatic challenge manifests itself in less explicit ways than the typical language of negation in the *Praefatio*. For instance, a comparison of one passage from early in the poem and another from the latter third of the poem illustrates how the apophatic point of view remains a vital assumption in the *Psychomachia*'s discourse. The apophatic and theological language of *Psych.* 78–84, which *Pudicitia* blurts out, possesses a counterpart in the response of *Discordia* to the questions, which the virtues ask concerning her identity and background at *Psych.* 709–14. It will help to quote *Psych.* 78–84 again:

> Verbum quippe caro factum non destitit esse   (*Psych.* 78–84)
> quod fuerat, verbum, dum carnis glutinat usum,
> maiestate quidem non degenerante per usum
> carnis sed miseros ad nobiliora trahente.
> Ille manet quod semper erat, quod non erat esse
> incipiens; nos quod fuimus iam non sumus, aucti
> nascendo in melius.
>
> For the Word made flesh has not ceased what it was before,
> that is, the Word, by attaching to itself the experience of flesh;
> its majesty is not lowered by the experience of flesh, but raises
> wretched men to nobler things. He remains what he always was,
> though begins to be what he was not; but we are no longer what
> we were, now that we are raised at our birth into a better condition.

> "... Discordia dicor,   (*Psych.* 709–14)
> cognomento Heresis; deus est mihi discolor" inquit,
> "nunc minor aut maior, modo duplex et modo simplex;
> cum placet, aërius et de fantasmate visus;
> aut innata anima est, quotiens volo ludere numen.
> Praeceptor Belia mihi, domus et plaga mundus—"
>
> She says, "I am called Discord, and my other name is Heresy;
> god to me is variable, now lesser, now greater, now double,
> now single; when I please he is unsubstantial, a mere apparition,
> or again the soul within us, when I choose to ridicule his divinity.
> My teacher is Belial, my home and country is the world—"

We notice immediately that the first passage is an apophatic *tour de force*, replete with negations, vague indirect statements, and subordinate clauses; while the second passage, possessing no negations, predicates many qualities of God. *Psych.* 78 is a direct allusion to *John* 1:14 and the rest of the passage represents an exegetical interpretation. *Pudicitia* affirms nothing concerning the Word. The nearest affirmations are . . . *carnis glutinat usum* and . . . *quod non erat esse incipiens.* Although these phrases allude to the Word becoming flesh, they do not advance the referential meaning of *John* 1:14 at all—we still cannot conceive of the meaning of the Word as flesh. The only concrete affirmation of the passage is a description at *Psych.* 81 of the direction and goals toward which humans or souls are led by the Word (*ad nobiliora*). On the other hand, the second passage is readily affirmative, *deus est*, and gives a list of predicates that portray God as changing and changeable: *discolor, minor, maior, duplex, simplex,* and *innata animus. Discordia* ignores negative theological restrictions and, as a result, she spews heresy and nonsense about the godhead. It is no surprise then that her tongue is the first part of her body to be damaged (*Psych.* 718). Such pretentious and mistaken predications of God will not be tolerated. Knowledge of God does not begin with predicates of God but rather from an apophatic position that acknowledges the epistemological and empirical limitations of human beings.

Other hints of an apophatic point of view occur when the poet describes the soul with phrases such as *arcana recondita mentis* (secret recesses of the soul; *Psych.* 840), *latebrosa pericula* (hidden dangers; *Psych.* 891), and *in nebuloso pectore* (in our dark heart; *Psych.* 893). The first phrase certainly conjures up the apophatic and mysterious quality of the soul, but, unlike the first phrase, the latter two have a distinct moral tone originating in the typical model of darkness as evil and light as good.[78] A sense of unknowability also accompanies this light/dark language, however, since darkness, for instance, is associated with evil because it is impenetrable to the seeker of knowledge. These phrases near the end of the *Psychomachia,* along with *Discordia*'s inappropriate predications, provide solid evidence that the apophatic point of view explicitly established in the *Praefatio* and in the first 100 lines of the poem proper, has sustained its presence until the end of the poem. In addition, both the *Praefatio* and *Psych.* 755–915 assert the centrality of faith in the search for divine knowledge, though the latter section of the poem strongly asserts reason's role in the form of wisdom in comprehending the nature of the soul and its divine interaction. The final section of the *Psychomachia* reminds the reader of the apophatic challenge, how to describe the soul and God with words, a challenge Prudentius answers with a typological and, ultimately, allegorically rich temple. The reader has been brought full circle to the *Praefatio*'s established purpose: to pose the apophatic challenge and to respond with typologies that build on allegorical description of the soul, God, and their relationship.

The Response: Typological Offerings to God, Christ, and Peace

A typological line of thought that emerges in this section of the poem focuses on the concept of peace. Between *Psych.* 782 and 787, Prudentius refers to *Eph.* 4:26 and 5:2[79] and says that peace

> occasum lucis venia praecurrere gestit,   (*Psych.* 782–87)
> anxia ne stabilem linquat sol conscius iram.
> quisque litare deo mactatis vult holocaustis,
> offerat in primis pacem. Nulla hostia Christo
> dulcior, hoc solo sancta ad donaria vultum
> munere convertens liquido oblectatur odore.
> [peace] is eager to pardon before sunset, uneasy lest the conscious
> sun leave behind it an enduring anger. Whoever would worship God
> properly with whole burnt offerings, let him above all offer peace.
> No sacrifice is sweeter to Christ; this gift alone pleases him with a pure
> aroma when he turns his face toward the holy altar.

Eph. 5:2 portrays Christ as a sacrifice which Prudentius imitates with *hostia Christo*, but he alters the meaning by asserting that peace is being offered, *offerat in primis pacem*, and this is the sweetest sacrifice to Christ. The scene is one of old-fashioned pagan/Jewish sacrifice, indicated as well with *mactatis . . . holocaustis* (*Psych.* 784) and *liquido* (or *puro*) *odore* (*Psych.* 787). Prudentius succesfully relates typologically two notions in this passage: Christ as sacrifice and peace as sacrifice—a clear innovation on *Eph.* 5:2. The meaning of *hostia* has undergone a slight change from the biblical passage. At *Eph.* 5:2 Christ as sacrifice has the connotation of not merely an "offering" but a sacrifice in the sense of "scapegoat." That is, the Christian idea of Christ as sacrifice assumes the notion of Jesus dying for humans and their sins. But in the *Psychomachia* the situation is different in the case of peace. Peace should not be sacrificed as atonement for some human imperfection, but it should be continually offered on earth to placate Christ and the Father and demonstrate a soul's readiness to meet God.

Peace must remain part of the human world, both within the city and especially within the soul. Given this difference with *Eph.* 5.2, we can say that, typologically speaking, Christ prefigures peace, which in turn is applied to the soul. The language in the text further defines peace as a sacrifice to be offered up to God, as Christ was offered up. By association, the peaceful soul is figured as an offering to God in the form of the temple about to be constructed. Prudentius has led the reader through a typological progression, which posits Christ, peace in the city, and peace in the individual soul as sacrifices in the pagan and Jewish sense of the word. Each is offered up to appease God. The typological schema of Christ-as-sacrifice/peace-as-sacrifice has been integrated into the orthodox typology of the old and new temples. Peace becomes a quality of the soul because it becomes part of the temple/soul. Part of the text's preparation for the description of the temple is to explain allegorically the proper conditions (qualities), which must obtain in the community and the individual soul.

The Typology of the Sceptre and *Sapientia*'s Authority

At the end of the *Psychomachia*, the apophatic-laden typology between the scepters of Aaron and *Sapientia* (*Psych.* 878–87) functions in much the same way as the Christ/peace typology. Prudentius combines it with the temple typology to delineate *Sapientia*, a divine quality of the soul, and the role of Christ in the soul. *Psych.* 878–87 makes reference to *Num.* 17:8[80] and/or *Heb.* 9:4 (*Psych.* 884),[81] both of which discuss the staff of Aaron, which is not manmade and burgeons with life. Prudentius gives his version at *Psych.* 884–87:

> Huius forma fuit sceptri gestamen Aaron
> floriferum, sicco quod germina cortice trudens
> explicuit tenerum spe pubescente decorem
> inque novos subito tumuit virga arida fetus.
> This is the scepter that was prefigured by the flowering
> rod that Aaron carried, which, pushing buds out of its dry bark,
> unfolded a tender grace with burgeoning hope, and the parched
> twig suddenly swelled into new fruits.

Sapientia holds the uncrafted sceptre which originates directly from nature. Although it has no contact with the ground it possesses blooming flowers, including blood-red roses that intermingle with white lilies (*sanguine tinctis / intertexta rosis candentia lilia*, *Psych.* 881–82). This scepter is prefigured by Aaron's staff, which behaved in a similarly supernatural fashion. Prudentius' poetic language of thrusting (*trudens*), blooming (*floriferum*), swelling (*tumuit*), dryness and moisture (*arida, umor*), youth (*pubescente*), and life (*vivum, fetus*) is rich and lavish.

Whatever power the scepter possesses comes directly from God and is not part of human ways of understanding. Prudentius embellishes the mystery by remarking on the scepter's ability to flourish as if planted in the ground though it has no contact whatsoever with the earth (*Psych.* 880). This apophatic power of Aaron's scepter is typologically transferred to *Sapientia*'s scepter[82] so that clarity is brought to the otherwise opaque struggles within the soul. Prudentius accomplishes this by expanding the scepter's meaning from a purely apophatic vision. For example, *Sapientia*'s scepter is also a source of virtue (*Psych.* 886). This leads to an acknowledgement of Christ's role in human beings' attempt to understand the mysterious struggles within the soul: *Tu nos corporei latebrosa pericula operti / luctantisque animae voluisti agnoscere casus* ("You wanted us to learn the dangers that lurk unseen within the body, and the vicissitudes of our struggling soul," *Psych.* 891–92). Without the aid of Christ, whose power and message emanates from the scepter, humans cannot understand the nature of the ideal soul and its parts. The life and message of Christ defines concretely the function of *Sapientia*'s scepter.

The presence of *Sapientia* with her divine scepter is what remains for and within the human soul. Christ and the other parts of the Trinity emanate in the human soul through the scepter. For instance, Prudentius has already established the presence of the Holy Spirit as overseeing the inner chamber of the temple/soul where *Sapientia* wields her scepter, and the scepter emits the Holy Spirit's grace and the hope that Christ brings (*explicuit tenerum spe pubescente decorum, Psych.* 886).[83] The typology of Aaron's scepter and Wisdom's scepter unifies a series of terms in this section of the poem. Having begun with the Holy Spirit, which is represented by the apostles, we progress to *Sapientia* as lawgiver and king, to Christ as the same. Thus the typology of the scepter, which is instrumental to this allegorical vision of the soul, translates into the following, more abstract, sets of typological progressions: from the Holy Spirit to the apostles, and from Old Testament *Sapientia* to Christ and finally to *Sapientia* of the *Psychomachia*. The foundation for these typologies is Aaron's scepter, which "unfolds" or "expresses" (*explicuit, Psych.* 86) its "grace" in the form of the Christian message instantiated by the incarnation of Christ.

The end of the poem reminds the reader of all that has been accomplished allegorically through the use of biblical typologies.[84] The final lines are a distillation of this response to the difficult problem of divine knowledge. When the typological sequence finally reaches Christ at *Psych.* 889–90, Prudentius revisits the language of sacrifice (*meritosque sacramus honores ore pio*), reminding the reader of the typological relationship between Christ and peace.

The temple is finished (the soul perfected) and is now ready to be dedicated to Christ. First, in ring composition, Prudentius returns to Christ, with whom he began the poem and who facilitates the usurpation of the throne by *Sapientia* from *peccatum*. But the ring composition is slightly mitigated by the fact that the final words of the poem are about *Sapientia, Sapientia regnet* (*Psych.* 915). This may indicate Christ maintaining his status as a separate divine entity. I have already mentioned the separate but equal positions of faith and wisdom in the temple allegory, but, by the end of the poem, the association of *Sapientia* and Christ is apparent. Two forms of *regno* ("to rule") are used of Christ (the equal of God) and of *Sapientia* (. . . *Christus Deus . . . regnaverat* and *Sapientia, Psych.* 910, 912, and 915), showing that *Sapientia* and Christ both hold sway in the soul, though from different ontological positions.[85] It is *Sapientia* who rules in the last line of the poem and whose very existence in the soul depends on the soul's successful emergence from the trial of *Psychomachia*.

It is common in Christian thought to understand biblical typologies as inevitably leading to Christ. Hence, at the end of the *Psychomachia*, even though, as part of the godhead, the ontological status of Christ remains separate from the soul simultaneously as he contributes to the soul's ethical development, Christ is an activator of typologies, the mediator through whom the meaning of historical events and the actions of persons form an allegorical meaning. Christ's complex role defines the *Psychomachia*'s allegory of the soul and the soul's relation to God, originating from the apophatic point of view. The exploration of a specific typology, in this case from Aaron and the temple of the Old Testament to *Sapientia* and the new temple (soul) of the *Psychomachia*—mediated by Christ of the New Testament, as well as the acknowledgment of the presence of typological vocabulary, clarifies and elevates the position of the human soul by endowing it with palpable, divine credentials and connections. Language used to describe the temple (*gemmas, aurea templi / atria, texat, ornamenta*) and the abstract language of soul and virtue (*virtutum, peccatum, animae*) crash together in the last lines of the poem (*Psych.* 911–15). This juxtaposition confirms the material temple's representation of the immaterial soul and the presence of typology as instrumental to the recognition of this allegory (*texat*).[86]

Conclusion

The section of the *Psychomachia* in which the temple is built functions as the summation of the allegory of the soul and points to the major argument of the poem: that a soul must be without vice and at peace, possessing the ultimate virtues of wisdom and faith that originate in God's power as represented by the Holy Spirit through the mediation of Christ's life and message. This is the answer to the apophatic dilemma outlined throughout this chapter. Only in such a condition of knowledge and understanding is the soul ready to offer itself up to God as a candidate for immortal life.

Rather than understanding typology only as a historical instrument of meaning, biblical typologies in the *Psychomachia* produce nonhistorical, allegorical effects. This is because the *Psychomachia*'s allegory of the soul, constructed from historical typologies based on exegesis of biblical texts, is also an ethical, epistemological, and theological allegory. Properly understood, the poem's allegorical effects teach the soul of the reader that virtue leads to knowledge of God. As we saw in the preceding chapter, Prudentius uses typology to construct salvation history that enacts an ambitious poetic program. In this chapter, typology and exegesis combine in response to an apophatic theological stance to create the allegory of the poem. This combination of the historical and the ahistorical—the nonliteral, if you will—constitutes the essence of Prudentius' allegory and thus also his poetic originality.[87]

CHAPTER FOUR

Pagan Philosophy and the Making of Allegory

As his appropriation of Vergil's *Aeneid* shows, Prudentius does not hesitate to embrace his pagan literary heritage. In this chapter, I explore further the pagan intellectual inheritance that is present—and underrepresented in the scholarly literature—in Prudentius' poetry with a focus on the *Psychomachia*. By "pagan intellectual inheritance" I mean the rich philosophical tradition that Prudentius imbibed, directly or indirectly, beginning with Plato and extending to the Epicurean and neo-Platonic traditions.[1] The *Psychomachia* contains imagery and ideas from these intellectual traditions that help form the poem's allegorical effects. I have argued that particular biblical interpretations are crucial to the poem's typologies and therefore to the signifiers of the *Psychomachia*'s allegorical universe: the personifications, the battle narrative, and the temple. I argue that the poem's Christian reception of pagan philosophical content also contributes to the construction of these markers of allegory. This combination of pagan and Christian elements lie behind the *Psychomachia*'s sustained allegory. Any explanation of Prudentian allegory must include a reckoning of pagan philosophical ideas in his poetry.

Prudentius' relationship to pagan philosophy and its Christian reception is fertile terrain to examine his poetry and allegorical practice. In particular, Prudentius integrates several philosophical doctrines of the soul that contribute to the *Psychomachia*'s allegory of the soul. The following ideas, which have their roots in pagan philosophy, find expression in Prudentius' poetry: The Platonist metaphysical and political analogy of city and soul, the Platonist doctrine of ascent and descent of the soul, the Epicurean idea of the mortal soul, and, finally, the late-fourth-century idea of the soul as a Platonist reflection of the Trinity (Father, Son, and Holy Spirit). These philosophical resonances furnish a significant portion of the allegorical language of the *Psychomachia*. Specifically, they help to portray vices and virtues, which are typologically related to both historical figures and the reader.[2]

Prudentius and the Pagan Philosophical Past

The ties between late fourth-century Christian intellectuals in the West were close, and they were bound together in part by training in the pagan philosophical tradition and its transmission through Jewish and Christian apologetics. Ambrose, whose influence on Augustine is documented in the *Confessions* (6.3.3), knew well the works of Plotinus and philosophically aware writers such as Philo, Origen, the Cappadocians, Tertullian, and Cyprian.[3] In his exegetical works Ambrose borrows freely from Plotinus and Porphyry; in particular, the images of the soul's ascent to God and death as a release from prison.[4] Ambrose was tutored by Simplicianus, a bishop of Milan, who also was instrumental in the conversions of two main figures regarding the reception of Greek philosophy in the West, Augustine and Marius Victorinus.[5] Ambrose, Victorinus, Jerome, and Augustine followed the Origenist view that Greek philosophy must be subordinated to scripture through a form of allegorical interpretation.[6] As a result they did not enforce a strict separation between pagan philosophy and Christian theology in their own literary and exegetical practice, though sometimes from their severe rhetoric, a reader might conclude otherwise.[7] Rather, their approach to the pagan philosophical inheritance was to privilege scripture over the classics, to challenge the ancient philosophers and, in so doing, construct an alternative Christian *paideia*.[8]

Although Prudentius is not known to have had contact with this circle, he shares their intellectual background. His corpus represents a complex example of the pagan philosophical tradition filtered through his patristic forebears. He received a similar education and, from his doctrinal and apologetic poetry, we can detect a familiarity with patristic Platonist writings, as well as with other philosophical doctrines from pagan Latin poets. Prudentius has provocative things to say about pagan philosophers. Yet it will become clear that certain philosophical doctrines, especially those of Platonism, are determinative of Prudentius' allegorical program in the *Psychomachia*.

Apoth. 200–11 reflects the ambivalence that Prudentius had toward pagan philosophy. On the one hand, the poet pejoratively mentions Plato, the Cynics, and Aristotle (e.g., *deliramenta Platonis, Apoth.* 200). Their acceptance of pagan sacrifice is inscrutable (*Apoth.* 204–206), and their ravings are labyrinthine and meandering (*hos omnes . . . labyrinthus et error / circumflexus agat, Apoth.* 203–204). The writings of the great pagan philosophers distract humans from the meaning of scripture. On the other hand, according to Prudentius, these thinkers are rational and logical (*Apoth.* 206–207). The conclusion of their arguments—that there is one divine force in the universe (*numen in unum, Apoth.* 209)—is consistent with the Christian story. Prudentius even cites the classic pagan argument from design for the existence of God. Prudentius' treatment of the pagan philosophers parallels, for example, Augustine's ambivalent attitude toward Cicero's *Hortensius* (*Conf.* 3.4.7–3.6.10).

In the only other direct reference to Plato and his work, Prudentius refers to the common Platonic idea of the Philosopher king at *Symm.* 1.30–32 (*Rep.* 473c11–d3). He does so without vilification in order to argue that Theodosius is an example of a Platonic philosopher-king (*dux sapiens, Symm.* 1. 36).

> Nimirum pulchre quidam doctissimus: "Esset
> publica res" inquit "tunc fortunata satis, si
> vel reges saperent vel regnarent sapientes."
> To be sure a most learned man says finely,
> "the state would then be prosperous enough,
> if either kings were wise or wise men kings."

Even if Prudentius' praise of Theodosius amounts to no more than a panegyrical topos, the poet's intellectual assumptions inherited from the pagan philosophical tradition help to legitimize "truths" about theology and politics. In other passages, Prudentius may call pagan philosophers "followers of Hercules" (*Ham.* 402–403) and "bearded sophists" (2 *Sym.* 890–91), yet he deploys their ideas without hesitation to strengthen Christian ideology. In this way, his use of the pagan philosophical past parallels the use of late-fourth-century Christian intellectuals such as Ambrose, Jerome, Augustine, and Victorinus.

Julian's decree of 361/62, which barred Christians from teaching in the schools, compelled Christian intellectuals to carry on this seemingly duplicitous relationship with the pagan literary inheritance. From the last quarter of the fourth-century western churchmen and pagan aristocrats squared off in opposing rhetorical camps. As R. A. Markus puts it, "Jerome, Augustine, Prudentius, and Orosius belong to the world of Praetextatus, the Symmachi, and the Flaviani: a world in which the age-old tensions between paganism and Christianity were as sharply crystallized as they were never again to be."[9] This polarization, however, did not prevent Christian intellectuals from appropriating pagan ideas. Jerome, for example, made extensive, though unacknowledged, use of pagan philosophical texts.[10] Similarly, Augustine owes much to the prominent contemporary neo-Platonist Manlius Theodorus, though he never explicitly mentions him.[11]

Some scholars believe that Manlius Theodorus introduced Augustine to Platonic texts, which he could have read in Greek. For the Greekless reader, four translated Platonic dialogues were well known in Late Antiquity. Cicero is responsible for two of them: the *Protagoras* and the *Timaeus,* both mentioned by Jerome.[12] Apuleius' *Phaedo* is cited by Sidonius Apollinaris (c.423–c.480 AD).[13] Calcidius' rendering of the *Timaeus,* which became the most influential translation of the Middle Ages and, though incomplete, was accompanied by his commentary on the text.[14] If indeed he spent his time in Spain during the first half of the fourth century,[15] his output could be seen as evidence for the availability of Plato in the original in Spain in the first half of the fourth century. This is because it is likely that Calcidius read Plato in Greek.[16] In addition, several strong examples of doctrinal and linguistic parallels have been discovered between Calcidius and Porphyry, especially Porphyry's *Sententia.*[17]

Caution is best regarding questions of transmission and influence, but in the past few decades scholars have been able to improve our understanding of the spread and influence of Platonist texts and ideas. R. Klibansky and S. Gersh, for instance, have distinguished between the indirect and the direct traditions of Platonism.[18] The former consists of Latin and Greek writers (available in translation) of late antiquity who were read extensively in the Middle Ages. In the work of these writers, Platonist doctrine undergoes modification according to each author's religious and philosophical assumptions; examples include the traditional list of Latin church fathers (Tertullian, Lactantius, Ambrose, Augustine). The direct tradition is defined as earlier translations of Platonist dialogues such as those of Cicero, Apuleius, and Calcidius.[19] Indeed, it is difficult to keep separate the influence each one of these authors had on fourth-century Christian writers. It is necessary to have a complete understanding of the points of thought and language at which these sources would most likely be used. There are two clear examples of this concept. Augustine employs Platonist terminology and ideas concerning the Incarnation. He also cites various Platonic and neo-Platonic texts and authors to show that their theories are insufficient concerning the knowledge needed to know God.[20]

Pierre Hadot, in agreement with Courcelle, has referred to Porphyry (c.232–c.303 AD) as the major figure of neo-Platonism in the fourth-century West.[21] For this conclusion, scholars rely primarily on Augustine, who, during his time in Milan (386–391 AD), came into close contact with neo-Platonic philosophy through Manlius Theodorus[22] and the *platonicorum libri*,[23] Latin translations of Greek Platonist texts. Much has been written concerning the nature and contents of these books.[24] Augustine's demonstrated knowledge of Plotinus and Porphyry[25] and his statement that Marius Victorinus (281/291–post 362 AD) translated Platonist works,[26] however, makes it probable that these books were translations of a set of texts by Plotinus and Porphyry.[27] We may cautiously conclude that these Greek neo-Platonists owe their dissemination in the Latin West at this time to two of the most prominent Western neo-Platonists of the fourth century, Manlius Theodorus and Marius Victorinus. Victorinus appears to have been influenced primarily by Porphyry.[28] Of the seventy-seven titles we have of Porphyry's works, only thirteen (most of them minor and specialized) survive. This was not an accident of history but was caused by his work *Against the Christians* (κατὰ χριστιανῶν), which offended Christians to the extent that Constantine condemned his writings. It is no surprise that *Against the Christians* was not well known in the West in the second half of the fourth century. Jerome is one of the only writers who seems to have had an idea of its contents though not through direct reading, but rather through published Christian rebuttals of Porphyry's arguments.[29] Augustine knew the anti-Christian polemic by the time he wrote *De Consensu Evangilistarum,* which can be dated anywhere from 399–415.[30] Whatever the depth of Augustine and Jerome's knowledge of the anti-Christian side of Porphyry, it did not prevent both of these Christian bishops from being significantly influenced by him.[31] There can be no doubt that Porphyrian texts were indeed available in the Latin West; although Porphyry may have had an anti-Christian reputation, committed Christians of the late fourth century still permitted themselves to read him and employ his metaphysics and psychology, which had much in common with Christian belief. Prudentius was no exception. He was familiar with neo-Platonic, Platonist, and other pagan philosophical approaches through translations and handbooks. Further on, I show the crossover in the *Psychomachia* in which the Porphyrian imagery of ascent, for example, infuses the poem's narrative and description of the soul.[32]

City and Soul

At the end of the *Psychomachia*, Prudentius transforms the literal building of the temple within the walls of a city into an allegory of the soul.[33] Rather than focusing on the typical metaphor of the temple as the body that houses the soul, Prudentius develops the idea of the temple as the seat of monarchic authority in the soul (*Praef. Psych.* 799–822 and 823–87).[34] This monarchy within the soul comes to life through a manipulation of the metaphorical relationship between city and soul. By shifting deftly from the perspective of the city to that of the soul and back again, *Fides'* announcement of the building of the temple in the city of virtues (*Praef. Psych.* 814–15) becomes a metaphor of the temple as the soul, with *Sapientia,* the emanation of Christ, as king. In the last twenty-seven lines of the poem, the temple represents the nature of an individual soul and the political structure of a monarchy. *Psych.* 816–19 reflect this combination by indicating that peace (defined as a lack of vices) is a necessary—though insufficient—condition for a healthy soul and that the other necessary condition, the new temple inhabited by Christ, has become the allegory of the dominant governing entity of the human soul.

> Nam quid terrigenas ferro pepulisse falangas   (*Psych.* 816–19)
> culparum prodest, hominis si filius arce
> aetheris inlapsus purgati corporis urbem
> intret inornatam templi splendentis egenus?
> For what is the advantage to have driven out the earthborn
> phalanx of the sins, if the son of man, having descended from high
> heaven, enters the unadorned city of the cleansed body,
> and he is lacking a shining temple?

The phrase *purgati corporis urbem* ("the city of the cleansed body," *Psych.* 818) is an image of purity and cleansing (*sanguine . . . terso, Psych.* 809; and *toga candida, Psych.* 821). The meaning of the parallel phrase *purgata . . . corpora* of

Psych. 97 focuses on the cleansing of worldly sin from a person's body, an appropriate point of view that emphasizes the battle posture between the virtues and the vices. By broadening the phrase to mean the cleansing of a city, *Psych.* 818 triggers a version of the binary city and soul, which furnishes the dominant metaphor of the final hundred lines of the *Psychomachia*.

The phrase *purgati corporis urbem* explicitly links the city and soul into a mutually descriptive relationship; the city and the soul are to be adorned with a temple, its most important artifice, giving it a sense of order, purpose, and divine presence. In addition, when *Sapientia* is enthroned within the temple, she proceeds to establish government and laws to protect humankind.

> Hoc residet solio pollens Sapientia et omne   (*Psych.* 875–77)
> consilium regni celsa disponit ab aula
> tutandique hominis leges sub corde retractat.
> On this throne powerful Wisdom sits and
> from her high court she arranges every plan of
> her government and she considers again in
> her heart laws for protecting humankind.

This Platonist, civic language confirms the idea that the new temple stands for the rational governing center of the soul. Prudentius introduces the earthly notions of government and laws, which originate as worldly expressions of *Sapientia*. The city and citizen language, foregrounded in the allusions here to *Rev.* 21[35] and *Eph.* 2:18–22[36] and emphasized in much of patristic literature, is initially ignored by Prudentius. At *Psych.* 875–877, however, Prudentius explicitly establishes this level of meaning, confirming that the city/soul binary helps fix the allegorical meaning of the temple as the governing center of the human soul. In this way, the poem signals the transition to the new temple, the constituents of which express the nature and structure of a healthy human soul that is prepared to meet the godhead.

The city/soul binary is also implied in Prudentius' treatment of biblical texts and of their exegeses by previous Christian thinkers.[37] At *Psych.* 823–54 and essentially to the end of the poem, Prudentius mines *Rev.* 21 for the description of his poetic temple.[38] Although the allusion to *Eph.* 2:18–22 is not specific, several of the passage's fundamental themes are contained at *Psych.* 823–54: approaching the Father in one spirit, humans as citizens based upon the teachings of the apostles and prophets (cf. *Rev.* 21:14), Christ as cornerstone that connects all as parts of a temple, and the individual as a dwelling for God through the Holy Spirit. Paul makes the distinction between the temple as a holy place and the temple/body as a dwelling (1 *Cor.* 6:19) for God. Unlike Paul, Prudentius describes the Holy Spirit, which "goes around" or "surrounds" (*ambit, Psych.* 841) the hidden recesses of the mind (*mentis, Psych.* 840). These hidden places are where the vices can grow (*Psych.* 900–907). As a result, the Holy Spirit surrounding and being infused into the mind is the best way to fight against vices. In both the Pauline and Prudentian passages, the political dimension is emphasized and citizens and the building of a city are foregrounded; however, for Prudentius, the temple is a powerful allegory not for the body, as in Paul, but for the soul and its relationship to the divine. The prominence of *Sapientia,* combined with Platonist language of monarchy, civil discord, and bondage (e.g., *discordibus armis, inter vincla spiritibus pugnant, praesidio, regnaverat,* and *regent*; *Psych.* 902–15) gives a picture of the soul's relationship to God and thus constitutes a development of the city/soul analogy, a vital allegorical expression of the characteristics of the soul.[39]

Even with the biblical precedents, it is still possible to recognize the Platonist origins of the *Psychomachia*'s temple and its occupation by *Sapientia.* The allegorical character of the temple fits within the history of Platonist ideas from Plato's *Republic* to the Judeo-Christian response in Philo and the church fathers, examples of which include Ambrose, Jerome, and Augustine. The *Psychomachia*'s allegory of the soul, culminating with the establishment of the temple depends on the Platonist isomorphism of city and soul, which begins from a psychological isomorphism of internalization and externalization. The soul internalizes norms that enter it from its connections to the *polis,* and, in turn, the *polis* is a product of each soul's externalizations of norms.[40]

Two passages in the *Republic* show the essence of the relationship between city and soul. The first occurs at 435b1–2: "So the just man will not differ at all from the just city, so far as the character of justice is concerned, but will be like it."[41] The structure and character of the just, good, and harmonious soul, resembles the social arrangements of the just, good and harmonious city. Plato converts external virtue, traditional Greek morality, into an internal calm state of mind: "It seems then that real justice is not concerned with external behavior, but with what goes on inside, concerning the individual himself and his own affairs" (*Rep.* 443c9–d1).[42] Groups of souls constitute the source of a city's justice and injustice. The slippage in these two passages between the concepts of resemblance and membership appear in the *Psychomachia* as well.[43] Prudentius exploits the simultaneous presence of the virtues as individuals and the landscape of a single soul that the gates of city walls (*Psych.* 665–66) and the temple represent. Thus, the reader confronts a single soul, which is constructed in the likeness of a city, and simultaneously a city with many members—as implied by the army of virtues—that determine its character.[44] The expulsion of *Discordia-Heresis* from inside of the walls, indicated by the scattering of her body parts over land, sea, and air (*Psych.* 720–25), reinforces this double meaning by making both the soul and the city pure, peaceful, and just: ... *extincta est multo certamine saeva / barbaries, sanctae quae circumsaepserat urbis / indigenas* ("with a great struggle cruel savagery, which had surrounded the inhabitants of the holy city, has been wiped out," *Psych.* 752–54).

Both the early and late writings of Augustine employ the concept of Christian *imperium*, not as a phase of salvation history but rather as "a recognition of orthodox Catholic Christianity by Christians who hold office in the state, a summons to them to serve the church."[45] For Augustine, Roman power, in the form of state officeholders, is a tool to root out heresies.[46] In chapter 2 we saw that Prudentius understands Rome's political and military success as integral to the history of salvation. What is more, like Augustine, the poet connects earthly Rome's power with the task of eliminating heresies. In the *Psychomachia*, *Fides* and *Concordia* expel from the city *Discordia-Heresis* who blasphemes God as *discolor . . . / nunc minor, aut maior, modo duplex et modo simplex* (variable . . . now lesser, now greater, now double and now single; *Psych.* 710–11). The two virtues are associated with the monarchical and powerful state of Rome by their epithets (*Concordia princes*, *Psych.* 747; *regina Fides*, *Psych* 716), by their equal share of legal and political clout (*aequo iure potestas*), and by their status as law-givers: ... *quidnam / victores post bella vocet Concordia princeps, / quam velit atque Fides Virtutibus addere legem* (["They await] why *Concordia*, their leader, summons the victors after the war and what law *Fides* wants to put to the Virtues," *Psych.* 746–47). Prudentius appears to agree with Augustine that Roman Christian *imperium* should be an instrument that purifies Christian cities of heretical elements.

In addition, a specific aspect of the idea of the "two cities," which appears in the exegetical literature of the second-century writer Philo of Alexandria and reaches full expression in Augustine's *City of God*, animates the ideological architecture of the *Psychomachia*'s temple. Prudentius appears to share with Philo a version of the two cities motif. For both writers, two cities, one pure and other beset with vice, exist within the soul.[47] Prudentius' poetry does not fully reflect the Augustinian large scale and externalized conception of the two cities, one heavenly and the other earthly—with the latter to be rejected. He is writing at the high water mark of Roman Christian triumphalism and thus sees Rome as a direct reflection of the heavenly city, and understands the ideal soul as a reflection of heaven's order as well. Writing after the sack of Rome by Alaric, a period in which triumphalist Christianity, typified by Eusebius' writings (and Prudentius' work), was on the wane, Augustine distinguishes between Rome as the earthly city populated by those who live in the present moment according to the flesh and the heavenly city whose inhabitants, though pilgrims on earth, live according to Christian teachings and hope for the afterlife.

Philo figures the troubled soul as a city undergoing civil strife (*stasis*).[48] Philo begins with an antithesis between the cities of Cain and Abel-Seth. The contrasting themes include peace versus war, unity versus multiplicity, and goodness versus vice.[49] Elsewhere, he summarizes the two city idea: "The Lawgiver thinks that besides those cities which are built by men's hands upon the earth, of which the materials are stone and timber, there are others which men carry about established in their souls."[50] Philo takes his cue from the image and function of the demiurge in Plato's *Timaeus*. Philo's analogy between the mind of the architect and the earthly city, on the one hand, and the mind of God and the cosmic city, on the other, reflects a later Stoic view, also influenced by the *Timaeus*, of the divine craftsman as a supreme deity who oversees a rationally organized cosmos. But note that Philo glosses the metaphor of the divine craftsman with the image of the architect and king. Monarchy, which parallels the political structure of the Roman Empire, becomes Philo's dominant metaphor for the workings of the soul. A ruler exercising control over the city represents the dominance of the rational soul over the desires and weaknesses of the body.[51]

In the *Psychomachia*, Prudentius adopts this relationship between the Roman Empire and the soul. He employs Hellenistic language of monarchy and the language of the restored Republic under the Principate in order to illustrate the soul as a city (like Rome) in conflict between virtues and vices. Both *Sapientia* and Christ are monarchs within the soul: Christ is *rex* (*Psych.* 850) and *Sapientia* rules as king (*regent, Psych.* 915). The top virtues—*Concordia* and *Fides*—represent authority under the Principate of a restored Republic. *Concordia* is *Princeps* (*Psych.* 747) and both virtues, which possess qualities of Roman generals and magistrates (or even perhaps consuls: *aequo iure pot-*

estatis, Psych. 737–38) mount a platform (*tribunal, Psych.* 730 and 736) to speak to the rest of the virtues. The word *tribunal* refers to the platform that a Roman general mounted to address his troops; however, the word also refers to a platform for magistrates to pronounce judgments in a political context. *Tribunal* represents the poem's transition from the military to the political. Prudentius effects a transition from Roman military discourse of the battle between the virtues and the vices, which takes up the first two-thirds of the poem, to the image of an orderly, Roman, governing structure within the soul, indicated in the last third of the poem by the contemporary roles of *Fides* and *Concordia* as symbols of unity, the construction of the temple and the monarchic roles of *Sapientia* and Christ. The term *tribunal* and words referring to the restored Republic consequently coexist with monarchic language, thereby reflecting directly the contemporary political, and ideological, structure of the Christian Roman Empire, which in turn contributes to Prudentius' allegorical representation of the soul.

Prudentius develops the city/soul binary from merely an inherited Platonist idea to a trope that reflects contemporary Roman political ideology. The presence in the *Psychomachia* of both the language of monarchy and post-Republican politics merges into the idea of monarchy as Hellenistic kingship. Although patristic literature viewed the emperor as not subject to human law, it nevertheless does not consider him divine—this being the only major difference between a Roman, Christian emperor and a Hellenistic king. The pagan emperor Julian in the early 360s emphasized Platonic and Aristotelian political principles and not Hellenistic ideas of kingship. For Julian, a ruler's power comes from the people's consent, not from God, and the ruler himself is indeed subject to human law in the form of the laws of the Roman Senate.[52]

Yet, for most of the fourth century, the emperor was seen to be the only source of law on earth as it conformed to God's law. Ambrose expresses this idea and goes further, asserting that the empire is the guarantor of peace[53] and that one god implies both one empire and one emperor: "No Roman Christian of Ambrose's time could have failed to identify the interests of the church with those of the empire."[54] Monotheism's implications for human government culminated in theological monarchism. Gregory of Nazienzus reflects well the age's affinity for monarchy and dislike for Greek and Roman ideas of democratic and representative government: "We are not impressed by a crowd of gods, each ruling in his own way. For to me it is all the same to be ruled by none as to be ruled by many . . . strife means division, and division means

dissolution . . . so I find nothing divine in the government of many."[55] Prudentius favors one ruler as well, but he is loath to call that ruler on earth *rex*.
Divine beings such as Christ and *Sapientia* may be referred to as *rex* and enact
regal rule (*regent, Psych.* 915), but the emperor is styled "Father of the country,"
"director of the people and the senate," "leader of the military," "dictator," and
a host of other formal and informal titles.[56] The legacy of Rome's aversion to
the idea of a king may have still resonated with Prudentius who, through this
careful distinction, expresses the hierarchy between God, emperor, and Roman citizen.

Prudentius' *Psychomachia* is an allegory of the soul in which a monarch,
Christ/*Sapientia*, rules over evil desires and misguided ideas. Prudentius represents this allegory through a fourth-century version of Plato's city/soul analogy. By the fourth century, the "city" had become the Roman state, ruled over
by an emperor who, though not divine, maintained a close connection to the
divine as the siphon through which God's laws came to earth. The Roman state
was also an empire, which was synonymous with peace. The properly ordered
soul imitates the structure and success of the Roman state with its own emperor and its own borders to protect. Christ/*Sapientia* projects its direct connection to God through virtues that operate within a freely chosen struggle
against vices. *Concordia* results from a successful struggle and represents inner
peace. Prudentius' poetry reflects the development of Plato's analogy seen in
Philo and Ambrose's idea of the soul as a monarchy that must resolve the
constant threat of civil war. The last third of the *Psychomachia*, which includes
the expulsion of *Discordia-Heresis* and the transition from army camp to city
with a temple, shows how deeply "one-god one-ruler" was to define both the
personal and political identities of Christians for centuries to come, and this
concept, received by Prudentius via the twists and turns of a Christianized, and
Romanized, intellectual history, nourishes the *Psychomachia*'s allegory of the
soul as a city (and vice versa).

The Descent of the Soul and Other Platonist Doctrines

In the work of Plato, the ascent of the soul to the realm of ideal forms, to
perfect knowledge, and, finally, to divinity in the guise of the Good proved to
be an idea of extraordinary influence and reach. A major current in Augustine's work between the years 386–97 (just before the composition of the
Confessions) is the language of ascent.[57] From fifth-century Athens to fourth-

century Rome, and beyond, intellectuals adapted this concept to fit their views on the immortality and salvation of the soul. The idea of ascent and descent plays a significant role in the *Psychomachia*'s construction of its allegory of the soul. The portrayal of the soul's interior and its exterior relations with other souls is made vivid through the manipulation of the theme of ascent and descent. Moreover, the *Psychomachia* reflects the development of the Platonist idea in the third and fourth centuries and takes its place in the spectrum of neo-Platonic and Christian deployments of the theme. A survey of the theme in the *Psychomachia* not only confirms this intellectual historical argument but also illustrates the importance of pagan ideas in Prudentius' literary program.

The myth of the charioteer in Plato's *Phaedrus* and the structure of the soul implied by it, as well as the doctrine of the soul with its attendant imagery in the *Phaedo*, have resonances in the *Psychomachia*. Prudentius adapts the language of chains, bondage, and the soul as a prison, which have long histories beginning with the *Phaedo, Republic,* and *Cratylus*. The charioteer myth of the *Phaedrus* implies the soul's "fall" because of some kind of failing. The implication of the *Phaedo*'s view of the soul is that the soul should flee the body to be polluted as little as possible by the body.[58] We have already seen how Prudentius exploits the Platonic parallel between the structure of the city and the structure of the soul throughout the second half of the poem—especially from *Psych.* 606 (the beginning of *Operatio*'s speech) to the end. This results in a particular vision in the *Psychomachia* of the soul's nature and relationship to God. Platonist motifs of the soul's fall and bondage help to animate the *Psychomachia*'s vices as vivid, pagan typologies that represent wrong choices for the Christian soul.

In the *Phaedo* and the *Phaedrus,* Plato foregrounds the language of descent, one half of a binary pair (ascent of the soul/descent of the soul) that the neo-Platonists under Plotinus and Porphyry further developed. Neo-Platonists explained how the human soul comes to inhabit the human body through the concept of descent. In his metaphysics Plotinus creates a cosmic structure of four main hypostases in which the One and the Mind (Νοῦς) occupy the first and the second hypostases. The third hypostasis is the Soul, an image of the realm of the Mind; and the fourth, and in a sense "the lowest," hypostasis is matter (ὕλη).[59] For Plotinus descent is the first principle of coming to be.[60] The human soul descends from the third hypostasis, the world soul, which imposes form onto matter and thereby gives life to matter.[61]

Although in his own works Porphyry developed and modified Plotinus'

specific doctrines, he maintained the same basic general approach to hypostases while adding to the notion of the soul's descent.[62] Porphyry employs
several interesting images and motifs in his various descriptions of the soul's
descent. The fall happens because of the soul's weight.[63] The soul is sent away
naked by God on a sojourn abroad.[64] On its way down the soul grows wet,[65]
imbibes forgetfulness,[66] experiences estrangement, and is sleepy.[67] Porphyry
sees honey as the pleasure associated with descent.[68] Pleasure is part of the neo-
Platonist picture of descent because the soul is vulnerable to the desire for
corporeal form, the driving force of which is pleasure.[69] Poetry itself represents
the temptation of pleasure both in Plato and Plotinus. The neo-Platonist view
of poetry as symbolic rather than mimetic is a response to mimesis' association
of poetry with the pleasures of emotions.[70] Once making contact with the
human body,[71] the soul is diffused through a person's parts.[72] When the soul is
embodied, it exists in ignorance and is blinded, holds false opinions, is forget-
ful of the past and desires pleasure, and, finally, is under tyranny and enslaved
by the passions, which are compared to fetters and chains.[73]

Other pertinent metaphorical and doctrinal features of Porphyry's views on
the soul, its structure, and nature are to be found in his *Ad Marcellam*.[74] In this
work, he carefully creates a relationship between reason and its temple, the
soul.[75] The soul can be a dwelling place for evil as well.[76] Vices can prevent the
soul from reaching or seeing God, which can result in a battle within the soul.[77]
It is at this point that human choice and responsibility appear, because humans, not God, are the causes of evil.[78] Reason is food for the soul,[79] but hope,
as well, can nourish the soul.[80] Indirectly related to this language is Porphyry's
understanding of three types of law that humans must acknowledge: divine
law, the law of mortal nature, and the law of cities.[81] The law of cities for
Porphyry is an arbitrary agreement between citizens governing social interaction. The law of mortal nature sets the limits concerning the body's needs, and
divine law is rooted in the Stoic conception of divine law as the law of the
cosmos.[82] An underlying principle to the discussion of the soul's capability of
reaching God is the apophatic nature of both God and divine law: θεοῦ γὰρ
γνῶσις ποιεῖ βραχὺν λόγον ("knowledge of God renders a short account")
and μετὰ σιγῆς μὲν φθεγγόμενος τὴν ἀλήθειαν τὸν δὲ θεῖον αὐτῆς ἐξελίτ-
τειν ("uttering the truth in silence and exposing the divinity of it").[83] Regarding the soul's ascent, Porphyry calls the final goal σωτηρία τῆς ψυχῆς[84] or
expressed differently in Latin, *animae liberandae*.[85] Also Porphyry often uses
language such as "the way which leads to the gods" (τὴν μακαρίαν εἰς θεούς

ὁδόν; *Ad Marc.* 7.130–31).[86] Finally, through Platonic reminiscences, Porphyry uses tyrant/despot and slave language to stress the view that reason and not the passions must guide the soul.[87]

The Greek pagan tradition is the source of the language and imagery of the soul's incarceration: Plato's *Phaedo* 59e–60a, 62b, 67d; *Republic* 514a–17c; and *Cratylus* 400b9ff; as well as the neo-Platonist Porphyry adopted the motif (e.g., *Ad Marc.* 7.17–122). Socrates says at *Phaedo* 62b3: ὡς ἔν τινι φρουρᾷ ἐσμεν οἱ ἄνθρωποι καὶ οὐ δεῖ δὴ ἑαυτὸν ἐκ ταύτης λύειν οὐδ᾽ ἀποδιδράσκειν . . . ("that we men are in a prison and it is not necessary indeed to free oneself from it nor to run from it"). The body as prison and the notion of release appear in the *Republic*'s cave allegory and in the *Republic* and *Phaedo*'s language of incarceration and release: δεσμώτας (prisoners; *Rep.* 515a4); δεσμωτήριον (prison; *Rep.* 515b7); λύσιν τε καὶ ἴασιν τῶν δεσμῶν καὶ τῆς ἀφροσύνης . . . ("release and healing from bonds and folly"; *Rep.* 515c2); λύσις καὶ χωρισμὸς ψυχῆς ἀπὸ σώματος ("release and separation of the soul from the body"; *Phaedo* 67d4–5, repeated verbatim at 67d9–10).[88]

Release (λύσις) became a technical term in neo-Platonic philosophy.[89] The Latin translation, *liber* and its cognates, appear four times in the *Praefatio* to the *Psychomachia*,[90] much of which is occupied with describing the freeing of Lot from his bondage. Prudentius makes it clear that Lot's bondage is analogous to the bondage of the soul. Images of slavery, capture, and chains,[91] which occur in the main body of the poem, litter the preface: *cordis servientis* (the enslaved heart; line 14), *servire duris . . . vinculis* ("[Lot] enslaved under harch shackles"; line 21), *captis tenebant inpeditum copiis* ("[the enemy] hindered by captured abundance"; line 25), *ruptis expeditus nexibus* ("[Lot] released by the rupturing of his chains"; line 32), *quae capta foedae serviat libidini* ("[the body] which is captured and enslaved to disgusting desire"; line 54). This language has a long Platonist tradition.[92]

The *Praefatio* skillfully brings the reader into the interior realm of the soul[93] and its struggle to achieve a state that is "full of God," as Prudentius says of the great example of pity, Abraham (*plenus deo,* line 26; cf. *inplebit,* line 68). In this condition Abraham strikes down the enemy, who is described twice as weighed down by his material wealth garnered from military victories (*tenebant inpeditum,* line 25; and *graves,* line 27). On the one hand, there is Abraham, full of God, as a liberated and ascended soul should be, and, on the other, there is the enemy, weighed down and representing the state of a corrupted soul. This recalls Porphyry's description of the soul in its descent as heavy and weighed down (τὸ βαρὺ πνεῦμα; *Sent.* 29.18.14).[94] In the allegorical story of the *Praefatio*, Prudentius employs neo-Platonic imagery and language of the soul to establish the opposition within the soul, which will be played out in the rest of the poem.

Throughout the main body of the *Psychomachia*, ascent and descent are dominant metaphors. *Psych.* 86, *nosmet dona ad caelestia vexit* ("[God] has lifted us to heavenly gifts"), forms a the climax of ascent language and looks back to *Psych.* 68, *vera . . . virtus terrena in corpore fluxit* ("true power has flowed into an earthly body"), and 80–81, *maiestate . . . non degenerante . . . /. . . miseros ad nobiliora trahente* ("[The Word's] majesty is not lowered by the experience of the flesh, but raises wretched men to nobler things"). Platonist language of ascent/descent binds these lines together. Earlier, *Psych.* 68 had foregrounded *virtus* as the "force" or "power" that "flows" into the human body.[95] For Prudentius, this takes place in the context of salvation history as when Judith defeated Holofernes, indicating typologically the Incarnation. Prudentius combines salvation history's Incarnation and language of descent into a Christian Platonism representative of the age.[96] *Psych.* 80–81 provides the comparison between humans and the divine with respect to ascent/descent. The phrase *non degenerante* indicates that the Word "does not depart from its kind,"[97] when it undergoes incarnation. There is no directional language of ascent/descent used here. Just a line below, however, the directional language is used of human beings (*miseros*) whom the power of the Word "draws toward nobler things." This brings the reader to the parallel *ad caelestia vexit* of *Psych.* 86, which explicitly gathers the ascent/descent language of *Psych.* 68 and 80–81 to form a climax of the section full of the Platonist language of being.[98] Thus, *Psych.* 68–86 contains Platonist language of being and ascent/descent to create a complex Christian Platonist point of view.

Perhaps the most striking example of Platonist descent in the *Psychomachia* occurs at *Psych.* 190–93, which describes *Superbia*'s horse within an extended description of *Superbia*'s entrance into the battle:

> Nec minus instabili sonipes feritate *superbit*   (*Psych.* 190–93)
> inpatiens *madidis frenarier ora lupatis,*
> huc illuc *frendens obvertit terga negata*
> *libertate* fugae *pressis*que tumescit *habenis.*
> Her horse is no less insolent with its unpredictable savageness
> unable to bear her mouth bridled by the wet bit,

gnashing its teeth this way and that it turns its back,
since its liberty of flight has been denied, and swells with anger
because of the pressure of the reigns.

Parallels to *Psych.* 191 are found both in Ovid and in Horace.[99] The portrayal of the horse, however, is reminiscent of the evil stallion of Plato's *Phaedrus* 254e2–5:

ἔτι μᾶλλον τοῦ ὑβριστοῦ ἵππου ἐκ τῶν ὀδόντων
Βίᾳ ὀπίσω σπάσας τόν χαλινόν τήν τε κακηγόρον
γλῶτταν καὶ γνάθους καθήμαξεν. . .
[The charioteer], pulling the bit backward even more violently
than before from the teeth of the insolent horse covers
his scurrilous tongue and jaws with blood.

The two passages are similar in thought and language. Both horses are connected directly or indirectly to arrogance. Both the rider in the *Psychomachia* passage and the charioteer in the *Phaedrus* passage have to apply great pressure to the reins, which causes the bridle bit to draw blood in Plato and to expose moistened (with blood?) teeth in Prudentius.[100] Moreover, *Psych.* 305–309 has much in common with *Phaedrus* 256d3–e2:

Dixit et auratis praestringens *aëra pinnis*   (*Psych.* 305–309)
in caelum se virgo rapit. Mirantur euntem
virtutes *tollunt*que *animos* in vota *volentes*
ire simul, ni bella duces *terrena* retardent.
Confligunt vitiis seque *ad sua praemia* servant.
She [Hope] spoke, and striking the air with her golden wings
the maiden takes herself to heaven. The virtues marvel at her as
she goes, and they raise their spirits in longing, desiring to go
at the same time, if earthly wars were not delaying their leaders.
They join the battle with the vices and preserve themselves
for their own rewards.

ἄπτεροι μέν, ὡρμηκότες δὲ πτεροῦσθαι ἐκβαίνουσι τοῦ
σώματος, ὥστε οὐ σμικρὸν ἆθλον τῆς ἐρωτικῆς
μανίας φέρονται· εἰς γὰρ σκότον καὶ τὴν ὑπὸ γῆς
πορείαν οὐ νόμος ἐστὶν ἔτι ἐλθεῖν τοῖς κατηργμένοις
ἤδη τῆς ὑπουρανίου πορείας. . .   (Phaedrus 256d4–8)
When they [souls] depart from the body, they are

not winged, but their wings have begun to grow, so that the
madness of love brings no small reward; for it is the law that
those who have once begun their upward progress shall not
pass into darkness and the journey under the earth . . .

Prudentius depicts *Spes* as winged[101] and flying *in caelum* while the rest of the virtues want to go with her. Danuta Shanzer notices that aside from this passage, *Spes* is never winged in Latin literature but it is in Greek literature.[102] She goes on to argue that Prudentius is making a historical reference to the restoration of the Altar of (winged) Victory in the Senate house after 405, attested to by Claudian at *6 Cons. Hon.* 597. However this may be, Prudentius is primarily displaying his familiarity with the *Phaedrus* myth and certain neo-Platonic images of the soul.[103] The phrase *animos . . . volentes* stands for the desiderative part, which houses the desire to go immediately (*ire simul*) with winged *Spes* (*auratis pinnis*) but cannot be indulged since there are earthly battles (*bella . . . terrena*) to be fought in order to secure future rewards (*sua praemia*). The *Phaedrus* passage concerns the lover's soul within which Plato continues the charioteer metaphor. The main issue is desire, which, if properly understood, becomes transformed into a life of continence,[104] something with which Prudentius surely sympathized. The soul's structure aside, these two passages have much in common, including the language of "wings," "reward," "earthly/heavenly," "rising," and "journey."[105]

Taken in light of the two preceding passages, *Psych.* 253–54, . . . *rapidum . . . urget / cornipedem laxisque volat temeraria frenis* ("she spurs on her swift horse and flies wildly with loose reins"), which portrays the charioteer (*Superbia*) disastrously giving free rein to the reckless and impetuous horse, recalls Socrates' admonition that allowing too much slack in the reins of the desirous horse will cause the lover to fail in his approach to the beloved (*Phaedrus* 254a–e). *Psych.* 255 furthers this thought by associating *Superbia* and the horse with unrestrained desire (*hostem. . . . cupiens . . . / sternere* ["desiring to lay low her enemy]"), which results in a fall, *cadit in foveam praeceps* ("She falls headlong into a pit," *Psych.* 257), eventually causing the deaths of the horse (*eques*) and the charioteer (*equi*).[106] The fall of *Superbia* and her horses strikingly recalls the Platonic myth of the charioteer and evil horse. But, more important, the image of descent, Platonist in its origins, is an integral part of the portrayal of the vice, *Superbia*.

Three more instances of the wing and chariot language occur in the next section of the *Psychomachia: Psych.* 321, *curru invecta venusto* ("carried along in a magnificent chariot"), places another vice, *Luxuria*, in the role of charioteer; *Psych.* 323, *ales*, is an adjective modifying the noun "arrow"; and *Psych.* 334–35, *currum varia gemmarum luce micantem / mirantur* ("they wondered at the chariot gleaming with the darting light of gems"), presents a description of the chariot which will later be applied to the description of the temple. The soul's be-jeweled appearance is a reckless chariot that will later become a harmonious temple. Elements of the *Phaedrus* myth reappear as a superficial temptation that the virtues must resist—*Sobrietas* will later encourage such. *Psych.* 335–39 specifies further this temptation but includes the telling addition of heaviness (*ponderis, Psych.* 336)[107] regarding the gold and silver. In addition, *crepitantia* (rattling, crashing), which is said of the chariot as it rolls along, conjures up the reckless nature of the machine and its pilot. *Luxuria*, like *Superbia*, is heading for a fall. Again, not only are aspects of the Platonic myth applied to the portrayal of a vice, but the corrupt soul itself is implied through the Platonist language of falling and heaviness.

Spes is a concept with which Porphyry is familiar. To engage in ascent, the soul has to nourish its "good hopes" (ἐλπίσιν ἀγαθοῖς).[108] The phrase *futuri / spem boni* (*Psych.* 232–33) echoes the same idea. Prudentius recalls the pagan philosophical context further by portraying *Spes* as ascending. At *Psych.* 300–301, *me tunc ille puer . . . secutus . . . / . . . sursum in mea regna tetendit* ("at that time that boy followed me and he rose upwards to my kingdom"), *Spes* herself employs the language of ascent, which is clearly distinct from the allusion to *Matth.* 23:12 at *Psych.* 290 that those who are low shall be high and *vice versa*. At *Psych.* 302–304 she again uses language of ascent in the process of describing her home underneath the feet of the omnipotent God: *certa . . . domus . . . / . . . sub pedibus Domini . . . ad sublime . . . / . . . capessunt* ("there is a certain home at the feet of the Lord . . . they reach towards the highest region"). The pagan intellectual tradition, which portrays *Spes* in terms of ascent, is integral to Prudentius' understanding of the virtue.[109]

Virtues such as *Fides* and *Spes* live in a higher realm but one that subsists below that of God. Humans, who are represented by the constituents of the army of the virtues, occupy another level below the higher virtues and God. These beings reach up or stretch out toward the upper realms by destroying vices. This section of the poem establishes a metaphysical hierarchy for the universe: from God, to Virtue (Hope), and finally to mortal. If one includes the netherworld, which Prudentius mentions at *Psych.* 89–90, there are four distinct levels of reality that furnish the levels of ascent for the human soul. The metaphorical structure of ascent brings with it an exteriority in which the soul moves outside of the body toward an external goal. In this way the *Psycho-machia* maintains a simultaneously internal and external view of the soul.[110] In addition, the metaphor of ascent can be integrated into the typological schemes of the poem. The three-part typology assumes a connection between humans, virtue, and God.

The motif of the horses (with the addition of the chariot and charioteer) continues through the battle between *Luxuria* and *Sobrietas* (up to *Psych.* 416). This pagan philosophical motif is vital to the creation of these personifications. The *Phaedrus'* horse-and-charioteer picture of the impetuous and reckless soul descending and falling is developed further by Prudentius through neo-Platonic imagery and concepts. We have already touched upon a couple of these important images above. It is possible to expand upon what has already been said. When she enters the battle, *Luxuria* is drunk (*ebria, Psych.* 320). *Sobrietas,* in her speech of exhortation, describes *Luxuria*'s drunken feasts with language of wetness and alcohol: *conbibat infusum croceo religione nardum* (["a turban] with its yellow band to drink up the spikenard poured on"; *Psych.* 359); *inde ad nocturnas epulas ubi cantharus ingens / despuit effusi spumantia damna Falerni / in mensam cyathis stillantibus, uda ubi multo / fulcra mero veterique toreumata rore rigantur* ("and so to feasts that last into the night, where the huge tankard spills out wasted floods of foaming wine, while the ladles drip on the table, the couches are soaked with neat liquor," *Psych.* 367–70); *His vos inbutos dapibus iam crapula turpis / Luxuriae ad madidum rapit inportuna lupanar* ("and now after you have been steeped in these feasts savage drunken-ness takes you to the drunken brothel of *Luxuria*," *Psych.* 377–78). Neo-Platonic language of drunkenness contributes to the personification of this vice.

The feast provided by Christ (*his dapibus*) is set off against *Luxuria*'s "nightly feasts" (*nocturnas epulas, Psych.* 367). The opposition can be seen again in the *infusum nardum* (*Psych.* 359) of *Luxuria* and the *unguentum regale . . . et chrisma perenne* (*Psych.* 361) of Christ. *Luxuria* represents the side of neo-Platonism that images the soul as falling, drunk, wet, and descending. None of this language is applied to Christ's feasts. Instead, they are referred to as *angelicus cibus* ("food of the angels," *Psych.* 374), which is *de corpore Christi* (*Psych.* 376). At *Psych.* 380 *Sobrietas* repeats the neo-Platonic adjective of de-scent from *Psych.* 320, *ebria*.[111] At *Psych* 371, right in the midst of a flood of this language and at a climax of her speech, *Sobrietas,* nearly exasperated, asks whether the virtues have forgotten very important Old Testament stories, the memories of which would protect them from the influence of *Luxuria*: *excidit ergo animis eremi sitis* ("so has [the memory] of thirst in the desert fallen from your souls") and just ten lines later at *Psych.* 381: *State, precor, vestri memores, memores quoque Christi* ("stand! I pray, remember who you are and Christ as well!"). This appeal to memory (and thus the avoidance of forgetfulness) immediately follows some of the densest language of intoxication and wetness. As mentioned above, Porphyry commonly represents the descending soul as heavy with wetness and forgetfulness.

Luxuria's death at *Psych.* 407–53 combines Platonist images of the chariot-eer and wetness, for instance, *Fertur resupina reductis / nequiqam loris auriga comamque madentem / pulvere foedatur* ("the charioteer, leaning back, is carried along helplessly though she pulls back on the reigns and her dripping hair is soiled with dust"; *Psych.* 412–14). *Luxuria*'s hair is "soaked" just as neo-Platonic souls which are in the process of descent.[112] Prudentius carefully frames these lines with detailed description of the chariot. *Psych.* 408–409 and 414–16 together recall the last reference to the chariot at *Psych.* 336–39:

> et solido ex auro pretiosi ponderis axem
> defixis inhiant obtutibus et radiorum
> argento albentem seriem quam summa rotarum
> flexura electri pallentis continet orbe.
> And [they look longingly at] the axle of a costly weight
> made from solid gold, and the spokes of white silver, one
> after another, the rim of the wheel holding them in place
> with a circle of pale amber.

This description suggests the model of the concentric circles, which may represent hypostases. There is a progression of value from the axle of gold to the spokes of silver to the rim of amber. The center contains the most precious metal while the outer edge of the wheel consists of a more commonplace material.[113] In addition, the rim is described as "pale" (*pallentis*), which is also a possible expression of the neo-Platonic "pale emanation."[114] These same wheels at *Psych.* 414–16 "entangle" *Luxuria* as she "falls" under the axle: *tunc et vertigo rotarum / inplicat excussam dominam, nam prona sub axem / labitur et lacero tardat sufflamine currum* ("then the whirling of the wheels entangles their mistress who has been knocked out; for she falls forward under the axle and her mangled body is the brake that slows the chariot down"). The outer edge of the wheels "mangles" her and begins the process of destruction and dispersion of a vice's body, and therefore the bad soul it represents.

Psych. 432–46 re-describe *Luxuria*'s death as a scattering of the abstract qualities that define her. The expression *caede ducis dispersa . . . / nugatrix acies* ("at the slaughter of their leader her trifling followers scatter"; *Psych.* 432–33) commences an abstract dissipation, parallel to the physical mangling of *Luxuria*'s body, of those things which represent her essence: *Iocus, Petulantia, Amor, Pompa, Venustas, Discordia,* and *Voluptas.*[115] This movement from the physical to the abstract is an allegorical strategy of Prudentius in which the death of a vice represents the deconstruction of its fictional character into a set of abstract qualities that inhabit the soul. This scenario aids in the militaristic setting of the poem as a civil war, but also finishes off the section of the poem in which the poet vividly portrays the soul's descent into sinful materiality. Descent (and ascent) figured according to Platonist language and imagery is central to the poem's purpose of presenting to the reader positive and negative typological choices that employ both figures from history and ethical-spiritual concepts.

Descent and the Philosopher King

The end of the *Psychomachia* recalls the neo-Platonist-inspired idea that a philosopher-king's political activities should be understood as a descent from the intelligible realm of knowledge into the earthly realm of politics, a descent undertaken to facilitate a union of human souls on earth with God in heaven. For pagan Platonist thinkers of the third and early fourth centuries, the descent of the philosopher king to earthly political life for the sake of the salvation of his fellow citizens, as first suggested by Plato's myth of the cave, represents for the citizens the possibility of ascent to the Good, the One, or the divine intellect, which functions as the monarch of the universe.[116] D. J. O'Meara captures the essence of the neo-Platonist idea of politics as a descent into the world of appearances:

> Political life, a life in which a soul, as living in relation to the body, is confronted with problems of order both within itself and in relation to others, is thus a school of virtue, an extended version, so to speak, of the philosophical school, the ruler being consequently a kind of mentor or guide who brings order to political life, inspired by a privileged access to the divine.[117]

This neo-Platonic idea penetrates the end of the *Psychomachia,* on the one hand, through Prudentius' substitution of *Sapientia* and Christ as the highest entities of the soul on the other hand, through their political activities of ruling and teaching. They are the guides who descend to earth to save humans who require aid in their earthly struggle to vanquish desire and vice to attain virtue and a connection to the divine (Christ is described as *inlapsus, Psych.* 818). Prudentius here participates in what began with third-century Christian intellectuals—namely, "the displacement of culturally authoritative Greek texts by the Christian Bible." But a difference between Prudentius and other Christian intellectuals is that this "displacement" did not entail "a radical criticism of some of Platonism's most central affirmations."[118]

While Prudentius' allegory evokes the interior of the soul through its struggle against vice and union with *Sapientia* and Christ, it simultaneously operates at the level of exterior relations between individual souls. When the final third of the poem describes the securing of the city and the constructing of the temple, a slippage from inner to the outer world occurs because the personified virtues, as I have already argued, are portrayed as individuals under a monarchy tinged with characteristics of the Roman Principate. According to O'Meara, Iamblichus "links humanity to the divine through the virtue of wisdom. Wisdom derives from a transcendent divine intellect, and, inspired by this model, divinizes human institutions through the order she brings."[119] In the *Psychomachia,* Christ as the ruler of the cosmos sits above the city and temple while his regent, *Sapientia,* governs the virtues/citizens through the rule of law. In the neo-Platonic model, law is derived from reason, which originates in the divine intellect. Law comes down from on high as a transcendent good to be communicated to humans on earth through the wisdom of the monarch.

The Emperor Julian, whom Prudentius admired as an excellent earthly ruler,[120] adopted this neo-Platonic political model, seeing his mission as a descent to imperial rule following a vision of the gods.[121] What we might call the divinization of the political present at the end of the *Psychomachia* recalls this neo-Platonic thought world, which Julian attempted to put into practice in order to revive Hellenism. Julian's program of a return to state paganism caused anxiety and consternation that persisted in Christian politicians and intellectuals into the fifth century. Prudentius reveals this anxiety when he tells a story (*Apoth.* 449–502) in which Julian attends a sacrifice to the god Hecate (later in the passage named as Persephone).[122] It all goes wrong—the pagan priest cannot read the entrails—because of the presence of a Christian in Julian's retinue.[123] The sacrifice is ineffectual, the rest of Julian's retinue is converted to Christianity, and Julian himself scurries off alone, his pagan rites and gods shown to be feeble.[124] Immediately following the story Prudentius launches into a description of the new (Christian) temple made from the "Logos of the Lord" (*verbo domini, Apoth.* 524). This "everlasting" temple stands upon the ashes of pagan rites and replaces the temple of Solomon, which lies in ruins.

Prudentius' keen awareness of Julian's program to revive paganism through the restoration of temples, cults, altars, and sacrifices, and his admiration of the pagan emperor for his military achievements, law giving, learning, and oratorical skill are reflected in the *Psychomachia*'s transformation of the neo-Platonic story of the ruler's descent into the world. Julian preferred not to disturb ancient religions such as Judaism—in fact, he had decreed that the temple in Jerusalem be rebuilt (a point conveniently ignored by Prudentius)—but he did not tolerate religious innovations, especially Christianity. O'Meara has argued that Julian's program was a direct result of his neo-Platonic ideology, influenced by Iamblichus, who held that the practice of rituals and praying helped to elevate a soul fallen from the perfection of the divine intellect.[125] Julian also fostered local and regional pagan clergy whose involvement with the people in villages, towns, and cities, he believed, paralleled Platonic philosopher kings by imparting their wisdom to citizens.[126]

In the *Apotheosis*, Prudentius turns the tables on Julian's neo-Platonic political legacy by offering a vision of a new temple with Jesus as monarch, a temple that finds full allegorical form in the *Psychomachia* as both the hierarchical structure of the interior soul and of the exterior body politic. Both the Roman Christian soul and the Roman Christian Empire are evoked through Prudentius' allegorical city and temple, both of which spring from a neo-Platonic intellectual blueprint. Julian intrigued Prudentius because he envisioned a model of politics that Christians could appropriate by applying Jesus' story and identity as savior to the neo-Platonic idea of the leader who descends to earth.

Like Eusebius, the great church historian of the early fourth century, Prudentius substitutes Christian terms into a neo-Platonic metaphysical structure. Eusebius was the first to perform this intellectual maneuver by replacing the neo-Platonic first principle, the intelligible logos, which rules over the universe and its imperfect material component (earth), with the Christian god and logos.[127] Eusebius establishes a relationship of imitation between the actions of Constantine and the Christian logos.[128] Analogously, the *Psychomachia* employs a metaphor of the individual soul and Roman imperial state, which retains Christ as the logos that rules over the universe through the laws and administration of *Sapientia*. Whereas Prudentius still thinks in neo-Platonic terms of stages of ascent, later, the Augustine of the *City of God*, through the deployment of the "two-cities" concept, not only eliminates the neo-Platonic notion of the city and its political order as a stage of ascent to the divine but also discards the Christian substitution of a Christian Roman Empire as a means of ascent.[129] For Prudentius, by contrast, these ideas remain central to his poetic project.

The Vices as Epicurean Souls

The intensity and frequency of violence in the *Psychomachia* has elicited various explanations from critics, who, until recently, have pronounced judgments based more on an impulse of revulsion toward violence than on an analysis of the work's poetic conventions and philosophical program. Michael Roberts has helped to clarify the issue with regard to the *Peristephanon*, in which excessive and graphic images of violence dominate the poetic discourse.[130] He has pointed out that the torture and suffering of a martyr is directly proportional to the glory that martyr is to receive as a saint. In addition, Roberts uncovers a series of dialectics between "freedom and restraint," and "the liberation of the soul" and "the enchainment of the body."[131]

The *Psychomachia*, by contrast, presents different hermeneutic problems, for, unlike the violence displayed in the *Peristephanon*, it is not apparent what poetic purpose is served by having the virtues inflict extreme bodily harm on the vices. Scholars have handled the issue of violence in the *Psychomachia* in various ways. Some trace the violent language to the *Aeneid*.[132] Others see the violence done to the vices and by the virtues as a part of the epic battle conventions that Prudentius employed.[133] Macklin Smith views the use of the conventions as purposely ironic, for otherwise the hyperbole of such violent descriptions would appear absurd. Martha Malamud establishes language of dismemberment as a topos, since it also occurs in Claudian's *In Rufinum*.[134] C. S. Lewis, Gay Clifford, and Maurice Lavarenne are justifiably vexed by the apparent ethical contradiction of virtues wielding excessive force.[135] James Paxson has offered a fuller treatment and a noteworthy interpretation.[136] He studied four death scenes in which the destruction of the eyes, mouth, and throat are described: those of *Veterum Cultura Deorum* (*Psych.* 30–35), *Libido* (*Psych.* 49–52), *Luxuria* (*Psych.* 421–26), and *Discordia Heresis* (*Psych.* 715–18). These death scenes represent the symbolic dismantling of the trope of *prosopopoeia* (the technical term in Latin is *conformatio*, frequently translated as "personification"[137]). The root of the term suggests "putting on a face" or "dramatizing," and this is the relevant meaning in Prudentius. Thus, according to Paxson, to destroy the face by destroying its parts—i.e., the lips, teeth, and tongue (which produce speech), and the mouth and the eyes (which signify the face)—is to dismantle the trope, *prosopopoeia*.

This explanation is persuasive for the first three cases, and accounts for the stabbing of *Discordia*'s tongue. There is, however, more to say about *Discordia*'s dismemberment. Bodily dismemberment is the physical version of *Discordia*'s abstract meaning. Furthermore, Paxson's explanation does not apply to the other occurrences of graphic violence in the *Psychomachia*, such as *Ira*'s death at *Psych.* 153–54 and *Avaritia*'s death at 589–97. And there are many others.[138]

A more comprehensive approach is to understand these deaths according to the Epicurean doctrine of the dissipation of the soul. According to this doctrine, the soul is mortal and dies with the body. In fact, at the moment of death, the body, which is figured as a hollow vessel, gives up its cargo, the soul. The soul's atoms flit away, dispersed amongst the atoms of the universe. In the *Psychomachia*, the descriptions of the vices' deaths employ the language and imagery of this doctrine. Conversely, the impenetrability of the virtues, imaged as failed penetrations and breakings of vessels, represents the contrary of this doctrine, that is, Christian doctrine. Such an approach has two chief merits. First, it explains all cases of violence in the poem but, more important, it reveals again the poet's manipulation of philosophical doctrine in order to construct important features of the poem's personified virtues and vices that represent terms in typological pairs or triads.

In fact, the gore of the *Psychomachia* suggests a conscious awareness of the Epicurean doctrine of the soul's mortality. This awareness is seen in Prudentius' language of dissipation, penetration, and breaking, which can be traced within the tradition of Epicurean thought from Epicurus himself to the explications by Lucretius and Cicero. Significantly, this language is applied by Prudentius only to the souls of vices, which are mortal and pagan. As the vices, or souls replete with vices, die, so the virtues, or the souls constituted of virtues, live forever. Prudentius indicates this opposition by depicting the virtues as never being subject to or narrowly escaping penetration, dissipation, and breaking. Immortality and mortality are part of the very make-up of the poem's virtues and vices. In this way the poet uses an Epicurean idea to express the Christian conviction that with the birth of Christ, salvation history has reached the stage in which souls can attain eternal life.[139]

In the case of each death of a vice, with the possible exception of one, Prudentius applies language and ideas found in Epicurus himself as well as in Cicero's and Lucretius' version of Epicurean philosophy of mind.[140] I am referring specifically to the idea of the soul being diffused and dissipated at the moment of the body's destruction, a notion that prevails throughout the battle scenes in the *Psychomachia*. Piercing and penetration language, as well as a focus on the description of breathing and the organs of breathing, recall philosophical language and doctrine derived from the Epicurean view that the soul dissipates into nothing once the body is penetrated or destroyed.

In his extant writings, Epicurus[141] represents the death of the soul through the metaphor of the corporeal soul being contained within a vessel, the body, which once harmed or broken, dissipates into nothing: καὶ μὴν καὶ λυομένου τοῦ ὅλου ἀθροίσματος ἡ ψυχὴ διασπείρεται καὶ οὐκέτι ἔχει τὰς αὐτὰς δυνάμεις οὐδὲ κινεῖται, ὥστε οὐδ᾽ αἴσθησιν κέκτηται ("Moreover, when the whole aggregate disintegrates, the soul is dispersed and no longer has the same powers, or its motions, hence it does not possess sensation either," *Letter To Herodotus* 65);[142] and ὁ θάνατος οὐδὲν πρὸς ἡμᾶς· τὸ γὰρ διαλυθὲν ἀναισθητεῖ· τὸ δ᾽ ἀναισθητοῦν οὐδὲν πρὸς ἡμᾶς ("Death is nothing to us. For what has been dissolved has no sense-experience, and what has no sense-experience is nothing to us," *Principle Doctrines* 2).[143]

In Latin literature this doctrine is clearly stated, for example, by Cicero, who gives the Epicureans credit for the doctrine he mentions earlier in the *Tusculan Disputations* at 1.9.18: *alii* (sc. *censent*) *statim dissipari* . . . ("Others [the Epicureans] (think) that it (the soul) is immediately dissipated"; see also *Tusc.* 1.34.82). Moreover, Lucretius (*DRN* 3.425–44) presents the Epicurean argument for the soul's mortality—namely, that at death, the soul leaves its vessel and is scattered in the winds. The most striking example of a linguistic parallel between Prudentius and Lucretius is *spargat in auras* (*Psych.* 720) and *polluit auras* (*Psych.* 52) and *discedit in auras* (*DRN* 3. 436). Lucretius is even more specific:[144]

ergo dissolvi quoque convenit omnem animai   (*DRN* 3.455–58)
naturam, ceu fumus, in altas aeris auras,
quandoquidem gigni pariter pariterque videmus
crescere et, ut docui, simul aevo fessa fatisci.
Therefore, it is fitting that the whole nature of the soul
dissolves too, like smoke, into the high winds of the air,
since we see that it is born at the same time and grows at the
same time [as the body]; and, as I have instructed, that
simultaneously exhausted by age it becomes weak.

At *DRN* 3.456 we again encounter the line-ending *auras* imitated by Prudentius. Lucretius is at pains here to establish the interdependence of the body and the soul. Thus, whatever happens to the body directly impinges on the health and welfare of the soul. And this phenomenon establishes the mortality of the soul for Lucretius. Furthermore, if the soul were immortal, it would be impervious to any sort of harmful penetration. As Lucretius argues later:

Praeterea quaecumque manent aeterna necessest   (*DRN* 3.806–15)
aut, quia sunt solido cum corpore, respuere *ictus*
nec penetrare pati sibi quicquam quod queat artas
dissociare intus partis, ut materiai
corpora sunt quorum naturam ostendimus ante;
aut ideo durare aetatem posse per omnem,
plagarum quia sunt expertia, sicut inanest,
quod manet *intactum* neque ab *ictu* fungitur hilum;
aut etiam quia nulla loci sit copia circum,
quo quasi res possint *discedere dissolvique,*
Besides, all things that endure forever must either,
through having a solid body, repel impacts and allow
nothing to penetrate them which might separate their
tight-fitting parts from within, for example the particles
of matter whose nature we proved earlier; or be able to
endure through all time because they are free from blows,
like void, which remains untouched and is quite unaffected
by impact; or again because there is no place available
around them such that they might be able to
disperse and disintegrate,

Lucretius' language of penetration and of the rejection of blows is replicated at *Psych*. 672, 676–77 (*ictu . . . nec . . . / . . . sinerent penetrare*—the whole passage is quoted below). Lucretius presents twenty-eight separate arguments (3.417–829) in order to defend the Epicurean doctrine that the soul does not survive the death of the body.[145] The issue of the soul's mortality and immortality is framed by Lucretius, just as in the texts of Epicurus and Cicero, in a discourse which images the soul as possessing a solid body for protection (*DRN* 3.807, 820). This vessel experiences either an impact or a penetration from the outside (*DRN* 3. 809, 814) and, finally, disperses at the moment of physical destruction (*DRN* 3. 815, 817–18). For the Epicureans this is the model that unequivocally proves the mortality of the soul. The *Psychomachia* shows awareness of this model and manipulates it to associate its features with virtues and vices. The soul is incorporeal, immortal, and invulnerable when it possesses virtues and accepts Christ and his teachings. On the other hand, the soul is mortal and vulnerable when vices dominate it and it rejects Christian dogma.

The text of the *Psychomachia* portrays the vices as subject to language of violent penetration and breaking. The untouched virtues, however, behave according to an inversion of the doctrine (i.e., the soul's immortality); thus, the poem systematically represents virtues and vices according to the language of violence that accompanies their brutal interaction for a specific purpose— namely, to express the view that the soul is indeed immortal in the age of Christ. The language of violence is the instrument through which the discourse of Epicurean soul behavior at the moment of death is activated. In addition, Epicurean discourse of the soul does not merely stand in opposition to the Christian view of the soul; it also furnishes the semantic field within which the Christian view is constructed. The representation of vice-death is so consistent regarding language, imagery, and idea, that the poet in effect creates a topos of vice-death. This topos of vice-death becomes clear from the examination of the deaths of individual vices and several "near misses" of the virtues:

Veterum Cultura Deorum:

> . . . *animamque malignam*　　　　　　　　(*Psych*. 33–35)
> *fracta* intercepti *commercia gutturis artant*
> *difficilemque obitum suspiria longa fatigant.*
> and the shattered windpipe chokes off
> the scanty breath of the broken throat, and long
> gasps drag out a difficult death.

Libido:

Tunc exarmatae *iugulum* meretricis adacto   (*Psych.* 49–52)
transfigit gladio. *Calidos vomit illa vapores*
sanguine concretos caenoso, spiritus inde
sordidus *exhalans vicinas polluit auras.*
Then she [*Pudicitia*] pierces the throat of the disarmed
harlot with her sword having been plunged into it.
She vomits forth warm vapors clotted with filthy blood,
and from there her foul breath, belching out, pollutes the
air nearby.

Ira:

Rasile *figit* humi lignum ac se *cuspide* versa   (*Psych.* 153–54)
perfodit et calido *pulmonem vulnere transit.*
She plants the smooth shaft in the ground and
with the point turned up, she stabs herself and
punctures her lung with a warm wound.

Superbia:

Tunc caput orantis flexa *cervice* resectum   (*Psych.* 282–83)
eripit ac madido suspendit *colla* capillo.
Then, although she [*Superbia*] begs her, she [*Mens Humilis*]
bends her neck and tears out her head, having severed it,
and raises the head by the dripping hair.

Luxuria:

Casus agit saxum, *medii spiramen ut oris.*   (*Psych.* 421–26)
frangeret et recavo misceret labra palato.
Dentibus introrsum resolutis *lingua* resectam
dilaniata gulam frustis cum sanguinis inplet.
insolitis dapibus crudescit *guttur* et ossa
conliquefacta vorans *revomit* quas hauserat offas.
Chance directs the rock so that the breath-passage in
the middle of her face breaks and mashes together
her lips with her hollow palate. As her teeth are loosened
inside, her tongue, which has been torn to pieces, fills her
severed throat with bloody chunks. Her throat gags
because of the unusual meal, and gulping down mashed
bones, she vomits up again the morsels which she had swallowed.

sacerdotes Domini:

... vix *in cute summa*   (*Psych.* 506–509)
praestringens paucos t*enui de vulnere laedit*
cuspis Avaritiae. Stupit Luis inproba castis
heroum iugulis longe sua tela repelli.
... the spear point of Greed barely injures a few, grazing
them on the surface of the skin with an insignificant wound.
The wicked plague is stunned that her weapons are repelled
at a distance from the heroes' pure throats.

Avaritia:

Invadit trepidam Virtus fortissima duris   (*Psych.* 589–97)
ulnarum nodis obliso et *gutture frangit*
exsanguem siccamque *gulam;* conpressa ligantur
vincla lacertorum sub mentum et faucibus artis
extorquent animam, nullo quae vulnere rapta
palpitat atque *aditu spiraminis intercepto*
inclusam patitur venarum carcere mortem.
Illa reluctanti genibusque et calcibus instans
perfodit et *costas* atque *ilia rumpit anhela.*
The bravest virtue [*Operatio*] attacks the alarmed
[*Avaritia*] by strangling her with the harsh clench of her
arms and crushes her gullet, bloodless and dry, in her throat;
the fetters of her arms pressed together are tightened under
her chin and they twist out the breath from her narrow
throat which writhes, ravaged without a sign of a wound;
since the opening of the breath-passage has been blocked,
it suffers death shut up in the prison of her inmost parts.
She [*Operatio*], pressing on her with her knees and heels,
stabs her and breaks her ribs and breathless flanks.

Concordia:

excipit occultum vitii latitantis ab ictu   (*Psych.* 672–77)
mucronem laevo in latere. Squalentia quamvis
texta *catenato ferri subtegmine corpus*
ambirent sutis et *acumen vulneris hamis*
respuerent rigidis *nec* fila tenacia nodis
inpactum *sinerent penetrare in viscera* telum.

She receives a concealed sword in her left side from
the blow of a hidden vice. However, a stiff fabric
of interwoven iron-thread surrounds her body and
because of the stitched hooks, it spits out the sharp point
from the wound, and the firm threads with their rigid knots
do not allow the thrusting weapon to penetrate into her innards.

Concordia:

. . . Sed *non vitalia rumpere* sacri   (*Psych.* 691–93)
corporis est licitum, summo tenus extima *tactu*
laesa cutis tenuem signavit sanguine rivum.

. . . But it was not permitted that she [*Discordia*] break
through to the vital organs of the holy body; just
on the surface, the outermost layer of skin, having
been wounded by contact, displayed a thin stream of blood.

Discordia:

. . . Sed verba loquentis   (*Psych.* 716–25)
inpedit et vocis claudit *spiramina pilo*
pollutam rigida *transfigens cuspide* linguam.
Carpitur innumeris feralis bestia dextris.
Frustatim sibi quisque rapit, quod *spargat in auras,*
quod canibus donet, corvis quod edacibus ultro
offerat, inmundis caeno *exhalante* cloacis
quod trudat, monstris quod mandet habere marinis.
Discissum foedis animalibus omne cadaver
dividitur, ruptis Heresis *perit* horrida membris.

. . . But she [*Fides*] stops her [*Discordia*] speaking, and
she [*Fides*] closes shut the breath-passage of her voice
piercing her filthy tongue with the stiff point of a javelin.
The funereal monster is torn to pieces by innumerable right
hands. Each one grabs for herself [bits] piece by piece, so that
each scatters them to the winds, gives them to the dogs,
offers them freely to voracious ravens, shoves them into
the squalid sewers as filth fumes out, or entrusts them to the
monsters of the sea to have. The whole corpse, having been
torn apart, is distributed to foul animals; after her limbs have
been torn, terrible Heresy perishes.

I should preface the analysis of these passages by first calling attention to *Praef. Psych.* 34, where Abraham, the most important typological figure of the *Psychomachia*, is called *triumfi dissipator hostici*.[146] The noun *dissipator* is used of Abraham after he has driven away the fleeing kings who hold his kinsman, Lot, prisoner: *reges superbos . . . / pellit fugatos . . . (Praef. Psych.* 27–28). Such scattering will take place both on the concrete human level and the abstract level of the soul. As we have already seen, the analogy between the world of human beings and the soul is part of the allegorical strategy of the *Psychomachia*. After the virtues finally defeat the vices, they enter a walled camp, which is still vulnerable to the incursion of vice (*Psych.* 665–84 and 726–29), just as an individual soul is. As already argued, throughout the poem Prudentius plays upon the analogy between city and soul, or as in the case of Abraham, between the combatants' activities and the soul. Lot's evil enemies are scattered as the combatant vices are scattered and as the soul of a vice is scattered. The language of dissipation thus makes an early appearance in the poem.

Two categories of language from the preceding list of passages compellingly illustrate the doctrine of dissipation: soul/breath words and penetration or breaking words. In each death scene of a vice, words specifically referring to breathing or the life force occur—this includes the breath passage and organs such as the lungs: *animam* (*Psych.* 33), *suspira* (*Psych.* 35), *calidos . . . vapores* (*Psych.* 50), *exhalans . . . auras* (*Psych.* 52), *pulmonem* (*Psych.* 154), *spiramen, animam* (*Psych.* 593), *spiraminis* (*Psych.* 594), *ilia anhela* (*Psych.* 597), *spiramina* (*Psych.* 717), *auras* (*Psych.* 720), and *exhalente* (*Psych.* 722).

These words are joined by verbs of penetration and breaking: *fracta* (*Psych.* 34), *transfigit* (*Psych.* 50), *figit* (*Psych.* 153), *perfodit* (*Psych.* 154 and 597), *frangeret* (*Psych.* 422), *frangit* (*Psych.* 590), *rumpit* (*Psych.* 597), *transfigens* (*Psych.* 718), and *trudat* (*Psych.* 723). The consistency is striking, especially when set against the absence of this language in passages depicting the attacks on the virtues. In these scenes either verbs of repelling are employed—e.g., *repelli* (*Psych.* 509) and *respuerent* (*Psych.* 676)—or verbs of penetration are negated—e.g., *non rumpere* (*Psych.* 691) and *nec . . . penetrare* (*Psych.* 677).[147] The fate of the breath, life force, or soul forms the dramatic focus of these scenes. When the vessel of the soul is violated through penetration or other damage, as with the deaths of the vices, it escapes the vessel or is trapped in a defective vessel in which it is no longer able to live. Death is the final result. Vices and those who live the life of vice (to extend the analogy to the reader) die, but for the virtues or one who lives according to virtue, immortality is guaranteed, because nothing can penetrate the structure that houses the soul of the virtuous person.

The consistent use of language denoting soul/breath and penetration/ breaking points to the overall doctrine that at death the souls of the vices dissipate or are destroyed in some way.[148] As for the virtues, the opposite is the case. They are well protected behind armor, and when they are attacked by a vice, either the blows are repelled or their flesh is merely grazed. Examples of this phenomenon abound: *Patientia*'s armor repels the spear throw of *Ira* (*Psych.* 121–29); *Mens Humilis* is scantily clad (*Psych.* 204–205), but *Superbia* never reaches her; *Avaritia*'s javelin grazes the flesh of a few priests (*Psych.* 506– 509); the spear thrust of *Discordia* results in a flesh wound and fails to harm *Concordia*'s vital organs (*Psych.* 672–77 and 691–93).[149] On the literary level, the Epicurean features of each vice, and their negation in each virtue, contribute to their identity as personifications, and often these personifications function as terms in a series of opposed typologies from which the reader is invited to choose: for instance, *Superbia*/Goliath and *Mens Humilis*/David (*Psych.* 291–304).

When a soul is dominated by vice, it behaves in a more Epicurean way. Its vessel is penetrated, breaks, and dissipates, never to be reconstituted again. When the poet is concerned with virtues or good souls, the vessel never undergoes violence. Each virtue remains intact, impervious to bodily harm, an indication that the soul inside is safe and unharmed. This interpretative strategy reflects the poet's normative views on the soul, its structure, and behavior. A Christian soul is immortal because it is replete with or practices virtue. Further, Prudentius is, in effect, assigning pagan doctrine to a past history, to the sinners, and to a violent world in which the soul died. This is why there is a change in tone after the final battle of the poem and the victory of the virtues— indicated by a transparent preoccupation with peace.[150] Those older views, with their history and their adherents, are gone. It is not merely the case that a soul has been purified and renewed; a whole new world with a new future has been born.

The use of violence in the *Psychomachia* serves a wider and deeper poetic purpose than hitherto acknowledged. The view of the human soul and the behavior of the virtues and vices in the poem are traceable in part to a particular aspect of Epicureanism, a pagan philosophical doctrine, the history of which proceeds from the founder himself and finds an easily recognizable voice in Cicero and Lucretius. Prudentius again mobilizes a pagan intellectual tradition to portray the characters of his allegory. This time he exploits images and concepts traceable to the Epicurean doctrine of the mortal soul.

Prudentius and the Neo-Platonic Soul

The doctrine that human beings are created in the image of God (*Gen.* 1:26) had important implications for fourth-century views of the human soul. Christian intellectuals enthusiastically took up the pagan challenge that Trinitarian terms amounted to meaningless nonsense. Augustine developed a series of three-termed analogies (ternaries) between the soul and the Trinity on the premise that the soul possesses "traces" or "images" of the three-part Trinity.[151] The study and explication of these "ternaries" of the human soul represent self-knowledge, a way toward God figured as an ascent. Augustine, especially in *De Trinitate* and the *Confessions,* extends these ideas, influenced by Plotinus who, by seeking essences through self-contemplation, anticipated Descartes.[152] The conceptual trio of being, life, and reason is where Plotinus began in order to describe the essence of the soul. Augustine's version begins with *esse-nolle-velle* (*Conf.* 12.11); that is, the essence of a human being is "to exist, to know, and to will." Having established human existence based on cognition, Augustine further reduces the ternary to its foundation, *esse-vivere-intellegere* (to exist, to live, to understand; *De Trin.* 10.3.5; 10.8.11), which provides an accurate "trace" of the Trinity in humans.[153] Moreover, as a human reflects even further, more ternaries become apparent, the most important of which is *memoria-intelligentia-voluntas,* which "expresses self-reflection: what is in my consciousness (*memoria*) is the object of my understanding (*intelligentia*) by virtue of my will (*voluntas*)."[154]

Augustine was influenced by the neo-Platonic language of terneries found in the trinitarian psychology of Marius Victorinus. Victorinus sees the structure of the soul not as a direct reflection of Logos, but λογικός, that which participates in the nature of the logos. It is the image of the Trinity indirectly or an image of an image.[155] Therefore, the nature of the soul reflects *esse, vivere,* and *intellegere.* In book 3 of the *Adversus Arium* (chapters 4 and 5) Victorinus discusses this triad in order to focus on the identity and difference between the Son and the Holy Spirit and to explain that life and knowledge are indicative of the movement of being.[156] As a reflection of the Trinity, the human soul is defined by its life and intelligence. Even though these two characteristics are consubstantial with being at the level of the Trinity, being can either be lost or gained through vision or union with νοῦς. This consubstantiality allows the soul, if it chooses, to return to its higher state (*Adv. Ar.* 1.61.21–24).[157] Depending on the soul's choices, a direction of the soul's activity is created and thus determines the likeness of the soul to the logos. If the soul subjects itself to passion, change, and corruption, it will lose its likeness.[158]

The first 320 lines of the *Apotheosis,* in which Prudentius criticizes heretical doctrines is an excursus on the orthodox view of the Trinity and employs the ternary *esse—vivere—intellegere:*

> Haec *fore* cum veterum cecinissent organa vatum,   (*Apoth.* 234–42)
> nos oculis manibus congressu voce loquella
> experti heroum tandem *intelleximus* orsa
> priscorum et viso patefacta oracula Christo.
> Haec est nostra salus, hinc *vivimus,* hinc animamur,
> hoc sequimur: numquam detracto nomine nati
> appellare patrem, patris et sine nomine numquam
> natum *nosse* deum, numquam nisi sanctus et unus
> spiritus intersit natumque patremque vocare;
>
> After the lyres of the old prophets had sung that these things
> would come to be, we, with our eyes and
> hands, having come to know him through a union, through
> his voice and speech, *we* have *understood* at last the words of
> the ancient heroes and the prophecies that were laid bare by
> the appearance of Christ. This is our salvation, from this *we live*
> and from this we are given life. We follow this rule: never
> address the father without the name of the son, never *to know*
> God the son without the name of the father, never to call on
> the son and the father unless the one and holy spirit is present.

The context of this passage is a discussion of the ontological status of Christ, who holds sway in the three possible realms of creation: *carnis . . . medium, summum patris, et Stygis imum* ("the middle domain of the flesh, the highest domain of the Father, and the lowest domain of hell," *Apoth.* 228). Christ may have functioned as a mortal, but he maintains his identity as God (*Apoth.* 230). Just following these orthodox assertions concerning the Son's status within the Trinity, Prudentius explains how humans receive and understand this lesson in divine being. When humans *understand* the true identity of Christ and his role in the Trinity—i.e., that he *is,* then humans begin to *live* the true life. Reality (*fore/esse*), the existence and being of the Trinity in the universe, becomes understood (*intellegere*), engendering eternal life (*vivere*). The ternary is revisited at the end of the *Apotheosis* in the form of *esse-noscere-vivere* (*Apoth.* 1055/1061, 1062, 1067). In the passage surrounding this triad, Prudentius asserts what Christ is (*esse*) and consequently his (the poet's) personal knowledge (*nosco*) that he (the poet) will rise after death and live on (*vivit*). Again, the triads are traces of the Trinity, residues in the world and in the human soul of the godhead. Although Prudentius does not explicate them systematically, as do Augustine and Victorinus, his poetry displays an awareness of the idea that the Trinity is reflected imperfectly in triads concerning human nature and the soul.

Mention of the old prophets (*Apoth.* 234–42) indicates that Prudentius ties the ternary *esse-vivere-intellegere* to salvation history as expressed in scripture. A little further in the poem Prudentius says that if one doubts the *mystica Christi*, all one need do is read scripture, which are *dei signacula* (*Apoth.* 290–94).[159] The letters and words of scripture are "signs" or traces of divinity, a concept that Augustine develops in detail.[160] Prudentius associates scripture with the notion of Moses as the chronicler of creation (*Apoth.* 219, 234–35, and 302). Similarly, Augustine at *Conf.* 12.26 argues that Moses wrote words (*signa*) for those who understand the hidden meaning of scripture, but Prudentius adds a literary twist to the idea that salvation history as present in scripture expresses *esse-vivere-intellegere*. The lyres (*organa*) of the prophets (*veterum . . . vatum*), such as Moses, sang (*cecinissent*) the truth of the Trinity. The word *organum* can also mean the "tongue" of a man as Prudentius indicates in his poetic invocation at the beginning of the hymn to Saint Romanus (*Pe.* 2). The phrase *organa vatum* is a nod to traditional Roman poetics in which the poet as prophet expresses truth and knowledge. Not only can *esse-vivere-intellegere* be found in scripture as the *dei signaculi*, but also in Prudentius's new Christian poetry. Poetry is no longer the ignored stepbrother of patristic prose.

In the *Psychomachia*, three-fold traces of the Trinity help to structure and guide the poem's meaning. The first term of such a ternary, purification, occurs at *Psych.* 97–108, which describes the purification of *Pudicitia*'s sword after she kills *Libido*. The passage's two main concerns of the sacrament of baptism and the idea of purification occupy center stage. The almost unbearable attention (at least to a particular sensibility) Prudentius pays to descriptions of gore inevitably leads to language of purification (e.g., *purgata corpora, Psych.* 97; and *abluit infectum, Psych.* 100). Both the person and the bloody sword must be purified to enter the Catholic temple (*Psych.* 107). Thus, before any ascent is attempted, purification must be secured. *Pudicitia* is described as *docta,* which expresses her "deft" cleaning of the sword. One must know how to approach purification, the temple and, therefore, God.

The invocation of the concepts of purification and knowledge permit Prudentius to shift to more theurgic concerns and also to close the narrative of *Pudicitia* and *Libido.* But, more important, the passage stands as the first term in a Christian neo-Platonist ternary of ascent to God: purification-illumination-perfection.[161] Gregory of Nazienzus had linked together purification, illumination, and perfection as stages of ascent to God and as stages of humanity's development from paganism to Judaism to Christianity. In the *Psychomachia* there is a similar progression of concepts and religions. After the death of the vice, paganism, there is a rite of purification, followed by the illumination of the other six battle set pieces—including the exodus of the Jews from Egypt, and concluded by the achievement of a perfect Christian soul seen in the metaphor of the temple at the end of the poem.[162]

Prudentius writes that this new temple is the replacement for the Jewish temple (*Psych.* 811–19). The Christian temple represents the transformation of the Jewish temple in concrete ways. For example, Jewish sacrifice gives way to the idea of Christ's sacrifice and, most important, Jewish rules of daily behavior become an inner pattern of behavior based on the body of Christ. The end of the *Psychomachia* reflects this innerness.[163] In addition, the individual has become the temple (1 *Cor.* 3:16). The Trinity itself is within the soul: *Christus deus* (*Psych.* 910) and *Spiritus* (Psych. 840). Prudentius focuses on one of the traces of a ternary, "understanding" (*agnoscere, Psych.* 892; *novimus, Psych.* 893), which infuses the human soul in the guise of *Sapientia.* The poet retreats into a set of binaries in which two kinds of feelings (*ancipites . . . sensus, Psych.* 893) represent virtues or vices that continually battle. The addition of feelings to the description of the soul leads the reader into a more Aristotelian direction, where emotions play an important role in determining both good and bad actions.[164] The *Psychomachia,* however, exploits the Christian neo-Platonist thought that the soul is a reflection of the Trinity in the guise of ternaries and, accordingly, that union with God is possible through a three-step process.

Conclusion

The *Psychomachia* lays bare the allegorical meaning of scripture through its own allegory of the soul. In the *Praefatio* to his corpus, Prudentius gives a program for his poetry—to honor and praise god, explain the Catholic faith, argue against heresy and vanquish the nonbelievers, praise martyrs and apostles, and save himself (*Praef.* 36–45). This list of goals is no small challenge for poetry and forms part of the poet's claim that his Roman Christian poetry surpasses its pagan counterpart and rivals the cultural *gravitas* of patristic prose. The individual works of the corpus do appear to follow this program, though the *Psychomachia* does not fit neatly into any of the categories mentioned in Prudentius' preface to the whole corpus, except, perhaps, in that category that expounds the Catholic faith. It is with this in mind that I have laid out the *Psychomachia*'s use of pagan philosophy and its Christian reception. The poem expresses the divine truth of scripture through its allegory, much of which is constructed from Greco-Roman intellectual history. Philosophy plays its part in the formation of the new Christian poetry, according to which, poetry, like scripture, is a vehicle of divine truth.

Philosophical ideas and imagery from the Platonist and Epicurean traditions figure directly into the construction of the *Psychomachia*'s personifications and typologies. In fact, a pattern of the use of the pagan intellectual inheritance in Prudentius' work has emerged. On the one hand, Prudentius associates ideas and images that derive directly from pagan philosophical tradition with the personifications of vice and their attendant typological partners from biblical history. The ideas of descent and mortality prevalent in the Platonist and Epicurean traditions help to form the very essences of *Superbia*, *Luxuria*, and other Prudentian vices. On the other hand, the *Psychomachia* makes use of a series of ideas and images of a pagan intellectual heritage that was appropriated by the patristic tradition whose bulwarks were Philo, the Cappadocians, Ambrose, Jerome, as well as figures such as Marius Victorinus. Prudentius associates this Christianized version of pagan philosophical ideas with the portrayal of the virtues. Thus, he applies a patristic version of the ascent of the soul directly to *Spes* and to *Pudicitia* and her historical counterpart, Judith. The patristic ternary of purification-illumination-perfection accompanies the very structure of the poem; and the ternary of *esse-nosse-vivere* permeates Prudentius' assertions concerning the ontology of Christ and the human soul. Just as the allegorical qualities of the *Psychomachia* that purport to represent the inexpressible mysteries of God and the soul are not possible without the imaginative use of typologies, so the poem's use of the pagan intellectual inheritance contributes to the formation of its allegorical characters and vision.

Epilogue

Self, Poetry, and Literary History in Prudentius

I have argued for the centrality of typology in understanding Prudentius' poetry. The preceding chapters suggest various ways to show how typology is intrinsic to the poetry's literary ambitions, historiographical positioning, and intellectual inheritance. Typology and figurative reading (and writing) form the intellectual and artistic methodology of Prudentius's poetry.[1] The *Psychomachia* attempts to rival Vergil's *Aeneid* by rewriting the epic hero's descent and rebirth in the underworld, as the biblical Exodus in which the resurgent Jews are typological exemplars for both poet and reader. From the point of view of historiography, historical events and persons in the *Psychomachia* and *Peristephanon* contribute to a construction of a universal salvation history in the form of typologies from the Bible and Roman history. This project seeks the creation and consolidation of a Roman Christian self through the reader's acceptance of Christian salvation history. In addition, biblical interpretations and pagan philosophical ideas are crucial to the *Psychomachia*'s typologies and, therefore, to the signifiers of the poem's allegorical universe, which include the personifications of virtues and vices, metaphorical landscapes, and the temple, as well as the narrative of battles. These aspects are the foundation of the poem's allegorical stance and do not exist without the manipulation of the trope of typology. As an epilogue to these conclusions, I shall place Prudentius' use of typological thinking regarding the construction of the self in the context of fourth-century Christian views of the self. My main claim is that the self in Prudentius can be understood along two conceptual axes—the relational and the individualist—both of which merge into a vision of the soul and its relationship to God.[2] I conclude by exploring the implications of this and other claims I have made in this book in order to reassess Prudentius' position in literary history.

Prudentius' work defines the self as a relational subject through the typological triad of God—Christ—human. This typology is simultaneously ontological and historical because it situates the human creature in a hierarchy of being and is played out in salvation history. As a relational entity, the Christian self is realized through its connection to the divine. Furthermore, Prudentius represents the relational self as dependent on its earthly connections; specifically, that the Christian self exists in virtue of its associations to other Christian selves. In the *Psychomachia,* with the idea of association comes the political purpose of creating one Christian Roman at a time. In reading the poem, each Christian should experience a connection between himself, Christ, and God. These metaphysical *and* typological connections are reproduced on earth, outside of the poem, in the form of the church hierarchy and the community of enlightened Christians. These individuals recognize in each other the experience of self-realization in which the unknowable God becomes knowable. The recognition of such apophatic knowledge in others forms community and does not conflict with the prestige and history of imperial Rome.

In addition to a self constructed in relationalist terms, the self in Prudentius includes an individualist trajectory comparable to Augustine's idea of the "inward turn" as seen in the *Confessions.* Although relational in its core definition, the typological self of Prudentius is individualist because it is also understood as an "inner space" inside the person, and this inner space is the locus of moral conflicts and decisions, resolved and decided by means of freely chosen action. The Christian self, then, is discoverable through inner reflection and leads to a recognition of universal (divine) moral and metaphysical principles. The inner space of the soul, portrayed in the *Psychomachia,* is a metaphor for the self, rooted in the choices of how one is to live.

The soul's inner space is conceived of historically, as a place where signature events and characters stand for moral dilemmas. These dilemmas are nothing other than choices, which confront the reader, between typologies of virtue and typologies of vice: for instance, the reader is encouraged to choose between Lowliness—David—reader and Pride—Goliath—reader. The *Psychomachia* represents free will as an internal typological landscape where salvation history's actors and their abstract, moral personifications stage conflicts meant to stimulate spiritual improvement.

Within Prudentius' individualist concept of the self, however, we can make a further distinction based on categories delineated by Christopher Gill. On the one hand, the self is "objectivist-individualist" because the moral principles it discovers are universal and "objective" and are located "inside" each individual. On the other hand, the process of self-reflection and self-discovery requires a "subjectivist-individualist" stance because, as Gill observes about Sartre's ethics, "it is fundamental to our (human) existence as self-conscious agents that we are capable of exercising *radical* moral choice, that is, of choosing what our central moral values are."[3] Prudentius' language of free will presupposes Sartre's notion of radical moral choice. But, as we turn inward and reflect on possible choices of action, we find that the "right" choice, which we discover within us as a choice between historical typologies, falls in line with the divine cosmic order of God. Sartre denied the existence of a cosmic, moral order. Thus, in addition to a relational notion of the self, Prudentius' poetry assumes a self that is simultaneously objectivist-individualist and subjectivist-individualist.

The poem encourages the reader to turn inward to discover his power of freewill. As in Augustine's *Confessions,* to turn inward is to radically reflect, to attempt to think about one's own thinking. Reading Prudentius' poetry is a version of this process that should lead to a set of choices that are ultimately equivalent to a radical conversion and commitment to orthodox Christianity. The reader of the *Psychomachia* and the *Peristephanon* learns about choices and decisions from typological examples (Judith, Job, David, Adam, Agnes, Lawrence, Romanus, and so forth). Not only is history configured according to a typological structure but the derivation of free will also begins in the typological understanding of reality because it puts before the self a choice between virtue and vice. Thus, free will is proven through an historical, typological point of view, not from a philosophical argument. History with its typological exemplars establishes moral categories such as free will, which in turn, furnish the constituents of the self. All this amounts to a new claim, namely that the right kind of poetry can change and shape the moral condition of the Roman Christian self.

The Relational and the Individualist Self in Prudentius

Line 309 of the *Apotheosis,* with its overtly chiastic effect, establishes the "first" typological relationship at the core of Prudentius's work: *Christus forma patris, nos Christi forma et imago* ("Christ is the form of the Father, we are the form and image of Christ"). In arguing for the necessity of Christ as integral to the nature of God the Father, Prudentius yokes together in an archetypal and typological triad: God, Christ, and humans. This typology originates in the fundamental proposition from *Genesis* that God made humans in God's own image (*Apoth.* 308). Prudentius applies the language of typology—*forma* and *imago*—to link God and human through the mediation of the Word, Christ.[4] The self in its archetypal conception in history and ontology is relational. As noted in chapter 3, the reader and poet are figured as seekers after difficult knowledge, knowledge of their own souls, God, and their relationship. The point of this search is for the reader to rediscover—in Platonist terms, "to recollect"—his relationship to God through the typology God—Christ—human.

Prudentius explains the individualist side of the self that derives from an historical typology concerning free will.

En tibi signatum libertatis documentum   (*Ham.* 769–74)
quo voluit nos scire deus quodcumque sequendum est
sub nostra dicione situm passimque remissum
alterutram calcare viam. Duo cedere iussi
de Sodomis, alter se proripit, altera mussat,
Ille gradum celerat fugiens, contra illa renutat.
In this figure there is proof of your freedom whereby
God desired that we know that whatever way we are to follow,
lies in our power, and that we are free to tread upon
one of two paths. Two were ordered to leave Sodom;
one hurries away, the other hesitates, he hastens his
step as he flees, but she refuses.

The biblical event that Prudentius chooses to prove the notion of free will is Lot's escape from Sodom and Gomorrah. Lot's wife chose to look back at the cities, thus turning into a pillar of salt. By confronting the reader with this story, Prudentius associates the reader with a choice between Lot, who did not look back at the cities being destroyed, and his wife, who did. The implied typological choice for the reader is either Lot/reader or Lot's wife/reader.[5] Free will, then, is a function of choice, which in the story of Lot is determined by whether the human being has the right sense of faith. Lot listens to God, and his wife ignores God. Lot makes a good choice because of his faith, whereas his wife makes a bad choice because of her lack of faith.

In the *Hamartigenia, Contra Symmachum,* the *Peristephanon,* and the *Psychomachia,* the Christian soul exercises free will in order to choose between the Judeo-Christian God and godlessness and between good and evil. *Pe.* 2.217–20 illustrates the idea of a typological choice that takes place within a person: *Si forte detur optio, / malim dolore asperrimo / fragmenta membrorum pati / et pulcher intus vivere* ("If perhaps the choice is given I would prefer to suffer the breaking of my limbs with the harshest pain and to live within beautifully"). In this passage, the martyr Lawrence is speaking about the value of inner beauty, a state of the soul, which allows one to gain salvation with God. The reader is confronted with a choice between inner beauty, instantiated by the historical figure of Lawrence, or the ugly and foul inner state of his Roman persecutor. It is a choice made concrete through the historical types that populate the age of persecution. *Symm.* 2.471–87 is a strong assertion of free will by which a person can "know" God through correct choices. Consider Symm. 2–485–87: [F]*actorem noscite vestrum! / Libera secta patet. Nil sunt fatalia vel si / sunt aliqua opposito vanescunt inrita Christo* ("Know your creator! The way of freedom is open. Fate is nothing, or if it is something, it disappears and is useless when Christ stands opposite").[6]

Taken together, these two passages—*Symm.* 2.471–87 and *Pe.* 217–20—sum up the two aspects of the individualist self in Prudentius. *Pe.* 217–20 portrays an objectivist-individualist self, where a typological choice presented to the individual reader for inner reflection leads to an objective and divine principle. *Symm.* 2.471–87 exhorts a subjectivist-individualist self to make the radical leap to choosing for oneself. An inner and subjective space of the soul is implied in the very concept of free will; however, the self has a two-pronged *relational* goal: to discover the connection to Christ and God within the self and to form a community on earth with individuals who have made the connection to the divine. To reiterate, this goal of divine and human communion must begin with the individualist self that exercises free will through introspection as represented as a place within the individual.

Augustine, Paulinus, and Prudentius

Two other writers of the period provide examples of both relational and individualist language of the self. Paulinus of Nola's all-pervasive notion of

Christian friendship originating from "a life in Christ" indicates a relational view of self. Augustine's earlier works reveal an individualist view of self conceived of as inner space, a self whose communion with God is figured primarily as an ascent. In the work of Prudentius, the bonding of the self with God and other Christians occurs when the self independently and freely chooses Christianity and thus recognizes its typological relationship to God and Christ. In this way, typology overrides the more typical discourse of ascent as a metaphor for communion with God and other persons. For Prudentius, typology is the fundamental principle for reading and expressing ideas about sacred texts, history, and the self, and the concept of ascent, though still a metaphor for communion with God, operates as a complement to the trope of typology.

Augustine's earlier work teems with expressions of ascent for understanding the self's goal of uniting with God.[7] Several scholars rightly point to Augustine's requirement that the soul orient itself toward a higher reality.[8] The main scholarly observation concerning Augustine's vision of the soul and self, however, is that he inaugurated a turn inward, a first person standpoint that implies radical reflexivity and a language of inwardness.[9] Turning to reflect on one's own beliefs about the world and God represents a quest for self-knowledge, a premise of which is that God is inside a human being, not outside or "out there." This "inner space" is where immortality lies, in the form of the human soul's communion with God.[10] Humans themselves are not divine, but rather God is within and even "above" their souls. Inwardness makes possible the relation of human to God, because the soul animates the body and God animates the soul.[11]

Augustine's achievement was to furnish a theory of how a human could bond with God. The first prerequisite for such a bond is the proto-Cartesian proposition that a human as he reflects on himself establishes the truth that he exists. Thus, the act of reflecting about oneself, a process that requires a first-person standpoint, is the first step toward a human being's search for truth. The capacity to exist entails a capacity to live and living as a human being means the exercise of understanding or intelligence. This human trinity—*esse, vivere, intelligere*—becomes for Augustine the stuff of the human self and is a mirror-like image of the divine trinity represented by the Father, Christ, and the Holy Spirit. Reason as the "highest" part of human nature propels the self to conclude that there is indeed a higher truth: God in the form of the Trinity.[12] Only when a person discovers the truth of the human inner trinity can he bond with the higher truth of the divine trinity. Therefore, the typological triad of God—Christ—human, which is taken for granted by fourth-century Christian thinking on salvation history, is reinterpreted by Augustine as a metaphysical union, reflected in the triad, *esse—vivere—intelligere,* between God and humans that is located within the human soul.[13] The union hinges on an inward turn by a human being; in other words, a recognition of a sense of inwardness that forges a connection with Christ and then God within the soul's inner space. The root of knowledge, including knowledge of God, lies inside us.

This theory of human and divine communion is motivated in part by Augustine's reading of the Fall of Adam and Eve. In his interpretation of original sin, Augustine argues that sin is in each individual person: "you are born of Adam's loins."[14] When considering whether happiness can be found in the individual's memory, at *Conf.* 10.20.29 Augustine asserts that, although he will not consider the issue of whether human beings are happy individually or corporately, nevertheless, we are "in that man [Adam] who first sinned, in whom we all died (1 *Cor.* 15:22) and from whom we were all born into a condition of misery."[15] Augustine's view became standard in Western Christendom while the East adopted a more communitarian idea of sin in which sin is not in the person when he is born, but is already in the world into which he is born.[16] Augustine held that humans inherit sin directly from Adam rather than through exposure to a corrupt world that was caused by the Fall. And, if each individual carries the burden of sin in this way, it is not a significant leap to the argument that, in Augustinian thought, a radically reflexive self represents an inward turn and a struggle to transcend the self's connection to sinful flesh by recognizing the truth of its connection to God. Augustine, then, makes the self a more subjective and individualist entity by projecting original sin into each individual.[17] Yet, because of the Fall, according to Augustine, the capacity for free will is limited only to those who receive God's grace.[18]

Prudentius has constructed a radically reflexive self that searches for knowledge and communion with God. Prudentius, like Augustine in his earlier works, "dramatized the inner space" and "wrote a drama staged in that space."[19] Memory, which forms the basis of another of Augustine's triadic representations of the self (*memoria-intelligentia-voluntas/amor*) is invoked in the *Psychomachia* and forms the basis of Prudentius's use of typologies—namely, that the reader must remember the Old Testament stories, understand the connections to the Gospel narratives, and enact a moral choice these connections represent.[20] The inner landscape of the soul depicted in the *Psychomachia* can be seen as a repository of typological memories (and interpretations) animated as virtues, vices, the Roman landscape, and the architectural centerpiece of the temple at the end of the poem. Similarly in the *Confessions,* Augustine defines memory concretely, as an architectural object with an ethical dimension (*Conf.* 10.8.12).[21] Furthermore, at *Conf.* 10.25.36, memory becomes a secret hiding place for God: "Where in my consciousness, Lord, do you dwell? . . . What kind of sanctuary have you built for yourself? You conferred this honour on my memory that you should dwell in it. . . . But you were not there."[22] The architecture of the soul in the *Psychomachia* presents a similar vision; however, the reader must remember typologies that lead to the recognition of truth and God.

For Augustine, the remembering self is the self: "the memory . . . is awe-inspiring in its profound and incalculable complexity. . . . Yet this thing I am" (*Conf.* 10.17.26).[23] Augustine concludes that to confess one's thoughts and desires is to remember them and remembering is a never-ending process where thoughts and desires are collected and united, thereby constituting the self. The typological structure and examples of the *Psychomachia* also assume a deep and supple memory on the reader's part. Just like the writer of the *Confessions* who retreats into himself through writing, the reader of the *Psychomachia* retreats into himself through reading poetry. Through the text's suggestion, Prudentius's reader turns inward to his memory in order to collect the correct typologies that form a universal salvation history and a history of the self complete with a past, present, and future.[24] This is where the Prudentian self resides: in the memory where the choice of morally and doctrinally appropriate typological examples determines present behavior and future destiny. Thus, for example, the reader remembers Judith's chastity as a forerunner of Mary's miraculous chastity. This typological memory triggers in the reader a choice between chastity and promiscuity in the present and, consequently, at the end of time, between death and life.

The retreating into oneself through writing, known as the practice of *meditatio,* represents the hallmark of the individualist self and the inward turn in Augustine's *Confessions.* Prudentius in his preface to his works engages in moral and spiritual confessions similar to Augustine. The reader of both the *Confessions* and the *Psychomachia* is invited to turn inward to find God, but in the *Psychomachia* (and *Peristephanon*) the reader turns inward by choosing among typologies with moral, political, and spiritual implications. In addition, Michael L. Humphries has also observed in Augustine's writings a relational side to the practice of confessional *meditatio,* arguing, for instance, that confessional writing implies and intensifies social relations; because in exposing one's personal history of thoughts and desires, one invites the judgment and advice of others, thus bringing one's bodily desires and appetites under control and encouraging confession among others.[25] By contrast, the reader of the *Psychomachia* is encouraged not to confess her inner thoughts and desires to reach a higher moral and spiritual plane but, rather, to reach that plane through inner inspection of her thoughts and desires through the memory and choice of proper typological connections. Readers of the *Psychomachia* are bound together in common by the poem's radical purpose of changing its readers through introspection inspired by poetry.

Aspects of a relational self in the work of Prudentius come into even sharper focus when compared to the letters and poetry of Paulinus of Nola. On Paulinus' literary poetics, Dennis Trout has commented that, "as shared poetic and literary sympathies bound men in intellectual community and provided a language for social relations, so a new poetics was required to articulate a new relation to the world."[26] Catherine Conybeare is even more to the point: "For Paulinus and those he influenced . . . the self is essentially permeable to other selves, because it has been permeated by Christ; and what one is therefore depends fundamentally upon with whom one associates."[27] Both scholars interpret Paulinus' focus on the self as relational. According to Conybeare, Paulinus holds that Christ imposes himself on the human self so that the self will seek bonds with other "like-minded" selves on earth. Both Paulinus and Prudentius see one of the goals of becoming a Christian as fostering the bonds that make up a Christian community. The main difference between the two writers is that Paulinus understands Christ rather than the reader as the agent of self-realization in the reader. The relational idea of self in Paulinus' work, if Conybeare is right, overshadows any individualist formulation. With Prudentius, the dialectic of the relational and individualist is integrated into a theory of the soul and its relationship to God.

For Prudentius, as in the case of Augustine, the relational aspect of the soul is expressed on a spiritual plane and is possible only within an individualist act of looking inward. In the *Psychomachia,* Christ overlooks the soul as represented by the temple, ever watchful over the soul's appointed ruler, *Sapientia.* To recognize Christ in one's own soul requires a developed typological memory capable of making good choices. Ideally, the successful reader (and poet) realizes that the road to the Father begins with the reader himself and ends with a reckoning of Christ in the soul. The relational side of the self emerges from the "first" typology: God—Christ—human. In Gill's terms, the objective-participant self first emerges *within,* through a typology ontologically and historically connected to God. Paulinus of Nola, by contrast, expresses a version of the relational view of self through an outward-looking and socially oriented position. Parallel to the *Confessions,* Paulinus' work reflects the idea that the sharing of a conversion narrative implies a participatory idea of the self and is central to one's identity (*Ep.* 38.1).[28] His letters assert and negotiate bonds among him and his Christian friends, and letters between these friends create a system of communication with an accompanying notion of belonging to one group or body; hence the phrase "yours in Christ."

Conclusion

For Paulinus, this elevation of prose letters as a form of writing that conceives of a Christian self in terms of its relations to other Christian selves implies the inferiority of poetry as a mode of communication between Christians. Paulinus believes that poetry has reached this impasse because of its dominating pagan tradition. After all, he points out to his former mentor, Ausonius, the invocation of the muses "is addressed to nobodies . . . it is not sent to God" (*Carm.*10.113). Paulinus suggests the invention of a new poetry that addresses Christ, not the Muses, as its inspiration, and "repackage[s] biblical passages into classicizing verse for elite consumption." The *Natalicia,* which were completed in 407, achieved this end of "a divinely inspired Christian poetics of praise" and were read by an audience who was able to recognize Vergilian allusions and allegorically interpret texts.[29]

Prudentius's poetry claims divine inspiration for its content, employs classicizing verse and biblical passages, is read by an audience knowledgeable of Vergil and allegorical interpretation, and is a call for the reinvention of poetry to fit a new worldview. There is, however, a substantial gulf between the poetry of Prudentius and Paulinus. Prudentius' purpose is not merely to praise God but also to change or convert the reader. To accomplish this conversion, poetry must give knowledge of God and the soul's relation to God, both of which sit beyond normal, rational, human understanding. In typological terms, the *Psychomachia*'s epic presumption is that poetry can be the antetype to the type that is the Bible. By beginning with *Genesis* and ending with the temple of the new dispensation from *Revelation,* the *Psychomachia* stakes its claim to all of history and its meaning. What is more, Roman imperial prestige and power are included as fellow travelers. The *Psychomachia* in effect argues that poetry can express the truth of Christian dogma and universal history with absolute clarity, not in explanatory words, but in words that represent typological allegories that express the inexpressible. The *Psychomachia*—along with aspects of the *Peristephanon,* the dogmatic poems, and the *Cathemerinon*—argues that, while Vergil's poetic program in the *Aeneid* is indeed monumental, it is surpassed by the *Psychomachia*'s ambitions to change the individual reader into a "true" Roman citizen and promote a complete understanding of the universe.

It is more apt to compare Prudentius's poetic ambitions and program to the Augustine of the *Confessions.* In that work, reading leads to conversion (*tolle, lege*) and an opening up to a divine universe. In the *Psychomachia,* reading leads to the same place. In the *Confessions,* the expression of one's inner thoughts and desires constructed as memory furnishes the possibility of salvation for oneself and any other who may wish to imitate this process. In the *Psychomachia,* the carrying out of correct choices figured as typological pairs in the memory gives access to salvation for both the author and the reader. The crucial difference in this comparison, though, lies in the fact that Prudentius is writing poetry and Augustine prose. Prudentius has not only rivaled Vergil in his epic (and poetic) ambitions but has also aspired to match the church fathers as authorities on gaining knowledge and communion with God. Prudentius has reaffirmed poetry's status and developed for it a new mission, a level of literary accomplishment that, among centuries of literary historians, has been reserved for Augustine's *Confessions.*

Such a reevaluation of Prudentius's literary standing, I believe, flows from the arguments and analysis of this book. Prudentius continues to suffer in many literary historians' estimations because prose, relatively untainted by pagan religious and literary traditions, usurped poetry's traditional prestige. As a result, significant portions of Prudentius's achievement have been overlooked and ascribed to medieval or Renaissance poets. For example, Dawson, in his comments on Erich Auerbach's treatment of Dante as a figural poet, remarks that "Dante transformed figural reading into figural poetry."[30] Prudentius, however, makes a vital contribution to the birth of figural poetry. By taking up the apophatic challenge through his poetry's metaphors and typological choices, Prudentius points the way to a figural poetry that renders God and one's soul intelligible to oneself. By conceiving of poetry as a figural representation of the Bible that can change and define the Roman Christian self both individualistically and relationally, Prudentius reinvents poetry and establishes a benchmark for poets who were to follow him.

What I want to suggest here is a more prominent place for Prudentius in literary history than that which has been mapped out by two of the most influential medievalists of the twentieth century. Erich Auerbach and Ernst Curtius established a canonical view of literary history in which Dante's *Divine Comedy* "inaugurated modern European literature," was "the first . . . European poem comparable in rank and quality to the sublime poetry of antiquity," and had the status of "the classic in a modern European language."[31] While not expressing their views in such absolute terms, contemporary critics tacitly accept this view of Auerbach and Curtius when they discuss their formidable intellectual legacy.[32] Peter Godman asserts that Curtius' *European Literature and the Latin Middle Ages* "has become an international monument that towers above the landscape of provincial literary studies" and "a vision of European literary humanism" that "remains . . . provocative and imposing."[33] Edward Said proclaims that Auerbach's *Mimesis* "is the finest description we have of the millennial effects of Christianity on literary representation."[34] And Jan Ziolkowski comments that Auerbach's last major work, *Literary Language and Its Public in Late Latin Antiquity,* "demonstrates the best of Auerbach's historicist humanism" and may be his greatest book.[35]

This is not mere hyperbolic nostalgia for a great age of criticism gone by. In the past thirty years, Curtius has been one of the most frequently cited scholars in the humanities.[36] Auerbach's work has inspired contemporary critics to extend and criticize his theory of literary historiography and, most important, his concepts of *sermo humilis* and *figura* that led him to his reading of Western literary history.[37] In *Mimesis,* Auerbach lays bear his all encompassing view of Dante's figural realism, a concept that he traces in Western literature from Augustine in the early fifth century directly to Dante (though mediated in the sixth century by Caesarius of Arles, Gregory the Great, and Gregory of Tours). In the following extracts from *Mimesis,* Dante's inclusion of Rome and her historical figures functions as the basis of the *Divine Comedy*'s typological view of universal history:

> From the point of view of modern readers the most astounding instance, and in political and historical terms at the same time the most important one, is the universal Roman monarchy. It is in Dante's view the concrete, earthly anticipa-

tion of the Kingdom of God. Aeneas' journey to the underworld is granted as a special grace in view of Rome's earthly and spiritual victory (*Inferno*, 2,13ff.); from the beginning, Rome is destined to rule the world. Christ appears when the time is fulfilled, that is, when the inhabited world rests in peace in Augustus' hands. Brutus and Cassius, the murderers of Caesar, suffer beside Judas in the jaws of Lucifer. The third Caesar, Tiberius, is the legitimate judge of Christ incarnate and as such the avenger of original sin. Titus is the legitimate executor of the vengeance upon the Jews. The Roman eagle is the bird of God, and in one passage Paradise is called *quella Roma onde Cristo è Romano*. (195)

> . . . just as generally speaking every event and every phenomenon referred to in the Old Testament is conceived as a figure which only the phenomena and events of Christ's Incarnation can completely realize or 'fulfill' . . . so the universal Roman Empire here [in the *Divine Comedy*] appears as an earthly figure of heavenly fulfillment in the Kingdom of God. (195)

Auerbach sees Dante's figural approach as already present in Books 13–15 of Augustine's *Confessions*. For Auerbach and many critics who follow him, Augustine's work is a moment in literary history when the rhetorical strategy of *sermo humilis*[38] and the typological, historical outlook of the *figura* begin in earnest. In this reading of literary history, Dante inherits and develops these concepts from the church father: on the one hand, by applying a vernacular language and a humble rhetorical style to the sublime story of *status animarum post mortem* and, on the other hand, by bringing forward the universal Roman Empire as a figure to be fulfilled in the Last Judgment. Further, Auerbach's Dante posits himself as the fulfillment of Vergil and the *Divine Comedy* as the fulfillment of the *Aeneid*. The construction of literary history itself exists through the typological dynamic of figure-fulfillment, type-antetype. Thus, for critics like Brian Stock, Dante is indebted to Augustine because, "the following ten centuries of literary criticism is largely a gloss on [Augustine's] ideas."[39]

The implications of my argument concerning the poetry of Prudentius implies, I believe, an alternative view of literary history in which the *Psychomachia* and the *Peristephanon* contribute to the achievement that has been— and still is—reserved for Augustine and Dante. The figural representation of history becomes already in Prudentius a totalizing and fundamental component of epic poetry. Already in Prudentius, Rome's political and military success is universalized through a simultaneously diachronic and synchronic history of Christian salvation.[40] I have already sketched how Prudentius' view of history as dependent on memory that resides in the soul parallels Augustine's treatment of historical narrative and memory. As Stock has put it, Augustine understood that "a problem in the soul became a problem in narrative representation and with it, the inwardness of the mind identified with the inner discourse of the text."[41] As I have argued in chapter 2 and earlier in the epilogue, for Prudentius, the soul consists of stories and texts, which compete in the memory in the form of virtuous or evil typologies. The self achieves inwardness through the contemplation of narratives. The influence of Auerbach and Curtius has helped to exclude Prudentius from discussions of narrative, memory, and the self in Late Antiquity and the Middle Ages.

Auerbach sees Dante's figural realism as a seminal moment in the history of Western literature, a moment that would be taken up by Shakespeare, and more important for us moderns, by French realist novelists of the late nineteenth century.[42] If we understand "realism" as the inclusion of a contemporary reality in the divine historical scheme—for example, contemporary characters such as Beatrice and Dante himself in the *Divine Comedy*, who represent fulfillment of the self, we are justified in seeing Prudentius' martyrs and personifications as figures to be fulfilled in the person of the reader, a self-fulfillment, "which comprises the individual's entire past . . . involves ontogenetic history, the history of an individual's personal growth . . . the history of man's inner life and unfolding."[43] Auerbach wrote these words to describe Dante's figural realism, yet they could easily be said of Prudentius' achievement as well. Dante's insertion of Roman and Florentine historical figures, as well as the "Roman Monarchy" itself, is anticipated by Prudentius' inclusion of Roman figures, Rome herself, and the reader in his typological view of salvation history.[44] The reader of the *Psychomachia*, governed by his own free will, is asked to choose between pairs of a series of typological triads. Prudentius' use of figural thinking so that the reader may reflect and *decide* on the state of his own soul is also grounded on the ideas of "personal growth" and "the history of man's inner life."

The focus on Dante is certainly merited, because the *Divine Comedy* does develop figural thinking differently from late antique works. For instance, Dante's use of contemporary Florentine figures to achieve a full sense of figural fulfillment and to connect all historical ages and their souls is a significant innovation in the history of epic poetry. In considering the similarity between the use of Vergil's *Aeneid* by Prudentius and Dante, however, it is clear that the late antique author has anticipated his early modern successor. According to

Curtius, Dante's "spiritual meeting" with Virgil has no parallel in European literature.[45] Curtius asserts that *Aeneid* 6 is the *Divine Comedy's* "solemn center" and "august model,"[46] arguing that Dante's *bella scuola* of poets, in which by implication Dante includes himself, originates in the image of the pious poets of Elysium in *Aeneid* 6. Although Prudentius is less concerned to trumpet so explicitly his connection to the Roman epic tradition, he nevertheless emulates and endeavors to surpasse Vergil through the *Psychomachia's* sophisticated allusive program in which he combines the Romanized *katabasis* of *Aeneid* 6 with the Judeo-Christian *Exodus* of the Bible. With this epic innovation, Prudentius, like Auerbach's Dante, sets the individual soul within the context of salvation history and provides an explanation of how the soul may achieve communion with God.

Curtius argues that the *Aeneid's* synthesis of history and "the transcendent," as well as "the philosophico-theological epic of the Latin Middle Ages," form the foundation of the *Divine Comedy*.[47] Like Auerbach, Curtius emphasizes Dante's juxtaposing of ancient pagan, Hebrew, and Christian exempla. Curtius cites examples from the *Purgatorio*, for instance, David and Mary with Trajan (*Canto* 10), or Mary with the women of ancient Rome, Daniel, and John the Baptist (*Canto* 22).[48] In chapter 2, I argued that Prudentius uses just this kind of typological scheme—though certainly not as varied—to form a new version of Christian salvation history. The best examples in Prudentius for this argument are the *Peristephanon's* connecting of Christ with the imperial and religious legacies of Romulus and Numa, and the *Psychomachia's* tableau of Roman civil war that parallels and exemplifies battles in the soul. Prudentius represents these battles simultaneously as being between personified virtues and vices, historical figures, and the two conflicting sides of the reader's soul.

Prudentius' works reflect and manipulate the pagan and Christian philosophical and theological traditions. If we project this claim forward to Curtius' literary historical idea of the "universal poet theologian" or "philosophico-theological epic," we again find that Prudentius has been left out of the conversation. Curtius calls the twelfth-century writers Bernard Silvestris and Alan de Lille the first universal poet theologians of the Middle Ages. He also refers to Petrarch's critical assertion that "[p]oetry is in no sense opposed to theology. I might almost say that theology is poetry which proceeds from God."[49] Jerome is credited for "bequeathing" to the Middle Ages a "theological poetics," which binds the meaning of the Bible together with the practice of poetry. Curtius adds to this picture by explaining that Dante and his intellectual contemporaries, Giovanni del Virgilio and Alberto Mussato, championed a theological poetics. He concludes that Dante's *Divine Comedy,* as the central achievement of Western literary history, reconciles the old argument between poetry and philosophy. This standard view of a theological poetry is incomplete. Prudentius' creative use of typology in poetry, in order to address the apophatic proposition that the divine is not expressible in words (chapter 3), should be part of this particular story of literary history.

Contemporary literary critics and theorists of the medieval and early modern periods have often depended on the literary historical model of Curtius and Auerbach. That is, in their provocative treatments of, for example, Auerbach's self-reflexive use of the concept of *figura* or Curtius' view that medieval vernacular literature is rooted in earlier Latin literature, critics have either assumed or put aside the construction of literary history of Curtius and Auerbach that positions Dante as the fulcrum between the ancient (Augustine) and the modern (literary realism). The exclusion of Prudentius[50] from this scheme perhaps can be assigned to Auerbach's distinction between *figura* and allegory in which Dante, by means of the use of realist and more open-ended *figura,* was able to break the late antique and medieval penchant for allegories that "represent a virtue (e.g., wisdom), or a passion (jealousy), an institution (justice), or at most a very general synthesis of historical phenomena (peace, the fatherland)—never a definite event in its full historicity."[51] Yet Prudentius' use of typology as a way to furnish a Roman Christian individual with knowledge of God and his own soul, trumps this oversimplified view of what he accomplishes in his allegories: namely, both figuration and allegorical meaning. I am not arguing for a radical reassessment of Dante's fundamental position but, rather, am suggesting that this literary historical model is incomplete without a serious consideration of Prudentius' poetry and its achievement.

Notes

INTRODUCTION

1. C. Witke, "Prudentius and the Tradition of Latin Poetry," *Transactions and Proceedings of the American Philological Association*, vol. 99 (1968): 516, argues that in this passage, Prudentius is not concerned, like Horace, with the power of the text to achieve immortality, but rather with the process of praising God which ultimately will promote salvation. In Witke's view, Prudentius writes poetry to praise God, which facilitates personal salvation. Witke sees this passage in relation to the programmatic strophes of *Cathemerinon* 3 in which Prudentius' pronouncements on poetry's function and purpose is limited to hymns—i.e., poetry of praise. Witke's article is full of important observations and analyses, but in this case his discussion is overly narrow, neglecting the other poems' concerns with textuality, empire, and theology.

2. M. Smith, *Prudentius'* Psychomachia: *A Reexamination* (Princeton, N.J.: Princeton University Press, 1976), xi; and the Bentley comment is from V. Edden, "Prudentius," in J.W. Binns, ed., *Latin Literature of the Fourth Century* (London: Routledge and Kegan Paul, 1974), 161.

3. Books include Smith *Prudentius'* Psychomachia; S. G. Nugent, *Allegory and Poetics: The Structure and Imagery of Prudentius'* Psychomachia (Frankfurt am Main: Peter Lang, 1985); A. Palmer, *Prudentius on the Martyrs* (Oxford: Oxford University Press, 1989); M. Malamud, *A Poetics of Transformation: Prudentius and Classical Mythology* (Ithaca, N.Y.: Cornell, 1989); and Michael Roberts, *Poetry and the Cult of the Martyrs* (Ann Arbor: University of Michigan Press, 1993). Some recently published articles include C. Witke, "Recycled Words: Vergil, Prudentius and Saint Hippolytus," in *Romane Memento: Vergil in the Fourth Century*, ed. R Rees (London: Duckworth Press, 2004), 128–40; D. Rohmann, "Das langsame Sterben der *Veterum Cultura Deorum*," *Hermes* 131 (2003): 235–53; L. Pégolo, "La alegorí cívico-militar de la *Fides* en la *Psychomachia* de Prudencio," in *Discurso, poder y politica en Roma*, ed. E. Caballero de Del Sastre and B. Rabaza (Sante Fe, Argentina: Homo Sapiens, 2003), 271–83; J.-L. Charlet, "Signification de la preface á la *Psychomachia* de Prudence," *Revue des études latines* 81 (2003): 232–51.

4. A few examples are C. Conybeare, "The Ambiguous Laughter of Saint Laurence," *Journal of Early Christian Studies* 10.2 (2002): 175–202; Ch. Kässer, "The Body Is Not Painted On: Ekphrasis and Exegesis in Prudentius *Peristephanon* 9," *Ramus* 31.1 & 2 (2002): 158–75; and P. Cox Miller, " 'The Little Blue Flower Is Red': Relics and the Poetizing of the Body," *Journal of Early Christian Studies* 8.2 (2000): 213–36.

5. F. Young, L. Ayres, and A. Louth, eds., *Cambridge History of Early Christian*

Literature (Cambridge: Cambridge University Press, 2004). The same is the case in E. J. Goodspeed and R. M. Grant, *A History of Early Christian Literature* (Chicago: University of Chicago Press, 1966); however, A. Dihle, *Greek and Latin Literature of the Roman Empire: from Augustus to Justinian,* trans. M. Malzahn (London: Routledge, 1994), 584, says that Prudentius "was also the first herald of a Christian idea of Rome."

6. See notes 3 and 4 for recent articles. These are important lines of inquiry that yield interesting results.

7. J.-F. Lyotard, *Introducing Lyotard: Art and Politics,* ed. B. Readings (London: Routledge, 1991), 63, discusses grand and meta-narratives. See also J.-F. Lyotard, "Universal Histories and Cultural Differences," in *The Lyotard Reader,* ed. A. Benjamin (Oxford: Blackwell, 1989), 321.

8. M. Currie, *Postmodern Narrative Theory* (New York: St. Martin's Press, 1998), 2.

9. D. Quint, *Epic and Empire: Politics and Generic Form from Virgil to Milton* (Princeton, N.J.: Princeton University Press, 1993), 8–9. Quint develops the idea that two traditions of epic, the Vergilian epic of winners, and the Lucanian epic of losers, work their way through European literary history (Quint 1993, 8). The former represents imperialism, empire, and monarchy, while the latter more oligarchic and Republican notions—still including imperialism. Regarding the losers, Quint adds, "[T]he defeated hope for a different future to the story that their victors may think they have ended once and for all" (Quint 1993, 9). The Marxist critic Fredric Jameson, in his *The Political Unconscious: Narrative as a Socially Symbolic Act* (Ithaca, N.Y.: Cornell University Press, 1981), comments that the focus on "codes in structuralist and post-structuralist theory envisions history as a repository for 'clear' communication from the past offering a master narrative under whose aegis the occult meanings of texts can be solicited and allegorically rewritten." Quoted in G. Spiegel, *The Past as Text: The Theory and Practice of Medieval Historiography* (Baltimore: Johns Hopkins University Press, 1997), 20.

10. P. Hardie, *The Epic Successsors of Virgil: A Study in the Dynamics of a Tradition* (Cambridge: Cambridge University Press, 1993), 2.

11. C. Conybeare, *Paulinus Noster: Self and Symbols in the Letters of Paulinus of Nola* (Oxford: Oxford University Press, 2000), 132, comments regarding Augustine's *Confessions* that "what has come to constitute our vocabulary of personhood is . . . nascent in this period." D. E. Trout, *Paulinus of Nola: Life, Letters, and Poems* (Berkeley: University of California Press, 1999), 79, similarly comments, "[A]s a shared poetic and literary sympathies bound men in intellectual community and provided a language for social relations, so a new poetics was required to articulate a new relation to the world and God." It is time to include Prudentius in this ongoing discussion of the important intellectual issues having to do with self and community.

12. Prudentius was born under the consulate of Salia in 348 CE (*Praef.* 24). He claims three cities as his own: Caesaraugusta (modern Saragossa) (*Pe.* 4.141), Calagurris (modern Calahorra) (*Pe.* 1.116, 4.31), and Tarraco (modern Tarragona) (*Pe.* 6.143). There are two further references to his homeland at *Pe.* 2.537 and 6.145.

13. Palmer, *Prudentius on the Martyrs,* 14, says that Prudentius does not follow Augustine in his rejection of rhetoric—for, according to Palmer, Prudentius's preface, written last, shows knowledge of the early books of Augustine's *Confessions,* written in the late 390s. P. Brown, *The Body and Society: Men, Women, and Sexual Renunciation in Early Christianity* (New York: Columbia University Press, 1988), 388, dates the work

"around" 397. Palmer dates the *Praefatio* of Prudentius to about 404–405). Concerning the issue of Prudentius's "lying" to his audience regarding the *Praefatio*'s relationship to the literary chronology of his work see Palmer, *Prudentius on the Martyrs*, 16–17 and A. A. R. Bastiaensen, "Prudentius in Recent Literary Criticism," in *Early Christian Poetry: A Collection of Essays*, ed., J. Den Boeft and A. Hihorst (Leiden: Brill, 1993), 101–34.

14. Prudentius equates his education to learning how to *falsa loqui* (*Praef.* 8).

15. M. Smith, *Prudentius' Psychomachia*, 38 and 70 says, "Not that he ever was a Pagan, but for most of his lifetime he may have been a nominal Christian, unbothered by the spiritual implications of Christianity and comfortably at home with traditional Pagan culture" and that Prudentius had a "conversion of spirit." Palmer, *Prudentius on the Martyrs*, 11, imagines Prudentius's "causus scribendi as a 'conversion' from a worldly career to a single-mindedly Christian way of life." Roberts, *Poetry and the Cult of the Martyrs*, 2 further asserts that, in agreement with Fontaine, it is likely that Prudentius had a conversion experience, withdrew to his own estate, and devoted himself to the life of the *conversus*—i.e., "lay convert to an ascetic way of life." Roberts parallels Paulinus of Pella and Paulinus of Nola's correspondent, Sulpicius Severus.

16. R. Thomas, *Reading Vergil and His Texts: Studies in Intertextuality* (Ann Arbor: University of Michigan Press, 1999); S. Hinds, *Allusion and Intertext: Dynamics of Appropriation in Roman Poetry* (Cambridge: Cambridge University Press, 1999); G. B. Conte, *The Rhetoric of Imitation: Genre and Poetic Memory in Vergil and Other Latin Poets*, trans., C. Segal (Ithaca, N.Y.: Cornell University Press, 1986); B. Weiden-Boyd, *Ovid's Literary Loves: Influences and Innovation in the* Amores (Ann Arbor: University of Michigan Press, 1997); and J. Pucci, *The Full-Knowing Reader: Allusion and the Power of the Reader in the Western Literary Tradition* (New Haven: Yale University Press, 1998) are good examples of the progress in understanding allusive technique and reception.

17. M. J. Roberts, "Vergil and the Gospels: The Evangeliorum Libri IV of Juvencus," in *Romane Memento: Vergil in the Fourth Century*, ed. R. Rees (London: Duckworth Press, 2004), 50, note 17, comments that Herzog anticipates Conte's distinction between "exemplary model" and "model as code." Also S. McGill, *Virgil Recomposed: The Mythological and Secular Cantos in Antiquity*, series 49, American Philological Association (Oxford: Oxford University Press, 2005), makes use of the scholarship on allusion.

18. At *Ham.* 852–62, the soul returns to the bosom of *Fides*. In fact, Prudentius refers to the soul as the "nursling" of *Fides* (*Alumnam*, 853).

19. The verb form *invenies* is common in patristic prose for reading and studying scripture. Pagan prose writers use the form mostly of persons and inanimate objects. An exception is Seneca who uses *invenies* in connection with quoting a comic poet (*Ep.* 9.21) and reading philosophers (*Ep.* 64.3, *Nat. Quaes.* 6.17.3). But at *Helviam Matrem de Consolatione* 6.4 he uses *invenies* with *percense*, just like Prudentius, but not concerning the reading of texts but rather concerning the viewing of islands. The difference between pagan and Christian is clear since Prudentius and his fellow Christians see all literature as based on a quotable, citable sacred text, whereas the pagans cited authoritative texts much less frequently. Christian literature has a heavily textual orientation.

20. L. Edmunds, *Intertextuality and the Reading of Roman Poetry* (Baltimore: Johns Hopkins University Press, 2001), 32–33, refers to S. Levin, *The Semantics of Metaphor* (Baltimore: Johns Hopkins University Press, 1977), which theorizes that poems begin with a submerged sentence that has both illocutionary and perlocutionary effects: "I imagine (myself in) and invite you to conceive of a world in which (I say to you)." The

establishment of the poet with empirical credibility helps to engender a suspension of disbelief in the reader thus granting the poem a truth-value.

21. J.-L. Charlet, "Aesthetic Trends in Late Latin Poetry (325–410)," *Philologus* 132 (1988): 74. C. White, *Early Christian Latin Poets* (London: Routledge, 2000), 6, identifies three main purposes of Early Christian poetry: (1) to communicate the truth of Christianity, (2) to argue against heresies and paganism, and (3) to praise God.

22. Reinhart Herzog has briefly pointed out that late fourth-century poetry took an exegetical turn. See Charlet, "Aesthetic Trends," 82–84.

23. T. Whitmarsh, " 'Greece Is the World': Exile and Identity in the Second Sophistic," in *Being Greek Under Rome: Cultural Identity, the Second Sophistic and the Development of Empire,* ed. Simon Goldhill (Cambridge: Cambridge University Press, 2001), concerning the relationship of Greek writers to the Roman Empire says that the "process of self-definition against the classical past extends from literary fashioning to political revisionism; that the writers under examination strategically reorientate the language of self-definition which was current in that earlier period, configuring (sometimes explicitly) the relationship between self and polis in terms more appropriate to the enormous world empire of the Roman Principate." Christian writers between the rise of Constantine in 312 CE and the sack of Rome in 410 CE appear to follow the pattern Whitmarsh finds in the Second Sophistic.

24. Goodspeed and Grant, *A History of Early Christian Literature,* 191: "[Eusebius's] *Chronicle* provided a skeleton for the *Church History,* which is more a history of early Christian literature than a real history of deeds or of thought."

25. White, *Early Christian Latin Poets,* 7, argues that Paulinus of Nola "rejects the literary and aesthetic ideals of his mentor Ausonius," having the view that poetry is not "something essentially lightweight, a form of amusement rather than a vehicle of serious truth." The general proposition about literature does obtain in Paulinus' case, but it remains to be seen if Paulinus has poetry specifically in mind as a vehicle of truth. The case is clearer with Prudentius. It is suggestive that White's selection of early Christian Latin poets is published under a series entitled *The Early Church Fathers.* Are we to understand these poets, some of whom fall under the traditional category of "church fathers," as now being included in the category?

26. Paulinus of Nola was known in his time not as a poet (notwithstanding his famous poems on St. Felix), but as a prominent interpreter of Plato.

27. See McGill, *Virgil Recomposed.*

28. See R. Herzog, *Die Bibelepik der Lateinischen Spätantike* (Munich: Wilhem Fink, 1975), xv–lxxiii; C. P. E. Springer, *The Gospel as Epic in Late Antiquity* (Leiden: E. J. Brill, 1988), 9–18; and M. J. Roberts, *Biblical Epic and Rhetorical Paraphrase in Late Antiquity* (Leeds: Francis Cairns, 1985).

29. Witke, "Recycled Words," 128, comments that Vergil "corrected and deconstructed by Prudentius could offer a framework of reference for the follower of Christ who is also a Roman citizen educated, critically aware, and often highly placed." See also Witke 2004, 135, 138–39.

30. M. Vessey, "Jerome and Rufinus," in *The Cambridge History of Early Latin Literature,* ed., F. Young, L. Ayres, and A. Louth (Cambridge: Cambridge University Press, 2004), 321, says, Jerome is the first to theorize the art of [biblical interpretation] and to make its practice the main burden of the Christian *literatus.*"

31. Vessey, "Jerome and Rufinus," 320.

32. Vessey, "Jerome and Rufinus," 321.

33. G. O'Daly, *Augustine's City of God: A Reader's Guide* (Oxford: Oxford University Press, 1999), 20.

34. J. M. Rist, "Basil's 'Neoplatonism': Its Background and Its Nature," in *Basil of Caesarea: Christian, Humanist, Ascetic,* ed. P. J. Fedwick (Toronto: Pontifical Institute of Mediaeval Studies, 1981), 138.

35. Criticism of Prudentius over the past decade or so has put aside the question of his contributions to the history and theory of allegory, preferring to see the *Psychomachia* in particular as merely an incipient or limited stage of allegorical writing.

O N E : An Epic Successor?

1. M. Smith, *Prudentius' Psychomachia: A Reexamination* (Princeton, N.J.: Princeton University Press, 1976), 234, makes the claim that one in ten lines of Prudentius borrow from Vergil. A. Mahoney, *Vergil in the Works of Prudentius* (Cleveland: J. T. Zubal, 1934), gathers together and categorizes the linguistic and thematic commonalities between the two authors.

2. Thus, Smith, *Prudentius' Psychomachia,* chapter 4, for instance, discusses his reading of the *Aeneid* as a whole, employing his interpretation of Vergil to reveal how Prudentius read Vergil. Prudentius' reading of the *Aeneid* directly effects the composition and meaning of the *Psychomachia.* This kind of approach still informs the reception of Christian epic in literary history. As P. Hardie, *The Epic Successors of Vergil* (Cambridge: Cambridge University Press, 1993), 57, asserts, Vergil had "ensured that the epic genre had a vigorous afterlife; through the transposition of the theme of universal power from the terrestrial to the celestial plane the Virgilian epic easily became the Christian epic." For good or for ill the *Aeneid* and the *Psychomachia* have been and remain closely linked.

3. S. G. Nugent, "Ausonius' 'Late-Antique' Poetics and 'Post-Modern' Literary Theory," in *The Imperial Muse. Ramus Essays on Roman Literature of the Empire II,* ed., A. J. Boyle (Victoria: Aureal Publishers, 1990), 39. R. Thomas, *Reading Vergil and His Texts: Studies in Intertextuality* (Ann Arbor: University of Michigan Press, 1999), 1–2, confirms intertextuality as a starting point that "functions as a larger receptacle" for the process of allusion where there exists an "active collaboration between poet and learned reader." Thus, in my approach both parties, the poet and the (implied) reader, play active roles in the construction of meaning. The alluding poet is the "first reader of allusive incorporation," who focalizes the allusive account (S. Hinds, *Allusion and Intertext: Dynamics of Appropriationn in Roman Poetry* [Cambridge: Cambridge University Press, 1998], 103. The reader is expected to recognize the poet's allusive activity, especially in the case of an allegorical poem like the *Psychomachia* in which "hidden meanings" form the basis of an interpretation and are designed to persuade. It is unnecessary to become mired in a debate about the theoretical efficacy of isolating what the poet wants to communicate and what the reader comprehends. While in theory a reader-oriented intertextuality combined with an intentionalist view of the poet presents areas of slippage, in practice the approach suits the *Psychomachia,* because it dovetails with the assumptions behind the work. More generally, however, this approach facilitates a productive analysis of the shared discourse between the *Psychomachia* and the *Aeneid.* See Hinds, *Allusion and Intertext,* 50.

4. Of the many twentieth-century dissertations on the subject, the most useful are Mahoney, *Vergil in the Works of Prudentius* and S. M. Hanley, "Classical Sources of Prudentius," dissertation, Cornell University, 1959. See also, S. Döpp, "Vergilische Elemente in Prudentius' *Contra Symmachum*," *Hermes* 116 (1988), 337–42.

5. Smith, *Prudentius'* Psychomachia, 164–66, sees the relationship in adversarial terms, arguing that "not at all does it [the *Psychomachia*] value epic's basic idea" (Smith 1976, 166, and 236). For Smith, warfare and temple worship are biblical metaphors divorced from the pagan epic tradition. Hence, Smith can speak in terms of "the hard and agonizing death of epic" spawning "the birth of a new genre of spiritual allegory" (Smith 1976, 165). A. Dihle, *Greek and Latin Literature of the Roman Empire: From Augustus to Justinian* (London: Routledge, 1994), 583, subordinates epic to allegory. My approach does not envision such literary antipathy between Prudentius and the Latin epic tradition. Although Prudentius' nurturing of the "spiritual allegory" does indeed constitute a major innovation to be imitated in the Middle Ages, the *Psychomachia* falls squarely in the Roman epic tradition. In this chapter, I trace several defining characteristics of Roman epic to show that the *Psychomachia* is a serious and successful attempt to perpetuate and revivify epic's literary role in the Christian state. Later authors such as Dante and Milton are the direct inheritors of Prudentius' work. When Smith views the poem in the context of the Roman epic, he concludes that the *Psychomachia's* effect is comic (Smith 1976, 184 and 214), ironic (5), and mock-classical (236). In his approach, the Christian and the pagan are separate: "The mingling of the two literary systems is too obtrusive not to be spiritually shocking. The contradictions between Vergil and the Gospels are not smoothly resolved or synthesized—yet the display of these contradictions is morally instructive" (237). Smith assumes an opposition between the two traditions that may have not existed for Prudentius' audience. To write epic in fourth-century Rome was to engage Roman epic tradition. This engagement is not completely oppositional nor contradictory.

6. K. Thraede, *Studien zu Sprachen und Stil des Prudentius, Hypomnemata Heft* 13 (Göttingen: Vandenhoeck and Ruprecht, 1965); J. Fontaine, "Le mélange des genres dans la poésie de Prudence." *Forma Futuri in onore di M. Pellgrino.* Torino 1975; reprinted in J. Fontaine, *Études sur la poésie latine tardive d'Ausone á Prudence* (Paris: Société d'Édition les Belles Lettres, 1980), 758; Charlet, "Aesthetic Trends," 74–75.

7. In a brief but suggestive paragraph, M. Von Albrecht, *Geschichte der römischen Literatur,* vol. 2 (Munich: K. G. Saur Verlag, 1992), 1077, asserts that Prudentius was competing with epic poets and that the anti-Vergilian element should not be overemphasized. Rather, and in addition, the Christian poet is "striving" after the epicists like Lucretius and the Presocratic poets. Von Albrecht sees Prudentius seeking a valid mode of expression through the use of Vergil.

8. Prudentius is often included in studies of fourth-century Latin literature: M. Fuhrmann, ed., *Christianisme et formes littéraires de l'antiquité tardive en occident,* Entretiens 23 (Genève: Fondation Hardt, 1977); J. W. Binns, ed., *Latin Literature of the Fourth Century* (London: Routledge & Kegan Paul, 1974); and A. J. Boyle, ed., *The Imperial Muse: Ramus Essays on Roman Literature of the Empire II.* (Victoria: Aureal Publishers, 1990). But in recent studies that focus exclusively on the history of Roman epic, Prudentius is conspicuously missing—e.g., A. J. Boyle, ed., *Roman Epic* (London: Routledge, 1993); E. Burck, *Das römische Epos* (Darmstadt: Wissenschaftliche Buchgesellschaft, 1979); M. Von Albrecht, *Roman Epic: An Interpretative Introduction*

(Leiden: Brill, 1999). Whereas the *Psychomachia* is recognized as epic in studies dedicated exclusively to that work, the aforementioned epic histories include Claudian as the only fourth-century representative. Perceptive critics such as M. Smith, *Prudentius' Psychomachia*, 105–106, while acknowledging the *Psychomachia*'s epic features, sees Prudentius' contribution to the genre as its ultimate destruction: "Unlike Juvencus, Prudentius does not compose epic; he uses epic to compose allegory. The history of medieval literature will verify that while allegory grew to vigorous life, epic never fully recovered from Prudentius' treatment of it." Perhaps this sort of conclusion underlies Prudentius' exclusion from the canon of Latin epicists, for, in his hands, epic was transformed, rather than used only as an instrument of allegory. Moreover, the new epic Prudentius creates could be said to be responsible for the survival of epic, rather than the conventional epic productions of contemporaries such as Claudian. The literary phenomenon of biblical epic is certainly a new direction in Latin epic, but it does not engage the pagan Roman tradition as directly as Claudian and the *Psychomachia*. D. Quint's *Epic and Empire: Politics and Generic Form from Virgil to Milton* (Princeton, N.J.: Princeton University Press, 1993) convincingly shows that epic lived a vibrant life long after the end of the Roman Empire in the vernacular forms.

9. The claim that Prudentius programmatically engages *Aeneid* 6 means that he is actively reworking the purpose, content, form, and inspiration for epic poetry. This is accomplished by a systematic allusive program that primarily concentrates on *Aeneid* 6. Allusion as "systematic" reads an individual case of allsusion not locally, that is as "[privileging] the individual highly wrought moment," but within a broad pattern of narrative allusion (S. Hinds, *Allusion and Intertext*, 140–41).

10. L. Gosserez, *Poésie de lumière: une lecture de Prudence, Bibliothèque d'études Classiques* 23 (Louvain: Peeters, 2001), 95–103, suggests connections between the *Psychomachia* and *Aeneid* 6. She pursues the relationship between asceticism and *katabasis*, which she argues is figured in terms of the imagery of light and darkness. She does not treat the allusive relationship systematically, nor is her focus Prudentius' status as an epic successor to Vergil.

11. In analyzing this intertextual relationship, the question arises: why prioritize the *Psychomachia*'s allusions to *Aeneid* 6 over the rest of the Vergilian allusions? The answer has two parts. First, it is well known that the *Psychomachia* takes most of its allusions from the second half of the *Aeneid*, especially the fighting language and imagery. On the surface, this is because the series of battles in the "Iliadic half" of the *Aeneid* provide a handy source of descriptions for the battles between the virtues and the vices. I argue in chapter 4 that these descriptions of fighting and death exploit Epicurean and Platonist discourse that is associated with the defeated vices. In effect, these Vergilian allusions do not function programmatically, but within a hierarchy of allusive associations, whose preeminent member is pagan philosophical imagery. The allusions to the *Aeneid* found in battle sequences point to pagan thought which is associated with the losers, the vices. Second, and, most important, Prudentius' allusions to *Aeneid* 6 are systematic, in that they occur at the very beginning, middle, and end of the poem forming a clear set of connections that drive the poem. And often, when allusions to other books of the *Aeneid* occur near allusions to *Aeneid* 6, they directly recall the context and tone of the underworld narrative. It is the presence of this system of allusions to *Aeneid* 6, which expresses the *Psychomachia*'s central purpose of describing the fate of a soul and its place in the Christian city. Therefore, beginning with *Psych.* 1 and continuing

throughout the poem, many of the allusions to *Aeneid* 6 tend to function programmatically, not hierarchically; that is, they indicate the poem's content and epic ambitions. See Thomas, *Reading Vergil and His Texts,* 196, for the notion of primary and
secondary references.

12. Dihle, *Greek and Latin Literature of the Roman Empire,* 584 and 586: "Prudentius
was also the first herald of a Christian idea of Rome . . . as being at the head of the
empire which united civilised humanity . . . [this] was at the core of their [i.e., educated
people of the Imperial Age] political and cultural consciousness." Rome can then "truly
exercise its cultural mission as described already by Virgil."

13. Texts and Translations for the *Aeneid* with minor adjustments are from: Virgil,
The Aeneid, 2 vols., trans. H. R. Fairclough and rev., G. P. Goold. Loeb Classical Library.
(Cambridge Mass.: Harvard University Press, 1999); for the text of Prudentius, see M. P.
Cunningham, ed., *Aurelii Prudentii Clementis Carmina,* Corpus Christianorum: Series
Latina 126 (Turnhout: Brepol Press, 1966) and for translations with adjustments, see
Prudentius, vol. 1, trans. H. J. Thomson. Loeb Classical Library (Cambridge, Mass.:
Harvard University Press, 1949).

14. See *Apoth.* 402–21, where Prudentius in the context of his critique of the Jews
attacks the notion of Apollo as a source of poetic inspiration.

15. In another programmatic passage, Paulinus of Nola (*Carm.* 15. 30–33) replaces
Apollo with Christ as the source of poetic inspiration, but he does not allude to Vergil.
*Non ego Castalidas, vatum phantasmata, Musas / nec surdum Aonia Phoebum de rupe
ciebo; / carminis incentor Christus mihi, munere Christi / audio peccator sanctum et
caelestia fari.* "I shall not summon Castalian Muses, the ghosts of poets, nor rouse deaf
Phoebus from the Aonian rock. Christ will inspire my song, for it is through Christ's
gift that I, a sinner, dare to tell of his saint and heavenly things." (P. G. Walsh, trans., *The
Poems of Paulinus of Nola,* vol. 40 of *Ancient Christian Writers* [New York: Newman
Press, 1975]). Paulinus alludes directly to *Aen.* 6. 56 at *Carm.* 18. 261 (*Natalica* 6) in
which Apollo is replaced by Saint Felix: *Felix sancta, meos semper miserate labores.* This
is said by a poor farmer who blames Felix for the theft of his only two oxen. Of course,
the oxen are returned to the farmer through the miraculous power of Felix. Earlier in
the poem (18. 67–70), Paulinus the narrator says that Felix is equivalent to Christ in
terms of his ontological status after death. R. Green, *The Poetry of Paulinus of Nola*
(Oxford: Oxford University Press, 1971), views the use of *Aen.* 6.56 as mock epic humor.
Walsh, trans. *The Poems of Paulinus of Nola,* 376, note 19, sees Paulinus' use of Vergil as a
temporary elevation of style for a sophisticated audience. There is no hint of the
programmatic purpose Prudentius employs at *Psych.* 1. The contexts of each Christian
poet's usage could not be more different, save for the replacement of Christ for Apollo.

16. R. Thomas, *Reading Vergil and His Texts,* 198, says that Vergil's single purpose is
"subsuming or appropriating an entire literary tradition" and that Vergil's use of
"reference" conflates, corrects and renovates Greece and Rome. My argument concerning the *Psychomachia*'s use of *Aeneid* 6 implies a similar consumptive literary and
ideological purpose.

17. A. J. Boyle, "The Roman Song," in *Roman Epic,* ed. A. J. Boyle (London: Routledge, 1993), 5. Statius provides a twist on this construction of literary history when he
engages Vergil through the trope of self-effacement, unabashedly announcing that he
could never live up to Vergil (. . . *nec tu divinam Aeneida tempta, / sed longe sequere et
vestigia semper adora, Theb.* 12.816–17). See Hardie, *The Epic Successors of Virgil,* 110–11.

18. G. B. Conte, *The Rhetoric of Imitation: Genre and Poetic Memory in Vergil and*

Other Latin Poets, trans. C. Segal (Ithaca, N.Y.: Cornell University Press, 1986), 76 and 82; also D. Kennedy, "Virgilian Epic," in C. Martindale, ed., *The Cambridge Companion to Virgil* (Cambridge: Cambridge University Press, 1997), 151, who cites G. B. Conte, *Latin Literature: A History* (Baltimore: Johns Hopkins University Press, 1994), 4 on the notion of genre as "allusion on a massive scale."

19. Kennedy, "Virgilian Epic," 153.

20. Hinds, *Allusion and Intertext,* 115, says that Greco-Roman epic has a "unified literary system," in which occur moments of negotiation between timeframes of narrated worlds and timeframes of the poetic traditions.

21. Abraham entertains the triple-formed image in his home and he gathers all his home-related resources to fight the battle to save Lot.

22. *Ham.* 553–636 states that the soul gives birth to its own sins and it is fruitless to blame the world. Prudentius recalls the story of David and Absalom in which the son attempts to kill the father. This biblical story is an allegory for human beings' tendency to give birth to accursed children (*Ham.* 569–70); we give birth to Absaloms who wish to kill us (*Ham.* 579–80). The section ends with a well-known tale from "the moralists" of infant snakes who kill their mother shortly after birth.

23. Dihle, *Greek and Latin Literature of the Roman Empire,* 585, suggests this line of thought: "[O]utward victories which cast nations of the globe down at the feet of Rome are finally succeeded by inner victory, through which Rome itself is freed from the rule of the demons, and now becomes the haven of true civilization."

24. Yet, in a different sense, the world is a source of suffering to be endured on the inside—by the soul, borne to keep the soul pure and ready for the communion with the divine.

25. Also, the word *labores* may possess the Alexandrian notion of the difficulties in perfecting a poem, further reinforcing Christ's inspirational role in literary creativity.

26. Prudentius uses the term in other places primarily to refer to Old Testament prophets. *Cath.* 4.96, 9.25; *Apoth.* 219, 234; *Ham.* 343, 574; and *Pe.* 10.625. *Pe.* 12.28 refers to Saint Paul in the capacity of prophet and the only use of the *vates* signifying a pagan god (i.e., Apollo) is *Symm.* 2.525.

27. Where she is mentioned in two places in the Prudentian corpus (*Apoth.* 440, *Sibyllinis . . . libris,* and *Symm.* 2.892) they are both extremely negative representations of pagan prophecy.

28. The effect adds nuance to the conventional wisdom on the position of the Christian poet vis-à-vis his work. Scholars have assumed Christian poets' aversion to explicit promotion of their originality and poetic skills, a marked difference from the statements on the matter by, for instance Horace (*Odes* 3.30). C. White, *Early Christian Latin Poets* (London: Routledge, 2000), 10–11, discusses Christian poets' views on literary immortality and the importance of poetry. M. Malamud, "Making a Virtue of Perversity: The Poetry of Prudentius," in A. J. Boyle, ed., *The Imperial Muse. Ramus Essays on Roman Literature of the Empire II,* 68–69, decodes the last line of the *Hamartigenia* into an anagram in which Prudentius claims glory for himself as a poet. Although this is not the place to undertake a discussion of such a rich topic, we can conclude from the first line of the *Psychomachia* that even though Prudentius never says so explicitly, he has simultaneously elevated the status of the Christian poet and eliminated, what may have seemed to him, the profane pronouncements of originality of past pagan poets.

29. S. G. Nugent, "Ausonius' 'Late-Antique' Poetics, in *The Imperial Muse. Ramus*

Essays on Roman Literature of the Empire II, ed. A. J. Boyle, 41–45, sees a similar relationship between the poet, Ausonius, and the reader: "Ausonius plays with the possibility of the text as an open space into which both author and reader may enter" (42). Moreover, while articulating a reader-response approach to Ausonius Nugent comments, "Ausonius may well be capable of seeing his own text as a transaction between author and reader, because that is the way that he, in his turn, approaches the text of Vergil (or Plautus or Ovid). It should not surprise us that the 'reader reading' consciously writes for the 'reader reading' like himself," (44). In *Ham.* 624–26 Prudentius directly addresses the reader: *Sanctum, lector, percense volumen: / quod loquor invenies dominum dixisse profanes / vera obiectantem mortalibus.* In these lines there is a pact struck between poet and reader. Both are part of making meaning from the words on the page. In this didactic and persuasive formulation of the relationship between reader and poet, the poet interprets scripture and the reader is persuaded by the poet's interpretation. The poet realizes the limitations of his position by appealing to the reader to look for herself if she does not believe the poet's version of scripture. The reader, on the other hand, is in a position of power, able to discard or accept any part of what the poet offers. There is, however, a balance of power maintained between the reader and poet. Both parties, active and engaged, are required to achieve "true" (*vera*) interpretation of scripture.

30. At *Aen.* 5.730–31, *gens dura atque aspera cultu/ debellanda tibi Latio est,* the context is similar to *Aen.* 6.853. In the *Aeneid* 5 passage Anchises is telling Aeneas what he must do to settle his people in the destined place. At *Aen.* 7.651, *Lausus, equum domitor debellatorque ferarum,* the context is the catalogue of Italian kings and their soldiers. The noun form of *debellare* is used in a quintessentially epic moment that lists the combatants, in this case the doomed ones, before the final battle takes place.

31. A. Mahoney, *Vergil in the Works of Prudentius,* 48–49.

32. Mahoney, *Vergil in the Works of Prudentius,* 64 and 68, isolates these allusions.

33. The phrases *dubia sub sorte duelli* and *insani . . . pericula belli* recall, according to a strict philological standard, the dark and uncertain environment created in the *Psychomachia*'s invocation. Vergil's language is used: *sed dubius mediis Mars cerrat in armis* (*Geo.* 2.283), *Martis sorte* (*Aen.* 11.110), *pugnae conterrita sorte* (*Aen.* 12.54); *saevit amor ferri et scelerata insania belli* (*Aen.* 7.461), *accendamque animos insani Martis amore* (*Aen.* 7.550), *temptare pericula belli* (*Aen.* 11.505).

34. The allusion to *Aen.* 11.505 reinforces this warfare context by conjuring up Camilla's words to Turnus as she is going off to meet the army of Aeneas. Like Turnus, she will meet a violent death.

35. The effect of this phrase in Vergil is at once surprising and real because it portends of the tortuous history of civil war that Rome was to endure. In addition, being placed in the Sibyl's speech and in the second invocation of the *Aeneid* where the poet is summoning the inspiration to tell of internecine wars, marks this phrase as one of the most important signifiers of an idea in the epic.

36. For further details on Vergil's allusion to this temple see R. G. Austin, *P. Vergili Maronis Aeneidos Liber Sextus* (Oxford: Clarendon Press, 1977), 64 on line 69.

37. *Psych.* 9's *praesidium* may be a resonance of *Aen.* 6.10's *praesidit,* though the meanings are different in the two passages. *Psych.* 9's *pro libertate* clearly recalls similar Vergilian language, for example at *Aen.* 8.648, the tone of which is dark because it refers to the Brutus of the early Republic who had his sons prosecuted and eventually ex-

ecuted. The Vergilian context further contributes to the uncertain, foreboding tone that both the beginning of the *Psychomachia* and *Aeneid* 6 posses. Both poems occupy the stage of the epic narrative right before the big battle. No matter what god one prays to, the uncertainty of future human events remains in the background. Thus, there is tension over the conquering of Italy in *Aeneid* 6 and over the victory of the virtues over the vices in the invocation and the epilogue of the *Psychomachia*.

38. See B. Otis, *Virgil: A Study in Civilized Poetry* (Oxford: Clarendon Press, 1963), 281–312, who covers the structure, action, and religious elements of Aeneas' descent into the underworld. Along these lines, much of what Otis says still stands despite the fact that at times he engages in overly Christianizing language. Otis argues forcefully that the readiness of Aeneas for the future is "symbolically indicated by his crossing of the line between past and future when he leaves the *arva ultima* of the mythological Hades. By undergoing the crucial ordeal of death, of the loss of his old self, he has finally put on the 'new man' of Roman destiny" (310). G. Luck, "Virgil and the Mystery Religions," *American Journal of Philology* 94 (1973): 147–66, and P. Hardie, *Virgil's Aeneid: Cosmos and Imperium* (Oxford: Clarendon Press, 1986), 42, confirm that the *katabasis* of Aeneas functions according to the poles of death and rebirth.

39. Otis, *Virgil*, 308, says that Aeneas undergoes the death of "his old Trojan and erotic self" and has "an experience of death and resurrection or its psychological equivalent, and emerges from the underworld as a new man."

40. W. Fitzgerald, "Aeneas, Daedalus, and the Labyrinth," in P. Hardie, ed., *Virgil: Critical Assessments of Classical Authors* (London: Routledge, 1999), 214; originally published in *Arethusa* 17 (1984), 51–65; Also, Otis, *Virgil*, 290.

41. Fitzgerald, "Aeneas, Deadalus, and the Labyrinth," 208.

42. M. Malamud, *The Poetics of Transformation: Prudentius and Classical Mythology* (Ithaca, N.Y.: Cornell University Press, 1989), 104–10, in analyzing *Pe.* 11, calls attention to Prudentius' description of Hippolytus' tomb as labyrinthine, thus connecting it to *Aen.* 5.588–91. She rightly concludes, as she cites Fitzgerald's article, that Prudentius' description is nether-worldly, emphasizing the "ease of access" to the underworld and its "strange illumination" found at *Aen.* 6.126–28 and 6.268–72. Also Malamud mentions the connection between the mind and the labyrinth (100).

43. See R. G. Austin, *Aeneid VI*, 210 on line 665 for references.

44. Statius *Achill.* 1.11 has *tempora vittis* in the same line position. The poet is wearing the headdress as he seeks the grove of the Muses to tell his story. Statius' use of the phrase reinforces the poet as sacred communicator and *vates*.

45. Mahoney, *Vergil in the Works of Prudentius*, 59–75.

46. We may detect a comment on Vergil's *regifico luxu* (*Aen.* 6.605) at *Psych.* 97, which says that the bodies of Christians should "be kept clean for their own king." Is this a Prudentian glance at *regifico luxu*? After all, the divine monsters, who recline in luxury in the Vergilian passage are also dining sumptuously (*epulae*). Note later in the *Psychomachia, Sobrietas*' description of those who follow *Luxuria* as reclining at *nocturnas epulas* (*Psych.* 367).

47. *Psych.* 92 also has a resonance with *Aen.* 4.25's language of shades and night: *vel pater omnipotens adigat me fulmine ad umbras, / pallentis umbras Erebro noctemque profundam.* This is an important passage in *Aeneid* 4 because these are the words of Dido who is foreshadowing her own death. Prudentius is concerned to reconstitute the *Aeneid*'s environment of death, both in the characters that experience death and the

landscape of the underworld with its diverse inhabitants. This picture ultimately becomes psychological, signaling a crucial, allusive maneuver from the underworld landscape of *Aeneid* 6, which is suggestive of psychological categories, to the explicitly spatiopsychological terrain of the *Psychomachia*.

48. The words *Tartara* and *Averno* are used by both pagan and Christians—though in this passage *Tartaro* is used of the place where Christian souls go to hell; and *abysso* is exclusively Christian in usage taken directly from the Greek, ἄβυσσος. Despite its occurrence on several Christian inscriptions (*Thesaurus Linguae Latinae*, vol. 8, 298), *manes* appears to be used primarily by pagan authors and when rarely occurring in Christian writers, signifies the pagan underworld. In addition, Tartarus and Avernus commonly evoke both Christian hell and the pagan underworld. The effect of all these words in the Prudentian passage is to characterize Christian hell in a decidedly pagan manner. A. Blaise, *Dictionnaire Latin-Francçais des Auteurs Chrétiens* (Belgique: Brepols, 1995), 513, lists only two Christian readings for *manes,* both from the translation of Eusebius' *Chronicle* by Jerome (1.20.4 and 1.20.3). The evocation of the pagan underworld at the *Psych.* 89–97, in addition to key sections of the poem, which recall *Aeneid* 6, advance the case for the *Psychomachia*'s dependence on *Aeneid* 6.

49. See Ovid, *Meta.* 1.662 and V. Flaccus, *Arg.* 4.231. Lucretius, *DRN* 1.1112, transforms the common meaning of arriving at the "gates of death" to the Epicurean notion that, at the moment of death, one's atomic particles disperse. J.-L. Charlet, "Prudence et la Bible," *Recherches Augustiniennes* 18 (1983): 85, lists more references for both pagan and Christian expressions for the gates of hell.

50. See also *Aen.* 6.429 and 11.28, both of which refer to the gates of the underworld and whose contexts are the deaths of infants and Aeneas' friend Pallas, respectively. *Geo.* 4.481–84 contains yet another Vergilian description of the gates and Tartarus.

51. Biblical epic marginalizes itself by its openly hostile stance against Roman pagan epic tradition. It may use the language, but avoids dialogue with the literary, historical, and political authority of Roman epic. Prudentius engages Roman epic at many levels, including, metaphysics, politics, the status of the hero, and other epic categories. He enters the "literary system" as for instance Walcott does when he engages Homer, Vergil, and Dante in his epic, *Homeros.* Biblical epic refuses to engage in this way.

52. On this and other invocations in Vergil, see Austin, *Aeneid VI,* 115 on lines 264–67.

53. Both Malamud, *The Poetics of Transformation,* 109–10, and S. Spence, *Rhetorics of Reason and Desire: Vergil, Augustine, and the Troubadours* (Ithaca, N.Y.: Cornell University Press, 1988), 60–61, discuss Jerome's *Comm. In Hiez.* 40, where he recalls the feeling of horror (quoting *Aen.* 2.755) he experienced in the labyrinthine and hellish catacombs. Spence does emphasize the psychological aspects of Jerome's comments and Malamud develops Spence's notion of audience participation in the viewing of catacomb paintings.

54. This is M. Smith's position. Nugent, *Allegory and Poetics,* 39–40, views Prudentius' use of Vergil as an appropriation rather than a subversion. Prudentius is more interested in "transferring Roman excellences to Christian contexts" (40).

55. The adjective *malesuada* (*Aen.* 6.276), with which Vergil describes *Fames,* is used by Prudentius with a different personification, *Luxuries* (*Psych.* 404–5). This is an epic word used by Statius at *Theb.* 11.656 to modify *amor* and by Silius Italicus at *Pun.* 14.501 to modify g*loria.* Prudentius is clearly recalling the Vergilian usage.

56. On the Platonic context of *Aeneid* 6, see D. Feeney, "History and Revelation in

Vergil's Underworld," *Proceedings of the Cambridge Philological Society* 212, n. s., 32 (1986): 1–24. D. A. West, "The Bough and the Gate," in S. J. Harrison, ed., *Oxford Readings in Vergil's* Aeneid (Oxford: Oxford University Press, 1990), 237–38, establishes Plato as the source for understanding Aeneas' exit through the gates of dreams. R. Tarrant, "Aeneas and the Gates of Sleep," *Classical Philology* 77 (1982), 51–55, is the most convincing, arguing that the gates of dreams (*falsa insomnia*) through which Aeneas exits should be understood according to a Platonist account in which Aeneas returns to the inferior material world of shadows. For Platonist and other pagan philosophical elements in the *Psychomachia* see chapter 4.

57. *Aen.* 8.362, contains similar language and part of Aeneas' dramatic entry to the palace of Evander, a descendent of the Greeks, who exhorts Aeneas to enter only if he disdains wealth. The tension of the scene resides in the fact that Aeneas has just entered a hostile land, expressed clearly by Venus who appeals for help to Jupiter just as Aeneas enters the palace.

58. The epilogue, however, may be read as simply a rehashing in miniature of the successive battles of the body of the poem. The alternation between virtue as victorious in the soul and vice as triumphant, appears to mark the element of choice in the battle within the soul, for while we are on earth humans can never believe that the battle against vice is won. But in the epilogue both sides receive nearly equal time, suggesting that the choice is always before us.

59. Lactantius uses *ore pio* once (*De Ave Phoenice* 127); Ambrose once (*Hex.* 6.4.18); Augustine once (*Serm.* 51); Paulinus of Nola three times (*Carm.* 21.62—407 CE, *Carm.* 28.311—404 CE, and *Ep.* 33.2).

60. The expression is found eleven times in Cicero, fourteen times in Livy, and once in Caesar, Sallust, Vergil, Valerius Flaccus, and Silius Italicus. Prudentius, like his fellow Christian writers, "Christianizes" the expression, but given the connections to *Aeneid* 6 I have established, the claim to epic identity of the *Psychomachia*, a second reference to Aeneas' meeting with Deiphobus in the underworld and the substantial pagan usage of the expression, we can confidently read this expression, as Mahoney does, as an allusion to *Aeneid*.

61. A. Mahoney, *Vergil in the Works of Prudentius*, lists *Aen.* 12.140–41 as another allusion at *Psych.* 889, but it is difficult to see what the connection is between the two passages.

62. The history of the *Aeneid*'s reception has vacillated between two views. On the one hand, there is the melancholic, elegiac view that the tragedy of Turnus' death, as well as perceived ambiguities in the pageant of heroes and the shield passage, dominates whatever the propagandistic and ideological content of the *Aeneid* may be. On the other hand, the confident, imperial view understands the work as cosmic in reach, wherein the advent of Roman Empire confirms a universal order, inevitable and ultimately for the good. Rather than two detailed, opposing views, these readings represent general and beginning assumptions according to which a reader approaches language, scenes, and characters in the *Aeneid*. It does not mean, for instance, that each side's reading of a character or a scene is exclusive of the other side's reading. More accurately, the optimistic and pessimistic assumptions lead a reader to emphasize one aspect of the work at the expense of another; for instance, the *Aeneid*'s characters over its universal implications or *vice versa*. On the "voices" in the *Aeneid*, see M. C. J. Putnam, "Foreword," and S. Quinn, "Introduction: Why Words," in *Why Vergil? A*

Collection of Interpretations, ed., S. Quinn (Wauconda, Ill.: Bolchazy-Carducci Press, 2000), vii–xii and 8–17.

63. Smith reads pessimistically, seeing the *Aeneid* overlain with a tragic gloom that Prudentius reacts to with the grand universal vision of the *Psychomachia.* For Smith, the mortal characters of the *Aeneid* have "no salvational desire," a phenomenon indicated by the work's tragic tone. This is a reading heavily influenced by Christianity's emphasis on individual salvation (Smith, *Prudentius'* Psychomachia, 241). Aeneas, Dido, Turnus, and other characters do not see their purpose as personal salvation, but are clearly focused on the salvation of their peoples, whatever the cost to them individually. Prudentius understands this broader sense of salvation and recasts it as a consequence of individual Romans adopting Christian values and beliefs. The more individuals there are who adopt completely Christianity, the more likely will Rome's greatness survive. In addition, the point is frequently made in the *Aeneid* that the coming of Rome may not represent salvation to the actors in the narrative, but certainly does to the generations that follow Aeneas, Lavinia, and Ascanius; this salvation can be felt most pointedly by the original reader himself who was the beneficiary of Roman citizenship in the first century BCE. The tragic fates of Dido and Turnus represent the exact opposite of salvation, namely, generational and national extinction. So, if we read the *Aeneid* in this way, the *Psychomachia* takes on a different meaning from what critics have said of it in the past.

64. H. J. Thomson "The *Psychomachia* of Prudentius," *Classical Review* 44 (1930): 109–12, and W. T. H. Jackson, "Allegory and Allegorization," *Research Studies* 32 (1964): 161–75, with whom Smith disagrees, read the *Aeneid* optimistically and thus emphasize the idea that the *Psychomachia* represents a cosmic vision, mirrored on earth as a "civilizing struggle." Thomson argues that the Aeneas/Turnus conflict informs the *Psychomachia,* especially as expressed in "the contest of the divinely commissioned Trojans with the present inhabitants of their promised land under 'proud Turnus.'" Thomson further argues that "Prudentius conceived the war of Aeneas as in a way 'prefiguring' the moral warfare of the soul, divine law and peace subduing ungoverned selfish passions" (112). Jackson says, "The *Psychomachia* assumes, as does the Vergilian epic, a struggle between two opposed views of existence—the new Trojan and the old Italian in the *Aeneid,* the combats between the brothers in the *Thebaid* of Statius, and it assumes also the possibility of the resolution of the struggle between these forces by the outcome of one titanic conflict. . . . By using these epic techniques, Prudentius lends to the Christians' daily struggle with evil the grandeur and majesty as well as the authority of epic. . . . The implication of an epic struggle dignifies the effort to make virtue conquer vice and universalize it" (quoted in Smith, *Prudentius'* Psychomachia, 165). In Jackson we witness a forerunner of Hardy's focus on epic's universalizing tendency and the transmission of this from Vergil to the proceeding Roman epicists.

65. See R. D. Williams, *Virgil Book III* (Oxford: Oxford University Press, 1962) on *Aen.* 3. 274 for the connection to Actium and the shrine restored there by Augustus.

66. Smith, *Prudentius'* Psychomachia, 190. In note 18, Smith wonders whether these lines are "a central miniature of the action of the *Psychomachia*" (192). And Smith comments on the end of the *Psychomachia,* "Through the process of defeating the vices, of experiencing reversals in the moral struggle, of maintaining a watchful guard against the Barbarian attackers of Satan, the virtues have gained a glimpse of Hell and have passed on to their reward" (204). Smith does not develop these perceptive observations into a coherent view.

67. The scene of the virtues surrounding *Discordia* recalls the scene of the Greeks surrounding Sinon at *Aen.* 2.67ff. Specific linguistic references are as follows: *Psych.* 685/*Aen.* 8. 702–703; *Psych.* 700/*Aen.* 11.746 *Psych.* 703/*Aen.* 11.812. Other linguistic references for *Psych.* 699–715 are as follows: *Aen.* 12.662–63, 2.333, 2.449, 11.746, 11.812.

68. Hardie, *The Epic Successors of Virgil*, 4–11.

69. In Vergilian and Flavian epic, the hero has a synecdochic or metonymic quality where "Rome," and its attendant metaphysical, political and historical connotations, is reduced to one man. The hero is "the individual who stands for the totality of his people present and future, part for the whole" (Hardie, *The Epic Successors of Virgil*, 4). Hardie comments further that the succession of such heroes in epic leads to the Adam and Christ of Milton (4–10). This standard theme of the *unus homo* takes different forms in the Flavian epicists but is radically altered in Prudentius. Regarding terminology, "synecdoche" can work in two directions, either the part for the whole or the whole for the part. In addition, "metonymy" is a one-to-one relationship where one name stands for another name. The two can be used interchangeably, though in certain cases, the whole/part relationship is instructive.

70. The only time when the virtues engage in self-destructive behavior (*Psych.* 328ff.), they are figured according to the description of the vice *Luxuria*. The winners in epic "experience history as a coherent, end-directed story told by their own power," while the losers, "experience a contingency that they are powerless to shape to their own ends"(Quint, *Epic and Empire*, 9). The virtues and vices parallel this idea directly, and if we further understand them as representing Christian and pagan doctrine respectively—the connection to the political is not far. For, as the *Contra Symmachum* explicitly shows, Prudentius deeply engages the struggle that, although all but settled politically by the end of the fourth century, remains ideologically and spiritually in play. Each individual must be fought for, each person convinced or persuaded that immortal life is only possible through faith in the Trinity.

71. M. Smith, *Prudentius'* Psychomachia, 275. Smith does not mention nor discuss the further parallels the text encourages and I give in the rest of the paragraph.

72. Hardie, *The Epic Successors*, 75, says of Milton's *Paradise Lost*, "The contrasting claims of God and Satan for the admiration of the reader arise out of the thematization within the epic narrative of *the need to make a choice* (my italics), intellectual and moral, between good and evil, such being the condition of our fallen selves once the apple has been tasted." Moreover, as Hardie mentions, Milton problematizes the choice by making good and evil similar. In the *Psychomachia*, this is also the case. See S. G. Nugent's discussion of *fraus* in the *Psychomachia* in her *Allegory and Poetics*, 87–93. Good cannot be discerned because evil is disguised as good—i.e., the wolf in sheep's clothing. And good becomes assimilated to worldly goods that are temporary and cater to humans' desire for pleasure. Prudentius deserves credit for transposing Roman epic dualism from political and historical issues to the individual. What is left of the political and the historical mission of Rome is syncretized in a universal history that includes pagan Roman history. In addition, the mechanism for the problematization of the individual reader is the doctrine of free will which I will treat more comprehensively. The reader becomes part of the *Psychomachia*'s typological architecture as the final term in the series and thus epic's ultimate purpose, which consisted of national and heroic concerns, becomes personal. Yet, since this "personal" epic is a product of the Roman epic tradition, it maintains a political point of view.

73. The final prayer of the *Hamartigenia* portrays the poet/narrator in the abject

position of a believer undeserving of a place in heaven and full of sin. This is not the heroic confidence and active stance of the virtues in the *Psychomachia* and the martyrs in the *Peristephanon*.

74. Prudentius, *Symm.* 2.649–768, personifies Rome, giving her a speech in which she confirms her identity as a Christian state. *Symm.* 1.287–902, 2.583–640, and *Pe.* 2.413–40, describe Rome's cosmic and sacred historical mission.

75. Yet the *Punica* seems to reconfirm traditional Roman values in the guise of Scipio. Valerius Flaccus' *Argonautica* is shot through with references to contemporary Roman customs in order to show the origins of imperial institutions. The voyages of the Argo set in motion historical cycles of civilization that lead to the Roman Empire (1.536–41). Statius' *Thebaid* revisits themes of political power and civil war but is not as directly concerned with Rome's imperial and cosmic roles.

76. Of course, the Christian golden age occurs before the Fall and is brought back through the Incarnation of Christ. As a Roman, Prudentius displaces this mythological and theological story into the actual condition of third- and fourth-century Rome. For more on epic golden ages, see Hardie, *Epic Successors,* 2–3, with references. For the primary texts see Lucan, *Bell. Civ.* 1.61–62, Valerius Flaccus, *Argon.* 1.555–67, and Silius *Pun.* 3.622–24.

77. Nugent, *Allegory and Poetics,* 40, extrapolates from the historical context that the religious and the political are in conflict: "The battle fought in the soul of man has repercussions also for the confrontation between the body politic and the mystical body of the church."

78. Nugent, *Allegory and Poetics,* 61, suggests one interpretation of the *Psychomachia*'s new temple as a triumphal military arch of the Roman Empire. The temple signifies the founding of a civilization.

T W O : Christian History and the Narrative of Rome

1. See D. Quint, *Epic and Empire,* chapters 1 and 2 on the *Aeneid* in which "narrative itself" is "ideologically charged" and the reason for "historical identity" (45). The *Aeneid* "is the struggle not of the individual psyche but of a collective political nation" (51). The *Psychomachia* combines both the individual psychological struggle with political definition by using the latter as a resolution to the former.

2. See H. White, *The Content of the Form* (Baltimore: Johns Hopkins University Press, 1987), on the idea that allegoresis is the fundamental way to describe what the narrative historian is doing. D. Quint, *Epic and Empire,* 43 comments on how "epic shapes a master narrative of history." In the preliminaries to his postmodern critique that the metanarrative of the Enlightenment eliminates "little narratives" in the modernist quest for emancipation from history, J.-F. Lyotard, "Universal History and Cultural Differences, in *The Lyotard Reader,* ed. A. Benjamin (Oxford: Blackwell, 1989), 321, aptly describes the authority of grand or master narratives: "The power of the narrative mechanism confers legitimacy . . . being diachronic and parachronic, it ensures mastery over time, and therefore life and death. Narrative is authority itself. It authorizes an unbreakable 'we,' outside of which there can only be 'they.'" For the definitions of and relationship between "metanarrative" and "little narratives" see B. Readings, *Introducing Lyotard: Art and Politics* (London: Routledge, 1991), 63–64.

3. J. Burckhardt, *The Age of Constantine the Great,* trans., M. Hadas (New York:

Pantheon, 1949), 283, sees Eusebius as "the first thoroughly dishonest historian of antiquity" who participated in the creation of an imperial theology by not revealing "Constantine's true position" and "uttered no word of displeasure against the murderous egoist who possessed the great merit of having conceived of Christianity as a world power and of having acted accordingly" (293). See also A. Momigliano, "Pagan and Christian Historiography," in *Essays in Ancient and Modern Historiography* (Middletown, Conn.: Wesleyan University Press, 1977), 108–19; T. Barnes, *Constantine and Eusebius* (Cambridge, Mass.: Harvard University Press, 1981), 105; and A. Cameron and S. G. Hall, *Eusebius: Life of Constantine* (Oxford: Clarendon Press, 1999), 46 (Cameron and Hall represent current approaches which situate Eusebius as a biblical scholar and Christian apologist and not as a "scientific" historian); and, finally, E. Breisach, *Historiography: Ancient, Medieval, and Modern,* 2d ed. (Chicago: University of Chicago Press, 1983), 82.

4. Just as the careers of Sallust's Jugurtha and Marius can be understood as analogies or metaphors for the decline of Rome, and therefore the corruption of a Republican *Romanitas.*

5. *Pe.* 11.1–22; and in the first twenty lines of *Pe.* 9 Prudentius portrays himself interviewing the caretaker (*aedituus*) of Saint Cassian's tomb.

6. *Symm.* 2.343–46: *ipsum / sanguinis Hectorei populum probo tempore longo / non multos coluisse deos rarisque sacellis / contentum paucas posuisse in collibus aras;* they ignored crucial events to defend their position: e.g., *Symm.* 2.309–11: *quid mihi tu ritus solitos, Romane senator, / obiectas cum scita patrum populique frequenter / instabilis placiti sententia flexa novarit?* It is especially noteworthy that Prudentius feels no compunction about lecturing Symmachus on the history of Roman pagan religion. In addition, at *Symm.* 2.312–15 (*nunc etiam quotiens solitis decedere prodest / praeteritosque habitus cultu damnare recenti, / gaudemus conpertum aliquid tandemque retectum, / quod latuit*), Prudentius augments his critical and teleological views of history by arguing that the study of history allows humans the flexibility in the present to change and adapt. Old ways that do not work must be discarded for new ones. Roman history is rife with such examples, but the poet does not reject altogether the old ways.

7. M. Smith, *Prudentius' Psychomachia,* chapter 3, skillfully discusses typology and history in the *Psychomachia* from an exclusively Christian perspective without a major consideration of the pagan Roman contribution.

8. Quint, *Epic and Empire,* 30, relates the use of history to universal historical narrative and "the *principle of history*—whereby identity and power are transmitted across time in patralineal succession."

9. Conventional scholarly wisdom rightly concludes that one purpose of fourth-century Christian historiography was to unify the history of the empire and sacred history—e.g., Momigliano, "Pagan and Christian Historiography," 110. Breisach, *Historiography,* 78–79, and 82; also, G. A. Press, *The Development of the Idea of History* (Montreal: McGill-Queens University Press, 1982), 127. But even though the separation between sacred and Roman history persists for many poets of this era, including Juvencus, Proba, Damasus, Ambrose, and Paulinus—and for those Christian poets who follow Prudentius: Sedulius, Arator, Victorius, and Avitus—Prudentius' *Psychomachia* and *Peristephanon* are serious attempts at unification.

10. This trope's effect is best measured as "a literary device" that constructs a "sacred story." N. Frye, *The Great Code, The Bible and Literature* (New York: Harcourt, 1982),

explains that of the many figures used in writing narratives causality and typology move in time. Whereas causality is past-oriented, based on reason and observation, typology is forward-looking, future-oriented, and based on faith and hope. Frye sees typology as a metaphorical language of proclamation, the basic expression of which is "this is that." This language is applied within the historical frame of salvation history, which Frye understands as a series of revelations. Thus, typology plays a central role in salvation history. In Prudentius' work, the correspondences that define typology are the means for the construction of his historical narrative, which enacts an allegoresis—that is, it means something other than what it literally says. Typology is necessary but not sufficient to form a Christian theory of history; it may participate in forming such a theory by playing the role of creating a historical narrative that, when taken as a whole, results in a meaning different from its constituents (events)—i.e., salvation history. The *Psychomachia* in particular operates in this manner, but the same can be said to a lesser degree of the *Peristephanon* by itself and when juxtaposed with the *Psychomachia*. F. Young, "Typology," in *Crossing the Boundaries: Essays in Biblical Interpretation in Honour of Michael D. Goulder,* eds. S. E. Porter, P. Joyce, and D. E. Orton (Leiden: E. J. Brill Press, 1994), 48. T. Fabiny, in his *The Lion and the Lamb,* writes eloquently about Frye's views of typology worked out in *The Great Code.* The intertextual element is expressed in typology's correspondences between personages, events, words, and concepts derived from historical circumstances that constitute particular manifestations of the broad category of allegory. See M. D. Goulder, *Type and History in* Acts (London: SPCK, 1964) and Young, "Typology," 39.

11. This typological method is part of a poetics of history in which the past, as a construction of writing, is, "pregnant with the future"—i.e., the Fall prefigures salvation—Fabiny, *The Lion and the Lamb*, 20.

12. Prudentius' historical narrative in both the *Psychomachia* and the *Peristephanon* manifests itself through the distribution of allusions from the three major historical traditions he controls: the pagan, Christian, and Hebrew traditions. In other words, the construction of the historical narrative is represented through a series of organized and carefully chosen allusions from these traditions. In the *Psychomachia,* the historical narrative is not the surface narrative of the battle between the virtues and the vices and is assembled from allusions to "real" events that happened "in time." The surface narrative is straightforward, and perhaps monotonous, summed up as merely a series of set piece battles with the victory of the virtues and the building of a temple. The bridge which connects the surface narrative of virtue/vice battles and the subnarrative of historical allusions is the comprehension of these two narrative levels by readers themselves. For the *Psychomachia* assumes that they experience the struggle between the virtues and the vices, and, hence, the readers' own time, the present, becomes intertwined with the history, the past, constructed through Prudentius' allusive technique. The argument of the poem is that the present individual is part of salvation history. In this way sub- and surface narratives merge, the present becomes bounded to the past. A similar argument can be made for the *Peristephanon.* The surface narrative of this series of poems is the deaths of martyrs that took place in the near past, but a subnarrative, made up of events even further in the past, I submit, results in the conjoining of Roman and martyr historical traditions. Prudentius sprinkles each poem with allusions to Rome's pagan past in order to merge the surface narrative of the martyr with the bulk of Roman history.

13. R. G. Collingwood, *The Idea of History* (New York: Oxford University Press, 1946), 50, sums up the Christian approach to historical events: "[Providential history] . . . will attach a central importance . . . to the historical life of Christ," and discusses Eusebius' *Chronicle* as a universal history "where all events were brought within a single chronological framework . . . inspired by a new purpose, the purpose of showing that events thus chronicled formed a pattern with the birth of Christ in its center" (51).

14. The discourse of Christian personhood takes different forms according to its theological, ethical, political context. In this chapter, I move freely between these contexts but always assume, as I believe Prudentius does, that the portrayal of the soul determines how one talks about the Christian person. My use of the term "self" functions as a locus for the theological, ethical, and political discourses of the individual.

15. Augustine *De Doct. Chr.* 2.28.42–44 says that profane, worldly history does give useful knowledge for understanding scripture since it is under God's control—i.e., somehow divinely directed. The notion of history is also part of Augustine's radical theory of subjectivity in which time is synchronic and the past and the future exist only as a "present of things past, a present of things present and a present of things future because these temporal entities exist in the mind and nowhere else. Memory therefore is the present of things past." See J. Coleman, *Ancient and Medieval Memories* (Cambridge: Cambridge University Press, 1992), 97 and *Conf.* 11.8. In "early" Augustine, then, sacred and profane history are combined into a synchronic view in which human memory, as it distinguishes the past and the future in the now, sees the past as "ever present and ever relevant" (J. Coleman 1992, 100). Likewise, when looking to Prudentius' use of typology, it is clear that past events merge into the present and future through the development of a person's ability to hold simultaneously in her mind past, present, and future events. This is the point at which a person constructs meaning.

16. Charlet, "Prudence et la Bible," 93, lists the New and Old Testament books alluded to in the *Psychomachia* and the *Peristephanon*.

17. Spiegal, *The Past as Text*, xiii, refers to N. Frye's notion of emplotment, which accounts for the creation of a (historical) narrative: "a text's structural characteristics and narrative economy, as the submerged vehicle of meaning." See also White, *The Content of the Form*, 51.

18. Prudentius uses *fabula* to indicate a general idea of lies and falsity at *Symm.* 2.50, when he blames the poets (*poetica fabula*) for propagating false gods. See also *Pe.* 10. 956–58 where stories about Christ are not "fictional," *fabulosa* and *Symm.* 1. 191, which gives a typical literary meaning of the word as stories about heroic men. But in other passages there are signs of Prudentius expanding the meaning of the word. For instance, at *Apoth.* 294–309, *fabula* at first glance is set in opposition to historical sources which come from Moses' meeting with God on Sinai (*scrinia primi scriptoris, Apoth.* 295–96). True stories, history, can only come from god via an intermediary like Moses or Christ whom, in this passage, Prudentius argues has always been with God (*orbis principio, Apoth.* 303) including the time when he instructed Moses. Prudentius projects a Platonist ontology onto storytelling. The stories of history occupy the realm of the divine, Human stories are one level removed from this absolute truth because they admit of falsity. Thus, they must be carefully scrutinized. *Fabula*, however, is a general word for narrative story, the form in which all information, whether of God or not, is communicated. For human beings to receive true stories, they must put their trust in

Christ as the mediator of divine history. The notion of story then spills over into the human world because of our relationship to God as having been created in his own image. We are in a typological relationship (*Apoth.* 309) with God and Christ, which not only proves our relationship to the Father, but also bespeaks our ignorance of true *fabulae* without the mediation of Christ. For Prudentius, typology, history, and narrative (*fabula*) have a necessary and complicated relationship. *Apoth* 1018–19 again uses *fabula* to connote a human life in which Christ takes part yet is clearly beyond. For a more direct association of *fabula* with typology see *Ham. Praef.* 25–31, which associates Marcion the heretic with the fratricide Cain. *Pe.* 2. 313–20 links *fabula* with *figura*, but in service to a mocking and false type of storytelling—namely, automime.

19. Prudentius has a literary sense of *fabula* in mind at *Apoth.* 1017–18 and preserves this sense at *Pe.* 9. 17–20 and *Praef. Ham.* 25–26 to link *fabula* with a typological notion of history. His usage differs from Livy *Ab Urb. Cond.* 1.11.8, for instance, where he describes a *fabula* about the Sabines that describes their bracelets. Prudentius does not have in mind an ornamental notion of *fabula* as pithy legend. Augustine uses the word in its range of senses in his earlier works. For *fabula* as fables, untrue stories, or wondrous accounts see *Conf.* 5.10, *De genesi contra manichaeos* 2; as gossip, *Conf.* 5.9, Paulinus *Carm.* 11.45; as trivial Greek literature, *Conf.* 1.14, Paulinus *Ep.* 16.7, 23.30, 49.8, *Carm.* 10.34; as lies, *Conf.* 4.8, *De Genesi Contra Manichaeos* 1, and *De Doct. Christ.* 2.25; as literary deception engaged in by poets, orators, philosophers, and heretics, *Conf.* 5.3 and *De Doct. Christ.* 2.35, Paulinus *Ep.* 13.24, 16.4, 40.6.

20. M. Currie, *Postmodern Narrative Theory* (New York: St. Martin's Press, 1998), 88 summarizes S. Greenblatt's claim that "history has to renew itself by moving away from 'realist' assumptions about the meaning of a historical text toward the recognition that history and literature are discourses which construct rather than reflect, invent rather than discover, the past." Athough it is almost certain that Prudentius understood his poetic composition as reflecting and discovering history, from the point of view of the early twenty-first-century critic, his literary activity falls under Greenblatt's characterization. Even Prudentius himself would have to admit, along with postmodern narratological conventions, that the reader plays an active role in the constructing of the historical narrative allegorically expressed in the *Psychomachia*. A literary work that depends on the proper understanding of allegories, relies heavily on the reader to construct meaning, but nevertheless retains the presence of the author who furnishes a carefully presented and structured set of literary data which guides the reader's understanding.

21. Prudentius uses forms of *noto* at *Pe.* 9.16 and 82. The passages emphasize the perverse use of writing skills that Cassian innocently taught his students. The act of writing letters in the classroom has become an act of murder and ironically a means of transcendent immortality. But as *notata* at *Praef. Ham.* 26 indicates, writing is the vehicle for storytelling, which is precisely what Prudentius wishes to do regarding his subject, Cassian. See J. Ballengee, "The Wound That Speaks: Prudentius' *Peristephanon Liber* and the Rhetoric of Suffering," *Crossings* 5/6 (2002–2003): 107–43.

22. Currie, *Postmodern Narrative Theory,* 2:"[N]arrative is central to the representation of identity, in personal memory and self representation or in collective identity of groups such as regions, nations, race, and gender."

23. In *Apoth.* 1017–18, the allusive twist on the Homeric motif of human lives as leaves is unmistakable. Like Homer, Prudentius' metaphor of the winds reflects the

futility of mortality. The epic *fabula* of great men's deeds is feeble in itself. The story becomes great only when the typologies of salvation history are applied to a human life, to that person's story, with the result of true immortality. The old epic (pagan) *fabula* remains a piece of writing as part of this world and of nothing beyond.

24. J. D. Dawson, *Christian Figural Reading and the Fashioning of Identity* (Berkeley: University of California Press, 2002), 86, appeals to Auerbach's three features of figural (i.e., typological) reading: that there be two persons or events from different historical periods, that there be a relation between them, and that an act of interpretation expose the relationship between them. Dawson extends this idea of figural reading by commenting that figural meaning "describes the intelligibility discovered in the relation between two events comprising a single divine performance in history." Dawson, similar to his readings of Auerbach and Origen, is concerned to preserve the historicity of both the figure and its fulfillment, a task that flies in the face of, he believes, modern and postmodern notions of meaning with their preoccupation with the textual signifier. Rather than meaning as abstraction or allegory, Dawson, 87, understands figural meaning as a relationship between real (historical) entities. Meaning is the literal relationship between two historical events or persons that preserves the historical reality.

25. Dawson, *Christian Figural Reading,* 96, in agreement with both Auerbach's and Boyarin's idea that allegorical reading "reduces objects of its interpretation to abstractions," comments that figural reading regards the object of interpretation as simultaneously text and history. According to Dawson, this has the further effect of preserving historical reality and its textual representation. Allegorical reading disregards historical reality by viewing texts as collections of signs independent of historical events. This may be the case, but Dawson, in my view, has not satisfactorily shown that figural reading itself does not participate in a comparable maneuver that an allegorical reader performs when interpreting a "historical" text. Figural meaning as a relation between x and y still is an add-on in the same way an allegorical meaning originating from a textual signifier is. Dawson, while discussing Origen (chapter 5), admits to the generally allegorical character of figural meaning but maintains his stance that figural reading must not become figurative—i.e., nonliteral. A figural interpretation perhaps is more closely tied to the content of events x and y, but, as a result, x and y do not gain "more" historicity than a semiological interpretation of x and y as expressed in words. Figural interpretation remains in the realm of words that are signs to be interpreted according to a human projection of the world onto them.

26. *Apoth.* 1017–18 and *Praef. Ham.* 25–26 contain a literary series of connections, events—story—typology—history/allegory, all of which help to define an individual human life. For the view of self typology underwrites see the epilogue.

27. Dawson, *Christian Figural Reading,* 133, shows that Origen accepts the proposition that events may alter the character of prior events; a good example being the notion that Christ's arrival transforms what has come before into "gospel." Origen signals this view by describing the Old Testament prophets and patriarchs as "initiated in types." See Dawson, 128–31.

28. Poetry is surely implied by *recto . . . pede.*

29. Fabiny, *The Lion and the Lamb,* 22–25.

30. Hence the reader's role in the process of allegory is to make this correct application. But the author plays a central role in guiding the reader's response, though he can not ultimately control the reader's response.

31. We can tell that Prudentius has an interest in Rome, the imperial state, because he connects the adoption of correct doctrine to the health of the state (e.g., *Pe.* 10. 402).

32. The first two lines of *Pe.* 11 refer indirectly to Prudentius' "archival" research: *Innumeros cineres sanctorum romula in urbe / vidimus, o Christi Valeriane sacer* (*Pe.* 11.1–2).

33. Prudentius' use of *apices*, "letters," reinforces the notion that the genre of history is invoked here through the writing of historical events. But the word does even more work. M. J. Roberts, *Poetry and the Cult of the Martyrs,* 151–56, acknowledges Prudentius' historiographical mission and focuses on *apices* as "the strokes that make up an individual letter" (151), which emphasize "the element of decipherment" and an investigator's actual search for a martyr's remains (153–54). "Traces *(apices)*" of the inscriptions on the tombs are parallel to "traces of past events *(rerum apices veterum)*." In a less developed view of the passage, Palmer, *Prudentius on the Martyrs,* 116 mentions Prudentius' "insistence on his personal observation and experience" as well as on "autopsy." It is possible to push the polyvalency of the word even further. In addition, an *apex* is also a felt tip of a roman priest's cap, as well as a crown of victory. It is not a giant leap, especially considering the poet's careful use of language in programmatic parts of his poetry, to see *apices* as a pivotal programmatic word. This word alone alludes to three separate but connected categories: history (written letters), religion (an accoutrement of a priest), and major Christian heroes (the crowned martyrs).

34. As I argued in chapter 1, both poet and reader are subsumed under the category of "reader."

35. Examples abound in the *Natalicia* in which Felix is compared to Old Testament figures—e.g., 15.84ff., 26.195ff., 26. 246ff.—and for a more generalized moral exemplar see 16.129ff. Because this set of poems by Paulinus is often concerned with the *res gestae* of Felix—i.e., miracles and achievements—Paulinus is able to think of himself as a historian as well. But his two main historical activities in these poems are recounting the events of Felix's life and retelling the narrative of the Old and New Testaments. The most fascinating statement of this project is at *Carm.* 20. 28–61, where Paulinus draws the classical and now Christian distinction between the "truthfulness of the historian" and "the deceit of the poet," saying that his poetry will be a version of the former without the latter (20.28–29). The passage goes on to exploit the metaphor of the lyre, a sophisticated typological device that stands for the body. But here it is the body of a mortal person, David, Christ, and the unified body of the people of the world under Christian doctrine of immortal life. The lyre of course stands for poetry as well. Thus, like Prudentius, Paulinus sees a new poetry whose inspiration is the figure of Christ that cuts across and unifies all geographical and temporal boundaries. What Paulinus manifestly lacks is a detailed and systematic vision of how Old Testament, New Testament, Roman pagan, and Roman Christian historical traditions come together to form universal salvation history. Prudentius undertakes this project and makes his task even more difficult by trying to include Rome's political and literary successes in that vision. Paulinus simply does not go this far.

36. The "T" (tau) represents the cross and the capital "I" (iota) and "H" (eta) are the first two letters of Jesus' name.

37. I understand "Christian doctrine" as distinct from "Christian ideology." The former refers to the religious ideas that drive the definition of Christian religion such as the doctrines of the soul and Trinity, canonized—to some extent—at the Council of

Nicaea in 325. The latter is a concept in which Christian doctrine is exploited for the creation of a Christian historical memory to advance a political program, such as a divine Roman empire.

38. P. Brown, *The Rise of Western Christendom: Triumph and Diversity* (Oxford: Blackwell, 2003), 14, writes, "Christians might not convert everybody; but they could, at least, be everywhere. The possession of sacred Scriptures made of them a potentially worldwide 'textual community.'"

39. Here defined as the doctrine itself or the sacrament.

40. Smith, *Prudentius' Psychomachia*, 232: "The *Psychomachia* contains many typologically related temples: the temple of Solomon, the temple of the pure heart, the anagogic temple of the New Jerusalem, and the temple of *Sapientia*.

41. Compare *Titulae Historiae* 31.21, where a stone of the old temple is used for the foundation of the new temple.

42. This is the reading of scripture and history that Dawson, *Christian Figural Reading*, 7 wishes to avoid. He seeks rather a "Christian figural reading that can remain true to its vocation of fashioning Christian identity while simultaneously cherishing human diversity."

43. See notes 3 and 9.

44. This is not to say that both pagan historians did not have a bias or that the populations regarding whom they produce historical discourse separate religion from politics.

45. A salient example of Eusebius' and Christian historiography's practice of wedding the political and the religious is at *Vita Constantini* I.2.1, where Eusebius claims he will not treat Constantine's military campaigns but will focus only on his religious actions. Yet throughout the *Vita* he does indeed narrate and linger over the emperor's military exploits. Rome's peace and prosperity are inseparable from God. Eusebius presents Constantine's victories as a divine endorsement that binds together Rome's imperial mission and Christian identity. See A. Cameron and S. Hall, *Eusebius: Life of Constantine* (Oxford: Clarendon Press, 1999), 45–47.

46. The word *saeculum* is primarily a word of historical discourse rather than of typology. As we shall see, however, it is inseparable from Prudentius' typological language and thought. *Conbibere* as well is not a technical, typological term but the way Prudentius uses it in this passage and others indicates a strong typological sense of the word—unique to Prudentius.

47. For instance, Ovid *Ars Am.* 2.326, *Met.* 13.944, 13.410, and 15.275.

48. *Fin.* 3.9.

49. The literal meaning of the passage is about a golden headband drinking up spikenard. Thus the meaning of "drinking up doctrine" requires the reader to make an allegorical leap. If one's dress or appearance depends on the consumption of such luxury products, one's character is easily corrupted. *Ham.* 608 contains another occurrence of the verb in which the soul is depicted as "drinking up" snake venom, again the idea of corruption is present on a figurative level. Still another usage at *Pe.* 10. 1040 is a part of the famous description of the *taurobolium* ritual in which the priest, while standing in a pit below a bull as it is slaughtered, "drinks up" the sacrificial animal's blood. Such imbibing leaves the pagan priest "defiled" (*inquinatum*). The reader again can infer that bad doctrine has been taken into the body and as a result, pollutes the soul. *Conbibere* is doing significant work in these passages.

50. Tertullian at *De Baptismo* 4 speaks of various bodies of water that can be employed for the sacrament of baptism because they "imbibe" the power to sanctify through the Holy Spirit: *Igitur omnes aquae de pristine originis praerogativa sacramentum sanctificationis consecuntur invocato deo: supervenit enim statim spiritus de caelis et aquis superest sanctificans eas de semet ipso et ita sanctificatae vim sanctificandi conbibunt.* Arnobius (*Ad. Nat.* 5.10) criticizes a pagan theory of creation in which stones "absorb" semen and create humans.

51. The Latin text of Paulinus is from the edition of G. de Hartel, *Paulinus Nolanus: Epistulae.* Vol. 29 of *Corpus Scriptorum Ecclesiasticorum Latinorum,* 2d ed. (Vienna: Verlag sterreichischen Akademie Der Wissenschaften, 1999).

52. This is P. G. Walsh's translation of *tristi . . . crapula.*

53. Interestingly *conbibere* is not associated with the eucharist in Christian writing of the fourth century.

54. For example, Tertullian, *De Baptismo* 4, *Adv. Iud.* 14.

55. Saint Jerome uses the word very often. It appears that he is more interested in the usage that has to do with naming something, at least in his *Epistulae.* In his textual criticism, he uses it to obelize a phrase or word; however, the typological usage is present in his works as well.

56. Paulinus is discussing the basilica at Nola: *Omne cubiculum binis per liminum frontes versibus praenotatur, quos inserere his litteris nolui.*

57. It is surprising that late fourth-century Latin church fathers use forms of *adumbrare* infrequently. The use of the participial form in a typological sense is very rare. Augustine uses the verb the most, but, more surprisingly, Tertullian never uses the typological sense. Ambrose, Jerome, and Augustine all use the term in its technical, typological sense: e.g., Jerome, *Comm. In Ez.* 1.4; Ambrose, *De Spiritu Sancto* 1.7; Augustine, *Civ.* 16.3 and 17.5. For *adumbrare* as "obscure" or "counterfeit, see Tertullian, *De Pudicitia* 17; Ambrose, *De Fuga Saeculi* 4.18; Jerome, *Adv. Iovanian.* 2.14; Augustine *Conf.* 6.7.

58. *Instructionum Libri* 1.36.4–5: *Rex aeternitatis per crucem diros adumbrat, / ut sibi non credant.* The passage is difficult to translate because the meaning of *adumbrat* is unclear, or at best, extremely abstract. The text is from J. Martin, *Commodiani Carmina. Corpus Christianorum: Series Latina* 126 (Turnholt: Brepols, 1960).

59. I give lines 363–68: *inde sub antiquo legitur velamine Moyses / Iudaeis nebula cordis opertus adhuc, / quam de luminibus mentis mihi creditus aufert / Christus, adumbratas discutiens species / seque docens prisca velatum legis in umbra / iamque revelatum corporis in facie.*

60. A search of the database *CETEDOC Library of Christian Latin Texts,* CLCLT-4, ed., P. Tombeur (Turnhout: Brepols Publishers, 2000), yielded eight occurrences besides Prudentius in the Patristic era.

61. The other occurrences come from Tertullian, Pseudo-Jerome, *Historia Ecclesiastica Tripartita,* and Cassiodorus. The Tertullian passage (*Adv. Valent.* 27) contains the two words, but they are syntactically distinct. The church father is describing the Valentinian heretical view of Christ's nature and thus there is no typological usage implied here. Pseudo-Jerome (*Expositio Evangelii Secundum Marcum* 15) uses the expression to indicate how in nature the form of the cross is present; for instance, a bird takes on the shape of the cross when it flies. The occurrence at *Historia Ecclesiastica Tripartita* 6.1 refers to the famous sighting of the cross by Constantine before the battle

of Milvian Bridge. And Cassiodorus (*Expositio Psalmorum* 21) describes how the body looks like the shape of the cross when stretched out on it. It is clear that Prudentius is the only writer in late antiquity to use the expression in a historical typological fashion.

62. *Carm.* 19. 612–15: *forma crucis gemina specie conponitur: et nunc / antemnae speciem navalis imagine mali / sive notam Graecis solitam signare trecentos / explicat existens,* . . . And *Carm.* 19. 665–67: *ergo eadem species formam crucis exerit illam, / quae trutinam aequato libratam stamine signat / subrectoque iugum concors temone figurat.*

63. See Walsh's helpful notes and bibliography which explains the iconography behind the fourth-century church's representation of the cross (P. G. Walsh, *Ancient Christian Writers* 40, 383–84 with notes 77–84). The written symbol encompasses Greek letters, *chi, rho, iota, sigma, tau,* and *omicron.*

64. Dawson, *Christian Figural Reading,* 91 and see also 84–91.

65. The word *principes* at *Pe.* 10.626, as well as *virtute* and *bellis* of line 627, are markers of Roman pagan historical characters and events. Paulinus of Nola at *Carm.* 24. 475 uses *principes* as clearly referring to Roman pagan rulers.

66. Here "historical" has to do with the unification of seemingly disparate narratives. The political aspect lies in the idea that with the inclusion of pagan Rome in salvation history, Christian Rome's identity infuses the individual reader.

67. There are 168 occurrences of forms of *saeculum* in Paulinus' corpus; of them, 38 are in the *Carmina.*

68. There are of course various criteria for categorizing an author's use of a term. Many times the subject and purpose of a poem determines how an author will use a term; for instance whether the word occurs in a poem about St. Felix, is addressed to Ausonius, or a paraphrase of scripture; however, we have enough of a sample, and will sufficiently contextualize each member, that clear and accurate patterns of usage do result. Thus, for example, Paulinus is fond of *saeculum*'s meaning as "this contemporary age" or "this world" (e.g., *Carm.* 7.44; 21.179, 208; 24.473, 481, 508, 719, 754, 823, 824, 929, 930; 17.173; 31.387).

69. I list the senses of *saeculum* and the passages in Paulinus' *Carmina*: a lifespan (16.299, 21.116, 22.119, 31.385); a past age(s)/generations (6.250, 323; 9.37, 21. 231, 558, 574, 800; 22.152); new or old age of immortality (6.171, 10.180, 328; 22.63; 23.25; 26.15; and 6.241); a space of time (11.50, 18.161); and all ages taken together (6.329; 22.53).

70. P. G. Walsh, *Ancient Christian Writers* 40, 414, note 37, comments that Paulinus is thinking "of such utterances as the 'Sibyllic' prophecy mentioned by Augustine (cf. *Civ.* 18.23), which foretold the Final Judgment, and which has been immortalized in the *Dies Irae* (*teste David cum Sibylla*)."

71. See note 35 for examples from the *Natalicia,* which are concerned with comparing the extraordinary qualities of Felix to past personages in scripture.

72. Walsh, *Ancient Christian Writers* 40, 387 note 29, corroborates that the term *mysticus* is part of typology's semantic field.

73. For other examples of moral exemplar typology see also the passages that surround *saeculum/saeclum* at *Carm.* 6.250 and 6.323.

74. At *Carm.* 239ff. Paulinus offers himself and his ancestor as a parallel case in which freedom of choice is mentioned.

75. The semantic extension of typological terms through their juxtaposition with historical markers does not occur in Paulinus, nor in other fourth- and early fifth-century poets.

76. See Paulinus *Carm.* 21.231; Prudentius *Apoth.* 606–607 and *Cath.* 9.25.

77. Although Paulinus uses *saeculum* and *crux* in another passage, there exists no relationship as seen in the Prudentian passage: *Huic iam et potentes saeculi curvant genu / Deduntque cevices deo, / Regemque Christum confitentur principes / Et sceptra submittunt cruci* (*Carm.* 24.473–76). The meaning of *saeculi* in this passage is "of this age," not "past ages", and is tangentially related to *cruci* of line 476 because the "powerful ones of this age"—i.e., the *principes,* are submitting to the doctrine of the cross. This is a statement about the contemporary state of affairs, even perhaps about current political conditions in Roman territories, rather than any sort of historical or typological approach directed at the reader's spiritual condition. Absent in this passage of Paulinus is typological language and *saecula* as referring to past historical periods within the context of a grand metaphysical and historical vision.

78. For example, *Symm.* 2.682–83; *Pe.* 2.581–84, 14.94–111, 5.5–8, 10.86–89, 10.386, 10.541. As in the case of Paulinus, Prudentius frequently means "this age of corruption" or human imperfection.

79. Paulinus does this once in his poetry at *Carm.* 24.473–76, when he also speaks of *potentes saeculi* (i.e., *principes*), except Paulinus means here the men who hold political power in Rome.

80. See also *Symm.* 1.511–13 (Rome, the age of martyrs) 1.652–55 (post-Constantinian age of peace) and *Symm.* 2.428 (the republican period of Rome).

81. For Greed see *Psych.* 522–23 and for the soul see *Ham.* 889–90. Compare *Ham.* 922–27, where the soul is trapped in hell for the eternity of ages.

82. M. P. Cunnigham brackets *Cath.* 5.161–64 as an add-on. Because the lines are in the major manuscripts and do not display any disruption of sense, bracketing amounts to speculation.

83. See M. M. Van Assendelft, *Sol Ecce Surget Igneus: A Commentary on the Morning and Evening Hymns of Prudentius* (Groningen: Bouma's Boekhuis B. V., 1976), 197, on the expression *saecula saeculis.* She mentions that the meaning of *continuat* (line 163) is "extend in time" where Christ's *bonitas et pietas* extend in time his kingdom, but she says nothing about *texens* and its historiographical significance.

84. Other passages in which Prudentius uses a form of *saeculum* to promote unification of various ages of history are as follows: *Cath.* 9.112–14, *Cath.* 11.25–32, and *TH* 31.121–24. The last passage binds the history of the Old and New Testaments together through the building of the new temple with a remaining rock of the Jewish temple (*structus lapide ex illo, TH* 31.122).

85. What theological explanation does the poet possess for such a literary and historical strategy? An answer to this question begins with the benefits of a typological construction of history in which Christ and the cross, for instance, function as interpretative markers of the passage of time. God stands outside of this unified chronological expanse, imposing himself through the intervention of Christ. Thus, it would seem that the unification of all *saecula* for Prudentius takes place from the theological perspective of God outside of time. Other passages show Prudentius' theological perspective of Christ as intervener in world history. At *Symm.* 1.278–96 we encounter *saeclis* as the ripeness of time, when all past ages reach the climax of God's intervention through Christ. This is expressed in a vivid poetic metaphor at *Cath.* 11.57–64, where Christ is envisioned as coming into history as if coming out of a womb and thus ushering in a new age (*novellum saeclum*).

86. For *imperium sine fine*, see *Symm.* 1.542–43: *imperium sine fine docet* [Cicero], *ne Romula virtus / iam sit anus, norit ne gloria parta senectam*. Compare *Symm.* 2.640–47, where the ages of history correlate to Rome's political power. Prudentius wants this legacy for Christian Rome.

87. Reinforced in the passage by humans' status as *Christo procreati* (*Pe.* 1.58).

88. See F. Heim, *La théologie de la victoire de constantin a théodose* (Paris: Beauchesne, 1992), 269, who argues for the assimilation in Prudentius' poetry of the love of glory and the allegorical notion of humility herself; and C. White, *Early Christian Latin Poets* (London: Routledge, 2000), 6–11. Whereas White argues for the notion that early Christian poets viewed poetry as a medium of serious ideas, she holds the view that poetry is an offering to God and mere window dressing for the communication of doctrine. I am arguing that Prudentius, consciously or not, presents his poetry as a sacred text that informs, converts, and contains all other sacred texts.

89. A. Palmer, *Prudentius on the Martyrs*, 126, points out that in *Pe.* 2, Prudentius "wants to make an optimistic statement about the conversion of Rome which has been 'officially' completed in his own day and about his Christian view of this as the climax of Rome's imperial history." This Christian view is expressed in what Palmer calls a "spiritual triumph represented by the victory of martyrdom [as] an extension of traditional Roman values of courage, glory and achievement" (127). Palmer (128–29) fleshes out this position by arguing that the pageant of heroes at *Aen.* 6.756ff. forms the basis of *Pe.* 2.1ff. and *Pe.* 2.417–32, a set of allusions that functions to replace Augustus with Christ as founder of Rome, just as for Vergil, Augustus replaced Romulus. Palmer's argument is compelling and raises further issues of the use of history. Her concern is to show that through the replacement of Augustus with Christ, for instance, Prudentius constructs a new Christian patriotism. Because of this original contribution, she recognizes Prudentius' value to the history of Latin poetry: "Prudentius' originality lies in his translation of his own involvement in martyr cult and its literature into a poetic form which represents both a revivification of the forms and language of the secular poetic tradition, and a new departure in the development of martyr literature" (205). But my concern is broader, consisting in the negotiation or lack of compromise between the historical traditions that Prudentius combines. My interest in these passages is in the way Prudentius uses the names of Romulus, Remus, Numa, and Quirinus to unify the disparate historical narratives of pagan and Christian Rome. Rather than seeing what appears to be at first glance a paradoxical usage of these Roman names as an unintended result of Prudentius' poetic program, we should take the phenomenon more seriously. The mention of Roman kings as possible Christians is a historical use of typology that "absorbs" the figures of Roman history and the narratives of these figures into salvation history by means of Christian doctrine. In carrying out this project, he again reasserts poetry's narrative, historical, and political function.

90. *Symm.* 1.102, 193, 2.45; and as a pagan who nevertheless had some common sense, *Apoth.* 215. The only mention of Numa in Paulinus of Nola's poetry is *Carm.* 19.64, where he refers to Rome as a Christian city. Compare *Ep.* 13.15 and 29.13.

91. It is instructive to compare Prudentius' and Paulinus' use of the name *"Romulus"* in their poetry. Nowhere in the *Carmina* of Paulinus do we encounter a comparison between Romulus and Christ as in Prudentius. Before Augustine's *City of God*, Tertullian appears to be the only church father who compares the two directly (*Adv.*

Marc. 4.7): *Indignum denique, ut Romulus quidem ascensus sui in caelum habuerit proculum adfirmatorem, christus vero dei descensus de caelo sui non invenerit adnuntiatorem, quasi non sic et ille ascenderit isdem mendacii scalis. Sicut et iste descendit.* The ascent of both figures is compared, the difference being that Christ's ascent has no witness. Paulinus uses the adjectival form of "*Romulus*" six times, all of which refer to the city of Rome. Three occurrences have no significant historical or political meaning (*Carm.* 10.257, 19.483, 538). At *Carm.* 19.334 Paulinus refers to Rome (*Romuleam . . . urbem*) in order to hold it up as a standard to which the new imperial city, Constantinople should aspire. At *Carm.* 26.273 Felix is portrayed as able to calm the city of Rome (*Romuleis . . . terris*), which is suffering from anxiety over the Barbarian invasions of 402CE. *Carm.* 21.32 once again refers to the city of Rome, but this time the adjective *Romuleos* is set within the context of history where the martyrs, especially Peter and Paul, have aided in "the continuance of Roman safety and existence of the state." This poem was written in 407 CE after the battle of *Faesulae* (406 CE) in which a Christian Roman force under Stilicho destroyed the invading barbarian army of Radagaisus—though the barbarians were allowed to overrun northern Italy for six months. Paulinus is asserting that Christians could contribute to the preservation of Rome and, in fact, Felix did. Prudentius uses the words "Christ" and the adjectival form of "*Romulus*" in close proximity three times. At *Apoth.* 444 the juxtaposition is hostile with the poet urging that pagans mourn Roman emperors' antipagan laws. God is running Romulus' city now. At *Pe.* 11.1–2, Prudentius is keen to make the points that martyrs are buried in Romulus' city and that the political ruler in that city is a servant of Christ, Valerian. Each one of the thirteen other occurrences of a form of "*Romulus*" is either in the *Contra Symmachum* or the *Peristephanon*, two works that are overtly concerned with history. Some arresting examples are the following. At *Symm.* 1 *praef.* 80, Christ is fashioned as the savior of Romans (*salvator generis Romulei*). *Symm.* 1.181, 542, and 2.298 clearly use the name in Prudentius' argument for history as developmental. *Symm.* 2.767–72 contains *Romuleas* and *Christus* and is a clear statement of imperial theology where Christ is the ruler, whom the forts of Romulus follow and thus they are protected by good government. The *Peristephanon* passages with a form of "*Romulus*" add more ideological and historical depth to the previous examples by emphasizing the syncretism of the pagan and Christian traditions. For instance, both *Pe.* 12.57 and 14.1 force together unlikely partners: in the first case it is the "people of Romulus" on their way to a festival of Peter and Paul; and in the second case (in line 1!) Agnes is described as buried *Romulea in domo*. At *Pe.* 10.411–13 Prudentius asks the question to which the subsequent 200 lines or so of the poem, and, indeed, much of what I have been describing in other poems, is a response to: *Ubi iste vester tunc erat summus deus, / divum favore cum puer Mavortius / fundaret arcem septicollem Romulus?* He certainly has this question in mind at *Pe.* 10.611–12 when he says, *Antiquitatem Romuli et Mavortium / lupam renarras primum et omen vulturum.* Prudentius' attitude in the *Peristephanon*, while hostile to paganism in this passage, focuses on the unification of the two opposing historical traditions. These examples pose the problem of syncretism and the extraordinary passage at *Pe.* 2.443–44 offers a bold answer worked out through typological connections that establish a continuous historical narrative.

92. O'Daly, *Augustine's City of God*, 22. O'Daly sees Prudentius', Ambrose's, and Augustine's version of the Christian apologetic in both Theodosian and post-Theodosian contexts as a "new articulation of Roman values" (38), which, in Prudentius' case, takes the form of a renewal of Rome's greatness through martyrdom.

93. Compare *Symm.* 1.566–77, where again Prudentius emphasizes the senators as Christians whose characters will thus serve the country well.

94. The parallel to keep in mind here is Hippolytus (*Pe.* 11) who, as we saw earlier, put himself on the righteous path after disastrous beginnings. The responsibility of choice colors both of these examples (i.e., Hippolytus and Judas/Achar).

95. See White, *The Content of the Form,* 48 and 53, on Ricoeur's notion of historical narrative understood as "always a figurative account" and "an allegorization of the experience of within-time-ness." Also, White says, "narrative figurates the body of events, that serves as its primary referent and transforms these events into intimations of patterns of meaning that any literal representation of them as facts could never produce" (45). Dawson, *Christian Figural Reading,* would take issue with such an analysis of biblical historical narrative. Regarding the relationship between typology and history, Dawson asserts we must assume the historicity of biblical texts in order to understand their theological relevance. He says, "[A]ny effort to understand Christian figural reading as fundamentally a matter of texts and the presence or absence of meaning, rather than a matter of rendering God's historical performances intelligible, is doomed to theological irrelevance, however much contemporary theoretical sense it may make" (6). For those readers and writers "in the fold" the veracity of events contributes to the theological view that God by acting in history, transforms it. White's approach, however, does not contradict Dawson's, for even Dawson, when pushed, will admit that figural reading constructs a narrative with meaning, albeit relational. Ultimately, the reader, whether a believer or not, is an interpreter of words even though he may believe those words to represent or be equivalent to real events. The crux of the distinction Dawson wishes to preserve between reading for meaning and reading for relations between historical events performed by God (i.e., figural reading) ultimately depends on a pronounced theological assumption that God is actually acting in history. Dawson's nuanced, but dogmatic (see Dawson, "Acknowledgments," x) view of theology is preserved regardless of whether the sensible appearance of both the figure and fulfillment is assumed.

96. H. White, *The Content of the Form,* 53. Hence typology is a form of allegory with historical reality as a defining characteristic. It is possible to isolate two levels of allegory in Prudentius: The first is more typological and is clear in the formulation $x = y$, where an event, character, or object x corresponds to another event, character, or object y by means of an overarching idea. See Goulder, *Type and History in* Acts, and Young, "Typology," 39. The idea can be described in doctrinal terms as, for example, Christ as God who is the bringer of immortal life. The second level of allegory can be expressed as $x + y = z$, where z is equivalent to a narrative, or in the case of the *Psychomachia* and *Peristephanon,* a historical narrative. When combined, the x and y form a narrative that subsumes both terms; for example, understanding Passover as prefiguring the passion of Christ. The blood on the doorposts is the type for the antitype of Christ's blood. This would be the level of $x = y$, where the two terms are related in the first place because of doctrinal assumptions having to do with the status of Christ. The further effect of marrying the two historical phenomena, x and y, is the formation of a continuous narrative z from the Old to the New Testaments, i.e. $x + y = z$. Salvation history itself is formed; but, again, the assumption of Christ's extraordinary function lies behind this formulation as well. The allegorical process begins and ends with doctrine, a circular exercise presenting no logical difficulties for Christians. Augustine is well known for his approach to exegesis where in order to understand the

"truth" of scripture, one must already be a believer—i.e., have faith. One brings the assumption of Christian doctrine to the interpretation of texts.

97. For a concise and comprehensive overview of Roman historiography see C. B. R. Pelling, "Roman Historiography," in *The Oxford Classical Dictionary*, 3rd ed., ed. S. Hornblower and A. Spawforth (Oxford: Oxford University Press, 1996), 716–17.

98. A. Momigliano, ed., *The Conflict between Paganism and Christianity in the Fourth Century* (Oxford, 1963) draws the differences between pagan and Christian historiography. A. Cameron, "Remaking the Past," *Late Antiquity: A Guide to the Post-classical World* (Cambridge, Mass.: Harvard University Press, 1999), 1–20, glosses over the uncritical nature of Christian historiography by setting the Christian's unnostalgic view of Rome's past within the context of an unselfconscious Christian's abiding need to connect with the past. One of pagan historiography's qualities, political and moral critique, perhaps can be traced to the tradition's lack of a metaphysically authoritative set of texts that anchor the origin and destruction of the world.

THREE: Christian Theology and the Making of Allegory

1. M. Quilligan, *The Language of Allegory: Defining the Genre* (Ithaca, N.Y.: Cornell University Press, 1979), 19, says that Prudentius was the first to make allegory a narrative genre; and J. Whitman, *Allegory: The Dynamics of an Ancient and Medieval Technique* (Cambridge, Mass.: Harvard University Press, 1987), 85, gives Prudentius credit for expanding personification into a continuous narrative. J. J. Paxson, *The Poetics of Personification* (Cambridge: Cambridge University Press, 1994), 70, says that Prudentius' originality lies in his use of personifications that speak and narrate. Quilligan, *The Language of Allegory*, 19, in a general statement says, "No doubt that the late rise of narrative [compositional] allegory is due to the effect Christian theology had on notions of classical rhetoric; by adding historical dimension to the classical Greek logos, Christianity gave to classical rhetorical figures . . . a capacity for massive narrative extension."

2. N. Frye, "Allegory," in *Encyclopedia of Poetry and Poetics*, ed., A. Preminger (Princeton, N.J.: Princeton University Press, 1965), 12.

3. W. Harmon and C. H. Holman, *A Handbook to Literature*, 8th ed. (Upper Saddle River, N.J.: Prentice Hall, 2000), 12, comment that a literary allegory has "a dual interest, one in events, characters, and setting presented, and the other in the ideas they are intended to convey or the significance they bear." According to Frye, for the interpreter of the allegorical text, there is a tension between the consistency and importance of the fiction presented—in the *Psychomachia*, for example, the virtue/vice battles and temple building—and the poem's additional historical, moral, and religious meanings. Frye, "Allegory," 12, mentions this tension as a function of simple as opposed to complex allegory, which possesses an ironic tone because it pretends to discuss one series of events as it really is focusing on another. This issue is treated by K. Glau, "Allegorie als Reflex der Origenischen Hermeneutik der *Psychomachia* des Prudentius," in *Hortus Litterarum Antiquarum: Festschrift für Hans Armin Gärtner zum 70 Geburtstag*, ed. A. Haltenhoff and F.-H. Mutschler (Heidelberg, 2000), 166–67, who summarizes the views of Ch. Gnilka, *Studien zur Psychomachie des Prudentius* (Weisbaden: O. Harrassowitz, 1963), 9–18; R. Herzog, *Die Allegorische Dichtkunst des Prudentius* (Munich: Beck, 1966); P. F. Beatrice, "L'allegoria nella Psychomachia di Prudenzio," *Studia*

Patavina 18 (1971), and Cotogni, "Sovrapposizione di visioni e di allegoria nella Psychomachia di Prudenzio," *Rendiconti della R. Accademia Nazionale dei Lincei, classe di scienze morali, storiche e filologiche*, series 6, vol. 12 (1936): 441–61. Glau herself revives Beatrice's thesis that Prudentius knew the threefold exegetical approach ("dreifachen Schriftsinn") of Origen (Glau, "Allegorie," 168–69). See my doctoral thesis, "The *Psychomachia* of Prudentius: A Reappraisal of the Greek Sources and the Origins of Allegory," which acknowledges the Origen-Prudentius connection and traces the relationship between Prudentius' and the Cappadocian Fathers' use of biblical texts.

4. S. A. Barney, *Allegories of History, Allegories of Love* (Hamdon, Conn.: Archon Books, 1979), 78, concludes that the poem's complete expression of interior human conflicts paradoxically rids the poem of an engaging sense of human conflict; "a personification cannot have a tragic flaw. The successive descriptions of battles, after all, are not interesting." R. Lamberton, *Homer the Theologian: Neoplatonist Allegorical Reading and the Growth of the Epic Tradition* (Berkeley: University of California Press, 1986), 146: "The 'secondary' level of meaning is obtrusive and takes on greater importance than the action itself, which has lost all claim even to a coherent surface meaning." C. Van Dyke, *The Fiction of Truth: Structures of Meaning in Narrative and Dramatic Allegory* (Ithaca, N.Y.: Cornell University Press, 1985), 34–40, attempts to resolve "inconsistencies" in the *Psychomachia*.

5. It is curious that C. Whitehead, *Castles of the Mind: A Study of Medieval Architectural Allegory* (Cardiff: University of Wales Press, 2003), 5, says that she does not treat "the construction of the temple at the close of the *Psychomachia*," because this poem and others cannot "be shown to have exercised some kind of influence upon the academic allegorists of the twelfth century, or the vernacular allegories of the later Middle Ages." She does acknowledge the *Psychomachia*'s role as one of the first architectural allegories and its connection with allegorical poems such as the *Ancrene Wisse* (thirteenth century) and the *Castell of Perseverance* (c. 1405–25). In her chapter entitled "Knowledge" (Whitehead, *Castles*, 201–29), she admits that the *Psychomachia* "is probably the earliest example . . . of extracting the house in *Proverbs* from its biblical surroundings and subjecting it to a process of imaginative elaboration . . . [with] more examples . . . to follow." These admissions seem to fly in the face of her pronouncement in her introduction.

6. J. Pelikan, *Christianity and Classical Culture: The Metamorphosis of Natural Theology in the Christian Encounter with Hellenism* (New Haven, Conn.: Yale University Press, 1993), 40–74 and 200–31, has shown the importance of negative theology to the Cappadocian Fathers' notions of the relationship between pagan philosophical views of rationality and Christian doctrines of faith, the Trinity, and the soul. Although the Cappadocians did not reject reason, they realized that apophatic theological language limited rational inquiry because it set proper limits to human inquiry (Pelikan, *Christianity and Classical Culture*, 50). Human rational inquiry simply cannot produce knowledge of the divine because it is impossible to explain the divine, as pagan philosophy purported to do, in human terms or in affirming human language. Thus, the Cappadocians employed a large amount of negative prefixed words in their discourse about God—a much larger amount than their Latin Christian counterparts. The only thing comprehensible about God's nature is that it is indeed incomprehensible and infinite. Human language about earthly things and human language about the Creator are superficially similar, but the latter, through apophatic restrictions, has "at one and

the same time, a human sound but not a human meaning [ἀνθρωπίνη συνήθεια]" (J. Pelikan, 207, quoting Gregory of Nyssa, *Eun.* 1. 300–301). Dawsen, *Allegorical Readers,* 91–92, commenting on Philo, *De Mutatione Nominum* 15, asserts that humans' inability to know God originates in our inability to establish determinate correspondances between words, meanings and objects. Because we are functioning under such an epistemic limitation there are meanings hidden in normal language. Allegory assists the epistemic project because it allows expression of the extraordinary meaning embedded in the normal, inadequate language of the sacred text. Thus, Philo justified his practice of subjecting biblical language to τὸ κατακρήσις/ *abusio,* which forces words away from their customary usage. Concerning terms such as God, the Son, the soul, and the Trinity, which in Cappadocian exegetical literature are defined according to apophatic language and assumptions, it is difficult to avoid the practice of allegorical interpretation, which locates meaning not in the literal sense of words but in a different or sometimes completely unrelated sense of the words.

7. Also, *Apoth.* 564–71 exploites the language of negation in a discussion of Christ's birth.

8. M. Smith, *Prudentius' Psychomachia,* 231, describes Prudentius' achievement in using the *De Abraham* of Ambrose as "[accepting] the typological connection between Scripture and detailed psychology."

9. Charlet, "Aesthetic Trends," 82–84, gives a cogent summary of contributions by P. de Labriolle, *A History of Latin Christian Literature,* 3d ed. (Oxford: Clarendon Press, 1947), and W. Ludwig, "Die christliche Dichtung des Prudentius und die Transformation der klassischen Gattungen," *Fondation Hardt, Entretiens* 23 (1977): 303–63. Herzog's examination of late Antique poetry and exegesis is in his "Exegese-Erbauung-Delectatio: Beiträge zu einer christlichen Poetik der Spätantike," in *Formen und Funktionen der Allegorie* (Stuttgart: J. B. Metzlersche, 1978), 54–58. M. Smith, *Prudentius' Psychomachia,* 25–26, traces the critical tradition which sees the *Psychomachia* as a poem concerned with allegorical exegesis.

10. Prudentius refers to biblical people, stories, and passages throughout his works, but systematically so in the *Psychomachia.* The literary use of biblical material in the poem presupposes an interpretation of the biblical passage/story—that is, an exegesis, formed (and recoverable) from the placement, context and effect of the story and words in the poetry. Charlet, "Prudence et La Bible," 3–149, gives a comprehensive list of the biblical passages used in each work and general comments on tendencies of usage within each work. His main emphasis, however, is the *Cathemerinon* for which he undertakes a useful investigation on Prudentius' allusive and exegetical techniques. My concern is with the *Psychomachia,* and my conclusions represent a different investigative emphasis and direction—namely, how the exegesis of biblical texts and stories in the *Psychomachia* reveals fundamental aspects of Prudentius' allegorical and poetic techniques and purposes.

11. The late fifteenth-century humanist E. Antonio de Nebrija, *Aurelii Prudentii Clementis V. C. libelli cum commento Antionii Nebrissensis,* ed. F. Gonzalez Vega (Salmanca: Ediciones Universidad de Salmanca, 2002, emphasizes Abraham as the stand-in for faith. On line 1 of the *Praefatio,* he comments on Prudentius' strikng use of *via* as referring to a person, Abraham, *Quam credituri debemus imitari.* Commenting on line 62, he says of Abraham's role, *per quem intelligimus victorem vitiorum.*

12. Although I discuss the role of reason, I leave several important issues to the discussion of reason in chapter 4, where I show how Prudentius uses pagan philosophy to help construct the poem's allegorical universe.

13. Gregory of Nyssa cites *Gen.* 14:18 and *Hebr.* 7:1 at *Eun.* 1.39 in the middle of a discussion about the transferability of substance between persons and their progeny, what he calls "a kinship of substance." He employs apophatic language to describe the Son as already existing in the Father. At *Eun.* 8.1, Nyssen uses *Heb.* 7:3 as part of a series of apophatic expressions that describe the Son's status. In another usage of *Heb.* 7:3 Nyssen criticizes Eunomius for employing affirming names of "him who, as the Apostle says, has neither beginning of days nor end of life." Rather, the vocabulary that must be used of the godhead is "anterior to all beginning un-generate, and again that which is circumscribed by no limit, immortal, and indestructible." It is clear that the most important meaning of these biblical passages revolves around apophatic conceptions of the godhead and its constituents. Gregory of Nazianzus at *Or.* 28.18 (*Second Theological Oration*) cites *Gen.* 18:18 (the Faith of Abraham; *Praef.* 1, *senex fidelis*) and *Gen.* 18:2 (visitation of the three men to Abraham) in a context of apophatic language concerning knowledge of God. The latter passage indicates to Nazianzen that Abraham saw God not as God but as a man. This has to be the proper interpretation of the biblical passage, according to Nazianzen, because God cannot be known any other way by humans. This passage has apophatic language, the interpretation of the tripleformed angel as a vision of one, and the prefiguring typology, all of which Prudentius expresses in his usage of the biblical passage. At *Or.* 38.2 Nazianzen uses *Heb.* 7:3 to draw the typology of Christ and Melchisedec. Although this typology is common among the church fathers, nearly the same words are used by Augustine at *Tract. In. Joann.* 8. Lactantius, who predates both Nazianzen and Augustine, at *Div Inst.* 4.13 adopts the typology and has very similar language. In *Ep.* 101, ("Against the Apollinarians"), Nazianzen cites *Gen.* 18:2–5 once again to make the point that God can only be known to us as a man. Knowledge of God is again the topic of discussion and the citation is preceded by apophatic language. With regard to Prudentius and Nazianzen, the point is that the apophatic themes and language are foregrounded in their usage of these scriptural texts. This trend is not to be found in the Latin Fathers, though there is one notable exception, Ambrose's *De Fide* 3.88. Like Nyssen, Nazianzen, and Prudentius, Ambrose understands *Gen.* 14:18 and *Heb.* 7:1–3 in an apophatic and typological way in order to explain the unity of the godhead. The rest of the Latin patristic literature does not overlap with Prudentius in these particular ways. A good example of this difference is Jerome's *Ep.* 46.2 (386 CE), which makes use of the typology but does not mention or foreground apophatic language and concepts, nor does it mention the triple-formed angel. Jerome follows a similar approach with regard to *Gen.* 18:1 and *Heb.* 7:3 in four other places. *Ep.* 46.11; *Ep.* 108. 11; *Ep.* 122.1; and *Adv. Jovanian.* 1.23. Jerome mentions the triple-formed angel at *Ep.* 46.11 and *Ep.* 122.1. These passages show how consistent Jerome was throughout his life concerning the exegesis of these texts. Ambrose uses *Gen.* 18.1 three times to show that Abraham is rewarded for his entertaining of the angel and to assert that Abraham saw three but "adored one" (*De Officiis Miniistrorum* 2.21.104, 2.21.107 and *De Fide* 1.13.80). Tertullian uses *Gen.* 14:18, *Gen.* 18:1–2, and *Heb.* 7:1–3 to discuss Melchisedec as a type and Abraham's vision of the angel (*Adv. Jud.* 2; *De Carne Christi* 3; and *Adversus Omnes Haereses* 7). He does quote the apophatic language

directly from *Heb.* 7:1–3 but does not elaborate or display awareness of its relationship to faith and knowledge of God. Instead, he sees such language as meaning that Melchisedec is superior and ends his exegesis.

14. Prudentius is retrojecting the figure of Christ into the Old Testament story by comparing Melchisedec, who provides food for the triumphant Abraham, to Christ who brings food for the *beatis . . . victoribus.* The Old Testament story prefigures the concrete events of later Christian history. Most important, though, the Old Testament story prefigures Christ when the *triformis angelorum trinitas* visits Abraham (*Praef.* 45). The method of typology, which both Latin and Greek exegetes engaged in, is here exploited by Prudentius.

15. These lines have been isolated as having textual problems. *Praef.* 41–42 do not appear in the oldest manuscript, A, but are in B, the second-oldest manuscript. Bergman and Lavarrene bracket them as interpolated. H. J. Thomson and M. P. Cunningham keep the lines preferring to have a parrallel with *Praef.* 60. *Praef.* 60 is problematic because the major manuscripts are faulty. Thompson prints *parente inennarabili atque uno satis,* acknowledging that even the line that he prints is "abnormal." Cunningham and Lavarrene print *parente natus alto et ineffabili,* and Cunningham comments, "*aliquot litterae rescriptae sunt in B, sed de lectionibus non est dubitandum.*" I assume that *Praef.* 41–42 are not interpolations. Whichever reading one chooses for *Praef.* 60, there is apophatic language.

16. Another interesting example is *Apoth.* 782–951, which this time discusses the nature of the soul. *Apoth.* 797, 799, and 800 refer to the soul as an *umbra* (e.g., *umbra dei, Apoth.* 797), a word that participates in Prudentius' typological discourse and once again suggests the typology God—Christ—Human. That is, the soul has a dual nature. Even though it is typologically related to God and is immortal and wise (*Apoth.* 803), nevertheless the soul is describable unlike God (*Apoth.* 809–10, 814, 872–78). The soul's divinity is not of the same metaphysical level as that of God (*Apoth.* 879–82) and is created in time (*Apoth.* 823–29); however, because the soul is incorporeal and immortal one cannot describe it in a straightforward manner. At *Apoth.* 834–36 Prudentius asserts that we can nevertheless gain knowledge of the soul: *In corpore discas / rem non corpoream sollers interprete Christo, / qui patrem proprium mortali in corpore monstrat.* This passage confirms the soul's quasi-apophatic status by asserting its incorporeality and relationship to the Father, but it nevertheless leaves open the possibility of describing the soul. In these lines Prudentius indicates what I claim to be actualized in the *Psychomachia*'s allegory of the soul: a description of the soul.

17. J. Pelikan, *Christianity and Classical Culture,* 216 and 220, cites Gregory of Nyssa *Vita Mos.* 1 (J. 7-I:22) and *Eun.* 2. 91–93. Faith, as seen in the *Praefatio* to the *Psychomachia,* is an individual human response to the "unknowability" of divinity and provides a fertile ground for allegorizing about such entities. Faith stands outside of the idea that the universe in all its facets is to be explained through reason and language. And, thus, the realm of faith is where divinity locates itself, a place exclusive of human reason and language, but not of knowledge. This exclusion of language and reason would have presented a predicament to Prudentius, a practitioner of poetic discourse, whose purpose in the *Psychomachia* is to celebrate God and describe the content and workings of the soul (*Praef.* 36: *saltem voce deum concelebret*). J. D. Dawson, *Allegorical Readers,* 2–3, finds a partial parallel of religious allegory's connection to apophatic theology to the deconstructionist approach to allegory: " . . . for the ancient inter-

preters . . . (in contrast to postmodern readers), apophatic assumptions are not herme-neutical (or rather, antihermeneutical) ends in themselves, designed to foster an un-ending thrill of indeterminate interpretation. Instead of reveling in the absence of meaning, these ancient allegorists tended to use apophatic claims rhetorically, as a way of justifying their own application of allegorical readings that were designed to show what the real meanings were (p. 3)." One can readily see that the author's intentions are central to the practice of ancient allegorical interpretation and for that matter, ancient allegorical composition. So J. D. Dawson, *Allegorical Readers,* 7; P. Rollinson, *Classical Theories of Allegory,* 19; M. Quilligan, *The Language of Allegory,* 224; N. Frye, *Anatomy of Criticism,* 90. For the reader as producer of meaning, see again Quilligan, 21, and 67–68.

18. If one says that the Son is "begotten" (γεννήτος) of the Father, the word "begot-ten" does have its normal literal human meaning, but, because God can not be repre-sented concretely in human terms such as this, the word takes on a transcendent meaning. As J. Pelikan, *Christianity and Classical Culture,* 207, says of Gregory of Nyssa, "Only then could such language become a 'symbol' for transcendent reality, containing a deeper meaning than the literal one."

19. Thomson translates the verb *formet,* "it takes some tempering shape." The noun *moderamen* is a political word used of government managing (Ovid *Met.* 6.677), but in the *Code of Theodosius* 11.30.64 it stands for "a means of moderating." The expression as a whole is vague and under apophatic assumptions this is indeed deliberate. It is not clear what aspect of the Father humans are seeing. On the other hand, one can see the connection between *moderamen* and Christ in his role as mediator between the Father and humans.

20. D. J. Nodes, *Doctrine and Exegesis in Biblical Latin Poetry* (Wiltshire: Francis Cairs, 1993), 30, says that the argument of *Apotheosis* 28–30 reflects in part an argument in Justin Martyr, *Dialogue with Trypho* 56, Origen, *Commentary on John* 2.144, and Novatian, *De Trinitate* 18.13, that the Father can not be seen, and, therefore, references to seeing God are really references to seeing the Son. Compare Tertullian *Adv. Marc.* 3.9. Of course, Tertullian was almost directly translating Justin's work of the same name. Nazienzen as well makes the same argument.

21. See Nodes, *Doctrine and Exegesis,* 30–33.

22. Some examples are *dogmata . . . prodita* (*Apoth.* 2); *species et imago / nulli visa umquam; nec enim conprendier illa / maiestas facilis sensuve oculisve manuve.* (*Apoth.* 6–8); *haud umquam testata deum potuisse uideri.* (*Apoth.* 10); *nulla acies . . . tuendo / . . . penetravit* (*Apoth.* 11–12); *inmensum* (*Apoth.* 14); *numquam visa* (*Apoth.* 16); *vis intacta* (*Apoth.* 17); *inspiciendum* (*Apoth.* 24); and *infinita* (*Apoth.* 26). Apophatic language continues through *Apoth.* 127, where Prudentius takes up God's apophatic ontology and the paradox of the father becoming flesh. Prudentius then through *Apoth.* 177 posits Christ as the mediator between the father and the human world.

23. At *Apoth.* 362–75 Abraham is taken for a Christian because he is able to see God, unlike the Jews, who ignore God in the form of Christ. Note *fidelis* (*Apoth.* 363), *creditus* (*Apoth.* 365), and *fide* (*Apoth.* 366), all of which are directed toward Abraham. Just as in the *Praefatio* to the *Psychomachia,* Abraham remains the quintessential hu-man symbol of faith.

24. These first two examples have the language of *Genesis* 15:6, *Credidit Abraham Deo.* On *Praef. Psych.* 1, see note 11.

25. I owe this translation to Christopher Francese.

26. The sacrificial language is revisited at the end of the poem as part of a typological line of thought that posits Christ as the type for peace in the city and the soul.

27. One witnesses the great flexibility of Prudentius' typologies with the association of Isaac with human flesh as regarding Christ being born from miraculous origins, and with the association of the reader of the *Psychomachia,* the every day Christian, with human flesh in the person of Abraham who is rewarded because of his faith.

28. The other necessary condition for a successful life, a capacity to reason, is hinted at in *vigilandum* ("keeping watch," using one's human capacities of sense and reason to recognize danger) and is clarified in the story of the visitation of the three angels (*Praef. Psych.* 45–46), as well as in the phrase *vicendi praesens ratio est* of *Praef. Psych.* 18 of the main text of the *Psychomachia.* As for the latter example, the important word is *ratio.* Throughout the *Psychomachia* the notion of reason and its personification is integral to the victory over the vices (e.g., *Psych.* 501ff.). At *Psych.* 502 *ratio* is described as *una / semper fida comes.* Faith and reason are an essential pair. In the *Praefatio* we have seen that Prudentius understands faith, if alone, as vulnerable, but, if the capability of "keeping watch," in the guise of reason, is joined with faith, success is assured. Reason alone is insufficient for the successful life. Although the *vicendi . . . ratio* may be before our eyes (*praesens*), it is only the first step. Abraham represents to our common sense a *credendi via,* that is, we understand faith as the next step after our recognition of Abraham's example through our faculty of reason. Reason must be the preliminary phase to the life of faith. It is reasonable for individuals to join the battle between the virtue and the vices. The rewards—immortality, for instance—constitute reasonable goads to action.

29. *Et Melchisedec rex Salem protulit panem et vinum fuit autem sacerdos dei summi.* For each biblical allusion I have tried to give the Latin Prudentius most likely was reading. When the old Latin text is not available, I give the text in English. There are three editions of the *Vetus Latina,* which I have used. For *Matthew, Mark, Luke,* and *John* I have used A. Jülicher, ed., *Itala: Das neue Testament in altlateinischer Überlieferung* (Berlin: Walter de Gruyter, 1938, 1940, 1954, and 1963); for *Genesis,* Fischer, ed., *Vetus Latina: Die Reste der altleinischen Bibel* (Freiburg: Verlag Herder, 1951–54); for 1 *Thessalonians,* 1 *Timothy, Philemon,* and *Hebrews,* H. J. Frede, ed. (Freiburg: Verlag Herder, 1981–87); for *Ephesians,* H. J. Frede, ed. (Freiburg: Verlag Herder, 1962–64); for *Philippians* and *Colossians,* H. J. Frede, ed. (Freiburg: Verlag Herder, 1966–71); for 1 *Corinthians,* U. Frölich, ed. (Freiburg: Verlag Herder, 1995–96). For the rest of the biblical passages, I have used P. Sabatier, *Bibliorum Sacrorum Latinae Versiones Antiquae Seu Vetus Italica* (Remis: Apud Reginaldum Florentain, 1743).

30. I give verses 1–3: *sic enim Melchisedech rex erat Salem sacerdos dei altissimi qui obviavit Abrahae regresso a caede regum cumque eum benedixisset et Abraham benedictus ab eo;* (2) *qui et decimam omnium divisit primum quidem qui interpretatur rex iustitiae deinde autem et rex Salem quod est rex paci;* (3) *sine patre sine matre sine genealogia neque initium dierum neque vitae finem habens simulatus autem filio dei manet sacerdos in perpetuum.*

31. I give verses 1 and 2: (1) *visus est autem ei deus ad ilicem Mambre sedenti illi ad ostium tabernaculi eius medio die adlevatis;* (2) *autem oculis suis vidit et ecci tres viri stabant super eum et cum vidisset occurrit in obviam illis ab ostio tabernaculi sui et adoravit super terram.*

32. I give verses 1–6: (1) *et dominus visitavit Saram sicut dixit et fecit deus Sarae sicut*

locutus est; (2) *et concepit et peperit Sara Abrahae filium in senectute sua et in tempore sicut locutus est illi dominus;* (3) *et vocavit nomen filii sui qui factus est ei quem genuit ei Sarra Isaac;* (4) *et tunc circumcidit Abraham puerum die octava sicut praeceperat ei deus;* (5) *Abraham autem erat annorum centum quando genuit Isaac;* (6) *dixit et Sarra risum mihi fecit dominus quicumque enim audierit congratulabitur mihi.*

33. Paul develops this argument in his Letter to the *Hebrews.* Compare *Psalm* 110:4, "You shall be a priest for life, a Melchisedec, because of me."

34. The mystic union achieved in the final lines of the *Praefatio* has a Christian neo-Platonic ring to it. The neo-Platonic notion of θεότης, union with or knowledge of God achieved through mystical strategies, is evoked. Prudentius sees such a union implicit and incomplete in the stories of Melchisedec and Sara, but attainable through the agency of Christ who provides the necessary knowledge. See further chapter 4.

35. I give here *Matth.* 25:7: *tunc surrexerunt omnes illae virgines et acceperunt lampades suas.* It is clear that Prudentius has assumed the other twelve verses of *Matthew* in his text, just as he has assumed *Judith* 13 and 14.

36. The Prudentian reference to the specific verse of *Matth.* 25:7 can be seen in *lampades* and *famulos famulasque* (compare *virgines* of 25:7).

37. The Cappadocians nowhere cite this passage and Latin patristic literature fails to employ the passage in a context similar to that found in Prudentius.

38. *[D]ixit autem maria ad angelum: quo modo fiet istud, quod virum non novi.*

39. *[E]t verbum caro factumest et habitavit in nobis et vidimus gloriam eius, gloriam quasi unigeniti (filii) a patre plenum gratia et veritate.* Prudentius writes, *Verbum quippe caro factum non destitit esse* (*Psych.* 78).

40. Jerome does not use John 1:14 and Luke 1:34 often. Two references indicate that Jerome understands the former as merely a statement of the actualization of Christ's birth; and the latter as a passage which raises the issue of Joseph's status (*Ep.* 108.10, 404 CE) and *Adversus Helvidium* 4). Ambrose, on the other hand, uses these biblical texts often and for a consistent purpose. He employs *John* 1:14 eight times in the treatise *De Fide* to explore themes of the unity of the godhead (*De Fide* 3.4.26), the meaning of the names and descriptions given to Christ (*De Fide* 2 intro. 2; 1.2.16; 1.8.56—"was," repeated three times, is equivalent to "eternal" and "infinite"; 1.14.89), the distinction between the Father and the Son (*De Fide* 1.7.50 and 4.9.102), and the uncompromised nature of the godhead after the incarnation (*De Fide* 4.8.87–88). In another treatise, the Bishop quotes the biblical passage to prove the *unigeniti gloria, et perfecti hominis natura* (*De Fide Resurrectionis* 2.103). Ambrose pays close attention to the words used of Christ, which he understands as affirmations of him more than as expressions of the human limits of knowledge of the godhead, but Ambrose does possess apophatic awareness; for example, at *De Fide* 4.8.87 he understands the "begetting" activity of the godhead as an exercise of authority that produces the Son *nata generationis arcano.*

41. Language of purification indicates the idea of proper preparation for meeting the godhead. In addition, as I discuss later in this chapter, such language at the end of the *Psychomachia* suggests a trial that the human soul must undergo.

42. Dawson, *Christian Figural Reading,* 122–23, shows how deeply ingrained typological reading is in ancient Christian readers.

43. J. Danielou, *From Shadows to Reality: Studies in the Biblical Typology of the Fathers,* trans. D. W. Hibberd (London: Burnes and Oates Ltd., 1960), 287–88, makes the point that the Alexandrine tradition of exegesis as represented in these fathers

endeavors to apply "the types of the Old Testament to the interior life of the Christian." (287). The *Psychomachia* falls squarely in this tradition thereby granting a significant nonliteral meaning to biblical stories and passages.

44. Examples include Chastity/Judith, Pride/Adam, Lowliness/David, and Greed/Judas.

45. D. L. Madsen, *Rereading Allegory: A Narrative Approach to Genre* (New York: St. Martins Press, 1994), 58, defines in part Christian figuralism as the continuity between the text, its interpretation, and the interpreting subject through shared participation in the word. The reader is a potent part of this allegorical process.

46. Job begins this series of three Old Testament, typological figures as primarily an instantiation of the virtue *Patientia*. This one-to-one correspondence is so strong because, unlike Adam and David, who are to follow, Job is actually a character in the narrative of the *Psychomachia*—though admittedly he appears at the end of the battle and is an add-on. The poet-narrator provides details of his story, whereas for the stories of Adam and David it is the vice *Superbia* and the virtue *Spes* who narrate.

47. Gen. 3:21: *et (tunc) fecit dominus deus Adae [Adam] et mulieri eius tunicas pellicias et induit illos.*

48. Again, the reader's ethical choice is present in the binary opposition of the clothed Adam and the naked Adam.

49. See C. T. Lewis and C. Short, eds., *A Latin Dictionary* (Oxford: Oxford University Press, 1998), 2. *habitus*, I.A. and II.A.

50. See J. Danielou, *From Shadows to Reality*, 40–43.

51. Other works of Prudentius mention the Adam/Christ typology directly. At *Apoth.* 687–91, 911–26, and 1004–19 a series of themes emerges from the typology. Christ remakes us into the "new Adam" who possesses the purity of prelapsarian Adam. We are like the "old Adam," whose original sin we carry deep within our souls. All flesh after the Fall is therefore "insubstantial," mere "aether." Christ corrects this state of affairs by taking on original sin, not as we humans do, but in a way that does not affect his divine being. *Cath.* 3. 113–40, 181–90, 9.17, 92 continue the theme of Adam as standard bearer for original sin, and particularize further Christ as a *nova progenies* (3.136) and an *alter homo* (3.137) who puts on human nature—but only to a certain degree. Christ's divine breath (*oris opus*, 3. 186) refashions the clay that went wrong in Eden. Typology stretches as far back as creation in the person of Adam and in the circumstances of paradise. These passages emphasize the making, shaping, and fashioning of a human being in the likeness of something else. Note the language of typology at *Apoth.* 689–91 (*figuram . . . finxerat*) and *Apoth.* 1010 (*fingas ab origine*). Typology appears to be a fundamental force in the divinely inspired and created universe.

52. Danielou, *From Shadows to Reality*, 30.

53. Both *Luke* 1:52 (. . . *disparsit superbos mente cordis ipsorum. Deposuit potentes de sede et exalta vit humiles*) and *Matth.* 23:12 (*Qui autem se exaltaverit humiliabitur; et qui se humiliaverit exaltabitur*) work together in the *Psychomachia* (*Psych.* 285–86, 289–90) to illustrate what should be learned from the story of David and Goliath, which occupies *Psych.* 291–301. *Luke* 1:51–52 portrays Mary speaking in a lyrical exhange with Elizabeth whom she meets after the Holy Spirit has visited her. To paraphrase: for those who believe, God's power can accomplish great things such as making Mary pregnant. Prudentius puts Mary's words in the mouth of *Spes* as she vaunts over *Superbia*, who

has been made headless by *Mens Humilis,* who herself was encouraged by *Spes* to inflict the death stroke. The words of *Matth.* 23:12 are spoken by Christ in a public attack on the Pharisees. Certain narrative choices Prudentius makes bind the story closely with the New Testament aphoristic assertions; Goliath taunting the Jewish battle lines (1 *Sam.* 17:26 and 36), young David achieving victory only with a sling and a stone (1 *Sam.* 17:50), and David beheading Goliath with the Philistine's own sword (1 *Sam.* 17:51). Prudentius also includes Goliath's awesome appearance (1 *Sam.* 17:4) while having *Spes* take credit for David's victory (*Psych.* 301). The irony is pronounced as *Spes* taunts a dead *Superbia* with this story of a taunter—i.e., Goliath.

54. The speech introduces the terms in a clear progression from the beginning, to the middle, and to the end: *puerilis, pueri, puer* (*Psych.* 292, 298, 300); *me, mea, mihi, meque* (*Psych.* 300, 301, 302, 303) and *victores* (*Psych.* 304).

55. Prudentius appears to have employed *Spes* as a surrogate for *Fides.* Hope's importance is emphasized in the poem. *Operatio* at *Psych.* 606–28 exhorts all human beings to cultivate *spem . . . invitiabilis aevi* (*Psych.* 626). See *Apoth.* 372–74 where Hope and Faith are strongly associated.

56. For Christ as culmination of a royal succession epitomized by David, see *TH* 20; *Ham.* 787; *Cath.* 12.49, 96; *Apoth.* 418, 999, 1012. *Apoth.* 1012 adds the nuance that David, though a king, is empty and flawed flesh that Christ took on. *TH* 19 gives a highly abbreviated summary of David's life. *Cath.* 9.4 portrays David as an epic poet and prophet who narrates and predicts the coming of Christ. *Psych.* 386's mention of David speaks to the issue of biblical history. *Ham.* 563 interestingly refers to the story of David and Absalom in which David is the father of an accursed child just as a human soul gives birth to "*diros . . . natos*" (*Ham.* 569). The language of inwardness here typologically connects David and events in his life to the activity of the soul, in this case an undesirable activity with an immoral result.

57. *Psych.* 545–46 distinguishes between two kinds of typological relationship; either between two figures (*exemplum generis*) or two sets of events (*forma exitii*). Typology is most recognizable in a "historical" figure regarding what they did and the qualities that motivated them to act. But, in addition, certain events and their sequence also serve as typological markers. The "form of one's end" focuses directly on the structure of a story that is to be repeated in the present or future. These lines with their aside quality and commenting tone parallel *Sobrietas'* comment on the story of Jonathan: *Sed quia paenituit. nec sors lacrimabilis illa est. / nec tinguit patrias sententia saeva secures* (*Psych.* 401–402). In this formulation of typology, Prudentius uses the "this is that" language (*illa est*) that N. Frye isolates as fundamental for allegorical exegesis. Moreover, the words *tinguit* and *patrias* are typological vocabulary that Prudentius employs here. With the negative *nec,* the fate of Jonathan the son is reversed, as if it were a typology unrealized. Jonathan's completely free-willed action of repenting— though, in the biblical version, Jonathan does not appear to be repenting, but merely admitting his guilt—reverses what seemed inevitable. And, what is more, the people come to his aid and plead for his life to his father Saul. Prudentius sees human choice everywhere and expresses it through the flexibility of typology—implied, explicit, unrealized, realized. Some scholars have attributed Prudentius' statement that Jonathan had a *regni . . . voluptas* (*Psych.* 399) to a confusion with Absalom's desire to depose King David (2 *Sam.* 15:7ff.). Absalom, however, never repents and, as we have already seen, Prudentius is not adverse to embellishing in order to confirm his Christian

assumptions. Thus, 1 *Sam.* 14:29–30 could be interpreted as Jonathan expressing a desire for power. In fact, given Prudentius' penchant for indirect associations between various biblical figures, personifications, and the reader, I would argue that Absalom is being recalled through the figure of Jonathan typologically since both are sons and both disobey their royal fathers. In these ways, the personifications' asides shed light on typology's flexibility in the *Psychomachia*, a flexibility that expresses possibility, dramatic tension, and finally, human free will.

58. There are four passages from *Matthew* littering *Operatio*'s speech: *Matth.* 6.34 (*Psych.* 615): *Nolite solliciti esse in crastinum; crastinus enim dies sollicitus erit sibi ipse; Matth.* 6:11 (*Psych.* 616): *Sufficit diei malitia sua Panem nostrum cottidianum da nobis hodie*—from the Lord's prayer; *Matth.* 6:26 (*Psych.* 617): *Respicite volatilia caeli, quoniam non serunt neque metunt neque congregant in horreis et pater vester caelestis pascit illa. Nonne magis vos pluris estis illis?*; and *Matth.* 10:29 (*Psych.* 620): *Nonne duo passeres asse veniunt?* But Prudentius refers to Matth. 6:29–34 throughout the speech of *Operatio.*

59. *Psych.* 642–643, *et Christum gaudere suis victoribus arce / aetheris ac patrium famulis aperire profundum,* is an echo of *Rev.* 3:21: *vincenti dabo sedere mecum in throno meo: sicut et ego vici, et sedeo cum patre meo throno eius.* In the patristic literature I have found only three very indirect references to *Rev.* 3:21 in Tertullian (*De Idololatria* 18, *Adversus Praxeam* 30, and *De Paenitentia* 8). He discusses the status of Christ in one of the passages, but not too thoroughly. There is nothing about being victorious or victory.

60. At *Psych* 650 J. Bergmann, *Aurelli Prudentii Clementis Carmina*, Corpus Scriptorum Ecclesiasticorum Latinorum, vol. 61 (Lipsiae: Hoelder-Pichler-Tempsky A.G.), 1926, has *Ex.* 15:14–15, whereas Cunningham has 15:1 and 15:20–21. Thomson rightly thinks that through *Psych.* 662 *Ex.* 15:1–21 is evoked. Cunningham lists *Ex.* 15:20 for *Psych.* 658. I give here all twenty-one verses: (1) *tunc cantavit Moyses et filii Israel canticum hoc Domino, et dixerunt dicere: cantemus Domino: gloriose enim magnificatus est, equum et ascensorem deiecit in mare;* (2) *adiutor, et protecto factus est mihi in salutem: iste Deus mesu, et glorificabo eum: Deus Patris mei, et exaltabo eum;* (3) *Dominus conterens bella, Dominus nomen est ei;* (4) *currus Faraonis et exercitum eius proiecit in mare: electos ascentores ternos stantes demersit in rubro mari;* (5) *pelago cooperavit eos, devenerunt in profundum tamquam lapis;* (6) *dextra tua, Domine, glorificata est in virtute; dextra manus tua, Domine confregit inimicos;* (7) *et per multitudinem gloriae tuae contribulasti adversarios: misisti iram tuam, et comedit illos tanquam stipulam;* (8) *et per spiritum irae tuae divisa est aqua: gelaverunt tanquam murus aquae, gelaverunt fluctus in medio mari;* (9) *dixit inimicus: persequens comprehendam, partibor polia, replebo animam meam: interficiam gladio meo, dominabitur manus mea;* (10) *misisti spiritum tuum, et cooperuit eos mare: descenderunt tanquam plumbum in aquam validissimum;* (11) *quis similis tibi diis Domine? quis similis tibi, gloriosus in sanctis, mirabilis in maiestatibus, faciens prodigia?*; (12) *extendisti dexteram tuam, et devoravit eos terra;* (13) *gubernasti in iustitia tua populum tuum hunc quem redemisti: exhortatus es in virtute tua, in requie sancta tua;* (14) *audierunt gentes, et iratae sunt: dolores comprehenderunt habitantes Philistiim;* (15) *tunc festinaverunt duces Edom, et principes Moabitarum; apprehendit illos tremor: fluxerunt omnes habitantes Chanaan;* (16) *cecidit super eos timor et tremor, magnitudine brachii tui: fiant tanquam lapis, donec pertranseat populus tuus, Domine, usquedum transeat populus tuus, Domine, hunc quem adquisisti;*

(17) *inducens plantato eos in montem haereditatis tuae, in praeparatam habitationem tuam quam praeparasti Domine: sanctificationem Domine, quam paraverunt manus tuae;* (18) *Domine, qui regnas in aeternum, et in saeulum, et adhuc;* (19) *quia introiit equitavus Pharaonis cum curribus et ascensoribus in mare: et adduxit super eos Dominus aquas maris: filii autem Israel transierunt per siccum in medio mari;* (20) *sumpsit autem Maria prophetis, soror Aaron, tympanum in manu sua: et exierunt postea omnes mulieres cum tympanis et choris;* (21) *praecedebat autem eas Maria, dicens: cantemus Domino, gloriose enim honorificatus est, equum et ascensorem proiecit in mare.*

61. Danielou, *From Shadows to Reality,* 207–12, has traced this tradition in connection with *Ex.* 15:4, *Matth.* 6:19–34, and *Deut.* 8:3. The dominant tradition in the Fathers is the sacramental exegesis of the Exodus, which sees Baptism and the Eucharist indicated. In the west, Ambrose, *De Myst.* 3.13 (*PL* 16.393) and *De Sacr.* 1.4.12 (*PL* 421), typify the sacramental interpretation; however, the tradition that Prudentius emphasizes portrays "the journey through the desert now . . . as a type of the soul's passage, progressively casting aside all the relics of the passions which remain in it; a passage which is continually enlightened by *logos*" (Danielou, 209). Some of the passages Danielou has gathered are: Philo, *Leg. All.* 2.86, 11.102, *De Sac.* 62; Origen, *Hom. Ex.* 5.5, *Hom. Num.* 26; Gregory of Nyssa, *Vit. Mos. PG* 44, 361C. Although Prudentius is not averse to the sacramental tradition of interpretation, in *Cathimerinon* 5 and the *Psychomachia,* he foregrounds the soul-journey exegesis.

62. See also *Apoth.* 711, where the same story of Christ feeding the multitudes is mentioned and interpreted as spiritual teaching (*dogmate*).

63. *Cath.* 5.31–136, 7.36–45, 12.134–204; *Apoth.* 32–35, 294–304; *Ham.* 339–45; *Pe.* 2. 363–68, 6. 85–99; *TH* 8, 9, 10, 11, 12, 13, 14.

64. Prudentius is familiar with the range of exegeses of the Exodus episode from both the patristic and catechetical traditions. *Cath.* 12.134–204 gives a litany of such interpretations and typologies: Jewish Passover/ the newborn Christ escaping Herod's decree/baby Moses abandoned and saved implied (134–35); Moses/Christ as protector of the people (143–44), as God's priest (153), and as transmitter/fulfiller of law (155–56), as slayer of Egyptians and liberator of Israel (150–60); Egyptians/enemy/sin (161–64); Red Sea episode/Baptism (165–67); Christ/pillar of light (168); Moses' outstretched arms to subdue Amalech/the cross (169–72); Joshua/Jesus (173); 12 stones of the River Jordan/12 Apostles (177–80). Prudentius sums up at 183–84: *cum facta priscorum ducum / Christi figuram pinxerint.*

65. For other instances of the Moses/Christ typology see *Apoth.* 32–35 and *Cath.* 7.36–45. At *Apoth.* 51, Moses' antitype, Christ, is described as *figura hominis* and similarly at *Apoth.* 309 (*nos Christi forma et imago*). Human beings constitute the final term in the typology Moses/Christ/humans. As we have seen in Chapter 2 Prudentius inderstands Moses as a *historicus,* the writer of universal history (*Apoth.* 294–304, 315, *Ham.* 340). In light of Christ's central role as Prudentius' muse and poetic inspiration, *Moyses historicus* of the Old Testament may prefigure *Christus Musa* of the New Testament and Prudentian corpus.

66. J. Danielou, *From Shadows to Reality,* 184–85, quotes the Persian sage Aphraates, *Demons* 12.8.

67. At *Pe.* 6.86 Prudentius recalls *Ex.* 3:5, where Moses takes off his shoes in preparation to meet God at the burning bush. In typological fashion the martyr Fructuosus takes his shoes off before his death, which includes walking through fire. At *Pe.* 6. 97–99

a spirit from heaven says, *Felices animae, quibus per ignem / celsa scandere contigit Tonantis, / quas olim fugiet perennis ignis!* Note that in this passage there is the same expression for "blessed souls" as at *Cath.* 5. 121, blessed souls whose opposite number, the souls from hell, are about to be described. In addition, at *Cath.* 5. 135 these accursed souls, which become progressively assimilated to the blessed souls in the passage and get relief from their punishment are described in a group that includes all souls as *populus liber ab ignibus.* The only other direct reference to the escape through the Red Sea in the corpus of Prudentius describes Moses after the collapse of the sea onto Pharaoh and the Egyptians in the following way: *patuit via libera Moysi.* The word *liber/libera* in these two passages is used to denote the state of a person's freedom after an extraordinary trial. Both the souls of heaven in *Cathemerinon* 5 and Moses just after the escape through the Red Sea are described in the same way. This set of textual associations shows that Prudentius understands the soul's journey to include a trial of fire; and that through Prudentian intratextual connections of language and Prudentius' association of the Vergilian underworld with the Exodus story, we can conclude that Prudentius associates the Exodus episode with a souls' trial by fire. See *Pe.* 2.363, where Moses' visage is completely changed after undergoing the trial of facing directly the burning bush. Also, *Cath.* 7.36–45 recalls Moses in the desert for forty days and nights, a trial that Christ was to undergo as well. *Cath.* 12.169–72 *and TH* 12 allude to *Ex.* 1:10–13 and *Num.* 21:8–9, respectively, where Moses' outstretched arms and hanging of a serpent on a cross prefigure Christ's death on the cross.

68. *Matth.* 6:34 and 6:26 assert God's ability and willingness to take care of everyone's basic needs and thus individuals should not worry about the future. God will provide. The allusion to *Matth.* 6:11 is from the Lord's Prayer and serves to add to the speech of *Operatio* not only the assurance that God will provide bread but also the instruction that one must pray for it.

69. *TH* 21 gives a sketch of the same typology for the new temple: Wisdom-Solomon's temple/Christ's temple. But, more important, these lines envision the new temple as a *templum hominis sub pectore,* a clear precedent for the temple as soul in the *Psychomachia.* M. Smith, *Prudentius' Psychomachia,* 232, gives a typological series for the temple: Solomon's temple/temple of the pure heart/temple of the New Jerusalem/temple of *Sapientia.*

70. The temple has several possible allegorical meanings, including a model of the soul, the concrete expression of the new Christian age in terms of a change in the soul's status, and the example of the harmonious hierarchy and relationship of a soul/city and God. The poem permits all of these meanings to stand.

71. 1 *Kings* 5:3–5: Solomon says, (3) *tu scis voluntatem David patris mei, et quia non potuerit aedificare domum nomini Domini Dei sui propter bella imminentia per circuitum, donec daret Dominus eos sub vestigio pedum eius;* (4) *nunc autem requiem dedit Dominus Deus meus mihi per circuitum: et non est satan, neque occursus malus;* (5) *quamobrem cogito aedificare templum nomini Domini Dei mei, sicut locutus est Dominus David patri meo, dicens: Filius tuus, quem dabo pro te super solium tuum, ipse aedificabit domum nomini meo.* 1 *Chron.* 28:2–6 (*Vetus Latina* is unavailable): David says, "I had prepared to build it, but God said to me, 'you shall not build a house for my name for you are a man of wars and shed blood.' . . . Now of all my sons . . . he has chosen Solomon . . . and he (the Lord) has said to me, 'Solomon your son shall build my house and my courts.'" Bergman does not list the 1 *Chronicles* allusion, but Cunningham is correct to see it as an alternative to 1 *Kings* 5:3–5.

72. *[N]ihilque erat in templo quod non auro tegeretur: sedet totum altare oraculi texit auro.*

73. *[E]t intulerunt sacerdotes arcam foederis Domini in locum suum, in oraculum templi, in sanctum sanctorum, subter alas cherubim.*

74. *Apoth.* 512–552 recall the destruction of Solomon's temple by Titus in 70 CE and announce a new Christian temple fabricated from the Word itself (*Apoth.* 524).

75. Pelikan, *Christianity and Classical Culture*, 45.

76. (45) *Iterum simile est regnum caelorum homini negotianti quaerenti bonam margaritam;* (46) *Inventa autem (una) pretiosa margarita abiit et vendidit omnia quaecumque habuit et emit eam.* Cunningham and Bergman list only verse 46, but Thomson lists both verses 45 and 46. Prudentius must have been looking at both verses.

77. *Sapientia aedificavit sibi; domum, et subdidit columnas septem.* Patristic literature typologically connects *Sapientia* to the word of God and Christ. See Smith, *Prudentius' Psychomachia*, 195.

78. By exploiting *Gal.* 5:17, Prudentius brings into clear relief the oppostions of flesh/soul and light/dark (*viscera . . . animam*, *Psych.* 904–905; *lux atque tenebrae*, *Psych.* 908).

79. *Eph.* 4:26: *irascimini et nolite delinquere. sol non occidit super iracundiam vestram. Eph.* 5:2: *et ambulate in caritate; sicut et Christus dilexit nos et tradidit semet ipsum pro nobis oblationem et nostiam deo in odorem suavitatis. Psych.* 782–86 expands the conceptual range of this biblical passage with the opposition between *venia* and *iram.*

80. *[F]requent die regressus invenit germinasse virgam Aaron, in domo levi: et turgentibus gemmis eruperant flores, qui, foliis dilatatis, in amygdalas deformati sunt.*

81. *[A]ureum habens altare et arcam testamenti tectam undique auro in qua urna aurea habens manna et virga Aaron quae floruerat et tabulae testamenti.*

82. Smith, *Prudentius' Psychomachia*, 216, connects Melchisedec with *Sapientia* because *Sapientia* fulfills the Levitical order of Aaron's priesthood. Smith does not discuss the apophatic language used of Melchisedec in the *Praefatio.*

83. Note *decoro . . . solio* at *Psych.* 914–15. At *Ham.* 264 *decore* is said of a woman who is not content with her "grace" (trans. Thomson).

84. Cunningham lists three biblical passages as allusions in the final lines of the poem *Psych.* 889–915: *Gal.* 5:17 *nam caro concupiscit adversus spiritum: spiritus autem adversus carnem: haec enim invicem adversantum ut nonquaecumque vultis, ista faciatis* (*Psych.* 908); *Ps.* 46:10 (*Vetus Latina* text is unavailable) "Be still and know that I am God; I am exalted among the nations, I am exalted in the earth" (*Psych.* 915); and 1 *Cor.* 1:24 *ipsis autem vocatis Iudaeis, et Graecis, Christum Dei virtutem, et Dei Sapientiam* (also a possible source of *Psych.* 915). Bergman does not acknowledge *Ps.* 46:10 and 1 *Cor.* 1:4 as allusions. He does recognize *Gal.* 5:17 but includes *Psych.* 904–908 as the referring lines. Cunningham also says to compare Augustine's *Enarr. in Ps.* 46:10: *dicit scriptura . . . animi iusti sedes sapientiae..* It is not difficult to see why Bergman left out two of the three references. The linguistic parallel is weak at best, but regarding the connection of wisdom to Christ, these texts are canonical.

85. The temple, which has been created for the soul, that is, as the soul, is a result of a trial (*spectamine morum, Psych.* 913).

86. See Ambrose's use of 1 *Cor.* 1:24 at *De Fide* 2.16.141–43 where in a discussion on faith in Christ we encounter the military metaphor of Christ as the leader of an army. To believe in Christ as "power and wisdom" is to "win the prize of victory for (one's) faith."

87. Dawson, *Christian Figural Reading*, 12–13, comments that Hans Frei's approach to Origen "[places] allegorical reading on a spectrum with typology, rather than casting allegory and typology as simple binary oppositions, Frei admits that figural reading is, in effect, a kind of allegorical reading, one properly governed by allegiance to the gospel's literal sense." Auerbach, for example, takes a strictly historicist view of typology which preserves the reality of the historical figures and narratives. For him, this is undermined by allegorical reading which he takes to be the Origenist way of reading scripture.

F O U R : Pagan Philosophy and the Making of Allegory

1. C. Gill, *The Structured Self in Hellenistic and Roman Thought* (Oxford: Oxford University Press, 2006), on the representation of character and emotions in literature, says that there is a "direct influence of philosophical ideas on other aspects of the culture . . . that helps to shape . . . the presentation of figures in works of literature" (408); and on the Aeneid that "philosophical themes . . . are integral with intertextual and political or ideological factors" (438). M. Colish, *The Stoic Tradition From Antiquity to the Early Middle Ages*, vol. 2 (Leiden: Brill, 1990), 107–108, describes the last twenty-five lines of the *Psychomachia* as possessing "a decidedly Neoplatonic coloration."

2. I use the term "Platonic" to refer to works authored by Plato and his ideas directly attributable to Plato. "Neo-Platonic" refers to the texts and ideas of Plotinus, Porphyry, Iamblichus, and their followers. "Platonist" is an umbrella term that includes Platonic, middle Platonic, and neo-Platonic images and ideas.

3. D. G. Hunter, "Fourth-century Latin Writers," in *The Cambridge History of Early Christian Literature*, ed. F. Young, L. Ayres, and A. Louth (Cambridge: Cambridge University Press, 2004), 309.

4. Hunter, "Fourth-century Latin Writers," 310. In *Conf.* 4.16.28 Augustine says that he has read Aristotle's *Categories* and goes on to list them. J. J. O'Donnell, *Augustine: Confessions*, vol. 2 (Oxford: Oxford University Presss, 1992), 264–65, argues that nevertheless Augustine's knowledge of the list comes via the neo-Platonic reception of Aristotle. In the fourth century, Platonist rather than Aristolian metaphysics held sway.

5. R. Markus, "Marius Victorinus," in *Cambridge History of Later Greek Philosophy*, ed., A. H. Armstrong (Cambridge: Cambridge University Press, 1970), 332.

6. J. D. Dawson, "Christian Teaching," in *The Cambridge History of Early Christian Literature*, 229.

7. Jerome, who maintained a strong rhetorical position against the use of the pagan literary inheritance, never gave up his favorite Roman authors and freely borrowed from pagan philosophers and poets. See M. Vessey, "Jerome and Rufinus," in *The Cambridge History of Early Christian Literature*, 320.

8. F. Young, "Christian Teaching," *The Cambridge History of Early Christian Literature*, 474.

9. R.A. Markus, "Paganism, Christianity, and the Latin Classics," in J. W. Binns, *Latin Literature of the Fourth Century* (London: Routledge and Kegan Paul, 1974), 12. The comment of Markus represents a rare instance in the secondary literature of Prudentius being mentioned with luminaries of the early church.

10. P. Courcelle, *Les Lettres Greques en Occident de Macrobe à Cassiodore*, 2nd ed.,

translated by Harry E. Wedeck. *Late Latin Writers and Their Greek Sources* (Cambridge, Mass.: Harvard University Press, 1969), 72–77, documents how Jerome uses without attribution Porphyry's *Isagoge* and *De abstinentia*.

11. J. J. O'Donnell, *Augustine* Confessions, vol. 2, 419–20, summarizes the scholarly debate on who introduced Augustine to the *platonicorum libri* and Manlius' influence on Augustine. See also B. Stock, *Augustine the Reader: Meditation, Self-Knowledge, and the Ethics of Interpretation* (Cambridge, Mass.: Harvard University Press, 1996), 329, note 217.

12. Jerome mentions the *Protagoras* translation at *Ep.* 57.5, 106.3, *Adv Ruf.* 2.25, and *Praef. In Pent.* He cites the *Timaeus* translation (which ends at 47b) at *In Amos* 2.5 (*PL* 25, 1038a) and *In Isaiam* 12.40 (*PL* 24, 409d). Augustine uses it at *Civ.* 13.16.

13. *Ep.* 2.9.5.

14. For bibliography see S. Gersh, *Middle Platonism and Neoplatonism: The Latin Tradition,* 2 vols. (Notre Dame, Ind.: University of Notre Dame Press, 1986), vol. 1, 13, and vol. 2, 421, note 2.

15. We are limited in our certainty as to the identity of Calcidius. He is a fourth-century figure, but our choices are between two personages. Either he lived in the first half of the century, as the dedication of the commentary to a certain Hosius, thought to be bishop of Cordoba (who lived between 296–357), might indicate; or he could have been a high Milanese official of 395 AD whose epitaph survives. For the arguments see S. Gersh, *Middle Platonism,* vol. 2, 421–25.

16. Gersh, *Middle Platonism,* vol. 2, 426 says, "There seems little doubt that Calcidius had direct access to the original texts (Plato) when composing his treatise since . . . he is found quoting at length from the dialogues in his own accurate . . . translations."

17. For references, see Gersh, *Middle Platonism,* vol. 2, 442–84.

18. R. Klibansky, *The Continuity of the Platonic Tradition during the Middle Ages* (New York: Kraus International Publications, 1982) with a new preface and four supplementary chapters (original edition published in 1939); and Gersh, *Middle Platonism,* vol. 2, 3–25.

19. Gersh, *Middle Platonism,* vol. 1, 25, has classified the indirect tradition further into five areas: pagan ancient Platonic, Christian neo-Platonic, and pagan neo-Platonic, middle Platonic, and Christian middle Platonic. Plato, Marius Victorinus, and Porphyry/Plotinus are examples of the first three of these categories, respectively. There are many names missing from this list, including church fathers and Macrobius. See chapter 2 for the former; and for the latter, references to *On the Dream of Scipio* will follow. For a useful distinction between Platonic and neo-Platonic see Gersh, *Middle Platonism,* vol. 2, 26–39. Note that late antique authors did not distinguish between Plato and the neo-Platonists such as Porphyry and Plotinus. They were subsumed under the category of "Platonists."

20. See J. J. O'Donnell, *Confessions,* vol. 2, 415. This raises issues of negative theology. Platonist theory and language do not provide knowledge of God, but the very fact of the Incarnation does. We know and do not know God simultaneously.

21. P. Hadot, *Porphyre et Victorinus,* Études Augustiennes (Paris: Firmin-Didot, 1968), 86: "On a donc pu dire très justement que Porphyre était, à partir du IVe siècle, le 'maître des esprits' en Occident. C'est lui qui révèle le néoplatonisme aux philosophes latins." In his statement, Hadot quotes Courcelle, *Les Lettres grecques,* 394 and *Late Latin*

Writers, 415, "The master mind was Porphyry." In the same pages Courcelle rightly states that Iamblichus was not known in the West until the end of the fourth century, and the major testimony, Augustine at *Civ.* 8.12, seems to have known him by name only.

22. On this central figure see A. H. M. Jones, J. R. Martindale, and J. Morris, *Prosopography*, vol. 1, under Theodorus 27; P. Courcelle, *Late Latin Writers*, 134–40; and O'Donnell, *Augustine*, vol. 2, 419–20. It was Manlius Theodorus who inspired Augustine to read the *De Regressu Animae* of Porphyry. According to Courcelle, *Late Latin Writers*, 135, Theodorus translated Celsinus' manual of Greek philosophers, read by Augustine, and containing information (as Claudian tells us, *In Laud. Manl. Theod.* 75ff) on the pre-Socratics as well as Plato and Epicurus.

23. Augustine *Conf.* 7.9.13.

24. See the full bibliography of J. J. O'Donnell, *Confessions*, vol. 2, 413–23.

25. See *Conf.* 7 and *Civ.* 10. O'Donnell, *Confessions*, vol. 1, i, xli comments on Augustine's interplay of images and patterns as "a feat possible in the fourth century only for someone who had read Plotinus, and read him very well"; and O'Donnell states that Augustine found in Porphyry "a Platonism that led him toward Christianity and that he would criticize mainly for not going far enough in that direction" (xlv).

26. *Conf.* 8.2.3. See J. J. O'Donnell, *Confessions*, vol. 2, 421 and vol. 3, 12–15, for information on Victorinus and a more cautious view of him as the translator of the *platonicorum libri*. See P. Hadot, *Marius Victorinus. Recherches sur sa vie et ses oeuvres* (Paris: Firmin-Didot, 1971), 25 for his date of birth; also P. Courcelle, *Les Confessions de saint Augustin dans la tradition littéraire* (Paris: Études Augustiniennes, 1963), 557–58. Porphyry's influence on Victorinus's work is clear from the fact that in his non-theological treatises, Victorinus cites Porphyry exclusively.

27. O'Donnell, *Confessions*, vol. 2, 423, represents the tide of scholarly opinion when he says that Plotinus and Porphyry came to Augustine as a package most likely in the form of Porphyry's *Sententiae* attached as a preface to selections from Plotinus. The most recent edition of the *Sententiae* is by E. Lamberz, trans., *Porphyrius Sententiae ad Intelligibilia Ducentes* (Leipzig: B. G. Teubner Verlagsgesellschaft, 1975). It is probable that we do not possess the complete text.

28. For a brief history of the scholarship on this issue, see M. T. Clark, *Marius Victorinus: Theological Treatises on the Trinity* (Washington, D.C.: Catholic University Press, 1981), 38–40. For the compelling arguments see P. Hadot, *Porphyre et Victorinus*, vol. 1, 102–46, and vol. 2, 157.

29. See Courcelle, *Late Latin Writers*, 74–76.

30. Traditionally this work has been dated at 399/400, but O'Donnell, *Confessions*, vol. 2, 422, wishes to push the date up, possibly to 415. Certainly by *Ep.* 82.2.22 (c.405) Augustine knew *Against the Christians*.

31. Thus, Augustine's acknowledged debt to the *platonicorum libri* for helping him to arrive at his Christian vision, and especially Porphyry's *De Regressu Animae;* also Jerome's wholesale plagiarizing of Porphyry, though he vilified him. For references see Courcelle, *Late Latin Writers*, 417 and 72–76, respectively.

32. This crossover must be approached with caution, since it is often difficult to attempt to disentangle pagan from Christian ideas. Consider *sapientia*. At times, Prudentius distinguishes two notions of *sapientia;* one pagan, and one Christian. But often, the *Psychomachia* settles on a syncretist and Christian Platonist construc-

tion of the concept. Sometimes he juxtaposes *Sapientia* and *Deus,* referring to them now as fellow creators and now as apophatic divine beings with no discernable origins (*Ham.* 345, 164). In another passage the poet invokes *Sapientia* as an offspring of the Father and therefore an ontological equal of Christ (*Hymn on the Trinity* 2). In all three passages, a Christian context is clear, but their debt to pagan metaphysics is clear from their concern with the ontology of the godhead. Conversely, the pagan *Sapientia* is sometimes clearly marked by Prudentius' pejorative language and attitude. At *Ham.* 378–405 *Sapientia* is a pagan personification carrying a Herculean club and is a direct cause of evil in the world. Here *Sapientia* is the ally of vice whose doctrines are arrogant and whose eloquence thunders to no good purpose. The vision of the temple and its inhabitants in the *Psychomachia,* by contrast, eschews the hard and fast distinction between pagan and Jewish-Christian *Sapientia,* preferring to combine the two.

33. Smith, *Prudentius'* Psychomachia, 232.

34. Ch. Gnilka, *Studien zur Psychomachie des Prudentius* (Weisbaden: O. Harrassowitz, 1963), 83–91, discusses in detail the *templum pectoris* motif.

35. *Rev.* 21:13–15 (with *Psych.* 830, 838, and 826): (13) *ab Oriente porte tres, et ab Aquilone portae tres, et ab Austro portae tres, et ab Occasu portae tres;* (14) *et muri civitatis habent fundamenta duodecim, et super ea nomina duodecim Apostolorum, et Agni;* (15) *et qui mecum loquebatur, habebat arundinem auream ad mensuram, ut meriretur civitatem, et portas eius, et muros eius. Rev.* 21:19–20 (with *Psych.* 854): (19) *fundamenta autem ex omni lapide pretioso, primum fundamentum, iaspis: fecundum, saphirus: tertium, calcedon: quartum, smaragdus;* (20) *quintum, sardonyx: sextum, sardius: septimum, chrysolitus: octavum, beryllus: novum, topasius: decimum, chrysoprasus: undecimum, hyacinthus: duodecimum, amethystus.*

36. *Eph.* 2:18–22 (with *Psych.* 840): (18) *quia per ipsum habemus consecuti simul in uno spiritu ad patrem;* (19) *iam peregrini at advenae sed concives sanctorum sed domestici dei;* (20) *superaedificati super fundamentum apostolorum et prophetarum cum sit summus angularis Christus in quo omnis aedificatio conpacta crescit in templum sanctum in domino, in quo et vos coaedificamini in habitatione dei spiritu.*

37. Prudentius exploits two meanings of *templum:* the meaning derived from ναός, "dwelling place" (Latin *habitatio*), and the meaning of *templum,* as a holy place formed by apportioning off a piece of land (*Psych.* 830). The phrase *purgati corporis urbem* implicitly possesses both meanings and establishes the temple as the soul itself through the suggestion of the city/soul analogy. We can see a similar ambiguity in Basil's usage of ναός at *Ep.* 8.11 (*To the Caesareans,* 360AD). He is interpreting 1 *Cor.* 6:19; "[Y]ou are the temple of the holy spirit which is in you." Basil says, πᾶς δὲ ναὸς Θεοῦ ναός. Εἰ δὲ ναός ἐσμεν τοῦ Πνεύματος του ἁγίου, Θεὸς τὸ Πνεῦμα τὸ ἅγιον. λέγεται δὲ καὶ ναὸς Σολομῶντος, ἀλλ᾽ ὡς κατασκευάσαντος. Εἰ δὲ οὕτως ἐσμεν ναὸς τοῦ ἁγίου Πνεύματος, Θεὸς τὸ ἅγιον Πνεῦμα. Ὁ γὰρ πάντα κατασκευάσας Θεός. Εἰ δὲ ὡς προσκυνουμένου καὶ ἐνοικοῦντος ἐν ἡμῖν, ὁμολογήσωμεν αὐτὸ εἶναι Θεόν. Basil moves comfortably from the temple as an actual artifice to the body as the temple of the Holy Spirit. The same distinction can be seen in Gregory of Nazianzus' *Or.* 8.11 (*On His Sister Gorgonia*), where he says of his sister: τίς δὲ ἧττον ἐφθέγξατο ἐν τοῖς γυναικείοις ὅροις τῆς εὐσεβείας μείνασα; ὅ δ᾽ οὖν ὠφείλετο τῇ γε ἀληθῶς εὐσεβεῖν ἐγνωκυίᾳ, καὶ οὐ καλὴ μόνον ἡ ἀπληστία, τίς μὲν ἀναθήμασιν οὕτω ναοὺς κατεκόσμησεν ἄλλους τε καὶ τὸν οὐκ οἶδ᾽ εἰ μετ᾽ ἐκείνην κοσμηθησόμενον;

μᾶλλον δὲ, τίς οὕτω ναὸν ἑαυτὸν τῷ θεῷ ζῶντα παρέστησεν; Nazianzen shifts from the literal structure of a temple in a city to the temple as a human being. Latin Patristic literature does not engage in the dual level discussion of "temple." But none of the Patristic literature uses the particular Old Testament texts as Prudentius does. He is original in this respect.

38. Prudentius's use of *Rev.* 21:19–20 provides the jewelry language with which Prudentius adorns his temple. *Psych* 826–27 uses the vocabulary of *Rev.* 21:15: *Aurea planitiem spatiis percurrit harundo / dimensis. Psych* 830 takes important vocabulary from *Rev.* 21:13: *Aurorae de parte tribus plaga lucida portis / inlustrata patet.* However, this language with *variatio* carries on through *Psych.* 834: *triplex . . . ad austrum / portarum numerus, tris occidualibus offert / ianua trina fores, totiens aquilonis ad axem / panditur alta domus* (*Psych.* 831–34). At *Psych.* 838 Prudentius adopts language from *Rev.* 21:14: *Portarum summis inscripta in postibus auro / nomina apostolici fulgent bis sena senatus.*

39. *Praef. Symm.* 1. 46 personifies *Sapientia* on a boat as the storm of the world passes over. The ship stands for the Christian ship of state (*Praef. Symm.* 1. 59), which *Sapientia* commands and whose holy law (*lex pia, Praef. Symm.* 1. 51) is wounded, probably referring to the Altar of Victory conflict which the *Contra Symmachum* addresses. Note the association of *Sapientia* with the religious state of Rome. *Sapientia* in Prudentius is associated both with the individual person and the state.

40. J. Lear, "Inside and Outside the *Republic*," in *Plato's* Republic: *Critical Essays,* ed. R. Kraut (Lanham, Md.: Rowman and Littlefield, 1997), 68.

41. Quoted in B. A. O. Williams, "The Analogy of City and Soul in Plato's *Republic*," in *Plato's* Republic: *Critical Essays,* ed. R. Kraut 49.

42. B. Mitchell and J.R. Lucas, *An Engagement with Plato's* Republic (Aldershot: Ashgate, 2003), 27. Plato establishes the metaphor of internal psychological battle a few lines later: "Injustice . . . must be some sort of civil war between these three elements, a refusal to mind their own business, and a determination to mind each other's, a rebellion by one part of the soul against the whole . . . the disorder and straying of the three elements produce injustice, indiscipline, cowardice, ignorance—evil of every kind, in fact." (444b1–8)

43. Mitchell and Lucas, *An Engagement with Plato's* Republic, 27. B. A. O. Williams, "Analogy of City and Soul," parses Plato's city/soul metaphor as a kind of confusion between the concepts of analogy and membership. The connections between the character of the *polis* and the soul are developed in a particular direction in the *Psycho-machia's* own expression of the pair soul/city.

44. In his failure to understand the dynamic of resemblance and membership, G. B. Ladner, *God, Cosmos, and Humankind: The World of Early Christian Symbolism* (Berkeley: University of California Press, 1995), 186 makes the misguided assertion that "in Prudentius the battle between virtues and vices does not take place in the soul, but outside." Ladner goes further, arguing that in Prudentius "the personifications of the virtues and vices that appear here are not only pure fabrications, they also lack the persuasive reality of major poetic inventions" (188). My project has been to show precisely the opposite of Ladner's position. Figurative reading in the form of typological allegory defines the essence of Prudentius' personifications, which produce a "persuasive reality" regarding the reader.

45. J. Van Oort, *Jerusalem and Babylon: A Study into Augustine's City of God and the Sources of His Doctrine of the Two Cities* (Leiden: E. J. Brill, 1991), 160; see 158–61.

46. Although Augustine does not explicitly express the connection between salvation history and Roman *imperium,* his willingness to use the power of the Roman Christian *imperium* to spread and preserve orthodox doctrine reveals a relationship between the Roman state and Christian doctrine.

47. The ecphratic presentation of two cities, one at war and the other at peace, dates all the way back to *Iliad* 18 in which the political and ethical condition of humankind is depicted as a relief on Achilles' massive shield.

48. Philo, *De Posteritate Caini* 183–84; *De Gigantibus* 51; and *De Confusione Linguarum* 46. D. T. Runia, "The Idea and the Reality of the City in the Thought of Philo of Alexandria," *Journal of the History of Ideas* 61.3 (2000): 370, comments that for Philo, "in the allegorical context, the city above all illustrates the inner workings of the soul." Also Runia says that the city is an "exegetical and allegorical theme" (377) and "the method of allegory enables [Philo] to bring forward the more theoretical and philosophical aspects of the theme [of the city] " (362).

49. Runia, "The Idea and Reality of the City," 377.

50. Philo, *De Confusione Linguarum,* 107–108, with Runia, "The Idea and Reality of the City," 369. Compare *De Somniis* 2.249: "The City of God is not only the cosmos but also the soul of the wise man. Its name Jerusalem means 'vision of peace.' This city should not be sought in the regions of the earth, for it is not made of wood and stone, but rather in the soul which sets for itself the goal of the life of peace and contemplation."

51. Philo, *Legum Allegoria,* 3.191, 224, and *De Sacr. Ab. et Caini,* 49, with Runia, "The Idea and Reality of the City," 369.

52. For these insights and the passages upon which they are based, see F. Dvornik, *Early Christian and Byzantine Political Philosophy: Origins and Background* (Washington, D.C.: Dumbarton Oaks, 1966), vol. 2: 660–65.

53. Dvornik, *Early Christian and Byzantine Political Philosophy,* 697, notes that Eusebius gives a biblical rationale for the empire as the guarantor of peace through his interpretation of Isaiah's messianic prophecy. Isaiah claimed that peace would come with the messiah and this peace Eusebius identifies with the Augustan *Pax Romana.* Given his emphasis on the typological allegory of peace at the end of the *Psychomachia,* Prudentius appears to recognize this association between the messiah and Roman peace.

54. Dvornik, *Early Christian and Byzantine Political Philosophy,* 680–82.

55. Gregory of Nazienzus, *Poemata Dogmatica,* 80 (*PG* 37, col. 865), with Dvornik, *Early Christian and Byzantine Political Philosophy,* 687.

56. *Symm.* 2.430–35: *tandem deprendere rectum / doctus iter caput augustum diademate cinxit / appellans patrem patriae, populi atque senatus / rectorem, qui militiae sit ductor et idem / dictator censorque bonus morumque magister, / tutor opum, vindex scelerum, largitor honorum.* Theodosius' speech to Rome in Contra *Symmachum* 1 never refers to the emperor as *rex.* He is "leader" (*duce,* 433), "first citizen" (*principis,* 478), and "a greathearted leader" (*magnanimo ductore,* 510).

57. O'Donnell, *Confessions,* vol. 1, xl. In the *Confessions,* Augustine expresses his most developed Platonist scheme of ascent. He lays out a seven-stage scheme of ascent, all of which depends on an acceptance of the Incarnation—for Augustine, a crucial

lacuna in the schemes of Porphyry and other neo-Platonists. See O'Donnell's comments with references on *Conf.* 7.17.23 and 7.18.24.

58. See Plotinus, *Enn.* 4.8(6).5 and 8. These two views seem incompatible with the pictures produced in the *Timaeus* and the *Republic*. The *Timaeus* envisions the soul's first incarnation, effected by the divine Demiurge, as a blameless event; and the *Republic* understands the embodiment of the soul as a result of universal necessity. It is possible to see how the notion in the two former dialogues of the soul's coming-to-be as a failing and resulting pollution could be in conflict with the explanation in the latter two dialogues of the soul's coming-to-be as a result of necessary and hence, blameless event, but Plotinus saw no contradiction and wanted to eliminate the language of falling which has connotations of deterioration. Rather, he thought that the soul remains as it was, divine and unseparated from Intelligence, but that the process of embodiment has somehow made the person unaware of this hidden life of the soul. This is not an equivocation on the problem presented by the Platonic texts, but Plotinus does manage to take both an optimistic and pessimistic view of the soul's coming-to-be. Optimistically, this is seen as an emanation that flows outward, therefore preserving a connection to the hypostasis of Intelligence. Pessimistically, the soul's emanation is still viewed as a fall implying the existence of the will and the punishment that such an instrument of choice necessitates.

59. Ancient introductions to the philosophy of Plotinus are Porphyry's *Sententiae* and *Vita Plotini* (*Plotinus*, vol. 1, ed. A. H. Armstrong. Loeb Classical Library [Cambridge, Mass.: Harvard University Press, 1966]). For recent introductions and specific references in Plotinus see M. Hornum's introduction to K. Guthrie's translation of the *Sententiae, Porphyry's Launching-Points to the Realm of the Mind* (Grand Rapids, Mich.: Phanes Press, 1988); P. Merlan, "Plotinus," in *The Encyclopedia of Philosophy*, ed. P. Edwards (New York: Macmillan and the Free Press, 1967), 351–59; J. M. Rist, *Plotinus: The Road to Reality* (Cambridge: Cambridge University Press, 1967); and D. J. O'Meara, *Plotinus: An Introduction to the Enneads* (Oxford: Clarendon Press, 1993).

60. Echoed by Porphyry at *Ad Marc.* 1.112. Augustine, like most Christians of his age, understands descent in a more moralistic and will-oriented way-that it is contingent on humans' chosen failure.

61. *Enn.* 1.1; 1.8; 2.4; 4.3.

62. For a detailed account of the differences and similarities between Plotinus and Porphyry see A. Smith, *Porphyry's Place in the Neoplatonic Tradition* (The Hague: Martinus Nijhoff, 1974), 1–78. On page 70, Smith names two of the most glaring differences. Porphyry decided that eternal transmigration of souls was irrelevant and should be eliminated from his theory of soul. Also, Porphyry, unlike Plotinus, recognizes the importance of the concepts of time and history which impose a beginning and an end to salvation. Both of these modifications were especially attractive to fourth-century Christians who despised the notion of reincarnation and saw the history of the world as a kind of progression to the incarnation of the savior.

63. *Sent.* 29.18.14 (τὸ βαρὺ πνεῦμα) and *Sent.* 29.19.16 (βαρεῖσθαι). Compare Macrobius's *pondus* at *In Scip.* 1.11.11 and 1.12.13; also Augustine *Conf.* 13.7.8 (*pondere cupiditas*) and 13.9.10 (*pondus meum amor meus*). Gersh, *Middle Platonism*, vol. 2, 585–87, says that Macrobius is following Numenius through Porphyry.

64. *Ad Marc.* 33.501–502 and 6.101.

65. *De Antr. Nymph.* 11.14.1–12,14,24; *Sent.* 29.18.14–19; *In Tim Fr.* 13. At *In Scip.* 1.12.8 Macrobius ascribes "intoxication" (*ebrietatem*) to the soul.

66. *De Abstin.* 1.28.2 and *De Regr. Anim.* fr. 11/1, 39. 19–22.

67. *Ad Marc.* 6.112–14. For the soul as sleepy see also *De Abstin.* 1.28 (referring to Homer *Odys.* 24.12), *De Antr. Nymph.* 75; and in Plato see *Rep.* 571c–72b.

68. *De Antr. Nymph.* 15,16,17–19, and 20.

69. *Sent.* 29.19.9–10 and Gersh, *Middle Platonism,* vol. 2, 583.

70. Dawson, "Christian Teaching," 224, refers to Plato's conception of mimetic poetry as being caught in "a labyrinth of narrative desire," the withdrawal from which was necessary in order to become an autonomous person whose actions are based on reasons.

71. Or, as Plotinus sometimes explains it, the body approaches the soul. See O'Meara, *Plotinus,* 27.

72. *Ad Gaur.* 13.53.2–27 and *Sent.* 37,43.11–16. At *In Scip.* 1.12.6 Macrobius writes *per hominis membra diffunditur.*

73. *Ad Marc.* 18.307–308, 17.291–92, 6.111–14, 34.523–25, and 7.115–20, respectively. For ignorance as a disease of the soul see Plato's *Republic* 609c–11a. Regarding shackle and chain language, the Platonic inheritance is significant: *Phaedo* 59e–60a and *Republic* 514a–17c. Chains are connected with the Orphic idea of the body as the prison of the soul. See *Cratylus* 400c and *Phaedo* 62b. For much of the Porphyrian language in Plotinus see *Enn.* 4.8.1.

74. The most recent editions are K. O'Brien Wicker, *Porphyry the Philosopher: To Marcella* (Atlanta: Scholars Press, 1987), references to the text are from this edition; E. des Places, *Vie de Pythagore; Lettre à Marcella* (Paris: Sociète d'Edition *Les Belles Lettres,* 1982); W. Pötscher, *Porphyrios Pros Markellan* (Leiden: E.J. Brill, 1969).

75. *Ad Marc.* 11.191–98; 19.316–20

76. *Ad Marc.* 11.201–202; 19.322; 21.333 (both of God and evil spirits); 21.338. Note that in sections 11, 19, and 21 Porphyry delineates the two-sidedness of the soul. It can either house God/reason or evil spirits.

77. *Ad Marc.* 13.221–26 and 233–37.

78. *Ad Marc.* 12.206–209; 23.367–69 and 373–74.

79. *Ad Marc.* 26.409–12.

80. *Ad Marc.* 24.381–82. This passage in context (376–83) discusses the τέσσαρα of which faith and hope are integral constituents of a knowledge of God. At 23.362–63 Porphyry appears to make a negative comment about faith as ἄλογος. But his point is that faith alone can not provide the neccessary divine knowledge. It must be supplemented with reason.

81. *Ad Marc.* 25.384–86.

82. See O'Brien Wicker's notes on these three categories of law: *Ad Marcellam,* 111–12.

83. *Ad Marc.* 20.331 and 26.417–18. 331 is paralleled in *Pythag. Sent.* 16 and *Sent. Sext.* 430.

84. Quoted in Eusebius *Praep. Ev.* 14.10.5.

85. Quoted in Augustine *Civ.* 10.32 (*De Regressu Animae,* fr. 12 J. Bidez, *Vie de Porphyre avec les fragments des traités* per περὶ ἀγαλμάτων *et De Regressu Animae,* Recueil de Travaux publiés par la Faculté de Philosophie et Lettres, xliii (Université de Gand, 1913).

86. See also *Ep. Ad Aneb.,* quoted in Iamblichus *De Myst.* 10.1 and fr. 12 Bidez.

87. *Ad Marc.* 521–25. Porphyry employs chain and binding language of the soul at 7.114–20 and 33.506–11. The former passage has to do with women weighing themselves down with the shackles of jewelry, while the latter equates chains with the various pleasure-seeking and fear-behaving organs of the body.

88. Socrates at *Phaedo* 59e–60a is released from his chains in the prison when his wife Xanthippe and his child briefly visit; also *Phaedo* 82d6: λύσει τε καὶ καθαρμῷ.

89. See Porphyry *Ad Marc.* 7.122.

90. *Psych.* 8, 29, 33, and 55.

91. I do not include *vernulas* (line 22) and *vernularum* (line 56) since these are household slaves, which are part of the family and are not intended to contribute to the bondage of the soul metaphor.

92. See also *Psych.* 591–92 and 595.

93. This is explicitly stated in lines 14 (*cordis servientis*) and line 52 (*in armis pectorum fidelium*). Note as well the language of home which foregrounds the soul: *domi* (the place where we gather our forces, line 55), *casam* (of the chaste soul, line 62), *domum* (the house of the Father, line 68). Abraham's *domus* is where he entertains the triple formed image of the Trinity.

94. See Plato, *Phaedo* 81c8–9 for the language of heaviness (βαρὺ, βαρύνεται).

95. Compare Macrobius *In Scip.* 1.9.1: *manare de caelo.*

96. Prudentius constructs this Christian Platonist conceptual scheme in the lines surrounding and including *Psych.* 68 in order to make clear his exegesis of the Judith story, which prefigures the Incarnation.

97. See C. T. Lewis and C. Short, *A Latin Dictionary, degenero* I. *Superbia* applies the adjective, *degener*, at *Psych.* 229 and *degenerem* at *Psych.* 248 to *Mens Humilis.*

98. *Psych.* 89–95 contain striking descent language, much of which seems to be overtly Christian or possibly pagan epic in its origin; however, besides having its directional orientation, the expression *ad mortis iter* (*Psych.* 89) picks up the earlier language of *credendi via* (*Praef.* 1) and *vicendi . . . ratio* (*Psych.* 18). All these nouns can be translated as "way". The soul gets submerged into Tartarus, *animas in Tartara mergis* (*Psych.* 90). *Pudicitia* commands the soul of *Libido* to "thrust into the dark depths of night" (*inque tenebrosum noctis detrudere fundum, Psych.* 93). *Psych.* 94–95 picks up *fluxit* of *Psych.* 68 with *volvant subter / vada . . . vada . . . / rotet per stagna sonantia vertex.* The context certainly consists of Christian notions of hell, but even here, certain signs of Platonist descent language can be seen.

99. Ovid *Amores* 1.2.15, *asper equus duris contunditur ora lupatis;* Horace *Carm.* 1.8.6, *lupatis temperet ora frenis.* Prudentius employs allusions to pagan Latin poets to construct a broader, Platonist resonance.

100. Note also Prudentius' use of *libertate*, which recalls neo-Platonic language of release from earthly bonds.

101. Compare the winged charioteer, ὑποπτέρου . . . ἡνιόχου, of *Phaedrus* 246a7.

102. D. Shanzer, "Allegory and Reality: Spes, Victoria, and the Date of Prudentius's *Psychomachia*," *Illinois Classical Studies* 14 (1989): 352: Hesiod *Op.* 97–98; *Anth Gr.* 7.420.1; Lucian *Merc. Cond.* 42.

103. D. Shanzer, "Allegory and Reality," 353, note 38, speculates that Prudentius may have gotten the notion of winged hope directly from Hesiod. Indeed, this assumes either Prudentius's knowledge of Greek or the availability of a Latin translation.

104. R. Hackforth, *Plato's* Phaedrus (London: Cambridge University Press, 1972), 107, says of 253c–56e: "The most that we can say is that continence is conceived as in one aspect intellectual, its source being knowledge or recollection of ideal beauty, and in another as emotional."

105. J. Bergman cites Vergil *Aen.* 9.14, *dixit et in caelum paribus se sustulit alis,* and Tibullus 4.1.209, *per liquidum volucri vehar aëra penna,* as parallels to *Psych.* 305 and 306. These allusions form but a small part of the *Phaedrus* language and imagery employed throughout the *Psychomachia.* And thus, as is the case with bits and pieces of scriptural texts used by Prudentius, such allusions take on a life of their own and are constituent of a broader allusion, in this case to Platonic imagery.

106. *Psych.* 270–73: *eques illa . . . / incidit . . . / Prona ruentis equi cervice involvitur . . . / pectoris inpressu fracta inter crura rotatur.*

107. Motifs of weight and heaviness of the soul were adopted by Plotinus/Porphyry (see note 63) from Plato.

108. See Porphyry *Ad Marc.* 24.376–83—ἐλπίσι γὰρ ἀγαθαῖς οἱ ἀγαθοὶ τῶν φαύλων ὑπερέχουσι.

109. *Psych.* 231–34 is a brief criticism of *Spes* put into the mouth of *Superbia.* She says that thinking which includes hope encourages idle expectation (*pigro rerum meditamine, Psych.* 234). She uses words of sluggishness and idleness (*lenta, desidiam*) that emphasize stagnation. Hopes are likened to "silly dreams of empty talk" (*vacuae frivola famae*) and are things "believed in" (*creduntur*). At *Psych.* 235 she calls hope lazy (*spes palpet iners*) and accuses her of not being able to rouse up the virtues. The metaphor of ascent is conspicuously absent in the vice's portrayal of the virtue.

110. See note 67 in Ladner, *God, Cosmos, and Humankind,* who mysteriously understands the battles of the virtues and vices in the *Psychomachia* taking place only on the outside.

111. See also *Ham.* 56–59, *in cerebro . . . ebrio . . . / madens.* Macrobius, in his neo-Platonic excursus on the soul, describes the descending soul as being in a state of drunkenness (*ebrietatem; In Scip.* 1.12.8).

112. Language of wetness and falling accompanies the description of *Amor* (*lita, lapsum, cadentem, Psych.* 436–37).

113. The word *electrum* can mean either "amber" or an "alloy of silver and gold." In this case, the color amber (and thus the material) is meant, especially considering the modifying adjective *pallens,* which is applied to the pagan underworld. The color of a sick and weakened person is foremost in the present context. See Lewis Short, *A Latin Dictionary,* A & B..

114. Plotinus, *Enn.* 3.4[15].3.25–27.

115. *Psych.* 448–49 is another example of *Luxuria's* dissipation, this time in terms of the things which were on her person: *damna iacent: crinalis acus redimicula vittae / fibula flammeolum strofium diadema monile.*

116. D. J. O'Meara, *Platonopolis: Platonic Philosophy in Late Antiquity* (Oxford: Oxford University Press, 2003), 74, illustrates the Plotinian use of the story of Minos, the legendary legislator, who, after communion with Zeus the monarch of the universe (equivalent to the divine intellect), legislates in the image of his union.

117. O'Meara, *Platonopolis,* 90.

118. Dawson, "Christian Teaching," 236.

119. O'Meara, *Platonopolis*, 91. O'Meara is interpreting a passage in a letter to a certain Asphalius, the text of which is preserved by J. Stobaeus, *Anthology*, eds., C. Wachsmuth and O. Hense (Berlin: Weidmannsche Verlagsbuchhandlung, 1958), vol. 3, 201, 17–202, 17. Iamblichus is following closely the language and imagery of Plato's *Rep.* 500e.

120. *Apoth.* 449–54: *Principibus tamen e cunctis non defuit unus / me puero, ut memini, ductor fortissimus armis, / conditor et legum, celeberrimus ore manuque, / consultor patriae, sed non consultor habendae / religionis, amans ter centum milia divum. / Perfidus ille deo quamvis non perfidus orbi.*

121. O'Meara, *Platonopolis*, 120. On the relationship between Julian's intellectual beliefs and his political program see P. Athanassiadi, *Julian: An Intellectual Biography* (London: Routledge, 1992); A. Cameron, "Julian and Hellenism," *The Ancient World* 24 (1993): 25–29; A Meredith, "Porphyry and Julian Against the Christians," in *Aufstieg und Niedergang der Römischen Welt*, II.23.2 (Berlin: Walter de Gruyter, 1980): 1119–49; and R. Smith, *Julian's Gods: Religion and Philosophy in the Thought and Action of Julian the Apostate* (London: Routledge, 1995).

122. See M. B. Simmons, "Julian the Apostate," in *The Early Christian World*, ed. P. E. Esler, vol. 2 (London: Routledge, 2000), 1252, for sources regarding Julian's daily ritual sacrifices. Libanius, *Or.* 12.82, says that Julian's fingers were stained red with the blood of sacrificed animals.

123. Lactantius, *Div. Inst.* 4.27 asserts that no pagan ritual will work nor a priest be able to read entrails when a Christian with an image of a cross on his forehead is present.

124. The passage makes it clear that the pagan gods are not non-existent, but rather are defeated by the one, true god whose authority consigns pagan gods to the status of demons or evil spirits.

125. On Iamblichus' influence on Julian, see M. B. Simmons and his references, "Julian the Apostate," 1252.

126. D. J. O'Meara, *Platonopolis*, 121–22. M. B. Simmons, "Julian the Apostate," 1254 emphasizes the idea that Julian's program of appointing pagan clergy is an anti-Christian maneuver above all else and parallels church structure with its regional clergy who have the authority to appoint priests with varying responsibilities in each city.

127. O'Meara, *Platonopolis*, 149.

128. O'Meara, *Platonopolis*, 147; for Eusebius' post-Constantinian, pre-Alaric triumphalism, see *HE* 4.26.7ff. and *Contra Celsum* 2.30; for the patristic literature's support of the close relationship between Roman *imperium*, the *pax Romana*, monotheism, and monarchy, see Van Oort, *Jerusalem and Babylon*, 156 with further references and Dvornik, *Early Christian and Byzantine Political Philosophy*, 676–96.

129. O'Meara, *Platonopolis*, 154–57, who follows Markus, *Saeculum*, chapters 1 and 2. For a qualification of Markus' view, see Van Oort, *Jerusalem and Babylon*, 160.

130. Roberts, *Poetry and the Cult of the Martyrs*, 55–76.

131. Roberts examines the various *topoi* associated with martyr narratives including a sequence of *tormenta*, exhaustion of the torturer, the growing enthusiasm of the martyr as he/she is tortured, the elements of a martyr death, etc. I would go even further. At *Pe.* 1006–50 Romanus describes in detail a pagan sacrifice of an ox only to deride it as senseless mutilation in the name of the "gods." Romanus goes on to accuse

pagans of being polluted by immersing themselves in such blood and gore. At *Pe.* 1091–1100 Prudentius explains that in the martyr narrative the polluting pagan ritual of blood and gore (i.e., sacrifice) is played out in reverse. That is, Christians in the time of persecution, and as represented in Prudentius' martyr narratives, turned this barbarity into a triumph. Thus, the violence is exclusively pagan since it derives from pagan sacrifice; and when pagans attempt to turn this violent behavior against Christian bodies, it is ineffectual. The idea is that Christians will live on no matter what happens to the body. Just as pagan sacrifice to false gods is futile, so violence done to a Christian of unshakable faith results in a glorious immortality.

132. M. Clement Eagan, *The Poems of Prudentius,* vol. 2, *Fathers of the Church* 52 (Washington, D.C.: Catholic University Press of America, 1965), 82.

133. Smith, *Prudentius's* Psychomachia, 280–96; and Van Dyke, *The Fiction of Truth,* 32–33.

134. Malamud, *A Poetics of Transformation,* 48–54. In *Rufinum* 2.410–20.

135. C. S. Lewis, *The Allegory of Love: A Study in Medieval Tradition* (New York: Oxford University Press, 1971), 69; G. Clifford, *The Transformations of Allegory* (London: Routledge and Kegan Paul, 1974), 28; and M. Lavarenne, *Prudence,* vol. 3, Collection des Universités de France, 3d ed. revised, corrected, and augmented by J.-L. Charlet (Paris: Budé, 1992), 11–12.

136. Paxson, *The Poetics of Personification,* 66–69.

137. See Paxson, *The Poetics of Personification,* 1–3.

138. Other examples are *Psych.* 153–54, 506–509, 589–97, 672–77, and 691–93. I also include *Psych.* 506–509, 672–77, and 691–93, even though little blood is spilled, because they are failed attacks. The goal of the attempts is the same type of death. In these cases the attempts fail because the intended victims are virtues. These contrasting results in an otherwise parallel situation express a picture of the Christian soul, which is distinct from the picture of the soul full of a vice. The latter dies, while the former attains eternal life.

139. Christian salvation history envisaged the coming of Christ as a turning point in the history of mankind. Before this event, humans were part of a pagan age in which God and salvation remained for the most part unacknowledged. In fact, the Roman Empire is understood as part of the evolution toward the age of Christianity, which commences with the birth of Christ and offers humanity an opportunity for eternal life. My implicit claim is that the souls of vices are relegated to a past time before the birth of Christ, a time when souls were indeed mortal owing to the false religious beliefs of the people and adherence to a pagan philosophical doctrine that simply does not apply in this new age of salvation history.

140. *Psych.* 33–35, 50–52, 153–54, 421–26, 506–509, 589–97, 672–77, 691–93, and 716–25. The only death scene that does not use this language explicitly is the death of *Superbia* (*Psych.* 280–84), but Prudentius does use the language in the story of David and Goliath, which prefigures the battle between *Superbia* and *Mens Humilis* (*Psych.* 294); also, just before *Superbia*'s death, *Psych.* 279 portrays *Spes* as she "breathes into" (*inspirat*) *Mens Humilis* the love of glory.

141. For the relevant texts, commentary, and scholarly bibliography, see A. A. Long and D. N. Sedley, *The Hellenistic Philosophers,* 2 vols. (Cambridge: Cambridge University Press, 1987), sects. 14A and 15A; A. A. Long, *Hellenistic Philosophy: Stoics, Epi-*

cureans, and Sceptics, 2d ed. (Berkeley: University of California Press, 1986), 49–56; R. W. Sharples. *Stoics, Sceptics, and Epicureans: An Introduction to Hellenistic Philosophy* (London: Routledge, 1996), 59–66, 94–99. Epicurus' theories of soul owe much to Plato, especially ideas seen in the *Phaedo.* For instance, Cebes at *Phaedo* 70a4–6 mentions the soul's dissipation after death (*diaskedasyeisa*), an idea that Socrates will argue against vigorously. Two of the cornerstones of the Epicurean argument for the mortality of the soul are that the soul is corporeal—unlike the Platonic and Christian conception—and the soul and body must work together in order to achieve sensation and consciousness. See Long and Sedley, *The Hellenistic Philosophers,* vol. 1, 71–72.

142. Text and translation are from Long and Sedley, *The Hellenistic Philosophers,* sect. 14A.

143. Text (as quoted by Diogenes Laertius) and translation of Epicurus are from R. D. Hicks, *Diogenes Laertius: Lives of the Eminent Philosophers,* vol. 2. Loeb Classical Library (Cambridge, Mass.: Harvard University Press, 1925), 664–65.

144. Text and translation of the Lucretius passages are from *Lucretius: On the Nature of Things,* W. H. D. Rouse, rev., M. F. Smith. Loeb Classical Library (Cambridge, Mass.: Harvard University Press, 1982).

145. Long and Sedley, *The Hellenistic Philosophers,* vol. 1, 71. E. J. Kenney, *Lucretius: De Rerum Natura, Book III* (Cambridge: Cambridge University Press, 1991), 134–92, follows C. Bailey, *Titi Lucreti Cari De Rerum Natura Libri Sex,* 3 vols. (Oxford: Oxford University Press, 1966) in isolating twenty-nine proofs in this section of book 3 for the death of the soul.

146. The word *dissipator* does not come into usage until the time of Prudentius. See A. Souter, *A Glossary of Later Latin to 600 A.D.* (Oxford: Oxford University Press, 1949), 109.

147. A similar pattern holds for throat words and words for things that penetrate and break. Regarding the vices, we encounter the following words: *gutturis* (*Psych.* 34), *iugulum* (*Psych.* 49), *gulam* (*Psych.* 424), *guttur* (*Psych.* 425), *gutture* (*Psych.* 590), *gulam* (*Psych.* 591), *gladio* (*Psych.* 50), *cuspide* (*Psych.* 153), *saxum* (*Psych.* 421), *pilo* (*Psych.* 717), and *cuspide* (*Psych.* 718). As for the virtues, the list is as follows: *iugulis* (*Psych.* 509); *cuspis* (*Psych.* 508), *tela* (*Psych.* 509), *mucronem* (*Psych.* 673), *acumen* (*Psych.* 675), and *ferrum* (*Psych.* 696). In the vice death scenes, Prudentius portrays throats, the seat of speech and the passage way for breath, damaged by weapons. But, in the virtue attack scenes, the poet renders these weapons impotent by virtue of the fact that the figures' precious throats are unharmed or slightly grazed. The throat as part of the protective vessel for the breath and soul remains contained, whereas, in the cases of the vices, the soul escapes through wounds or is trapped.

148. At *Psych.* 58–59 *Pudicitia* says to the dying *Libido: Tene, o vexatrix hominum, potuisse resumptis / viribus extincti capitis recalescere flatu.* And when *Avaritia*'s javelins are ineffectual against the *sacerdotes Domini,* she complains that no human used to be able to reject (*sperneret, Psych.* 516) or was impenetrable to (*inpenetrabilis, Psych.* 516) her influence. And then she explicitly states the mortality associated with herself as a conceptual vice: *ingenium omne neci dedimus* (*Psych.* 517).

149. I have quoted three of these passages above in the main text.

150. A section of *Concordia*'s speech at *Psych.* 750–87 is a literal panegyric in praise of peace. The poem has clearly shifted from the hardship and brutality of the war with the vices to the Christian ideal of peace and social harmony. This condition sets the stage for the building of the Christian temple in which *Sapientia* holds sway.

151. See F. Johansen, *A History of Ancient Philosophy: From the Beginnings to St. Augustine* (New York: Routledge, 1998), 601–17. H. Chadwick, "Augustine," 336, and Young, "Christian Teaching," 481, in *The Cambridge History of Early Christian Literature*, ed. F. Young, L. Ayers, and A. Louth (Cambridge: Cambridge University Press, 2004).

152. Johansen, *A History of Ancient Philosophy*, 605. R. Markus, "Marius Victorinus," in *Cambridge History of Later Greek Philosophy*, ed., A. H. Armstrong (Cambridge: Cambridge University Press, 1970), 337–38, outlines Victorinus' Trinitarian psychology in which the structure of the soul reflects the ternary *esse-vivere-intellegere*; see also Clark, *Marius Victorinus*, 38.

153. Because humans are made in the image of God, their souls reflect this divine ternary. But, since the human soul is created in time and exists logically posterior to the Father, it can never attain the level of being that the Father represents. Thus, the soul is defined more by its life and intelligence, both of which are consubstantial with being, but a lesser form of being than the being of the creator, which is incomprehensible and transcendent.

154. Johansen, *A History of Ancient Philosophy*, 615. This ternary reflects the Father (*memoria*), the Son (*intelligentia*), and the Holy Spirit (*voluntas*).

155. *Adv. Ar.* 1.63.7–18.

156. Clark, *Marius Victorinus*, p. 32.

157. See Markus, "Marius Victorinus," *Cambridge History*, 338.

158. Markus, "Marius Victorinus," *Cambridge History*, 339. Victorinus sees his triad in the scriptures at *Exodus* 3:13, *John* 1:1, and *John* 16:15. Augustine prefers two other trinitarian schemes: memory—intelligence—will (*Conf.* 13.11.12) and mind—knowledge—love.

159. *Signacula* means a seal or stamp at Tertullian, *Apologia* 21; Apuleius *Flor.* 2, sign of the cross; Tertullian *Marc.* 3.22 mark on forehead made at baptism. *Psych.* 360–61, *post inscripta oleo frontis signacula per quae / unguentum regale datum est et chrisma perenne*, reinforces the meaning of *signacula* as "signs" that connect worldly phenomena to transcendent divine mysteries; in this case, sacramental signs to Christ's power.

160. For Scripture as *dei signacula* see Augustine's semiotic explanation for the exegesis of scripture at *De Doct. Christ.* 1.2.2 and 2.1.1.

161. See I. P. Sheldon-Williams, "The Cappadocians," in *The Cambridge History of Later Greek and Early Medieval Philosophy*, ed. A. H. Armstrong (Cambridge: Cambridge University Press, 1967), 445–46.

162. Compare *Apoth.* 402–21, where Prudentius substitutes Christ for Apollo as an inspiration for poetry. The pagans appear to have understood the truth of this substitution—and thus have converted to Christianity, whereas the Jews have not. Christianity is the ultimate goal in the progress of religions.

163. C. Whitehead, *Castles of the Mind: A study of Medieval Architectural Allegory* (Cardiff: University of Wales Press, 2003), 10–11.

164. M. Colish, *The Stoic Tradition*, 108.

EPILOGUE

1. Dawson, *Christian Figural Reading*, 11, relying on Erich Auerbach (see "Conclusion") understands figural reading as, "a method of discerning the intelligibility of a

divine performance in history without relying on a conception of meaning as a concept signified by a textual signifier. The intelligibility of biblical narrative for the figural reader lies in the perception of divinely constructed figural relationships between persons and events in the world . . . preserving historicity means reading in such a way as to allow the text to have an appropriate ethical impact on the present-day reader." F. Young, "Typology," in *Crossing the Boundaries: Essays in Biblical Interpretation in Honour of Michael D. Goulder,* ed. S. E. Porter, P. Joyce, and D. E. Orton (Leiden: Brill Press, 1994), 36, draws a connection between typology and allegory that suits the work of Prudentius: "[T]he production of correspondences, whether or not the word 'type' actually appears, is what may constitute 'typology' as a particular definable form of the broader category 'allegory.' " See further, 39–40, for the variations of typological correspondences.

2. C. Gill, *Personality in Greek Epic, Tragedy, and Philosophy* (Oxford: Oxford University Press, 1996), 9–16, refers to individualist and relational concepts of the self as "subjective-individualist" and "objective-participant" respectively. In the former notion, the self (or personhood) is defined as "a unified locus of thought and will," autonomous, legislating its own moral principles, and abstracted from "localized interpersonal attachments." This summarizes what I mean by an "individualist" self. The latter notion envisions the self as a moral-reasoning entity that expresses its "reason-ruled" moral principles as a consequence of, and through, a shared "interpersonal and communal engagement." This encapsulates my idea of a "relational" self.

3. Gill, *Personality,* 445.

4. The linkage between God, Christ, and human implies a physical and psychological connection. Humans issue directly from God. Moreover, as one reads the *Psychomachia,* one looks into oneself to discover Christ for a connection to God.

5. In the *Praefatio* to the *Psychomachia,* the story of Lot appears once again, though it focuses on Abraham's earlier rescue of Lot.

6. *Symm.* 1.407–12 is another strong statement of free will.

7. See chapter 4, note 57.

8. C. Taylor, *The Sources of Self: The Making of Modern Identity* (Cambridge, Mass.: Harvard University Press, 1989), 128. C. Cary, *Augustine's Invention of the Inner Self: The Legacy of a Christian Platonist.* (Oxford: Oxford University Press, 2000), 5; Johansen, *A History of Ancient Philosophy,* 598.

9. Taylor, *Sources of Self,* 130–31; J. M. Rist, *Augustine: Ancient Thought Baptized.* (Cambridge: Cambridge University Press, 1994), 146; Cary, *Augustine's Invention of the Inner Self,* 65. My assumption is that the soul is equivalent to the self for most Christian thinkers of the fourth-century. See H. Chadwick, "The Philosophical Tradition of the Self," in *Late Antiquity: A Guide to the Post-Classical World,* ed. G.W. Bowersock, P. Brown, and O. Grabar (Cambridge, Mass.: Harvard University Press, 1999), 77.

10. Cary, *Augustine's Invention of the Inner Self,* 39: "God is not only within the soul but also above it. In the interval between the turning in and the looking up one finds oneself in a new place, never before conceived: an inner space proper to the soul different from the intelligible world in the Mind of God. The soul becomes, as it were, its own dimension—a whole realm of being waiting to be entered and explored." Compare Taylor, *Sources of Self,* 134: "By going inward, I am drawn upward."

11. *Conf.* 7.10.16: *Et inde admonitus redire ad memet ipsum, intravi in intima mea duce te, et potui, quoniam factus es adiutor meus. Intravi et vidi qualicumque oculo*

animae meae supra eundum oculum animae meae, supra mentem meam, lucem incom-mutabilem . . . ita erat supra mentem meam . . . sed superior, quia ipsa fecit me, et ego inferior, quia factus ab ea. Qui novit veritatem, novit eam, et qui novit eam, novit aeternitatem ("By the Platonic books I was admonished to return into myself. With you as my guide I entered into my innermost citadel, and was given power to do so because you had become my helper. I entered and with my soul's eye, such as it was, saw above that same eye of my soul the immutable light higher than my mind. . . . It transcended my mind. . . . It was superior because it made me, and I was inferior because I was made by it. The person who knows the truth knows it, and he who knows it knows eternity"). Translated by H. Chadwick (Saint Augustine: Confessions [Oxford: Oxford University Press, 1991]); Another key passage for Taylor, *Sources of the Self,* 129, is *De Vera Reli-gione,* 39.72: *Noli foras ire,in te ipsum redi; in interiore homine habitat veritas* ("Don't go outward; return within yourself. In the inward man dwells the truth").

12. Taylor, *Sources of Self,* 133.

13. Cary, *Augustine's Invention of the Inner Self,* 55, cites Augustine's *Ep.* 18.2 as evidence for a hierarchy of being: God-soul-bodies. Although not typological in its conception, this triad shows Augustine's preoccupation with an ascent to God through the connection of the immaterial to the material. His ontology maps on to the typology of God—Christ—human.

14. At *Conf.* 8.22 he comments on the source of his inner conflicts: *et ideo non iam ego operabar illam, sed quod habitabat in me peccatum de supplicio liberioris peccati, quia eram filius Adam* ("And so it was 'not I' that brought this about 'but sin which dwelt in me" [*Romans* 7:17, 20], sin resulting from the punishment of a more freely chosen sin, because I was the son of Adam"). See K. Stendahl, "The Apostle Paul and the Introspec-tive Conscience of the West," in his *Paul among the Jews and Gentiles* (Philadelphia: Fortress Press, 1976), 78–96.

15. *[I]n illo homine qui primus peccavit, in quo et omnes mortui sumus et de quo omnes cum miseria nati sumus.* C. Harrison, *Augustine: Christian Truth and Fractured Humanity* (Oxford University Press, 2000), 28, recalls Augustine's phrase, *massa pec-cati,* to refer to a human being after the Fall.

16. The tension between the individualist and relational sides of the self are manifest in the ways of reading the fall of Adam.

17. Cary, *Augustine's Invention of the Inner Self,* 117: "Without sin there could be no separation of souls and therefore no inner privacy."

18. Harrison, *Augustine,* 86–88.

19. The quotes are about Augustine from Cary, *Augustine's Invention of the Inner Self,* 78. Cary cites Augustine's *Soliloquia,* a dialogue with Reason as the interlocutor.

20. Rist, *Augustine,* 145–46, similarly argues that books 9–14 of Augustine's *De Trinitate* argue for another version of the Trinity's reflection in the human soul. A human being's inner psychological activities amount to self-memory, self-understand-ing, and self-willing/loving.

21. Whitehead, *Castles of the Mind,* 31–32.

22. *Sed ubi manes in memoria mea, domine . . . quale sanctuarium aedificasti tibi? Tu dedisti hanc dignitationem memoriae meae, ut maneas in ea . . . nec ibi tu eras;* and Whitehead, *Castles of the Mind,* 32.

23. *Magna vis est memoriae . . . profunda et infinita multiplicitas . . . et hoc ego ipse sum.*

24. K. Smolak, "Die Psychomachie des Prudentius als historisches epos," *La poesia*

tardoantica e medievale (2001): 125–30, discusses how Vergil, Lucan, Juvencus, and Prudentius connect history with the individual. Smolak deftly explains the interaction of Lucretian didactic epic and Vergilian narrative epic in the Psychomachia. He also argues that Prudentius' personification allegories are partly rooted in Greek philosophy.

25. M. L. Humphries, "Michel Foucault on Writing and the Self in the Meditations of Marcus Aurelius and *Confessions* of St. Augustine," *Arethusa* 30.1 (1997): 131–33.

26. D. E. Trout, *Paulinus of Nola: Life, Letters, and Poems* (Berkeley: University of California Press, 1999), 79.

27. C. Conybeare, *Paulinus Noster: Self and Symbols in the Letters of Paulinus of Nola* (Oxford: Oxford University Press, 2000), 147.

28. Conybeare, *Paulinus Noster,* 149.

29. Trout, *Paulinus of Nola,* 99, 164, and 181.

30. Dawson, *Christian Figural Reading,* 104, is analyzing the degrees of historicity of the biblical figure Joshua, who prefigures Jesus, and Vergil, who is fulfilled by Dante's Vergil.

31. E. Auerbach, *Literary Language and its Public in Late Latin Antiquity and in the Middle Ages,* trans. R. Manheim (Princeton, N.J.: Princeton University Press, 1993), 225 and 314; and E. Curtius, *European Literature and the Latin Middle Ages,* trans. W. R. Trask (Princeton, N.J.: Princeton University Press, 1990), 348.

32. Dawson, *Christian Figural Reading,* 104–105, assumes Auerbach's view of the centrality of Dante for the history of figural realism in order to highlight Auerbach's paradoxical assertion that Dante's Virgil becomes more historically real than even the historical Virgil because of his fulfillment in the otherworld as portrayed in the *Divine Comedy.*

33. P. Godman, "Epilogue," from Curtius, *European Literature,* 599, 653.

34. E. Said, "Introduction to the Fiftieth Anniversary Edition," *Mimesis: The Representation of Reality in Western Literature,* trans. W. R. Trask (Princeton, N.J.; Princeton University Press, 2003), xxii.

35. J. M. Ziolkowski, "Foreword" to Auerbach, *Literary Language and Its Public in Late Latin Antiquity and in the Middle Ages,* trans. R. Manheim (Princeton, N.J.: Princeton University Press, 1993), xi and xxviii.

36. See Ziolkowski, "Foreword" to Auerbach, *Literary Language and Its Public,* xvii, note 24, for references concerning the frequency of citations of Curtius.

37. S. Lehrer, ed., *Literary History and the Challenge of Philology: The Legacy of Erich Auerbach* (Stanford, Calif.: Stanford University Press, 1996), "introduction," 8, says, "[F]ifty years after the composition of *Mimesis,* Auerbach still stands as a touchstone for contemporary academic debates on the place of historical criticism in the construction of literary history, on the relations between intellectual activity and political action, and the function of the critic in reading-or effecting-social change." Auerbach's construction of literary history is, in general, assumed in many of these debates. Of particular interest on the ideas of *sermo humilis* and *figura* are the articles by Luiz Costa Lima, Stephen G. Nichols, Jesse Gellrich, Hayden White, Brian Stock, and Kevin Brownlee. For example, Nichols, "Philology in Auerbach's Drama of (Literary) History," 72, says of *Mimesis,* chapter 7, "It is a brilliant and subtle *Ausformung* of *figura* and *sermo humilis,* the two principles by which Auerbach transformed medieval studies generally and Dante studies in particular." For a more poststructuralist reading of Auerbach see E. Apter, "Saidian Humanism," *Boundary* 2, 31:2 (2004), who examines

how Edward Said's admiration for Auerbach's vision of literature intersects with "the association of humanism with Eurocentrism and Orientalism" (53). M. Dirda, "Dante: The Supreme Realist," *New York Review of Books* 54, no. 1 (2007): 54–58, celebrates the continued dominance of Auerbach's elevation of Dante as a central figure in Western literary history.

38. Auerbach, *Literary Language and its Public,* 25–66 treats the *sermo humilis* style adopted by early Christian writers (especially Augustine) in which there are no absolute levels of subject matter and "the highest mysteries of the faith maybe set forth in the simple words of the lowly style which everyone can understand" (37).

39. B. Stock, "Literary Realism in the Later Ancient Period," in *Literary History and the Challenge of Philology,* ed. Lehrer, 155. But Stock does note the limitations of Auerbach's preoccupation with Augustine as a literary wellspring for the Middle Ages— though Stock still pigeonholes Prudentius and other authors under the category of allegory: "The obvious weakness lay in the field of allegory, as witness his [Auerbach's] insufficient attention to writers like Prudentius, Johannes Scottus Eriugena, or Allen of Lille, who were all important influences on the medieval vernacular literature" (144). Curtius, *European Literature and the Latin Middle Ages,* 28, like Auerbach, asserts that the Middle Ages as the continuation of Rome originates in Augustine's philosophy of history—i.e., his notion of salvation history. Curtius moves from this point to Dante (29) who, he claims, has an Augustinian notion of history. In fact, on page 30 Curtius relates the two authors with the phrase "Augustinian and Dantean historical thought." Yet later, on page 371, note 57, Curtius says that, "Augustine . . . is systematically passed over by Dante." He does not attempt to reconcile these two statements. J. C. Warner, *Augustinian Epic, Petrarch to Milton* (Ann Arbor: University of Michigan Press, 2005), also falls in line with the Augustinian dominated notion of literary history by arguing that renaissance epics employ Augustine's idea of the spiritual ascent to God as a mainstay of their poetic program. Even the notion that through allegory Roman Christian epic furnishes knowledge of God and the soul, and thus achieves a communion with God, all of which I have argued as part and parcel of Prudentian poetics, is given over in Warner's study to Augustine's Christian purpose. I hope to have added a competing perspective to this view of medieval and early modern literary history.

40. In his essay, "*Figura,*" trans. R. Manheim, in *Scenes From the Drama of European Literature,* ed. Wlad Godzich and Jochen Schulte-Sassa (Minneapolis: *University* of Minnesota Press, 1984), 37, Auerbach focuses on Augustine's typological view of history put forward at Civ. 20:14; see also Dawson, *Christian Figural Reading,* 95 and 245, note 27. Auerbach, *Latin Literature and its Public,* 309, says, "Dante was the first and the last to undertake on the basis of his own historical existence a total view of the universe with the political life of man on earth as its arena an center." And see Auerbach, *Dante: Poet of the Secular World,* trans. R. Manheim (Chicago: University of Chicago Press, 1961), 17.

41. Stock, "Literary Realism," 154–55.

42. Stock, "Literary Realism," 149, posits Augustine as a central source for Auerbach's idea of literary realism, "in which distant persons and remote models of virtue are gradually replaced by those nearer at hand, that is, by individuals whose lives are recorded within the living memory of Augustine's own time." The martyrs and the role of the reader in the *Peristephanon* and *Psychomachia* function in a similar fashion. By being invited to come along on the Vergilian *katabasis* of Christian rebirth, the reader

of the *Psychomachia* inserts himself into the text, thereby collapsing the temporal and special distance between him and the "remote models of virtue." Prudentius' narratives of third-century Spanish martyrs close this distance as well.

43. Auerbach, *Mimesis,* 202.

44. On Auerbach's position that Dante is the font of literary realism, see Dawson, *Christian Figural Reading,* 104–105; Said, "Introduction" to *Mimesis,* xxix; Apter, "Saidian Humanism," 35, 39–40.; T. Bahti, "Auerbach's *Mimesis:* Figural Structure and Historical Narrative," in *After Strange Texts: The Role of Theory in the Study of Literature,* ed. G. S. Jay and D. L. Miller (Tuscaloosa: University of Alabama Press, 1985), 138. For Auerbach's earlier thinking on this issue, see his *Dante,* 174–79.

45. Curtius, *European Literature and the Latin Middle Ages,* 358: "The conception of the *Commedia* is based upon a spiritual meeting with Virgil. In the realm of European literature there is little which may be compared with this phenomenon."

46. Curtius, *European Literature and the Latin Middle Ages,* 359.

47. Curtius, *European Literature and the Latin Middle Ages,* 361.

48. Curtius, *European Literature and the Latin Middle Ages,* 363.

49. Curtius, *European Literature and the Latin Middle Ages,* 226, quotes and translates this passage from Petrarch, *Le Familiari,* 10.4.

50. Both Auerbach and Curtius praise Prudentius. For example, Curtius, *European Literature and the Latin Middle Ages,* 23, calls Prudentius "the first great Christian poet" and "the most important, artistic, and universal early Christian poet" (49). Auerbach, *Literary Language and its Public,* 336, includes Prudentius in a list of authors whom he calls "a heritage from antiquity." These compliments, however, are always in the context of Prudentius as an innovator in personification allegory and, more important, as only a Christian poet. Auerbach, *Latin Literature and its Public,* 195, makes this clear: "he far more than Claudian must be put down as a Christian writer, and we may prefer not to deal with Christian literature in the present context." For Auerbach, Prudentius is at best, "a transitional phenomenon" (195).

51. Auerbach, *"Figura,"* 54, quoted by J. M. Gellrich, *"Figura,* Allegory, and the Question of History," in Lehrer, *Literary History and the Challenge of Philology,* 119–20. Gellrich, like Dawson, *Christian Figural Reading,* explores the "strangeness" or "inbetweenness" of Auerbach's *figura,* which "postulates neither the truth of abstraction nor the disclosure of the accomplished fact . . . and thus kept alive the history he read and the history he was living" (123).

Works Cited

Apter, E. "Saidian Humanism." *Boundary 2*, 31:2 (2004): 35–53.

Armstrong, A. H., ed. *Cambridge History of Later Greek Philosophy*. Cambridge: Cambridge University Press, 1970.

———. *Plotinus*, vol. 1. Loeb Classical Library. Cambridge, Mass.: Harvard University Press, 1966.

Athanassiadi, P. *Julian: An Intellectual Biography*. London: Routledge, 1992.

Auerbach, E. *Dante: Poet of the Secular World*. Translated by R. Manheim. Chicago: University of Chicago Press, 1961.

———. *Literary Language and its Public in Late Latin Antiquity and in the Middle Ages*. Translated by R. Manheim. Princeton, N.J.: Princeton University Press, 1993.

———. *Mimesis: The Representation of Reality in Western Literature*. Princeton, N.J.: Princeton University Press, 2003.

———. *Scenes from the Drama of European Literature*. Edited by W. Godzich and J. Schulte-Sassa. Translated by R. Manheim. Minneapolis: University of Minnesota Press, 1984.

Austin, R. G. *P. Vergili Maronis Aeneidos Liber Sextus*. Oxford: Clarendon Press, 1977.

Bailey, C. *Titi Lucreti Cari De Rerum Natura Libri Sex*, 3 vols. Oxford: Oxford University Press, 1966.

Ballengee, J. "The Wound That Speaks: Prudentius' *Peristephanon Liber* and the Rhetoric of Suffering." *Crossings* 5/6 (2002–2003): 107–43.

Barnes, T. *Constantine and Eusebius*. Cambridge, Mass.: Harvard University Press, 1981.

Barney, S. A. *Allegories of History, Allegories of Love*. Hamden, Conn.: Archon Books, 1979.

Bastiaensen, A. A. R. "Prudentius in Recent Literary Criticism." In *Early Christian Poetry: A Collection of Essays*. Edited by J. Den Boeft and A. Hihorst. Leiden: Brill, 1993.

Beatrice, P. F. "L'allegoria nella Psychomachia di Prudenzio." *Studia Patavina* 18. 1971.

Bergman, J. *Aurelli Prudentii Clementis Carmina*. Corpus Scriptorum Ecclesiasticorum Latinorum, vol. 61. Lipsiae: Hoelder-Pichler-Tempsky, 1926.

Bidez, J. *Vie de Porphyre avec les fragments des traités* (περὶ ἀγαλμάτων) *et de regressu animae*, Recueil de Travaux publiés par la Faculté de Philosophie et Lettres, vol. 58. Université de Gand, 1913.

Binns, J. W., ed. *Latin Literature of the Fourth Century*. London: Routledge and Kegan Paul, 1974.

Blaise, A. *Dictionnaire Latin-Français des Auteurs Chrétiens*. Belgique: Brepols, 1993.

Bowersock, G. W., P. Brown, and O. Grabar. *Late Antiquity: A Guide to the Postclassical World*. Cambridge, Mass.: Belknap Press of Harvard University Press, 1999.

Boyle, A. J., ed. *The Imperial Muse. Ramus Essays on Roman Literature of the Empire II.* Victoria: Aureal Publishers, 1990.

———, ed. *Roman Epic.* London: Routledge, 1993.

Breisach, E. *Historiography: Ancient, Medieval, and Modern.* 2nd ed. Chicago: University of Chicago Press, 1983.

Brown, P. *The Rise of Western Christendom: Triumph and Diversity.* Oxford: Blackwell, 2003.

———. *The Body and Society: Men, Women, and Sexual Renunciation in Early Christianity.* New York: Columbia University Press, 1988.

Burck, E. *Das römische Epos.* Darmstadt: Wissenschaftliche Buchgesellschaft, 1979.

Burckhardt, J. *The Age of Constantine the Great.* Translated by M. Hadas. New York: Pantheon, 1949.

Burton, R. *Prudentius:* Psychomachia. Bryn Mawr, Penn.: Bryn Mawr Latin Commentaries, 1989.

Cameron, A. "Remaking the Past." In *Late Antiquity: A Guide to the Postclassical World.* G. W. Bowersock, P. Brown, and O. Grabar. Cambridge, Mass.: Harvard University Press, 1999.

———. "Julian and Hellenism." *Ancient World* 24.1 (1993): 25–29.

Cameron, A., and S. Hall. *Eusebius: Life of Constantine.* Oxford: Clarendon Press, 1999.

Cary, C. *Augustine's Invention of the Inner Self: The Legacy of a Christian Platonist.* Oxford: Oxford University Press, 2000.

CETEDOC Library of Christian Latin Texts, CLCLT-4. Edited by P. Tombeur. Turnhout: Brepols Publishers, 2000.

Chadwick, H. "Augustine." In *The Cambridge History of Early Christian Literature.* Edited by F. Young, L. Ayres, and A. Louth. Cambridge: Cambridge University Press, 2004.

———. "The Philosophical Tradition of the Self." In *Late Antiquity: A Guide to the Post Classical World.* G. W. Bowersock, P. Brown, O. Grabar. Cambridge, Mass.: Harvard University Press, 1999.

———, trans. *Saint Augustine: Confessions.* Oxford: Oxford University Press, 1991.

Charlet, J.-L. "Aesthetic Trends in Late Latin Poetry (325–410)." *Philologus* 132 (1988): 74–85.

———. "Prudence et La Bible." *Recherches Augustiniennes* 18 (1983): 3–149.

———. "Signification de la preface á la *Psychomachia* de Prudence," *REL* 81 (2003): 232–51.

Clark, M.T. *Marius Victorinus: Theological Treatises on the Trinity.* Washington, D.C.: Catholic University Press, 1981.

Clifford, G. *The Transformations of Allegory.* London: Routledge and Kegan Paul, 1974.

Coleman, J. *Ancient and Medieval Memories.* Cambridge: Cambridge University Press, 1992.

Colish, M. *The Stoic Tradition from Antiquity to the Early Middle Ages.* 2 Vols. Leiden: Brill, 1990.

Collingwood, R. G. *The Idea of History.* New York: Oxford University Press, 1946.

Conte, G. B. *Letteratura latina: Manuale storico dalle origini alla fine dell'impero romano.* Translated by Joseph B. Solodow. *Latin Literature: A History.* Baltimore: Johns Hopkins University Press, 1994.

———. *Memoria dei poeti e sistema letterario.* Translated by C. Segal. *The Rhetoric of Imitation: Genre and Poetic Memory in Vergil and Other Latin Poets.* Ithaca, N.Y.: Cornell University Press, 1986.

Conybeare, C. "The Ambiguous Laughter of Saint Laurence." *Journal of Early Christian Studies* 10.2 (2002): 175–202.

——. *Paulinus Noster: Self and Symbols in the Letters of Paulinus of Nola.* Oxford: Oxford University Press, 2000.

Cotogni. L. "Sovrapposizione di visioni e di allegoria nella Psychomachia di Prudenzio." *Rendiconti della R. Accademia Nazionale dei Lincei, classe di scienze morali, storiche e filologiche,* 6th ser., 12 (1936): 441–61.

Courcelle, P. *Les Lettres Greques en Occident de Macrobe à Cassiodore,* 2nd ed. Translated by Harry E. Wedeck. *Late Latin Writers and Their Greek Sources.* Cambridge, Mass.: Harvard University Press, 1969.

——. *Les Confessions de saint Augustin dans la tradition littéraire.* Paris: Études Augustiniennes, 1963.

Cunningham, M. P. *Aurelii Prudentii Clementis Carmina.* Corpus Christianorum, series latina, vol. 126. Turnholt: Brepol Press, 1966.

Currie, M. *Postmodern Narrative Theory.* New York: St. Martin's Press, 1998.

Curtius, E. *European Literature and the Latin Middle Ages.* Translated by W. R. Trask. Princeton, N.J.: Princeton University Press, 1990.

Danielou, J. *Sacramentum Futuri: Études sur les Origines de la Typologie biblique.* Translated by D. W. Hibberd. *From Shadows to Reality: Studies in the Biblical Typology of the Fathers.* London: Burnes and Oates, 1960.

Dawson, J. D. *Allegorical Readers and Cultural Revision in Ancient Alexandria.* Berkeley: University of California Press, 1992.

——. *Christian Figural Reading and the Fashioning of Identity.* Berkeley: University of California Press, 2002.

——. "Christian Teaching." In *The Cambridge History of Early Christian Literature.* Edited by F. Young, L. Ayres, and A. Louth. Cambridge: Cambridge University Press, 2004.

de Hartel, G. *Paulinus Nolanus: Epistulae.* Vol. 29 of Corpus Scriptorum Ecclesiasticorum Latinorum, 2nd ed. Viena: Verlag sterreichischen Akademie Der Wissenschaften, 1999.

de Labriolle, P. *A History of Latin Christian Literature.* 3rd ed. Oxford: Clarendon Press, 1947.

de Nebrija, E. Antonio. *Aurelii Prudentii Clementis V. C. libelli cum commento Antonii Nebrissensis.* Edited by F. Gonzalez Vega. Salamanca: Ediciones Universidad de Salamanca, 2002.

des Places, E. *Vie de Pythagore; Lettre à Marcella.* Paris: Société d'Edition *Les Belles Lettres,* 1982.

Dihle, A. *Griechische und lateinische Literatur der Kaiserzeit.* Translated by Manfred Malzahn. *Greek and Latin Literature of the Roman Empire: From Augustus to Justinian.* London: Routledge, 1994.

——. *The Theory of the Will in Classical Antiquity.* Berkeley: University of California Press, 1982.

Dirda, Michael. "Dante: The Supreme Realist." *New York Review of Books* 54, no. 1 (2007): 54–58.

Döpp, S. "Vergilische Elemente in Prudentius' *Contra Symmachum.*" *Hermes* 116 (1998): 337–42.

Dvornik, F. *Early Christian and Byzantine Political Philosophy: Origins and Background,* vol. 2. Washington, D.C.: Dumbarton Oaks, 1966.

Eagan, M. Clement. *The Poems of Prudentius*, vol. 2, *Fathers of the Church* 52. Washington, D.C.: Catholic University of America Press, 1962.

Edden, V. "Prudentius." In *Latin Literature of the Fourth Century*. Edited by J. W. Binns. London: Routledge and Kegan Paul, 1974.

Edmunds, L. *Intertextuality and the Reading of Roman Poetry*. Baltimore: Johns Hopkins University Press, 2001.

Edwards, P., ed. *The Encyclopedia of Philosophy*. New York: Macmillan and the Free Press, 1967.

Esler, P. F., ed. *The Early Christian World*. 2 vols. London: Routledge, 2000.

Fabiny, T. *The Lion and the Lamb*. New York: St. Martin's Press, 1992.

Fairclough, H. R., trans. (Revised by G. P. Goold) *Virgil*, vols. 1–2. Loeb Classical Library. Cambridge, Mass.: Harvard University Press, 1999.

Feeney, D. "History and Revelation in Vergil's Underworld." *Proceedings of the Cambridge Philological Society, No. 32 (1986): 1–24.*

Fischer, B., H. J. Frede, and U. Frölich, eds. *Vetus Latina: Die Reste der altleinischen Bibel.* Freiburg: Verlag Herder, 1951–96.

Fitzgerald, W. "Aeneas, Daedalus, and the Labyrinth." In *Virgil: Critical Assessments of Classical Authors*. Edited by P. Hardie. London: Routledge, 1999.

Fontaine, J. *Études sur la poésie latine tardive d'Ausone á Prudence*. Paris: Société d'Édition les Belles Lettres, 1980.

Frye, N. "Allegory." *Encyclopedia of Poetry and Poetics*. Edited by A. Preminger. Princeton, N.J.: Princeton University Press, 1965.

———. *Anatomy of Criticism: Four Essays*. Princeton, N.J.: Princeton University Press, 1973.

———. *The Great Code: The Bible and Literature*. New York: Harcourt Brace Jovanovich, 1982.

Fuhrmann, M., ed. Christianisme et formes littéraires de l'antiquité tardive en occident, Entretiens 23, Genève: Fondation Hardt, 1977.

Gersh, S. *Middle Platonism and Neoplatonism: The Latin Tradition*. 2 vols. Notre Dame, Ind.: University of Notre Dame Press, 1986.

Gill, C. *Personality in Greek Epic, Tragedy, and Philosophy*. Oxford: Oxford University Press, 1996.

———. *The Structured Self in Hellenistic and Roman Thought*. Oxford: Oxford University Press, 2006.

Glau, K. "Allegorie als Reflex der Origenischen Hermeneutik der *Psychomachia* des Prudentius." In *Hortus Litterarum Antiquarum: Festschrift für Hans Armin Gärtner zum 70 Geburtstag*. Edited by A. Haltenhoff and F.-H. Mutschler. Heidelberg: winter 2000.

Gnilka, Ch. *Studien zur Psychomachie des Prudentius*. Weisbaden: O. Harrassowitz, 1963.

Goodspeed, E. J., and R. M. Grant, *A History of Early Christian Literature*. Chicago: University of Chicago Press, 1966.

Gosserez, L. *Poésie de lumière: une lecture de Prudence, Bibliothèque d'études Classiques* 23. Louvain: Peeters, 2001.

Goulder, M. D. *Type and History in Acts*. London: SPCK, 1964.

Green, R. *The Poetry of Paulinus of Nola*. Oxford: Oxford University Press, 1971.

Guthrie, K., trans. *Porphyry's Launching-Points to the Realm of the Mind*. Grand Rapids, Mich.: Phanes Press, 1988.

Hackforth, R. *Plato's* Phaedrus. London: Cambridge University Press, 1972.

Hadot, P. *Marius Victorinus. Recherches sur sa vie et ses oeuvres.* Paris: Firmin-Didot, 1971.

———. *Porphyre et Victorinus.* Études Augustiennes. 2 vols. Paris: Firmin-Didot, 1968.

Haltenhoff, A., and F.-H. Mutschler, eds. *Hortus Litterarum Antiquarum: Festschrift für Hans Armin Gärtner zum 70 Geburtstag.* Heidelberg: winter 2000.

Hanley, S. M. "Classical Sources of Prudentius." Ph.D. dissertation, Cornell University, 1959.

Hardie, P. *The Epic Successors of Vergil: A Study in the Dynamics of a Tradition.* Cambridge: Cambridge University Press, 1993.

———. *Virgil's Aeneid: Cosmos and Imperium.* Oxford: Clarendon Press, 1986.

———, ed. *Virgil: Critical Assessments of Classical Authors.* 4 vols. London: Routledge, 1999.

Harmon, W., and C. H. Holman. *A Handbook to Literature.* 8th ed. Upper Saddle River, N.J.: Prentice Hall, 2000.

Harrison, C. *Augustine: Christian Truth and Fractured Humanity.* Oxford: Oxford University Press, 2000.

Harrison, S. J., ed. *Oxford Readings in Vergil's Aeneid.* Oxford: Oxford University Press, 1990.

Haug, W., ed. *Formen und Funktionen der Allegorie.* Stuttgart: J. B. Metzlersche, 1979.

Heim, F. *La théologie de la victoire de constantin a théodose.* Paris: Beauchesne, 1992.

Herzog, R. "Exegese-Erbauung-Delectatio: Beiträge zu einer christlichen Poetik der Spätantike." In *Formen und Funktionen der Allegorie.* Stuttgart: J. B. Metzlersche, 1978.

———. Die Bibelepik der Lateinischen Spätantike. Munich: Wilhem Fink, 1975.

———. Die Allegorische Dichtkunst des Prudentius. Munich: Beck, 1966.

Hicks, R. D. *Diogenes Laertius: Lives of the Eminent Philosophers,* vol. 2. Loeb Classical Library. Cambridge, Mass.: Harvard University Press, 1925.

Hinds, S. *Allusion and Intertext: Dynamics of Appropriation in Roman Poetry.* Cambridge: Cambridge University Press, 1998.

Hornblower, S., and A. Spawforth, eds. *The Oxford Classical Dictionary.* 3rd ed. New York: Oxford University Press, 1996.

Hornum, M. Introduction to K. Guthrie's translation of the *Sententiae, Porphyry's Launching Points to the Realm of the Mind.* Grand Rapids, Mich.: Phanes Press, 1988.

Humphries, M. L. "Michel Foucault on Writing and the Self in the *Meditations* of Marcus Aurelius and *Confessions* of St. Augustine." *Arethusa* 30.1 (1997): 125–38.

Hunter, D. G. "Fourth-century Latin Writers." In *The Cambridge History of Early Christian Literature.* Edited by F. Young. Cambridge: Cambridge University Press, 2004.

Jackson, W. T. H. "Allegory and Allegorization." *Research Studies* 32 (1964): 161–75.

Jameson, F. *The Political Unconscious: Narrative as a Socially Symbolic Act.* Ithaca, N.Y.: Cornell University Press, 1981.

Jay, G. S., and D. L. Miller, eds. *After Strange Texts: The Role of Theory in the Study of Literature.* Tuscaloosa: University of Alabama Press, 1985.

Johansen, F. *A History of Ancient Philosophy: From the Beginnings to St. Augustine.* New York: Routledge, 1998.

Jones, A. H. M., J. R. Martindale, and J. Morris. *The Prosopography of the Later Roman Empire,* vol. 1. Cambridge: Cambridge University Press, 1971.

Jülicher, A., ed. *Itala: Das neue Testament in altlateinischer Überlieferung.* Berlin: Walter de Gruyter, 1938, 1940, 1954, and 1963.

Kässer, Ch. "The Body Is Not Painted On: Ekphrasis and Exegesis in Prudentius *Peristephanon* 9." *Ramus* 31.1 & 2 (2002): 158–75.

Kennedy, D. "Virgilian Epic." In *The Cambridge Companion to Virgil.* Edited by C. Martindale. Cambridge: Cambridge University Press, 1997.

Kenney, E. J. *Lucretius: De Rerum Natura, Book III.* Cambridge: Cambridge University Press, 1991.

Klibansky, R. *The Continuity of the Platonic Tradition during the Middle Ages.* New York: Kraus International Publications, 1982.

Kraut, R., ed. *Plato's Republic: Critical Essays.* Lanham, Md.: Rowman and Littlefield, 1997.

Ladner, G. B. *God, Cosmos, and Humankind: The World of Early Christian Symbolism.* Berkeley: University of California Press, 1995.

Lamberton, R. *Homer the Theologian: Neoplatonist Allegorical Reading and the Growth of the Epic Tradition.* Berkeley: University of California Press, 1986.

Lamberz, E., trans. *Porphyrii Sententiae ad Intelligibilia Ducentes.* Leipzig: B. G. Teubner Verlagsgesellschaft, 1975.

Lavarenne, M. *Prudence.* 3 vols. Collection des Universités de France, 3rd ed. Paris: Budé, 1992.

Lear, J. "Inside and Outside the *Republic.*" In *Plato's Republic: Critical Essays.* Edited by R. Kraut. Lanham, Md.: Rowman and Littlefield, 1997.

Lehrer, S., ed. *Literary History and the Challenge of Philology: The Legacy of Eric Auerbach.* Stanford, Calif.: Stanford University Press, 1996.

Lesky, A., ed. *Thesaurus Linguae Latinae,* vol. 8. Lipsiae: B. G. Teubner, 1996.

Levin, S. *The Semantics of Metaphor.* Baltimore: Johns Hopkins University Press, 1977.

Lewis, C. S. *The Allegory of Love: A Study in Medieval Tradition.* New York: Oxford University Press, 1971.

Lewis, C. T., and C. Short, eds. *A Latin Dictionary.* 1879. Oxford: Oxford University Press, 1998.

Long, A. A., and D. N. Sedley. *The Hellenistic Philosophers.* 2 vols. Cambridge: Cambridge University Press, 1987.

——. *Hellenistic Philosophy: Stoics, Epicureans, and Sceptics,* 2nd ed. Berkeley: University of California Press, 1986.

Luck, G. "Virgil and the Mystery Religions." *American Journal of Philology* 94 (1973): 147–66.

Ludwig, W. "Die christliche Dichtung des Prudentius und die Transformation de klassischen Gattungen." *Fondation Hardt, Entretiens* 23 (1977): 303–63.

Lyotard, J.-F. *Introducing Lyotard: Art and Politics.* Edited by B. Readings. London: Routledge, 1991.

——. "Universal History and Cultural Differences." In *The Lyotard Reader.* Edited by A. Benjamin. Oxford: Basil Blackwell, 1989.

Madsen, D. L. *Rereading Allegory: A Narrative Approach to Genre.* New York: St. Martins Press, 1994.

Mahoney, A. *Vergil in the Works of Prudentius.* Cleveland: J. T. Zubal, 1934.

Malamud, M. *A Poetics of Transformation: Prudentius and Classical Mythology.* Ithaca, N.Y.: Cornell University Press, 1989.

——. "Making a Virtue of Perversity: The Poetry of Prudentius." In *The Imperial Muse. Ramus Essays on Roman Literature of the Empire II*. Edited by A. J. Boyle. Victoria: Aureal Publishers, 1990.

Markus, R. *Saeculum: History and Society in the Theology of St. Augustine*. Cambridge: Cambridge University Press, 1970.

——. "Marius Victorinus." In *Cambridge History of Later Greek Philosophy*. Edited by A. H. Armstrong. Cambridge: Cambridge University Press, 1970.

——. "Paganism, Christianity, and the Latin Classics." In *Latin Literature of the Fourth Century*. J. W. Binns. London: Routledge and Kegan Paul, 1974.

Martin, J. *Commodiani Carmina*. Corpus Christianorum, Series Latina 126. Turnholt: Brepols, 1960.

Martindale, C. *The Cambridge Companion to Virgil*. Cambridge: Cambridge University Press, 1997.

Mastrangelo, M. "The Epicurean View of the Soul in Prudentius' *Psychomachia*." *New England Classical Journal* 26.3 (1999): 11–22.

——. "The *Psychomachia* of Prudentius: A Reappraisal of the Greek Sources and the Origins of Allegory." Ph.D. dissertation, Brown University, 1997.

McGill, S. *Virgil Recomposed: The Mythological and Secular Cantos in Antiquity*. Series 49. American Philological Association. Oxford: Oxford University Press, 2005.

Meredith, A. "Porphyry and Julian against the Christians." In *Aufstieg und Niedergang der Römischen Welt*, II.23.2. Berlin: Walter de Gruyter, 1980.

Merlan, P. "Plotinus." In *The Encyclopedia of Philosophy*. Edited by P. Edwards. New York: Macmillan and the Free Press, 1967.

Migne, J.-P., ed. *Patrologiae Cursus Completus, Series Graeca*, (=*PG* and *PL* for *Series Latina*). Paris: Garnier, 1844–64.

Miller, P. Cox. " 'The Little Blue Flower is Red': Relics and the Poetizing of the Body." *Journal of Early Christian Studies* 8.2 (2000): 213–36.

Mitchell, B., and J. R. Lucas. *An Engagement with Plato's Republic*. Aldershot: Ashgate, 2003.

Momigliano, A. "Pagan and Christian Historiography." In *Essays in Ancient and Modern Historiography*. Middletown, Conn.: Wesleyan University Press, 1977.

Momigliano, A., ed. *The Conflict between Paganism and Christianity in the Fourth Century*. Oxford: Oxford University Press, 1963.

Nodes, D. J. *Doctrine and Exegesis in Biblical Latin Poetry*. Wiltshire: Francis Cairns, 1993.

Nugent, S. G. *Allegory and Poetics: The Structure and Imagery of Prudentius' Psychomachia*. Frankfurt am Main: Peter Lang, 1985.

——. "Ausonius' 'Late-Antique' Poetics and 'Post-Modern' Literary Theory." In *The Imperial Muse. Ramus Essays on Roman Literature of the Empire II*. Edited by A. J. Boyle. Victoria: Aureal Publishers, 1990.

O'Daly, G. *Augustine's City of God: A Reader's Guide*. Oxford: Oxford University Press, 1999.

O'Donnell, J. J. *Augustine: Confessions*. 3 vols. Oxford: Oxford University Press, 1992.

O'Meara, D. J. *Platonopolis: Platonic Philosophy in Late Antiquity*. Oxford: Clarendon Press, 2003.

——. *Plotinus: An Introduction to the Enneads*. Oxford: Clarendon Press, 1993.

Otis, B. *Virgil: A Study in Civilized Poetry*. Oxford: Clarendon Press, 1963.

Palmer, A.-M. *Prudentius on the Martyrs.* Oxford: Oxford University Press, 1989.

Paxson, J. J. *The Poetics of Personification.* Cambridge: Cambridge University Press, 1994.

Pégolo, L. "La alegorí cívico-militar de la *Fides* en la *Psychomachia* de Prudencio," In *Discurso, poder y politica en Roma.* Edited by E. Caballero de Del Sastre and B. Rabaza. Sante Fe, Argentina: Homo Sapiens, 2003.

Pelling, C .B. R. "Roman Historiography." *The Oxford Classical Dictionary.* 3rd ed. Edited by S. Hornblower and A. Spawforth. Oxford: Oxford University Press, 1996.

Pelikan, J. *Christianity and Classical Culture: The Metamorphosis of Natural Theology in the Christian Encounter with Hellenism.* New Haven, Conn.: Yale University Press, 1993.

Porter, S. E., P. Joyce, and D. E. Orton, eds. *Crossing the Boundaries: Essays in Biblical Interpretation in Honour of Michael D. Goulder.* Leiden: E. J. Brill Press, 1994.

Pötscher, W. *Porphyrios Pros Markellan.* Leiden: E. J. Brill, 1969.

Preminger, A., and T. V. F. Brogan, eds. *The New Princeton Encyclopedia of Poetry and Poetics.* Princeton, N.J.: Princeton University Press, 1993.

Press, G. A. *The Development of the Idea of History in Antiquity.* Montreal: McGill-Queen's University Press, 1982.

Pucci, J. *The Full-Knowing Reader: Allusion and the Power of the Reader in the Western Literary Tradition.* New Haven, Conn.: Yale University Press, 1998.

Putnam, M. C. J. "Foreword." In *Why Vergil? A Collection of Interpretations.* Edited by S. Quinn. Wauconda, Ill.: Bolchazy-Carducci Press, 2000.

Quilligan, M. *The Language of Allegory: Defining the Genre.* Ithaca, N.Y.: Cornell University Press, 1979.

Quinn, S. "Introduction: Why Words." In *Why Vergil? A Collection of Interpretations.* Edited by S. Quinn. Wauconda, Ill.: Bolchazy-Carducci Press, 2000.

Quint, D. *Epic and Empire: Politics and Generic Form from Virgil to Milton.* Princeton, N.J.: Princeton University Press, 1993.

Rees, R., ed. *Romane Memento: Vergil in the Fourth Century.* London: Duckworth Press, 2004.

Rist, J. M. *Augustine: Ancient Thought Baptized.* Cambridge: Cambridge University Press, 1994.

——. "Basil's 'Neoplatonism': Its Background and Its Nature." In *Basil of Caesarea: Christian, Humanist, Ascetic.* Edited by P. J. Fedwick. Toronto: Pontifical Institute of Mediaeval Studies, 1981.

——. *Plotinus: The Road to Reality.* Cambridge: Cambridge University Press, 1967.

Roberts, M.J. *Biblical Epic and Rhetorical Paraphrase in Late Antiquity.* Leeds: Francis Cairns, 1985.

——. *Poetry and the Cult of the Martyrs.* Ann Arbor: University of Michigan Press, 1993.

——. *The Jeweled Style: Poetry and Poetics in Late Antiquity.* Ithaca, N.Y.: Cornell University Press, 1989.

——. "Vergil and the Gospels: The Evangeliorum Libri IV of Juvencus." In *Romane Memento: Vergil in the Fourth Century.* Edited by R. Rees. London: Duckworth Press, 2004.

Rohmann, D. "Das langsame Sterben der *Veterum Cultura Deorum.*" *Hermes* 131 (2003): 235–53.

Rollinson, P. *Classical Theories of Allegory.* Pittsburgh: Duquesne University Press, 1981.

Rouse W. H. D. (Revised by M. F. Smith). *Lucretius: On the Nature of Things*. Loeb Classical Library. Cambridge, Mass.: Harvard University Press, 1982.

Runia, D. T. "The Idea and the Reality of the City in the Thought of Philo of Alexandria." *JHI* 61.3 (2000): 361–79.

Sabatier. P. *Bibliorum Sacrorum Latinae Versiones Antiquae Seu Vetus Italica*. Remis: Apud Reginaldum Florentain, 1743.

Said, E. "Introduction to the Fiftieth Anniversary Edition." In *Mimesis: The Representation of Reality in Western Literature*. Translated by W. R. Trask. Princeton, N.J.: Princeton University Press, 2003.

Shanzer, D. "Allegory and Reality: *Spes, Victoria,* and the Date of Prudentius's *Psychomachia*." *Illinois Classical Studies* 14 (1989): 347–63.

Sharples, R. W. *Stoics, Sceptics, and Epicureans: An Introduction to Hellenistic Philosophy*. London: Routledge, 1996.

Sheldon-Williams, I. P. "The Cappadocians." In *The Cambridge History of Later Greek and Early Medieval Philosophy*. Edited by A. H. Armstrong. Cambridge: Cambridge University Press, 1967.

Simmons, M. B. "Julian the Apostate." In *The Early Christian World*. Edited by P. E. Esler. Vol. 2. London: Routledge, 2000.

Smith, A. *Porphyry's Place in the Neoplatonic Tradition*. The Hague: Martinus Nijhoff, 1974.

Smith, M. *Prudentius' Psychomachia: A Reexamination*. Princeton, N.J.: Princeton University Press, 1976.

Smith, R. *Julian's Gods: Religion and Philosophy in the Thought and Action of Julian the Apostate*. London: Routledge, 1995.

Smolak, K. "Die Psychomachie des Prudentius als historisches epos." *La poesia tardoantica e medievale* (2001): 125–48.

Souter, A. *A Glossary of Later Latin to 600 A.D.* Oxford: Oxford University Press, 1949.

Spence, S. *Rhetorics of Reason and Desire: Vergil, Augustine, and the Troubadours*. Ithaca, N.Y.: Cornell University Press, 1988.

Spiegal, G. *The Past as Text: The Theory and Practice of Medieval Historiography*. Baltimore: Johns Hopkins University Press, 1997.

Springer, C. P. E. *The Gospel as Epic in Late Antiquity*. Leiden: E. J. Brill, 1988.

Stendahl, K. "The Apostle Paul and the Introspective Conscience of the West." In *Paul Among the Jews and Gentiles*. Edited by G. W. E. Nickelsburg with G. W. MacRae. Philadelphia: Fortress Press, 1976.

Stobaeus, Joannes. *Anthology*. 5 vols. Edited by C. Wachsmuth and O. Hense. Berlin: Weidmannsche Verlagsbuchhandlung, 1958.

Stock, B. *Augustine the Reader: Meditation, Self-Knowledge, and the Ethics of Interpretation*. Cambridge, Mass.: Harvard University Press, 1996.

——. "Literary Realism in the Later Ancient Period." In *Literary History and the Challenge of Philology*. Edited by S. Lehrer. Stanford, Calif.: Stanford University Press, 1996.

Tarrant, R. "Aeneas and the Gates of Sleep." *Classical Philology* 77 (1982): 51–55.

Taylor, C. *The Sources of Self: The Making of Modern Identity*. Cambridge, Mass.: Harvard University Press, 1989.

Thomas, R. *Reading Vergil and his Texts: Studies in Intertextuality*. Ann Arbor: University of Michigan Press, 1999.

Thomson, H. J. *Prudentius,* vols. 1–2. Loeb Classical Library. Cambridge, Mass.: Harvard University Press, 1949.

———. "The *Psychomachia* of Prudentius." *Classical Review* 44 (1930): 109–12.

Thraede, K. *Studien zu Sprache und Stil des Prudentius.* Hypomnemata Heft 13. Göttingen: Vandenhoeck & Ruprecht, 1965.

Trout, D. E. *Paulinus of Nola: Life, Letters, and Poems.* Berkeley: University of California Press, 1999.

Van Assendelft, M. M. *Sol Ecce Surget Igneus: A Commentary on the Morning and Evening Hymns of Prudentius.* Groningen: Bouma's Boekhuis B. V., 1976.

Van Dyke, C. *The Fiction of Truth: Structures of Meaning in Narrative and Dramatic Allegory.* Ithaca, N.Y.: Cornell University Press, 1985.

Van Oort, J. *Jerusalem and Babylon: A Study into Augustine's* City of God *and the Sources of his Doctrine of the Two Cities.* Leiden: E. J. Brill, 1991.

Vessey, M. "Jerome and Rufinus." In *The Cambridge History of Early Latin Literature.* Edited by F. Young, L. Ayres, and A. Louth. Cambridge: Cambridge University Press, 2004.

Von Albrecht, M. *Roman Epic: An Interpretative Introduction.* Leiden: E. J. Brill, 1999.

———. *Geschichte der römischen Literatur.* 2 vols. Munich: K. G. Saur Verlag, 1992.

Walcott, D. *Omeros.* New York: Noonday Press, 1998.

Walsh, P. G. *The Poems of Paulinus of Nola.* Vol. 40 of *Ancient Christian Writers.* New York: Newman Press, 1975.

Warner, J. C. *Augustinian Epic, Petrarch to Milton.* Ann Arbor: University of Michigan Press, 2005.

Weiden-Boyd, B. *Ovid's Literary Loves: Influences and Innovation in the* Amores. Ann Arbor: University of Michigan Press, 1997.

West, D. A. "The Bough and the Gate." In *Oxford Readings in Vergil's* Aeneid. Edited by in S. J. Harrison. Oxford: Oxford University Press, 1990.

White, C. *Early Christian Latin Poets.* London: Routledge, 2000.

White, H. *The Content of the Form.* Baltimore: Johns Hopkins University Press, 1987.

Whitehead, C. *Castles of the Mind: A study of Medieval Architectural Allegory.* Cardiff: University of Wales Press, 2003.

Whitman, J. *Allegory: The Dynamics of an Ancient and Medieval Technique.* Cambridge, Mass.: Harvard University Press, 1987.

Whitmarsh, T. " 'Greece Is the World': Exile and Identity in the Second Sophistic." In *Being Greek under Rome: Cultural Identity, the Second Sophistic and the Development of Empire.* Edited by Simon Goldhill. Cambridge: Cambridge University Press, 2001.

Wicker, K. O'Brien. *Porphyry the Philosopher: To Marcella.* Atlanta: Scholars Press, 1987.

Witke, C. "Recycled Words: Vergil, Prudentius and Saint Hippolytus." In *Romane Memento: Vergil in the Fourth Century.* Edited by R. Rees. London: Duckworth Press, 2004.

———. "Prudentius and the Tradition of Latin Poetry." *TAPA* 99 (1968): 509–25.

Williams, B.A.O. "The Analogy of City and Soul in Plato's *Republic.*" In *Plato's Republic: Critical Essays.* Edited by R. Kraut. Lanham, Md.: Rowman and Littlefield, 1997.

Williams, G. *Change and Decline: Roman Literature in the Early Empire.* Berkeley: University of California Press, 1978.

Williams, R. D. *Virgil Book III.* Oxford: Oxford University Press, 1962.

Young, F., L. Ayres, and A. Louth, eds. *The Cambridge History of Early Christian Literature.* Cambridge: Cambridge University Press, 2004.

Young, F. "Christian Teaching." In *The Cambridge History of Early Christian Literature.* Edited by F. Young, L. Ayres, and A. Louth. Cambridge: Cambridge University Press, 2004.

——. "Typology." In *Crossing the Boundaries: Essays in Biblical Interpretation in Honour of Michael D. Goulder.* Edited by S. E. Porter, P. Joyce, and D. E. Orton. Leiden: Brill Press, 1994.

Index

Aaron, 91, 113, 117

Abraham: as allegory of soul's battles, 83, 90, 135, 153; in creation of historical narrative, 48, 50; hospitality of, to triple-formed angel, 44, 86; as symbol of faith, 88, 89

Absalom, 185n22, 215n57

Achar, 28–29, 77, 104

Adam, 99; persuasion of, 6; as type for Christ, 100–101, 214n51; typology of, 6

Ad Marcellam (Porphyry), 134

adumbrata, 64–65

Adversus Arium (Victorinus), 155

Aeneid (Vergil): differing views concerning, 189n62; and the exodus story, 108–111, 189–190nn62–64; as national narrative, 4; piety expressed in, 34; in poetic genre, 7–8; Prudentius' adaptation of, 15–16, 183n11; salvation in, 190n63. *See also* thematic parallels in *Psychomachia* and *Aeneid*

afterlife, apophatic dilemma of, 108

Against the Christians (Marius Victorinus), 125

Alaric, 130

Albrecht, M. von, 182n7

Allecto, 23

allegorical reading, 197n25

allegory: of city and soul, 126–132; of exodus, 105–111; implied reader's discovery of, 52; Origenist view of, 122; pagan philosophy in making of, 11–12, 121–122; of Plato's cave, 135, 142; Prudentius' use of, 205n96; in *Psychomachia*, 82–83; and the soul, 133; of temple, 111–115; typology and, 11

allusion, 4–5, 181n3, 183n9, 183n11, 184n16, 194n12

Ambrose, 2, 8, 63, 71, 75, 85, 99, 109, 128; Platonist doctrine and, 124; on role of monarch, 131, 132; use of *adumbrare* by, 65; use of *forman crucis* by, 65–66; use of pagan literature by, 122, 123

Anchises, 20, 29, 34, 35

apices (letters), 198n33

Apocalypse, 68–69

Apollo, 34; Aeneas' prayer to, 18; Christ as parallel to, 25; as poetic inspiration, 16; as source of divine knowledge, 37–38; temples built in thanks to, 23

apophatic (negative) theology, 83, 207n6; Cappadocian Fathers on, 207n6; and Christ, 92–93; faith's role in, 87–88; on the godhead, 209n13; Judith typology and, 98; in patristic tradition, 86; in Prudentius' work, 83; in *Psychomachia*, 113–115; typologies as allegorical response to, 84–87

apostles, 110, 118

Apotheosis (Prudentius): and apophatic language, 86–87; narrative in defining identity, 46; on Trinity, 156; typology in, 48–49

Apuleius, 124, 125

Arator Victorius, 63

Aristotle, 123

art, as typology, 65

ascent of the soul, 132–142

Asclepiades, 54, 55, 78

Auerbach, E., 170, 171, 173, 175, 236nn36–43

Augustine, 2, 4, 8, 65, 145; on ascent of the soul, 132–133; on Christian *imperium*, 129, 225n46; on history, 195n15; language of self in works of, 164–169; on memory, 167; on original sin, 166; Platonism and, 122, 123, 124, 125, 128; on self, 161; on ternaries, 155

Augustus Caesar, 7–8